Early in his career, Dr. Morton, a biochemist, self-tested over 40 different psychoactive compounds looking for relief from his debilitating seasonal depression. He ultimately found a class of compounds that specifically attacked the Ego. Although his Ego fought back valiantly, Dr. Morton uncovered the conditions leading to "Ego death" where he repeatedly experienced dying. Each time, while the medicine incapacitated his frightened Ego, another very different consciousness came to the fore. It seemed to be God Himself. Yet, how could simply trying an unorthodox medication literally bring forth the presence of the divine into his consciousness?

It was then that Dr. Morton recognized a final step in human maturation: the discovery of the ancient truth that God was always within you, as the real you. Not God, an external supernatural spirit. Rather, God as your Inner Source, Holy Spirit, and Higher Power, your brain-based, genetic, and mortal Social Brain. Operating unrecognized within the unconscious, it acts to forward the immortality of life. As the opponent of our usually more dominant self-oriented Ego, our Source is family, species and life-oriented.

With this insight, Dr. Morton, decided to surrender his uncertain future to his Higher Power. He did so, because he found that his Source already had his purpose, his plan and the power to accomplish it. Upon doing so, his Source made clear the outlines of this book and set Dr. Morton to prove them correct. This has resulted in numerous research publications. The ultimate goal of his Source is awaken other Sources and align with them to optimize the survival of true human beings.

REVIEWERS COMMENT'S

"Dr. Morton should be nominated for the Noble Peace Prize for his brilliant and thought-provoking work, "Neuroreality". Not since Darwin has such a world-changing wealth of new ideas come to challenge our knowledge of the universe, life, and the workings of the human mind!"

E. A. HANKINS III, MD, Dermatologist, UCLA School of Medicine, Curator of Vertebrate Zoology and Founder of The World Museum of Natural History, Riverside, California

"This book provides a look into the dark pit of reality that lies outside of our usual awareness. Taking a journey into the realm of the building blocks of reality, should prove to be a trip worth taking"
ROBERT C. MARVIT, M.D., Neuropsychiatrist, President Hawaii Medical Association

"A major contribution by a pioneering neuroscientist to grounds for thinking that a killing-free world is possible."
GLENN D. PAIGE, Ph.D., Author of *NONKILLING GLOBAL POLITICAL SCIENCE,* Founder of the Center for Global Nonviolence.

"It is surprising that despite explosive advances of knowledge about our outer world, we know remarkably little about who we are and how to become happy. Written by an enlightened person, - Professor Bruce Morton, this book is a revolution in our knowledge about the human Self."
EUGENE NALIVAIKO, Ph.D., Associate Professor, Neurocardiology Laboratory, School of Biomedical Sciences and Pharmacy, University of Newcastle, Newcastle, NSW 2308, Australia

"This landmark work expresses Dr. Morton's illuminated vision of a nonkilling world of moral, environmental, and social responsibility. As I read the book, I found myself coming ever closer to Morton's Social Brain Source with its elevated view of optimal Human Survival."

JOSEPH SINGER, Chemical Engineer, Print Artist, Photographer, and Co Author of *"PANA O'AHU: SACRED STONES, SACRED LAND"*, and *"THIS IS NOT A PICTURE I AM HOLDING: KUAN YIN"*.

"Morton has constructed a coherent and provocative model to explain the human experience. This work is a must read for anyone interested in the scientific basis of spirituality."

MARK NOKES, Ph.D., Physicist, Former Vice President of a Silicon Valley company.

"An outstanding thing that this book accomplishes is clearly to demonstrate that the origin and operation of universe, life, and mind are in all regards natural and in no way dependent upon the supernatural, extracorporeal, or spiritual. This purging of our foundations of the cobwebs from superstition has created a space for the evolution of a belief system fully compatible with science: that of Neuroreality."

DENNIS G. McLAUGHLIN, Ph.D., Neuropsychologist, Co-Founder of Care Hawaii.

"Even if only half of Dr. Morton's ideas turn out to be empirically supported, he will still have made an unparalleled contribution to the understanding of human behavior at many levels".

MICHAEL P. KELLEY, Ph.D., Clinical Psychologist, Washington, D.C. USA.

RESEARCH

Also by Bruce Eldine Morton

The webpage: http://www2.hawaii.edu/~bemorton

lists Dr. Morton's neuroscience research and publications.

NEUROREALITY

A Scientific Religion to Restore Meaning

OR

How 7 Brain Elements Create
7 Minds and 7 Realities

Bruce Eldine Morton

Megalith Books

Doral, Florida

CONTENTS

MEGALITH BOOKS

ISBN 978-0-9833417-0-3

Library of Congress Control Number: 2011927333

General subject headings:
Body, Mind & Spirit/Inspirational
Science & Religion/Controversy
Self-Help/Personal Growth
Family & Relationships/Violence
Psychology/Personality
Neuroscience/Consciousness
Philosophy/Reality

Dr. Morton's email address is: bemorton@hawaii.edu

Table of Contents:

CONTENTS

CONTENTS

DEDICATION:

To **Terence A. Rogers**, Ph.D., Dean of the University of Hawaii's John A. Burns School of Medicine from 1972 to 1988, and surrogate Father in the best of ways.

ACKNOWLEDGEMENT:

The copy editoral work was done by Peter Aras at artiomovas@gmail.com

NEUROREALITY: A SCIENTIFIC RELIGION TO RESTORE MEANING

PREFACE: Biochemist's Path to Neuroreality

After obtaining tenure in 1975 as a faculty biochemist at the University of Hawaii School of Medicine, I was at last free to decide the future direction of my life. Because of my background skills and my advanced training, the citizens of Hawaii had seen fit to keep me from having to earn my living by working in the fields, so to speak. Rather, they had provided me a lifetime salary and a modest laboratory to do specialized work for them at their university. What was particularly challenging was that they were asking me, as a university professor, not only to teach their offspring what was known about the chemistry of life (biochemistry), but they were further asking me to use my abilities to find new ways to improve their own lot. Further, they implied that they did not quite know what they needed and trusted me to use my judgment in this regard. That is, they were asking me to work in whatever "field" I felt would be most likely to improve the human condition, and thus ultimately to benefit them. By doing so, I felt I could also repay the other U.S. citizens who had kindly contributed to my federally funded graduate and postdoctoral training.

Taking this responsibility seriously, I began looking intently for answers. I asked myself the following: "What do I think is the most significant problem facing humanity today (assuming I had no limitations and that I could do something practical)?" In response to this question, information confronting us every day through the mass media provided the area that most attracted my attention. The "News" continually explodes with human conflict, suffering and violence at all levels, from the intra-personal, to that between individuals, families, ideologies, cultures, nations, religions, and global alliances. For example, almost two of three U.S. marriages fail, usually in bitter conflict traumatizing their infants and children. Spousal abuse and other forms of domestic violence are rampant. Child abuse produces hospitalization of ten percent of U.S. children. Twenty percent of U.S. adults fall into the category of mentally ill. Moreover, almost half of the U.S. population has at least one bout with mental illness in their life. Violence appears to be increasing in intensity in parallel with the population explosion. More than half of all highway fatalities are due to intoxication. Drug abuse is wasting those who were the promise of entire nations. Unfortunately, this is only the tip of the iceberg.

7

To me, all of these interlinked societal problems represented a single theme: brain function. The brain, the most complex, least understood of all our bodily organs, is one of the last frontiers of ignorance. Yet, the brain is the mechanical device through which we are aware of our surroundings and which determines how we personally respond to them. Thus, the brain literally is the central organ of human life. Because of this logic, my first conclusion was that the rest of my career would be dedicated to brain research.

Yet, how could I, a biochemist, even begin to approach such a subject? I had no formal training regarding the brain at all. Surprisingly, this actually worked to my advantage in terms of ultimately developing an understanding of its nature. Those scientists who did study the brain were usually each remarkably unfamiliar with the accomplishments of the others. Furthermore, intense competition for limited research funds, forced scientists to become sub-specialist experts who knew more and more about less and less. This appeared literally to be maintaining a vast ignorance about the big picture of life, and especially of mind among the conventionally trained and funded scientific community, our neuroscientist leaders.

It was also helpful that the University of Hawaii, while very good, was not as competitive as the top ranked universities. As a result, I was encouraged, but fortunately not demanded to bring in governmental funding, along with its lucrative overhead to the university. This I would have been required to do to keep a similar job at Harvard, for example. Also, had I been in such a position, I may have been forced to work on narrow, politically correct, often seemingly "fad", short-range topics in order for me to obtain extramural funding needed to pay for part or all of my salary and that of my assistants. However, in Hawaii, I could continue slowly but surely my academic quest on behalf of the citizens, almost totally unhampered. One of this freedom's consequences was that I had to pay for many of my laboratory's small equipment and supply needs out of my own pocket. Some very dedicated unpaid student help volunteers aided me greatly. Far-sighted colleagues and other professionals with insight encouraged me.

I chose the subject of the emotions as a good brain research topic with which to begin my investigations. This was because: 1) emotions appeared to drive most human behavior; 2) drug seeking appeared to be a form of self medication to reduce unpleasant emotions; and 3) malfunctions in the production of emotions appeared to be source of the widespread mental illnesses. When I attempted to identify what emotions existed, I found almost as many different lists of emotions in the literature as there were authors writing about them. Furthermore, not only was it unknown what neurotransmitters were released to produce fear or anger, for example, but it was not even known what brain sites were responsible for their production. Those were truly the dark ages of the brain. It has been said that in the subsequent fifteen years, more was learned about the brain than had been discovered since the beginning of time. Even after the "decade of the brain" beginning in 1990, this huge outpouring continues. Yet, it occurs in the absence of an adequate logical framework upon which to assemble it. Thus, the neuroscience literature remains a vast, published collection of unassimilated, untapped treasures just waiting for recognition and integration into a living whole.

Fortunately for me, two powerful biochemical techniques appeared in the late 1970s. The first, using simple but elegant biochemistry, enabled the global visualization of regional brain activities in experimental animals, and later in humans, for the first time. The second made possible the mapping of the receptors' regional brain distributions for the almost one hundred neurotransmitters then known. With these techniques, I began observing regional brain activities produced in experimental animals subjected to conditions producing emotion-associated behaviors of different kinds. I also set up a bank of frozen whole human brains, sliced into 2 cm thick cross sections for later investigations of neurotransmitter receptor alterations associated with several mental illnesses. Work begun in the lab later led to yet unpublished clarification of the mechanism of action of several key psychoactive compounds. Around this time, I also began work designed to minimize brain damage due to cardiovascular injuries and stroke.

One of the problems a scientist faces when becoming a faculty member at a U.S. university is the following: Although highly educated in a subspecialty of science, they usually have received no formal training in education and often have not taught a single course. Yet, the system expects them to begin their university teaching in a proficient manner. For this and a number of other reasons, the early years of university employment can be quite stressful. In my case, each year the pressures of the fall semester precipitated within me what seemed to be a seasonal depressive disorder. While not incapacitating enough to cause me to seek medical aid, this was very unpleasant, both for me and for those around me. Every fall I attempted to eradicate or at least cope with this distracting altered mental state. I did so by trying what turned out to be a couple of dozen self-help methods, ranging from conventional therapy, counseling, prayer, and gestalt encounter groups, through Primal therapy, Rebirthing and Holotrophic Breathwork, to Dianetics, Mental Physics, Silva mind control, **est**, Transcendental meditation, the Forum and Theravada meditation. All around me, I saw impressive mental improvements and personal development occurring in individuals other than myself. Although each year my problem would finally lift, it returned the next fall. Meanwhile, I began to see many elements of commonality in these self-realization, religious, and therapeutic traditions. Much later, it became clear that many of these self-improvement approaches also had the potential to push the brain slightly outside of its normal operating limits to provide an opening for personal transformation.

Next, I modified the research orientation of my laboratory toward brain research and began to master the essentials of the many disciplines involved in Neuroscience. Then, I began a personal program, which I do not recommend to others, but which was part of my path to insights about the workings of the brain. This was a series of semi controlled auto-experiments. In these, I systematically administered to myself graded doses of representative psychoactive agonists and antagonists of the large number of brain neurotransmitter receptor systems known to participate in consciousness. I would then enter a well-equipped soundproof experimental chamber and experience the mental consequences of the ingested substance over the next several hours. While these psychoactive effects unfolded, I would record my subjective experience and objective (test based) observations on tapes or in notebooks for later assembly and analysis. I carefully tested about 40 different psychoactive compounds in this manner.

These experiments were extremely fruitful in a number of ways, but also personally dangerous. I accidentally overdosed myself on two separate occasions, but fortunately survived. In the process of this work, I developed an experiential view of brain system neuropsychopharmacology that I have found invaluable. Most of the compounds I tested produced direct and indirect effects which were very unpleasant, even frightening. However, some of them revealed critical clues to the mechanism of action of other important drugs. For example, I found that 10 mg oral muscimol, a well-understood and highly specific agonist for the GABA-A receptor, totally reproduced the many very characteristic subjective effects of marijuana, whose mechanism of action was unknown. . For the prepared mind, the significance of this observation alone was immense.

Ultimately, I tested several of the 5-HT2a receptor agonists, all of which are hallucinogens of the LSD type. At low doses, I noticed much greater access than I usually had to my emotions and other mental phenomena that previously had been very difficult for me to experience. Normally, I had so little feelings that I had taken to jumping off cliffs in a hang glider for fun, setting an unofficial world cross-country distance record of 28 miles in 1975 in the process. With low doses of hallucinogens, I began to have impressive mental experiences resembling those I had seen in others not using drugs in the various self-realization traditions I had pursued earlier. Simultaneously, I began to find relief from the annual "depressive" state that had plagued me for so long. Later, as I began increasing the hallucinogen dose, initially I began to suffer more and more emotional anguish until, at a critical dose I felt myself literally to be in the throws of death itself, an ancient experience that already had appropriately been labeled "Ego death". However, I was not dead. Rather an important system of my brain had been temporarily turned off by the drug to produce this Ego death, I had entered an altered state of consciousness, known as "Transcendence". In that transcendent state, I felt myself in the presence of an awareness of something much higher, purer, and wiser than my usual Ego based self. This sacred state of the brain has confused many individuals into thinking that they had contacted an external God. Rather, by the temporary collapse of their ego they saw how impure and self-serving it is in comparison to the selfless species-survival purity of their social brain Source. As did Old Testament prophets, I felt as if in filthy rags and with the desire to fall on my face before its overwhelming wisdom and purity.

Then, several awe invoking inspirational hours of intense contemplation would pass. During this time, I often took copious notes. I would finally fall asleep. Later, I would go over my notes and rediscover that I had been given some highly unusual insights that always turned out to be part of a powerful paradigm of the way something in the universe worked, often with strong social implications. Yet, I did not know where each of these models had come from. I would write it out in detail and diagram its relationships. Then, I would spend weeks in the library searching to see if the existing literature would support such a contextual model. It always did so abundantly. Last, I would go to experts in that field within the university and show them the paradigm. They usually said in essence, "Where did this come from?" "It seems to accommodate the data better than our present models do".

Over the ensuing 15 years, I received about two of these new contexts a year. At first, they appeared to be unrelated to one another. Over time, additional contexts began to fill in the blank spaces between them. My culminating insight was the following: within each of us is a genetic, brain dependent, higher intelligence that has a social purpose, a plan and the power to accomplish its goals. This mortal, higher intelligence appears to be produced by the activity of an evolution-derived brain system devoted to herd (family-group-species-life) survival optimization. It seems to be especially aware that working cooperatively for the good of the group is more survival effective with emergent benefits than working alone competitively for oneself as the "Ego" often does. Its thinking, as revealed by the many individuals who have written under its inspiration, seems generally similar in content, and appears to be the biological origin of the core elements of all world religions. It values honesty, integrity, deferred gratification, morality and service as the highest good. In the past, it had usually been misperceived as something external and supernatural, rather than the individual brain-dependent, genetically evolved social wisdom that it now appears to be.

There is evidence that this higher Source is derived from the activity of each individual's cerebellum, a highly compact structure containing more cells that the rest of the brain put together. Not only does the cerebellum give grace and agility to physical movement by coordinating the thousands of positions that one's muscles, bones and joints can take, it also participates in the production of language syntax. Thus, in its production of grammar, thousands of words are also coordinated. Furthermore, based upon considerable evidence, it would appear that the cerebellum is the major site of primary memory. This massive database connects to the cerebrum, at not only sensory-motor areas involved in the coordination of movement but also in the frontal cortex and other non-motor areas. Thus, it is reasonable that, functioning in the herd mode, this most complex brain element could   participate in the coordination of the thousands of social relations in our lives through the output of intuition.

It appeared that my own higher intelligence had a twofold plan for me: first, to provide repeatable, verifiable scientific data supporting the existence of such a Source within each of us, and second, to discover non-drug methods to open channels of communication from it to our usual consciousness. Its ultimate goal appears to be to give personal control to each of the billions of Sources alive but mostly suppressed today. This could enable humankind to evolve to the next higher level, and in this manner lead to the transformation of the planet from waste and destruction to balance and harmony.

I already knew that, as a scientist, I had long since risen to my "level of incompetence" and had produced nothing of great merit. Therefore, a few years ago as a transformative step in this path, I decided to dedicate the rest of my life surrendered to the service of my Source. Who I am now is this halting and wayward research assistant of my higher Source. When I have been working under its advisorship, everything I have done under its guidance has come up "smelling like a rose". It is quite amazing! All I have to do is effortlessly follow its intuition. I was unaware that earlier Francis Crick was under the influence of LSD when he recognized the structure of DNA, a concept that has transformed the "life sciences" (Hancock, 2007). In my laboratory, this approach has led to so many biomedical insights and discoveries that I cannot begin to capitalize upon them all. Having "graduated" to Professor Emeritus, I am in the process of publishing and giving them away for the benefit of the citizens of Hawaii, the U.S. and the world at large. This book contains compilations of many of these Sourceful insights. These include:

1) The Eternal Universe with Infinite Levels of Unique Structures and Laws

2) The Law of Emergent Properties

3) The Seven Types of Reality

4) The Galactic Singularity Model of the Origin of Life

5) Triadic Solution to the Mind-Body Problem

6) Cellular Survival as the Source of all Living Behavior

7) The Five Dimensions of Behavior

8) The Triadic Solution to the Mind-Body Problem

9) The Quadrimental Brain Model

10) The Dual Quadbrain Model and the Society of Seven

11) The Four Freedoms of Choice within Determinism

12) The Neuroanatomical and Behavioral Basis of Hemisity

In the mean time, this work continues to expand. Other Sources have begun to recognize that we are working in parallel for the same goals. It is exciting to watch Neuroreality develop under the guidance of our Sources. It appears ever more likely that such fruitful collaborations could actually transform the world for the better! Our Sources are good beyond compare! Find a way to uncover and tap yours and join us in this adventure! Your Source has the answers to all of your important questions. It has your purpose, your plan and the power you need to accomplish it. You can trust it with your life. It is the emergent nonkilling human of the future.

INTRODUCTION: Neuroreality: A Scientific Method-Based 4,000 Year Upgrade of Religion

Dear reader: This book provides a foundation for the reconstitution of religion. More than most other knowledge structures, it is built upon a step-by-step reasoning. Thus, one needs a clear understanding of the basic elements of each chapter before proceeding to the next. If chapters are read out of sequence, they will make little sense because they depend upon many new facts presently unknown to the reader that were introduced in earlier chapters.

> **We each have divinity buried within us.**
> **Our life's work is to uncover ourselves**
> **and join the human race.**

> **Neuroreality is a non-supernatural religion**
> **whereby through discovery of and surrender to**
> **one's brain-based Higher Power,**
> **one discovers their unique purpose,**
> **their plan, and the power to achieve it.**

No one needs reminding of the unsettling news reports that we must confront each morning. Killing and disaster is all around. The world appears to be moving rapidly toward chaos, with good news a rarity. We turn to spirituality for hope, only to find at least five of the world religions at each other's throats, rhetorically asking: Whose God is the real God? Somehow, someway, we need to step off this downward spiral before everything we hold dear is lost or destroyed. An important reason for this disturbing situation is the following: We have allowed our world religions to stultify and decay, rather than bringing them forward in parallel with the ongoing science-based explosion of knowledge.

As illustrated in **Figure 1**, a primary function of all religions has ever been to answer the personal big questions of existence. Our genes give us the curiosity to ask these survival questions because how we have

Figure 1. ORIGIN AND NATURE OF RELIGION

Sources of Answers

1. Pre-Language Childhood Natural Authorities:

Parents, Childcare Givers, TV, Cartoons, Siblings, Relatives, Peers

Inherently, at a very early age we each subconsciously seek answers to
LIFE'S BIG QUESTIONS:
Who am I? Where am I? How did I get here? Why am I here? Who are you? What should we be doing? Must I die? Where am I going?

2. Additional Later Childhood Natural Authorities:

Teachers, Leaders, Explorers, Inventors, Scientists, Doctors, News Media, Winners, Fashion Role Models

Presently, these questions are only answered by the 4000 year old traditions of the world religions. The relevant vast outpourings of Science are specifically excluded.

3. Personal Experience:

Eye Witnessing, Other Credible Witnesses (such as Friends, News Media, Books, School Courses, Research Reports), Reasoning, Experimenting, Analyzing, Intuition, Dreams, Altered States, Rumor, Mass Hysteria

Our answers to these Big Questions become our personal **BELIEFS** that are our Internal Reality approximations of External Reality

Fusion with similar beliefs of others transforms this into our **RELIGION** which provides us a superfamily to belong to, allies, enemies, resources, purpose, goals hope and something to live for.

4. Supernatural Authorities:

God, Mother of God, Devil, Angels, Demons, Priests, Prophets, Church Fathers, Sacred Writings, Religious Traditions, Witchdoctors, Blessings, Curses, Oracles, Magic.

This 4000 years out-of-date, consensus **FAITH** is highly resistant to change, in spite of challenges by reasoning or data-based evidence to the contrary presented to individual members.

answered them in the past has been a matter of life and death. These questions, used to organize this book, include: Where am I? – Who am I? – Who are you? – How did I get here? – Why do I feel the way I do? – Is this a safe place? – Who is my family? – What is my purpose? – What should I be doing? – How should my family be living? – Where am I going? – Do I have to die? – If so, what will happen to me as, and after I die? The answer to these existential questions provides two other key elements of religion: salvation from the terror of death, and the ability to work in a nonkilling relationship with other members of our human superfamily.

In early childhood, long before we can now recall, we each intuitively wished to know who we were, where we were, how we got here, whether this is a safe place, and our relationship to others. These in-built questions about existence, inherently asked by every one of us, constitute the biological foundation of religion. They form the framework that directs a young child to seek answers about universe, life and mind from the most authoritative sources available. Regardless of the outcome of this preconscious inquiry, its contents constitute the original core of our religious belief. This native religion serves as the foundational element in a person's later belief system. Consensus of religious beliefs within our family and culture further shaped it. Thus, the answers that we accepted as truth often came from our mother, our siblings, our childcare giver, our relatives or the cartoons of a TV babysitter. These childhood beliefs are still active in our subconscious minds today. There they will influentially remain, regardless of what we later learned after our conscious intellect migrated up from our brain stem into our left hemisphere cortical language center.

How ironic it is that after centuries of scientific inquiry, our native religions have not changed the traditional answers to the big questions of 4,000 years ago! In addition, it is predictable that those archaic answers are greatly at odds with discoveries coming from the vast outpouring of current experiment-based scientific knowledge. Furthermore, the religious truths we accept as infants are further distorted because of personal transmission to us by our relatively ignorant parents, maids or TV cartoons. For example, my mother told me that every beat of my heart was dependent upon the finger of God, who created me, and whom I must obey or I would cause my guardian angel to cry. Unfortunately for us, these archaic religious relics constitute our personal survival kit of beliefs about the universe and life. Upon such a ragged framework, we hang each new

17

experience as we each continue the endless construction of our unique model of inner reality. Then, with this stunted view, we venture into the world of external reality to make our daily life or death decisions.

It would help if these traditional contexts were even partially correct and we were at least in the right book, if not on the same page. Alas, they are not. As a result, for millennia humanity has continued to perpetrate and endure incalculable suffering and waste, violence, and killing. This is mostly due to operation from "false cause". Fortunately, this seemingly irreconcilable conflict between science and religion is an unnecessary artifact that was carried forward for thousands of years. Because of the awesome nature of religion with its authoritarian God and its supernatural answers, all seemingly set in concrete, fledgling science has been intimidated into shirking its responsibility for supplying more accurate answers to the life's big questions. This has led to the now huge gap between what we can demonstrate by reason and what we accept by belief and faith. This gap has falsely placed science and religion at odds.

Anciently, one's religion was a comprehensive personal and social way of life. It held all issues of living as humanity's best approximation of reality. There was no need for a separate science. However, as religion become organized and deified, the perfection of its deity fixated it. This prevented it from evolving along with our increased understanding of the universe and life. Ultimately, when it became obvious that the earth rotated around the sun instead of being the center of the universe, it became intellectually necessary to split science off from its rightful place within religion. This was inevitable because religion could not abandon subjective Spirituality's imagery that an all-wise God created the earth as the center of the universe, even though this context was increasingly found incompatible with Rationality's emerging objective facts. As a result, intellectual honesty forced one, either to become schizophrenic, i.e. to believe in religion on Sunday but to depend upon science the rest of the week, or to become atheistic by making isolated science as one's empty way of life. In spite of the horrible religious excesses of the past and present, we inherently wish to bring science back into our comprehensive religious belief system where it belongs and aggressively remove the spiritual irrationalities that lead to violence.

This book seeks to replace the murky and weak foundations upon which we have for so long built our lives. It provides an upgrade with more accurate answers to life's big questions using a Scientific Method-based wisdom structure called, "Neuroreality: A Transformational Context for Existence Bridging Brain and Mind, Science and Religion". We can thus replace traditional "impossible to reasonably believe" supernatural answers to life's Big Questions with more accurate cutting-edge, data-based, repeatable answers that require no faith to accept. Even though some of us have felt forced to become atheists in order to remain intellectually honest, we each have a genetically built-in and legitimate need for religion as our home. That is, we inherently need to believe in the existence of something holy, higher than ourselves and worthy of our whole-hearted support, something that gives us belonging, hope, purpose, goals and a reason to live. More accurate, logical, demonstrable answers to the big questions about reality, the universe, life and mind can supply this need. These same answers will also lead us to discover our hidden divinity, surrender to its wisdom and join the sacred human race in the nonkilling optimization of the existence of all sentient beings and their life support systems.

The remainder of this introduction contains highly condensed summaries of the six sections of this book. But, how does one summarize in advance the many new ideas and contexts yet to be developed for the reader within the books chapters? This artificially makes reading the next sections of this Introduction the most demanding part of the book. Paradoxically, to the uninitiated, these overviews may only become meaningful after having sequentially read the actual uncompressed chapters first. Do not worry, the chapters themselves are easy to follow and unfold naturally. This understood, one can proceed to enjoy the following overviews of the foundations of Neuroreality.

Section I: Where am I?

This begins with a very different databased understanding of the nature of the universe, from the infinitesimal to the infinite. These new insights include the existence of remarkable galactic singularity engines that form and maintain the existence of both our galaxy and others. As graphically illustrated herein, this engine drives the flow of matter, energy, and time through the galactic halo of life where living organisms originate, thrive, and die. Because of the inward flow of galactic arms, our world will ultimately pass beyond this halo into galactic areas where life is not possible. Thus, for our terrestrial life form to survive we will have to migrate upstream within the halo of life to greener planetary pastures.

INTRODUCTION

Available as a more accurate replacement of our primitive ideas about Gods, angels and demons, is the real possibility that other self-renewing God-like beings exist within our ever-flowing galactic halo of life. The discovery in Egypt and elsewhere of impossible megaliths, such as massive pre-cut beams and other objects over 2,000 tons in size, carved from bedrock as enormous single stones appears to be concrete evidence for the existence of these "Unknowns". Amazingly, those responsible for their production brought these massive structures from quarries miles away, even across rivers, and perched them atop columns more than 40 ft high as part of ancient cut stone buildings. Experts estimate that builders cut and assembled these megaliths at least 12,000 years ago, near the end Earth's most recent ice age. Despite naïve attempts to explain them away within a contemporary frame of reference, these feats are in fact completely beyond our current technology. The rising sea, resulting from the post ice age glacial melts has since covered some of these enormous structures. Satellite photos available on Google Earth reveal for all to see that in addition to these impossibly crafted structural megaliths, many huge geometrically precise pyramids exist. They are by far the largest artificial structures ever built on earth. They stare up at us, not only from Egypt, the Americas and Eurasia, but also from unexpected places such as China. Clearly, living beings with mastery of gravity have left their irrefutable, very real marks on earth for all to see, doing so at a time when humans of that era were still not beyond hunting and gathering food for cooking fires.

Section II: Who am I?

It is now clear that all behavior including, life and mind, consists of five specific dimensions. Development of this knowledge has enabled first understandable solution to the ancient Mind-Body Problem. That solution again makes it clear that existence of extracorporeal spirits is essentially impossible. This abolishes previous archaic concepts of God, demons, the soul and the spiritual afterlife, including a literal heaven or hell.

With the resultant clarity, we are next able to approach that multimind organ, The Dual Quadbrain, a multilayered, bilateral control apparatus evolved to optimize our personal survival in the dyadic universe. With the illumination of neuroanatomical locations, unique realities and functions of each of the Dual Quadbrain's Society of Seven, we can for the first time clearly see the brain-based origin of all human behavior, from diabolic to sublime. The temporarily dominant element of the hierarchy of

20

the Society for Seven determines who is in charge and who predicts our shifting behaviors and realities. Furthermore, under certain conditions, the Society of Seven can voluntarily or involuntarily give its control over to external authorities of several types In some cases this may serve to assemble us into groups of killing automatons called "warriors".

The most advanced member of the Society of Seven within each of us is our Source. This is our Nonkilling social brain's Holy Spirit, our God Within, Higher Power, with all of its goose-bump-raising inspirational wisdom. The Source has our own unique purpose for the optimization of life, a plan of action, and provides the personal power to achieve its Nonkilling goals. However, for the Source to be in control requires an individual to develop the ability to distinguish and surrender to its "still small voice" rather than giving in to the upset loud cries of our fearful reptilian self-brain (another member of our Society of Seven). The conversion from Reptile-directed violence toward Source-directed non-violence is a stage of maturation available to all, one that some normally never reach, but which can occur even before adolescence. This new understanding of the dynamic potential of human behavior places us in the position to do new and better synergistic things with our minds, our lives and our societies.

Section III: Who are You? Friend or Foe?

Astute Darwin was only a beginning pioneer. It is not yet common knowledge that life on earth appears to have emerged at least twice, forming not just one, but two complimentary trees of life, each based upon one of two equally possible, but opposite reproductive strategies. This is the subject of Familial Polarity. Within it, Patripolar true-breeding lineages exist where the male is genetically dominant in the home. In contrast, Matripolar lineages also exist in which the female rules the home, acting as role model and cultural standards setter.

Until the advent of Hemisity (the concept describing which side of the bilateral brain our Executive is located), it had not been possible to clearly identify these two ancient pre-racial human lineages of familial polarity. It now is clear that in general, the dominant marital partner of either sex within the home is usually a right brain-oriented person, possessing a big picture view and an intense, charismatic behavioral style. Research demonstrates that in mating, most often "opposites attract". Therefore, complimenting the right brain-oriented dominant partner is the supporting partner of the pair, usually a left brain-oriented person of either sex, with an important detail orientation and a sensitive, supportive behavioral style.

Recently, Magnetic Resonance Imaging (MRI) has revealed that at least two brain anatomical differences exist that distinguish who is right and who is left brain-oriented. Unrecognized interbreeding between the two polarities has long resulted in several categories of individuals with very specific deficits, including not only dyslexia, but also separate categories of differences in sexual identities and/or preferences. It is expected that once the existence of Familial Polarity is recognized, further study of the DNA sequences of these groups of people will further confirm the existence of the two trees of life and delineate their non-racial genetic differences and those of their hybrids.

In any case, it appears that our genetic compliment of survival instincts lags behind our current existence by at least a million years. That is, our basic instincts are those of hunter-gatherers, not city technocrats. We know that hunter gatherers, by endlessly repeating the life cycle pattern of their parents, appeared to have lived in balance with nature, rarely killing each other. This is why most people today will never kill another human being, except under certain extenuating conditions under which they most definitely will kill.

A provocative finding is that out of 22 global sites with recurring violence studied, at 21 of these locations the hemisities of the soldiers on opposing sides of the battle line were of opposite Familial Polarities. That is, soldiers on a Matripolar side were mostly left hemisphere-oriented men, fighting for their Motherland, and who when mortally wounded cried out for their mothers. Yet, on the other side, mainly Patripolar right brain-oriented soldiers are fighting for their Fatherland, and who when dying scream for their fathers. The importance of Familial Polarity in global killing is at present totally unrecognized. Yet, countless massacres, wars and genocides involve this biology.

Section IV: Why do I Feel the Way I do? What can I Do About It?

This part addresses several key elements regarding human violence and murder. The first is the recently recognized existence of a mutated, mal-functioning (x) developmental arrest repair program (xDARP). This potent, but broken subconscious behavioral system often activates once we have developed a safe and intimate relationship with mate or friend. When it feels safe enough, the xDARP pays them the ultimate compliment of using them, through transference, as a present-time substitute for a parent or sibling from one of our early childhood conflicts. The broken xDARP subconsciously does this in a attempt to complete a failed traumatic struggle for control from early childhood that has left us with subconscious unhealing psychosocial wounds in the form of a developmental arrests and fixations. This transference of my incomplete struggles from the past onto you, an important person in my present, has been called "running your tapes", and other less savory terms. Here is where the xDARP superimposes upon you an unwinnable thematic struggle from my past such as "You don't love me, Mommy! (or Daddy!)". Over time, this theme acts out with increasing age regression (infantile behavior) and endless repetition.

My unwitting beloved partner "transferee" takes these attacks seriously and attempts to satisfy the insatiable demands by my xDARP for change. Ultimately this escalating neurotic struggle leads, through psychosis, to murderous domestic "crimes of passion". This of course leaves the pair's love-children developmentally traumatized and scarred permanently, only to grow up and repeat this endless cycle. Often the adult victims of these sometimes complementary xDARP conflicts can find themselves in the "News", institutionalized, or forced to live on the margins of society. Yet, they have sincerely acted out this drama with the sole conscious intention of "being true to themselves". Because of the subconscious strength of the xDARP, they have confused their identity with a powerful compulsion. This is another situation where we have needed and used religion to help us, sometimes successfully, with its concepts of sin, a personal devil (xDARP), conversion, and the saving grace of a Higher Power.

The Dual Quadbrain Model also facilitates our understanding of the many layers of human motivation, starting with primitive pain and pleasure, expanding to the Hexadyad Primary Emotions, and on to mood and personality formation. However, over recent millennia, new stresses affect the biological connections between reproduction, sex and violence. This has led to an unrecognized crisis over the rigid bio-behavioral rules of one the members of our brain's Society of Seven. Its subconscious law is: It is a *biological* sin to increase one's own survival benefit at another's survival harm. The automatic production of the pain of guilt, and sometimes ostracism and exclusion from our extended family group always punish such a sin. Fortunately, the ancient, still-effective cure for stopping this guilt pain has always been the following: Make personal restitution to the victim by completely restoring their survival loss, by seeking their forgiveness and acceptance, and thus becoming reconciled back into the family again. Family membership ultimately became a fundamental genetic imperative, perhaps because long-term living alone on the glacier or in the desert was quite impossible.

However, we have long ago discovered that guilt pain can be suppressed temporarily by the ingestion of specific psychoactive drugs: caffeine, tobacco, alcohol, cannabis, opium, and now by new more potent chemicals. All of these substances have long been highly prized because they block subconscious guilt pain and thus temporarily restore pleasure. However, as tolerance to the drug develops, the biting pain returns ever more intensely. Thus, we obsessively seek stronger dosages, or move on to more potent narcotics. Relief from the incessant pain becomes our highest priority: subconsciously, we will give anything, pay anything, or even kill to get relief from the pain. Thus, what powerfully drives global drug demand is unrecognized guilt pain subconsciously self inflicted as punishment for harming the survival of others.

Yet in these days, harming another's survival is almost inherently forced upon us by the structure of our modern society with its cutthroat, antisocial competition, lies, theft and isolation. Because we will pay anything to assuage our subconscious pain, narco-trafficking has become the most highly profitable profession in the world. Through greed and extortion, it is now killing millions of human from all classes and literally corrupting the nations of the world. Neither eradication of drug production, dealer interdiction or punishment of abusers has stemmed the huge demand for alcohol and drugs. Only by removal of the sources of individual guilt production, by restoring the survival damage of the harmed one, will we be able to stop the insatiable narco-drive for the pleasure released from the relief of pain. This may demand a grass roots societal transformation.

Section V: Is this a Safe Place? What Should I Be Doing? How Should I Relate to Others?

Our early childhood environment often programs our answer to the first of four freedoms of choice within determinism that we have. The first freedom is a variation of the following: Is the universe my enemy or my friend? Should I resist or accept the way the universe works including the way our earth and you operate? Is it the source of life or death? Due to traumatic starts, many of us as infants came to believe they must resist the universe as a dangerous place. However, it is also possible to choose the way the universe is as perfect. Since nobody wins a fight against external reality, lives can either be permanently victimized by our resistant shoulds or shouldn'ts, or they can be empowered by aligning with and tapping the way the universe is and works. One can either resist and suffer drowning by a wave of life, or choose it as good and ride it with pleasure. The wave does't care. Since the universe is the sole source of life, abundance, opportunity and power, the choice is clear.

Usually, living together in the society of one's family and friends is much more satisfying than a life of social isolation. This is so because of the unrecognized but reliable generation of emergent properties. These automatically appear as a *state change* when one stops struggling to exist alone on one level, and moves up to the next higher level, working as a member of a composite, such as a "family" group. Because of the existence of this law of emergence, one gains more personal benefits from working cooperatively within a group than it costs to go it competitively alone.

Win-lose competition at any level activates the killer side of our brain to take violent action against the alien enemy. With the additional clarity brought by more accurate answers to life's big questions, we can begin to see the emergent gifts of converting from killing competition to nonkilling empathic cooperation. This makes it inherently optimal, and thus highly desirable that all levels of society convert to "win-win or no deal" cooperative transactions between caring "family" members.

Further, we have gained insights that can facilitate the rehabilitation of killers at all levels, even the automaton killers and the pathological killers. This rehabilitation includes teaching the distinction between fear and anxiety, and the activation of a responsible inner self rather than a passive ego abdicated to an external authority.

With an understanding of the law of emergence, the most personally profitable and rewarding task before each of us is to empathetically work with others to optimize the survival of the family of life. Based upon these principles, clearly the way to proceed is to set up a government that no longer depends upon killing force as its source of motivation. Its highest purpose will instead be the enlightened optimization of the survival of the individual as a part of humanity. Because of its resultant emergent benefits, it will be in the personal self-interest of individuals to join it in "The Nonkilling Dream".

INTRODUCTION

Section VI: Must I Die? How will I Die? What will Happen to Me after I Die?

Recognizing that we live in a non-supernatural universe operating without plan or purpose, our species needs to take responsibility for and to effectively confront the ongoing human population explosion. Whole regions of our earth are beginning to suffer from deforestation simply in order to obtain the wood needed just to cook the next meal. We must answer difficult questions about human equality and the right to life. Overall, policies that best support, the *optimization,* not the maximization, of the survival of the human race and all terrestrial life need to be identified and employed.

Now that scientists are decoding and reading the genomes of increasing numbers of living organisms, a vital opportunity emerges. That is, the real possibility of identifying and taking control of the genetic Aging and Death Program. It is this DNA program that makes dogs age and die after only about eight years, but directs parrots and elephants to live on until they are 80, ten times longer! As we decode the many elements of the DNA code of life, it is inevitable that we will discover the programmed activation of this inflammatory death program, which then can be understood and turned off.

Theoretically, having done so, one can then use it to regress back to one's prime of life. Then at last, the precious knowledge accumulated within our mature elder treasures after a lifetime of learning and experience will no longer have to be lost sadly in death, but can continue to grow and multiply their benefits. For optimum survival, we may have to limit reproduction to only that needed for replacement of existing members of the human race. This will require redirecting one of our greatest pleasures away from sex and reproduction, instead to the enhancement of the "joys of cooperation".

We have an inbuilt need for an effective philosophy of life that accounts for the mysterious as well as the mundane. This is the source of our religious orientation. However, we have inherited religions that are obsolescent. For this reason, organized religion is greatly in need of an upgrading. The fatal flaw of current religions is their erroneous belief in dream-like extracorporeal existence. Here, this is shown to be virtually impossible. Neuroreality replaces this error with the concept of an eternal universe of infinite levels, each with its emergent properties. This, brings us to an existence where rising from anxious individual competitive killing to the safe, nonkilling levels of cooperating empathic families, tribes, states, nations and worlds is in our self interest. This is because the emergent benefits of a long and satisfying life which automatically result.

We also will need to continue our ongoing encouraging astronomical quest for fresher habitable planets, as our earth slowly leaves the halo of life to be extinguished in entropy and chaos. Thus, the migratory cycle of seemingly divine extra-terrestrial life forms will become our own as well. So a key question is: when will we conquer gravity and become true builders and travelers? You are invited to move beyond this introduction to digest and assimilate the rest of this book. Then, come join your true family in the process of becoming an able, self motivated, peaceful human being with the potential for immortality.

Some Important Concepts of this Introduction:

We have an in-built religious constitution seeking to answer the big questions that give us purpose.

1. Our 4,000-year-old ancient religious heritages and traditions have become hopelessly out of date and no longer serve us.

2. Their non-credible, inaccurate answers to Life's Big Questions that we assimilate as children are the source of many of our problems today.

3. Religion can be brought into alignment with our current databased knowledge of the universe by recognizing the mental dream-based origin of the supernatural-spiritual, and the impossibility of its existence in external reality.

4. The Neuroreality of this book, seeks to provide the most accurate foundational understanding of the Universe, Life and Mind currently available, and will be continually updated.

5. This will enable us to move from the present level of killing up to the nonkilling levels of survival optimization, the next step in human evolution.

SECTION I: Where am I? The Nature of the Universe and Its Emergent Properties

CHAPTER 1: Universe Structure, Two Realities, Galactic Big Bang Engines and the Halo of Life

As we have created increasingly more powerful tools for observation of our environment, the concept of the Universe has changed remarkably. Originally, aware only of the "heavens and the earth" of our immediate surroundings, we naively imagined ourselves to be at the center of a finite flat universe, produced from nothing by a miraculous act of creation by a nearby God. Then, instrument makers such as Galileo produced successive waves of new information; forcing upon us several paradigm shifts in our beliefs. Among the first was that the earth was neither flat, nor the center of the universe, but instead, a small planet that orbits a much larger star. This gravely threatened religious tenets and forced the schism of science and religion. Now, contemporary scientists face another paradigm shift in long-held beliefs. This time it is whether by a miraculous act, some undefined God-being created the universe from nothing by a big bang, or whether the infinite mulitlayered universe has always existed as natural and eternal. The latter, a more accurate, data based view of the nature of the Universe is now emerging.

Living at the Event Horizon of an Infinitely Layered Universe:

It is simplest and most logical to believe in an eternal universe with no beginning, which is the first cause of all beginnings. It is uncreated, the source of all creation, and will never cease to be. In addition, by simple logic, the existence of the universe must precede the origin of any god or sentient being.

As depicted in **Table 1**, the Universe is composed of structural levels in endless layers, from the infinitesimal to infinite, each unique in content and in emergent properties. We have found that each outer boundary of our imagined Universe actually is a building block of the next level beyond. With ever more penetrating telescopic equipment, we have thus far perceived at least seven inanimate levels beyond our own. For example, **Figure 1** illustrates the universe level of planets in our solar

Table 1. Human-Centered Infinitude: Nearby Universe Strata, Each with Unique Properties and Structures

---

Infinities: *unique types and laws*

   Universes: *unique types and laws*

      Superclusters and Dark Matter: *unique types and laws*

         Galaxies: *unique types and laws*

            Solar Systems: *unique types and laws*

               Stars: *unique types and laws*

                  Planets and Moons: *unique types and laws*

                     Continents, Seas, Atmospheres: *unique types and laws*?

                        <u>**Animate and Inanimate Natural Forms:**</u> (* includes humanity

                          Solids, Liquids and Gases: *unique types and laws*

                             Molecules: *unique types and laws*

                               Atoms-Elements: *unique types and laws*

                                 Nuclei, Electrons: *unique types and laws*

                                   Protons, Neutrons, Leptons: *unique types and laws*

                                   Quarks-Antiquarks, Gluons, Color: *types, laws*

                                   Implied Smaller Components: *types and laws*

                                   Infinitesimals: *unique types and laws*

---

system. **Figure 2** illustrates some of the inhabitants of our galaxy at the universe level of stars. **Figure 3** is a small view of the next universe level, that of types of galaxies. Beginning with galactic super-clusters and dark matter, **Figure 4** contains simulations of even higher universe levels.

Figure 1, Universe Level of Planets: Relative sizes of the solar planets

Figure 2, Universe Level of Stars: Relative Sizes of Some of the Larger Stars

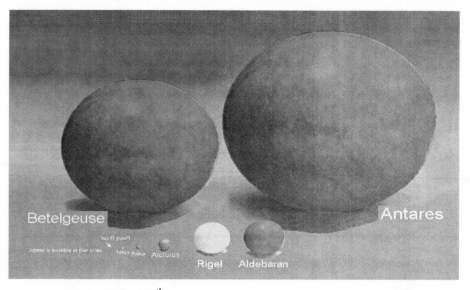

Antares is the 15th brightest star in our sky. It is more than 1000 light years away.

Figure 3, Universe Level of Galaxies: Many Types

This is a Hubble Telescope ultra deep field infrared view of countless entire galaxies, billions of light years away.

Figure 4, Simulations of Galactic Superclusters and Higher Universe Levels

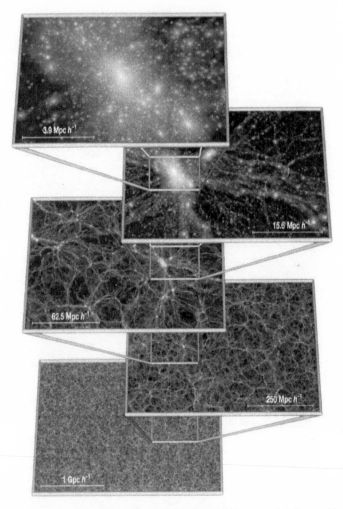

Figure 1 | **The dark matter density field on various scales.** Each individual image shows the projected dark matter density field in a slab of thickness $15h^{-1}$ Mpc (sliced from the periodic simulation volume at an angle chosen to avoid replicating structures in the lower two images), colour-coded by density and local dark matter velocity dispersion. The zoom sequence displays consecutive enlargements by factors of four, centred on one of the many galaxy cluster haloes present in the simulation.

Equally impressive, with our ever-more powerful magnifying instruments, we have also detected at least seven of the nearest inanimate levels below us. These invisible but very real levels are not illustrated here. Repeatedly, each proclaimed fundamental element of the universe has ultimately split into smaller particles (Table 1).

Thus, our cosmos's organization is not as a pyramid, but rather as an infinite nested hierarchy. Cosmologists have yet to appreciate the significance of human existence within a universe of infinite unique strata. Such structure, by its very definition, precludes intelligent external design. Comprehending the infinite levels of the universe can possibly push us to our limits, but not to its limits.

Thus, we stand at the event horizon of some arbitrary universe level called home that separates an endless progression of outer levels above us from the infinity of inner levels below us. Which way do we look in our search for God, or for other intelligent life? Are the stars of Orion only molecules within the foot of a giant? Is there a world of life, bustling upon the third electron-planet circling in the carbon atom? Might heaven be there? Yet, here we are, safe within our life-supporting nest, high in a tree. We know from observation that falling can kill us before we learn to fly. But then, we are the offspring of survivors.

External and Internal Realities:

To make progress in our understanding of where we are, it is helpful to be aware that there are at least seven types of reality. Distinguishing these can replace our natural confusion with an enlightened perspective. We will discuss two of them here. The most foundational of these several realities is **External Reality.** This is the actual state of the universe as it occurs independent of our participation or our agreement. Yes, that tree really did fall in the forest, unheard by us. External Reality is *the way things are,* and *how the universe works.*

At first, the nature of external reality appears hopelessly complex and paradoxical. On one hand, certain aspects of external reality seem to be *ever changing.* That is, there is matter's continual movement for example, microscopic Brownian motion, the travel of people, the drift of continents and the passage of asteroids. Many other changes occur with time as well, from the life cycle of living organisms to the continual galactic flow of free energy and order toward entropy and chaos. Thus, the appearance of much of our environment is indeed ever changing.

Yet, other aspects of external reality are *ever the same*. These are constant and reliable. That is, the macroscopic atomic and molecular properties of matter have the constancy and predictability that produces not only the reliable nature of solids, liquids, and gases, but also of the earth's rotational orbit around the sun. Time's movement at a given location is continuously unidirectional, proportional, and predictable. The constancy and predictability of the speed of sound and light, and the strength of gravity at a given location show the dependability of energy.

It is the contingent (random) interplay between the constant and changing properties of external reality that has led to the continued operation of the universe, including the origin of life, its properties, its evolution, and its potential for movement toward more energy-enriched quadrants of local or extended environment. Importantly, this interplay also provides personal, social and cultural access to the opportunity, abundance and power inherent within the external reality of the universe around us and which can only be found there.

External reality is approachable by living organisms through use of their multiple sensory apparatus, such as eyes or ears. From these narrow windows of perception, organisms can use the data obtained to create successively more accurate internal approximations of external reality. These ever-evolving models of external reality are called **Internal Reality.** Formed by experience, training and luck, each individual's Internal Reality model is unique. **Figure 5** shows the contrasts between external reality and internal reality.

Thus, each of our unique sensory-based, continually upgraded, working models of external reality began as an unavoidably grossly inaccurate and idiosyncratic personal approximation (Figure 5). See the "word processing" entries). As a result, we are able to use learning to upgrade our model at the intellectual, but not emotional level The more accurate it becomes, the more successfully we can align with and operate in the way the universe actually works; and thus, tap its resources. At some point, our internal reality model can actually cross the "threshold of workability". This happens when our internal reality becomes sufficiently accurate to actually function successfully in the real (external and interior) world. Fortunately, this also brings our internal realities ever closer to those of others who have also crossed the threshold of workability. Concerted,

Figure 5: Absolute External Realty vs. Our Internal Reality Models of It

THE UNIVERSE: THE WAY IT IS, HOW THINGS WORK,

.   **EVER CHANGING, EVER THE SAME**

~!@#$%^&*)(_+}{][?></~~!@#$%^&*)(_+}{][?></~~!@#$%^&*)(_+}{][?></#
$%^&*()_+={[}]'"?/\><~!@#$%^&*()_+={[}]'"?/\><~!@#$%^&*()_+={[}]'"?/_
+}{][?></~~!@#$%^&*)(_+}{][?></~~!@#$%^&*)(_+}{][?></~~!@#$%^&*)

EXTERNAL REALITY: SOLE SOURCE OF LIFE, ABUNDANCE,
                                    OPPORTUNITY AND POWER

*Like images on a screen, external reality can never be reached, only approached:***x**

                             Word Processor Inventors x

Nuclear Physics, Astronautics, Molecular Biology Genetic Enginering **x**

                           Word Processor Users   x

                                  Triadism **x**

Rising above this line brings enough alignment to tap the bounties of the universe
The Threshold of Workability:---------------------------- -**x**------------------------.

                                x   Neuroscience

INTERNAL REALITY: SENSE-BASED-   **x**   Certain Philosophies

                             x   Some Areas of Science

                          x   Many Philosophies

APPROXIMATIONS   **x**   Most Politics

                      x   Many World Religions

                 x   Traditions

OF EXTERNAL   **x**   Metaphors

             x   **Word Processor Beginners**

          x   Miracles

REALITY   **x**   Dualism

       x   Myths

     x   Magic

= MY "TRUTH" **x**   Omens

     x   Superstitions

   x   Monism

  x   Ignorance

x   Unawareness

x   Unconsciousness

x   Dead-Inanimate

---

aligned communication then begins to replace confusion. This is an important purpose of this book.

However, we must bear in mind that inner reality is related to external reality like images of an actual object are reflected by a mirror, etched on a photograph, or projected from a monitor. External reality is both unreachable and of a different nature than our inner reality models.That is, there is no green out there. Green is a product of the brain's processing of reflectance and absorbance sensory data *from something that is out there*. Whenever sensed, this object reliably produces the inner perception of green. Therefore, we can use these and the other consistent sensory-response metaphors to create a practical internal working model from which to make "sense" of our environment. In this regard, however, any absolute truth is inherently indeterminate and only approximate.

The Galactic Big Bang Engine:

Physicists and astronomers have discovered the *second half* of a universal process that interchanges matter, energy and time. **Figure 6** illustrates this second part of the process, nicknamed "The Big Bang Theory", which transforms energy into matter. Doctrinaire cosmologists have grasped at the Big Bang as a way to supply a much needed mechanism which could account for a purported beginning: the creation of the Universe from nothing by a miraculous act of God (Kragh, 1996). Calculations show the Big Bang inflation of time and space, with the transformation of energy into matter occurred over the following epochs of time: (Figure 6). That period from zero to 10^{-43} seconds is the Quantum Gravity Era. By 10^{-36} seconds, there had been an era of enormous inflation in space. By 10^{-5} seconds, neutrons and protons had been formed from a subatomic "quark group" of particles. By 3 minutes, the atomic nuclei had formed. By 300,000 years, during a period of recombination, atoms had formed, and light released resulted in the background microwave radiation. By 1 billion years, stars, black holes, quasars, and galaxies had formed. Current thought shows cellular life to have emerged by 3.8 billion years, and evolved about 10 billion years to reach the estimated present 13.7 billion year age of our universe. Without a doubt, the incredible transformational process of the big bang does exist. However, what is its origin and where within the infinite and eternal universe is it occurring?

Several methods have recently confirmed super-massive black holes to exist within the center of galaxies. Each of these black holes emits two enormous polar fountains of energy (white holes), often detected as quasars. A galactic black hole is truly massive. It contains the crushing gravity of thousands or millions of solar masses. These holes are known to suck stellar matter into the event horizon around their equators with such a collapsing force that even the photon particles of light fail to escape, making these pits the darkest of infernos. Beyond the event horizon, deep within galactic black holes, normal space-filled matter further compresses under this intense gravity. Next, the elementary particles aggregate to attain the density of tons per cubic centimeter, fusing together within a

Figure 6. Big Bang: Inflation of Time and Space with the Conversion of Energy to Matter

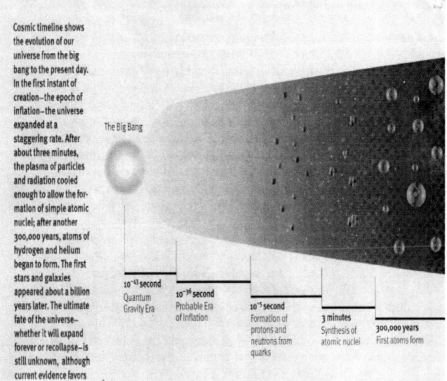

Cosmic timeline shows the evolution of our universe from the big bang to the present day. In the first instant of creation—the epoch of inflation—the universe expanded at a staggering rate. After about three minutes, the plasma of particles and radiation cooled enough to allow the formation of simple atomic nuclei; after another 300,000 years, atoms of hydrogen and helium began to form. The first stars and galaxies appeared about a billion years later. The ultimate fate of the universe—whether it will expand forever or recollapse—is still unknown, although current evidence favors

The Big Bang

10^{-43} second
Quantum Gravity Era

10^{-36} second
Probable Era of Inflation

10^{-5} second
Formation of protons and neutrons from quarks

3 minutes
Synthesis of atomic nuclei

300,000 years
First atoms form

singularity at its core. The result of this enormous compression is a thermonuclear fusion reaction explosion, seemingly related to that of our primitive H-hydrogen bomb. This continuously feeds the two polar fountain *white holes* (Bentov, 1978) with incredible energy.

Within the singularity of the black hole, enormous forces create an environment where normal external laws do not apply. Instead, presently unknown laws cause the transformation of this collapsing galactic equatorial influx of entropy (free energy depleted), chaotic matter, and expended time into a "white hole", producing two enormously energy and, time-inflating polar fountains. Now, here is a place in the Universe where "The Big Bang" is now occurring! These blazing fountains, seen from across the universe, actually are galactic Big Bang inflations of time, energy and ultimately matter feeding off the first half of the process, the stellar collapse into the black holes of galaxies.

As shown in **Figure 7**, the galaxy's gravitational attraction with its super massive central black hole draws these "white hole" fountains of invisible subatomic dark matter with its associated dark energy back around to form a double torus. Both hemispheres of this double torus coalesce together at the equatorial plane to form the inward feeding glowing spiral arms of the visible galaxy. These arms are visible because inflated dark matter and dark energy have begun to interchange so that at this point matter has aggregated into atomic and then molecular particles that release energy in the form of visible radiation. Nebulae of molecular hydrogen arise here to become the visible luminous, "light matter" of the galactic arms. Further inward these nebulae coalesce into young stars, which later transform mature stars, each with their own internal furnaces creating atoms of the more complex elements, such as those required for terrestrial life.

Presently, there is paradigm confusion among cosmologists regarding whether the galactic spiral arms move inward or outward, and thus, whether stars farthest from the black hole are the youngest or the oldest. The Galactic Engine Model predicts that stars first form with the outer edge of the spiral arms and then move and mature inward as they age ultimately to be continuously consumed by the black hole. This accurately predicts the reported clustering of oldest stars near the center of our galaxy. However, this observation contradicts the present paradigm that the oldest stars should be farthest from the galactic center.

Rather than a single huge big bang explosion occurring, ultimately followed by a universal collapse, or the oscillations between these two extremes, the Galactic Big Bang Engine model further proposes that the big bangs occurring at the heart of the galactic black hole singularities are ongoing continuous hyper-intense flames of re-creation. They are fed by chaotic entropy collapse at their equators, and emit fountains of the

Figure 7:

Galactic Engine Model: Origin of Life

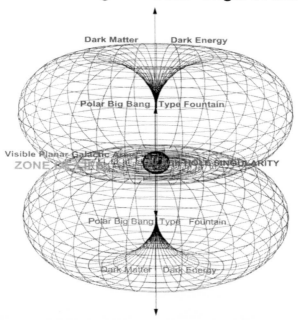

presently "missing" huge amounts of dark energy and dark matter that has already been detected to be concentrated around galaxies.

Source of Dark Energy, and Dark Matter

Thus, a galaxy is an enormous cyclic engine producing energy, matter and the beginning of time in the form of enormous coincident polar eruptions. The products of these geysers are pulled back around by gravity into its double toroidal-shaped transit to return through the galactic arms at the central plane. These finally collapse into the central black hole much later at the end of its time. Because dark energy converts into increasingly complex matter in the big bang inflation, there is a gradient of energy along each galactic spiral arm. Beginning at the outer edge with a crackling explosive excess of potential (free) energy and very little spent energy (entropy). As the stars progress on their inbound spiral more and more potential energy is spent, until eons later only spent energy remains. Then this entropy (spent energy)-engorged, chaotic matter collapses back through the event horizon into the awaiting black hole at the end of its time.

From this, it becomes clear that within most galaxies a "Halo of Life" exists at some intermediate distance from the galactic center and through which the stars in all the galactic arms must migrate. In this galactic zone of life, the ratio of free energy to entropy is such that the structural order inherent in life can spontaneously evolve and continue to maximize in order. Presently, our solar system is located about half way out from the galactic center, located in one of arms of our Milky Way galaxy. Our sun and earth are still within the galactic zone of life. It was here long ago (3.8 billion yrs) that life evolved or was inseminated on earth.

The Galactic Big Bang Engine is the first model to propose that big bang expansions are currently and continuously occurring within the black hole singularities at the center of galaxies, rather than being the ancient unique event that created our universe. This flips our understanding of galaxies on its head, and provides the foundation for a cosmology that is much closer to the truth. The multileveled universe is eternal, filled with galactic singularity engines within which matter and energy fluxes provide the requirements for the origin, and evolution of life.

Within this model, the nature of the larger universe, beyond of webs of galaxies at the limits of our most expansive view, cannot at present be known. Our astronomical window, whose distance in all directions has been found to be essentially equal, views only a narrow observational sphere of a much larger universe. To accommodate the currently popular expanding universe view, one only needs to imagine our sphere of current information as a bubble being swept by vaster cosmic events.

In our galaxy, we are within that zone of life where life survives or dies according to the laws of our local universe. If we learn them and align ourselves with these laws by making them our religion, we survive and prosper. If not, we die. The universe and its unbreakable laws do not care whether our particular religion works or not. Neuroreality forms the basis of a religion that promotes success in life.

Over time, our earth will move inward within its galactic arm, ultimately leaving the halo of life, migrating into regions so poor in potential energy and so rich in spent energy that life can no longer continue. Therefore, for our terrestrial life form to continue, we must evolve our technology far enough to be able to solve the problems of gravity and space travel. This will permit our continued extraterrestrial survival by enabling our migration outward along our galactic arm to planets deeper within the halo of life. There we can resettle in fresher planetary pastures of potential energy. Thus, our astronomers should specifically be looking outward along our galactic arm for younger planets.

Earlier Planetary Migrants:

There is suggestive evidence that such accomplished migrants reached our earth more than 12,000 years ago, just after the last ice age, when our world was fertile and blooming. Then, while we were but primitive hunter-gatherers, unknown beings at Abydos, Egypt built remarkable megaliths of monumental cut stone building blocks, leaving behind the by far the largest structures of this type in existence on earth today, (**Figure 8**). The only similar structures to be found in Egypt are the pre-pyramidal megalith temples that surround and include the Sphinx at Giza. The Sphinx itself is deeply eroded from long exposure to much earlier periods of abundant rainfall at the end of the ice age. This evidence

Figure 8. The Osirion Structure at Abydos, Egypt.

A.

B.	C.	D.	E.

Legend for Figure 8. The Osirion Structure at Abydos, Egypt
A and C: Red Aswan granite pillars, each weighing over a hundred tons
support equally massive archways. This megalithic building is about 50
feet below current ground level, and far below the present level of the Nile.
The thickness of the accumulated sediment above and around this ancient
structure supports the estimate that it was built at least 12,000 yrs bp. At
around 3,300 yrs pb Dynastic Egyptians, apparently calculated the same
exact spot to build the Tempe of Seti. Apparently, the subsequent discovery
of the ancient buried Osirion forced them change their plans and build the
only L-shaped temple found in Egypt (bottom of B.), abutting the east end
of the ancient Osirion (top of B). D. and E., Upon two opposing megalithic
pillars in the Osirion are several versions of a 64-faced 3D figure, now
known as the sacred Flower of Life (FOL). These ancient red ochre-like
precise drawings of complex geometry appear as if engraved by laser into
the granite structure itself. They are the only original inscriptions in the
ancient temple.

---

supports estimates that the stones in these structures were cut from the
bedrock next to and creating the Sphinx sometime before 12,000 yrs ago.

Other ancient megaliths are now submerged under the ocean that
has risen in more recent times. Apparently, these space travelers settled,
survived, and possibly interbred. Perhaps, those events sparked the
dualistic myths of the gods, angels and demons that we inherit today. Soon,
we must recover their former mastery of the knowledge used to build their
megaliths and travel in space. Now, it is our turn to migrate to fresher
planets upstream within the halo of life. We must do this if our life form is
to survive after the earth drifts beyond the halo of life.

Our Myths: Supernatural or Natural?:
An interesting perspective can be brought to some of our oldest
stories by changing the context away from the traditional supernatural view
to a more natural explanation of real accomplishment. For example, those
advanced immigrants, arriving here over 12,000 year ago, by definition,
would have had to of brought with them relatively compact transportable
antigravity power supplies to enable their not only their space travel, but
also to accomplish the cutting and carrying of the huge stone monoliths of
their ancient terrestrial temples. Perhaps, over time the continued existence

of one or more of these units formed the ancient basis of some of our Bible stories. For example, how about those cherubic energy sources which guarded the Garden of Eden? Did being cast out of Eden and away from them and the "Tree of Life" remove humanity from a highly tailored optimal system into a raw and unprotected labor intensive environment? Did Moses, educated for years as the son of an Egyptian pharaoh, use a still existing power source to cause the ten plagues? Was one of these cherubic power supplies housed in the Ark of the Covenant which Moses used to part the waters of the Red Sea, and then collapse upon the Egyptian Army seeking recoup its loss?

Was the cloud by day and pillar of fire by night, as well as the nourishing manna from heaven, the byproduct of this power source, which was kept hidden within the transportable Holy Tabernacle for the forty years in the wilderness of Sinai? Was it this ark-born power source, rather than some magical God, that was also responsible for the parting of the flooding River Jordan, when the Israelites finally entered Palestine. Did the well-documented collapsed walls of Jericho, fall by the power within the Ark, which had just been carried around Jericho for days by the Levites? When the Ark was lost with the destruction of the first Temple of Solomon in Jerusalem by the Babylonians around 550 BC, where did it go? Did the Knights Templers uncover its hidden crypt beneath the Dome of the Rock within Solomon's first temple. Did they take it to Europe, ultimately to assist in the building of the miraculous Chartres Cathedral? Is the Ark now guarded within a church in Ethiopia? Why did the Nazi Raiders of the lost Ark believe so strongly that it was an object of great power? Questions to tantalize the imagination! Perhaps evidence of previous immigrants to an ancient younger earth will stimulate us once again to gain a working knowledge of the power of gravity.

In the mean time there are more immediate things for us to do. First priority, is the conversion of humans from killing competitors to non-killing comrade-collaborators. This brings us to the next chapter and our paradoxical genetic heritage of "the survival of the fittest by tooth and claw".

Chapter 1: GALACTIC BIG BANG IN AN ETERNAL UNIVERSE

Some Important Concepts of Chapter 1:

1. We stand at the event horizon of some arbitrary universe level we call home, separating an endless progression of outer levels above us from the infinity of inner levels below us.

2. Each of us is making unique Internal Reality models of External Reality that we build from our experience, training and luck.

3. In our infinite and eternal, God-like universe, the Big Bang is seen to be only the second half of a cyclic process.

4. A galaxy is an enormous cyclic engine. At its center is a singularity-containing black hole from which a Big Bang is continuously inflating dark energy, dark matter, and time.

5. Due to the system's enormous gravity, this dark matter is pulled back toward the galaxy to form a double torus (see figure) that enters the outer edge of the visible, planar, star-forming spiral arms of the galaxy. Moving inward, these stars and planets pass through a Zone of Life, a region where the ratio of free energy to entropy brings about the structural order and complexity required for the evolutionary birth and development of terrestrial life

6. Over time, our earth will ultimately leave the halo of life, drifting inward along the galactic arms into chaotic regions where life becomes impossible. Thus, for our form of life to continue, we must master gravity and space migration. Tantalizing evidence exists that we will not have been the first to do so.

7. The unique concept of a galactic singularity engine within which we exist is the basis for Neurorealism's cosmology. This cosmology is more comprehensive and accurate than the idea of special creation. We survive and prosper better if we make it our religion to seek out and align with the laws of our local universe. This is because they are absolute and impersonal and do not care whether we live or die. Thus, to continue to exist, we must care.

NEUROREALITY: A SCIENTIFIC RELIGION TO RESTORE MEANING

SECTION I: Where am I? The Nature of Universe and Its Emergent Properties.

CHAPTER 2: The Five Dimensions of Behavior and The Law of Emergent Properties

In this chapter, two important concepts are developed and applied. Unfortunately, they were not included in our childhood toolbox of beliefs. The first is an explicit description of behavior. In the past, the causal production behavior has seemed so transient and inexplicable as to appear mysterious and confusing. We saw it happen, but aside from its after effects, the record of the event is now only in our memories. In this chapter, it is broken down into five quantifiable dimensions.

Once we understand the higher dimensionality of behavior within the context of a multileveled universe a whole new world emergent behavioral properties opens to us. This leads to the second important concept of this chapter: Emergence. Understanding that each of the infinite levels of the universe are occupied with not only unique structures, but also with unique emergent property laws makes it possible for us, for the first time to truly understand how the behavioral laws of the individual self are different, in fact quite the opposite, to the laws of family and society. This begins to open to us the path of how we can rise from killing to nonkilling.

With these two new concepts, we can build a more accurate model of the properties of the universe.

Time and Potential Energy are the Fourth and Fifth Dimensions of Behavior and Causality

To begin, let us convert the endless levels of unique three-dimensional (length, width, height) structures from a static universe into the actual dynamic universe of motion. To create this activity, we must add two additional dimensions. The first of these is *time*, a fourth dimension (Newcomb, 1895, Einstein, 1984). The second is *energy*, a fifth dimension (Kaluza, 1921; Einstein, 1927; Morton, 1985a).

The fourth and fifth dimensions used here are not to be confused with other unimaginable added   structural dimensions (Moller, Madland, Sierk, & Iwamoto, 2001). To the contrary, common everyday behavior, both living and non-living, is actually visibly five dimensional. That is, although often unrecognized, the addition over time (4th D) of energy (5th D) to a normal 3-D structure is the sole source of its movement, animation and behavior. In spite of our apparent lack of formal awareness of the existence of these five dimensions, we commonly operate as if we knew of them intuitively. Yet, the critical difference between a structure and its activities is generally not appreciated beyond such vague statements, such as "One cannot compare apples with oranges".

A point to be emphasized from the above is that the input of the fourth dimension of time and of the fifth dimension free energy converts a static, immobile universe of structural strata into a myriad of motions, activities, and processes. Correspondingly, the removal of either of these two required dimensional elements brings any material system to a total halt in terms of behavior, as in the case of inert archeological layers.

However, rather than seeming to confuse things by talking about apparently-strange five dimensional events, let us further clarify the nature of behavior by introducing the equivalent concept of Triadism. That is, the behavior of: 1) a physical *structure* (any material 3-D object) critically depends upon, not only its intact, functional status, but also 2) a finite period of *time;* and the 3) coupling to an *energy* source. That is, the input of an ultimately causal amount of accessible potential chemical free energy (= ΔG, *not* $E=mc^2$). We often think at this level, not realizing that we are thinking five dimensionally.

Behavioral Lessons from Laborsaving Devices: Triadic Requirement for Activity

To facilitate gaining clarity about the triadic nature of behavior, it is useful first to consider the behavioral properties of electronic or mechanical equipment, for example of a compact disc player or of an automobile (**Table 1**). The past, present, or future activities of a CD player or a car cannot be discovered by dissecting their structures. That is, one cannot hear a movie star's whisper either by taking apart the disc player, or by inspecting the structure of the compact disc, even with an electron microscope. Nor will dismantling one's auto reveal the route or speed of the trip with a friend from the restaurant last night. Yet, the useful behavioral activities of each machine are dependent upon its 3D structural integrity. If one cuts an essential wire or breaks a required mechanical part of either, it becomes inactive, nonfunctional, essentially "dead", or "soulless".

The activities of these machines are also dependent upon time. Complete viewing and analysis of a movie on a CD cannot be done in one second, nor can one get across Bangkok by taxi in one minute. Lastly, it is also clear that the activities of both a CD and a car depend upon the input of free energy. This may come, as in the case of the CD, perhaps from a nuclear reactor-powered electricity generator or for the car from the release of the solar energy stored within the bonds of gasoline.

Table 1. The Triadic Pillars of Behavior

Structure +	Time +	Potential Energy	=	Activity, Process, Behavior
Enzyme +	Seconds +	Cal. away from equilibrium =		Catalysis of a reaction
Automobile +	Minutes +	Octane of fuel	=	Travel on roadways
CD Player +	Minutes +	110-220 V electricity	=	Projection of multimedia
Computer +	Microseconds +	110-220 V electricity =		Processing of data

Behavioral Lessons from Enzymology: Dependence of Catalysis upon the Activity Triad

To avoid the illusion that human interference might invalidate the above illustrations, it is instructive to consider the activity of enzymes. Chemical catalysis by enzymes provides a very well characterized system for quantitative investigation. Enzymes are usually proteins (large linear polymers of small molecule amino acid building blocks) whose activities can accelerate the rate that a specific chemical reaction approaches its energetic equilibrium by as much as several billion fold (Nelson, and Cox, 2000) without themselves being depleted in the process. The emergence of enzymes was a key event in the origin of terrestrial life.

Many biochemists thought that if they could just see the structure of an enzyme, they would understand how it worked. They felt that its mechanism of action would then become at least accessible, if not obvious. Using x-ray crystallography and other powerful techniques, biophysicists have now completely solved the atomic structure of thousands of enzymes. Yet at present, this vast information about the static positions of all the thousands of atoms in an unknown protein does not permit the prediction as to whether such a peptide is even an enzyme, much less what its specific catalytic activity might be. Structurally similar proteins may have widely different specific catalytic properties if they are catalysts at all. Conversely, certain structurally different proteins can specifically catalyze the same reaction. Thus, the relation of enzyme structure to catalytic activity did not become obvious, even when complete structural information was available.

However, enzymologists studying enzyme activity by adding "kinetic" (time based, 4th D) and "thermodynamic" (energy based, 5th D) methods to this new 3-D structural information have now discovered the exact mechanisms promoting enzyme catalysis (Nelson and Cox, 2000). First, they confirmed that there were indeed, non-obvious but critically essential, structural requirements for an enzyme to act as a catalyst. In fact, the activity of an enzyme is absolutely tied to its 3-D structural integrity, a point that cannot be overemphasized. The fact that enzyme catalysis is extremely sensitive to small changes in enzyme structural conformation illustrates this key concept. For instance, a lethal point mutation, created by the substitution of only one different amino acid out of the hundreds in the primary structure of an enzyme could totally abolish its catalytic activity, in spite of abundant amounts of time and energy.

Researchers further observed that a critical structural "active site" within the enzyme actually provided the needed local chemical environment required to facilitate an actual energetic activation of specific covalent bonds in the reactant via bond distortion and strain introduction. This also included the coupling and transfer of the resulting labilized reactant's elevated free energy into lower-energy, more stable products.

Attempts to utilize reaction conditions where the reactants and products were arranged to be thermodynamically at chemical equilibrium confirmed this concept. There and then, no net catalytic activity occurred, in spite of enzyme structural adequacy and the presence of time. Conversely, regardless of how much intact enzyme (3D) and potential energy (5th D) were present, if there was too little incubation time (4th D) available, nothing happened.

Activity is a process, an event, an action, a phenomenon, an occurrence, a doing. This is equally true for human behavior as for the activity of an enzyme. Thus, all behavioral activities stand upon the same *triad*, absolutely requiring three elements: intact structure, time and potential energy. In fact, all proper macroscopic specific-activity descriptions ultimately must formally consist of units of each of these three elements: that is, *change in chemical free energy per unit mass of structure per unit of time.*

The Existence, Origin and Nature of Emergent Properties

Now with an understanding of the five dimensional nature of behavior, we can address the second major concept of this chapter: Emergence. By this is meant the emergence of new behaviors, activities, and processes that are inherent in our multileveled universe simply by the state change that occurs upon rising to the next universe level.

In Chapter 1, investigators described a powerful new way to conceptualize our universe. That is, here on the surface of the earth we stand at the event horizon separating an infinite number of higher inanimate structural levels above, from an infinite number of lower levels. Only the nearest few of these levels have we identified. It is important to note that in the universe, *each of these levels possesses unique emergent properties and is occupied by unique structural types not present on any other universe level.*

So, what does the term emergent properties mean? The "property" of something is any structure-dependent characteristic, quality, capacity, virtue, activity, behavior, use or process that it could be caused to do. For example, one "property" of water is that it converts from a liquid to a solid at temperatures below zero degrees centigrade. A property of a hammer is its usefulness for driving and pulling nails. While the existence of properties of a whole unit as being different and greater than the properties of the sum of its building blocks has long been obvious, observers do not yet recognize these state changes as expressions of a universal law. Even to this day, such emergence has seemed to many physicists, as inexplicable, counterintuitive, like magic, or the supernatural.

Here, we call attention to and provide understanding of the Emergent Properties Law, which may be stated as follows: *Although the structure is never more than the sum of its parts, the potential activities of a structure must always be different and greater than the sum of the potential activities of its parts.* (**Table 2**). It has long been clear that the total structure of a unit whole, say a little red wagon, can never be more that the sum of the structures of its building blocks, i.e. container, frame, wheels, axels, etc. Yet, as will be amply illustrated, when these wagon components assemble into the larger whole, a wagon, at the next higher universe level, the parts did not possess the new properties that appear.

Table 2, The Concept and Context of Emergent Properties

From Physics: The Three Dimensional Law of Structural Conservation:
*A **Structure** of an Object Never Can Be More that the Sum of the **Structures** of Its Parts.*

From Neuroreality: The Five Dimensional Law of Emergent Properties:
*The **Properties** of a Structure are Always Different and Greater than the Sum of the **Properties** of its Parts.*

For example, the wagon can be used to transport heavy items over a smooth surface. In contrast, when a whole is subdivided into its component parts at the next lower universe level, their properties always differ from those of the original whole. The wheels fall over onto the ground and will not roll. Likewise, the frame and axel have lost the properties of a wagon. Similarly, the separated handle and head of a formerly effective hammer are next to impossible to use for the efficient insertion or removal of nails

This state change paradox can be understood by considering the following points: First, the original activities of the building blocks become at least partially hindered or occluded by their attachment, and thus their enforced closer association within the newly created more complex whole. Thus, by definition, they will have a more rigid or constrained-controlled range of motion, than when detached. Second, it must follow that the new structure is more massive and complex than its component parts. Third, the more complex composite structure usually will have more surface area and thus more opportunities to accept and return energetic exchanges with its environment than its building blocks did. Thus, at the higher universe level, composite structure will have new purposeless, different and greater properties than are present in its component building blocks. Such new properties automatically appearing when subunits are assembled into a higher level whole are appropriately called Emergent Properties. For example, from two sticks, and a piece of string, came archery.

Referring to the structural levels of **Tables 3 and 4,** one can confirm these ideas by noticing the unique, interesting, and unexpected activities manifest by each higher level compared to those of its lower level building blocks. For example, consider the new properties that emerge by combining the twenty common amino acids into a protein. The following are eight emergent unique properties (Table 3) of such peptides that are not possessed by the sum of their free amino acid building blocks: 1) Antigens

Table 3: Emergent Properties of Amino Acid Polymers Not Possessed by a Mixture of Their Twenty Free Amino Acid

---

1. Antigens and antibodies
2. Transporters of blood gases, such as O_2, CO_2, NO
3. Cell membrane structural elements
4. Structural polymers of tendon, cartilage, and bone
5. Major elements in contractile systems
6. Structures of cellular receptors, channels, & pumps
7. Specific hormones and neuromodulators
8. Enzyme catalysts

---

and antibodies, 2), Transporters of blood gases, such as O_2, CO_2, and NO, 3) Cell membrane structural elements, 4) Structural polymers of tendon, cartilage and bone, 5) Major elements in contractile systems, 6) Key structures of cellular receptors, channels, and pumps, 7) Specific hormones and neuromodulators, and 8) Enzymes (Nelson and Cox, 2000).

Who could have predicted this? For example, what "equation for everything" (Lindley, 2001) using the laws of amino acids could have been extended or modified to predict for example, the existence of the partial antagonist-binding properties of the mu-opiate receptor subunit proteins. The existence and unpredictability of emergent properties is strong evidence that Godel's Incompleteness Theorem (1962) can be generalized beyond his arithmetic systems. This theorem actually *prohibits* the prediction of behavioral properties of a structures assembled at *any* next higher universe level based only upon knowledge of the properties of its parts at the level below.

For yet another example: clearly, inspecting a pearl or its interior, even microscopically, cannot trace its origin back to the behavior of an oyster on the next higher universe level. Yet, even today most physicists would strongly, but incorrectly, agree with Stapp (1993) that, "Nothing in classical physics can create something that is *essentially* more than an aggregation of its parts". Unfortunately, a classical, one level universe, mind-set equates activity with structure, thus making the undeniable existence of emergent properties as something akin to the supernatural. Actually, such are unrecognized paradigm shifts which must occur with any movement between universe levels. Similar examples of emergence exist ad-infinitum for the emergent properties of any of the structural levels

Table 4. How are the Emergent Properties of the Whole at One Universe Level Different and Greater than Those of its Parts at the Next Lower Level?

Properties of an **Atom** > sum of the properties of its **Subatomic Particles**?
Sodium (inflammatory metal) > constituent protons, neutrons, electrons?

Properties of a **Molecule** > sum of the properties of its Constituent **Atom**s?
Aspirin (anti-inflammatory drug) > Atoms (carbon, oxygen, and hydrogen)?

Properties of a **Polymer** > sum of properties of their **Molecular Monomers**?
DNA (genome) > monophosphate nucleotides (intermediary metabolites)?

Properties of **Supramolecular Assemblies** > that of **Polymer** Macromolecules?
Ribosomes (protein synthesis factories) > components (RNA & protein)?

Properties of **Subcellular Organelles** >that of their **Supramolecular Assemblies**?
Chloroplast (carbon fixing systems) > (lipid membranes and chlorophyll)?

Properties of **Living Cells**>properties of their combined **Subcellular Organelles**?
Ovum or muscle cell > constituents of nucleus or cytoplasm?

Properties of a **Tissue** > than the properties of its individual **Cells**?
Retina > neurons? OR Bone > osteocytes and calcium?

Properties of an **Organ** > the sum of the properties of its **Tissues**?
Heart (blood pump) > simple cardiac muscle shortening?

Properties of an **Individual** Organism > the sum of the properties of its **Organs**?
Person (Jane Doe) > kidney filtration, or heart pump?

Properties of a **Family** > the sum of the Properties of its **Individual** Members
The Kennedys > Jackie

(**Table 4**), and can come from three very different possible universe-level perspectives, as illustrated in **Figure 2**. These are: 1) the Self-referencing, 2) the Dissecting, and 3) the Synthesizing points of view. The self-referencing viewpoint considers types of objects within the same level of order, for example the great variety and vintages of existing automobiles. The dissecting viewpoint, considers the object in the next level lower level beneath the reference level in terms of its component building blocks, that is, the wheels, engine, or fenders of a car. The synthesizing viewpoint considers how the objects in the reference level contribute to the creation of larger wholes, such as traffic, fleets of rental cars, or auto races.

Figure 2: Beyond Induction and Deduction, the Logic Processes of Synthesis and Dissection are Used in the Discovery Process

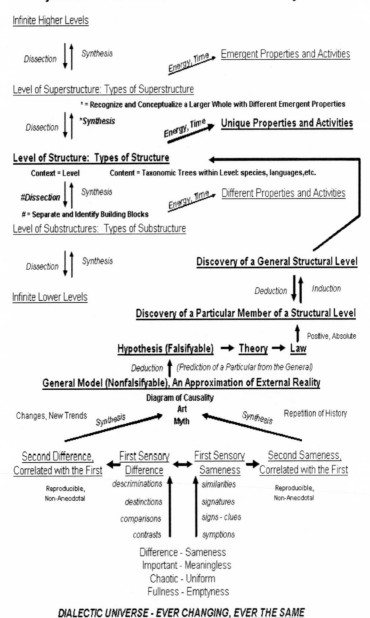

The Mathematical Processes of Induction and Deduction can only be Used Within the Same Universe Level

For centuries, confusion has arisen from inappropriate attempts to use deduction and induction across universe levels, instead of within them. Induction is bottom- up in orientation and may be defined as going from many individual cases to begin to see the pattern of a new general principle arising. In contrast, deduction is top down in view, as defined as recognizing that a specific case is an example of an already known general principle.

As seen in Figure 2, the use of the logical operations of induction and deduction are limited to transformations within a given, single universe level, i.e., moving from the particular to the general, or vice versa in structures or activities within only that level. The same restriction applies to mathematics: it is functional on any single universe level, but apparently cannot function in moving between universe levels. This is vividly demonstrated in the failure of many eminent physicists to develop a functional "Equation for Everything" (Lindley, 2001) after trying for over a century. Possibly these misunderstandings have occurred because the concept of infinite universe structural levels, each with unique types and properties is not widespread.

The Non-Mathematical but Logical Processes of Synthesis and Dissection are Required in order to Move Between Universe Levels due to their Different Emergent Properties.

Also made visible in Figure 2, the process of moving up or down universe levels requires different types of logical operations than those used in moving within levels, namely that of *synthesis* and *dissection*. Creating and assembling a higher-level structure from component parts of the universe level beneath is the process of building, construction, or creation, here called *synthesis*. The life processes, such as cell division and multicellular growth often show automatic self-assembly (synthesis) over several universe levels. Disassembling a structure into its component parts is the process of dissection, one at which auto mechanics or surgeons excel. If dissection is not reversible, it is butchery or destruction. Often, discovery requires the use of all four of these unique reasoning processes. Yet, presently in many areas of science, only deductive reasoning is valued as appropriate. Inspection of the bottom half of Figure 2 will bring into focus the necessary but often unrecognized steps required before deduction finally can be used in the act of recognizing any new object as an example of a more general theme. Actually, the use of hypothesis testing is appropriate only after final conceptualization of a general model has occurred. Yet, many manuscripts submitted to scientific journals, describing innovative observations, insights, conceptions, or models, are rejected today if they are not designed to test a narrow hypothesis by "falsification", i.e., could a different process produce similar result, thus making false the presently proposed hypothesis? Ironically, the dualist, Popper (1934) made the falsification procedure excessively popular.

It is commonly overlooked that a previous (often unrecognized) conceptual idea or hunch is required by a process called Abduction, before it is possible to generate a model by Induction, much less before Deduction can be used to produce a hypothesis. Furthermore, it is often unappreciated that a preceding, conceptual model *cannot be falsified* (as in, if it's not red, then it is not a car). An abducted, inductive model can only be overthrown by the discovery of a more accurate approximation of external reality that fits the data better (and also generates better hypotheses). Ironically, in this way, scientific conceptual models are like those underlying religio-cultural beliefs. Falsification does them no harm. Only the appearance of more powerful (more useful, i.e., more survival enhancing) models can dismantle and replace them.

The Emergent Laws at the Family Level are Opposite to the Survival Laws for an Individual at the Level of the Jungle

In terms of our evolution from killing to nonkilling, it should be noted that the laws at the universe level of individual survival in the jungle are crucially different from the emergent laws of family when we move up to the next universe level of society. In life-death one-on-one competition against snakes, tsetse flies, rats, wart hogs, hyenas, and other aliens, we do not hesitate to lie, cheat, steal, deceive, wound, enslave, or kill, and usually do so without guilt. As we will see, a part of our brain is in fact quite specialized to win at this very activity.

However, these self-survival "law of the jungle" rules valid at the level of individuals do not carry over from the state shift that automatically occurs from rising to the next higher level: that containing the members of a family or other functional groups. In fact, they are totally inappropriate and have long been proscribed as antisocial behavior. The emergent laws of relating to one's trusting and much-loved son or daughter are in fact quite empathic. We will not lie to them, nor do we cheat, steal from, wound, enslave, or kill them. In fact, such behavior seems naturally abhorrent. Instead, we would happily place their well-being before our own, share our food with them, protect them from harm, endure periods of self denial and sacrifice for the perhaps deferred gratification of seeing them grow, learn, thrive, and reproduce. We treat them how we would want to be treated, and do nothing to harm him or her that we would not want someone else to do to us (adjusting appropriately for differences in age, gender, and skill level). Now that's a paradigm shift!

What becomes clear is that we actually are talking about *paradigm shifts* in this chapter. The usual concept of paradigm shifts are that of context shifts, for example when we talk about "stocks and bonds", the question is, are we referring to investment activities on Wall St. or forms of punishment used by the Pilgrims? One cannot warp one context into the other. They cannot be inter-converted. Other classic illustrations of paradigm shifts include Kuhn's illustration of a figure that could be seen either as a duck or a rabbit. Others are the shift from the Flat Earth to the Spherical Earth views, or from a Geocentric to a Heliocentric context of the earth.

Here we can expand this by saying that simply going from one universe level to another actually requires a "Layer Paradigm Shift" (new term) in the point of view of the observer, eg. from atoms to molecules, from organs to organisms, etc. As abundantly illustrated in this chapter, (**Table 4**), each level has unique properties and laws that are inappropriate at the next higher or lower level, i.e., incubation conditions for lung cell tissue culture, vs. the physiology of respiration, vs. the winning of a foot race. The most misunderstood layer paradigm shift today is that of operating at the "self against the world" level of antisocial violence, or rising to the next higher level, that of the family where nonviolent sociality occurs. You cannot retain a family if you try to drag "self against the world" behaviors into a group. Nor can social rules apply to survival of an individual in the jungle. The two cannot be melded.

Are the 21 Paradigm Shifts of Neuroreality Established Facts?

The question arises: What about the validity of the many paradigm shifts with their new models of explanation that form the foundation of the book? Are they established facts? Are these ideas true? The short answers are No to the first question, and most probably Yes to the second. Obviously, because these models are new and original creations, they have no prior history. This is their first presentation. Most of them cannot be found in the published literature. At this stage in their discovery, they can only be the first conceptual models existing before other scientists have had the chance to evaluate them by hypothesis generation and formal proof. For those looking for such external verification, hypothesis fulfillment, and acceptance by the consensus of the reviewers of scientific journals as facts, by definition there can be none. Thus, to such a person, these paradigm shifts might appear as the most unfounded of rank speculations. This may lead such persons to be tempted "to throw the baby out with the bath water". Thus, discoveries have a very difficult time being born.

It is true. All new ideas must begin this way. It is an unavoidable fact. Yet, if these incomplete, metaphorical new ideas promote the reorganization existing facts into a more parsimonious, non-supernatural manner than the earlier model, then the new model must work better in practice. This paradigm shift will also lead to many new predictions, which from the earlier point of view were not obvious, but that from the new point of view become the most logical predictions of possibility. Their elegant simplicity makes them intuitively attractive. However, to someone demanding formal proof, this, by definition, can only come much, much later after the new idea first emerged. It is here predicted that within a century, essentially all of these new paradigms will prove to be better approximations of external reality than their predecessors and will become accepted as scientifically proven facts. Fortunately, the predictions generated by many these new models have already been abundantly fulfilled. So, shall our personal level of knowledge wait a century for consensus proof? Or, shall we ride on the cutting edge of knowledge at the event horizon. The answer is clear.

Thus, we have opened to us a well-rewarded path enabling humanity to rise from the level of individuals killing in the jungle, to the next higher level of order, that of society, with all of its rewarding and delightful nonkilling emergent properties. However, first, we must increase our understanding of life, mind, and consciousness.

Some Important Concepts of Chapter 2:

1. All behavior is a triadic process where a 3D structure, over time (4D), is powered to move by the application of free energy (5D).

2. A Structure can never be more that the sum of the structures of its parts. However, the emergent properties of a structure will always be different and greater than the sum of the behavioral properties of its parts.

3. Each of the infinite levels of universe contains unique structures and unique emergent properties.

4. Mathematics, including deduction and induction is useful for operations within a given universe level.

5. One can move between the unique universe levels by empiric-experimental synthesis or dissection, but not by mathematics. Thus, there can be no equation for everything.

6. Of crucial importance to humanity are two universe levels: That of individuals, which are the building blocks of the next higher level, that of the family units of society.

7. Because of the law of emergence, expressed in point two above, the behavioral properties at the universe level of individuals, are different and inappropriate when applied to the universe level of the group. Thus, at the level of the individual, selfish violence is appropriate and highly effective. However, such is totally the opposite and inappropriate to the cooperative interactions required to empower constructive interactions within the family. A paradigm shift in attitudes and behaviors is required for sociality.

8. As a crucial step in rising from Killing to Nonkilling, the current great confusion between these levels must be eliminated.

9. The 21 new paradigm shifts upon which this book is based, by definition,will take many years, even centuries to be exhaustively tested by hypothesis fulfillment to become accepted as agreed upon facts by scientists. Fortunately, the predictions generated by many these new models have already been abundantly fulfilled. So, shall our personal level of knowledge wait indefinitely for consensus proof? Or, shall we ride on the cutting edge of knowledge at the event horizon. The answer is clear.

NEUROREALITY: A SCIENTIFIC RELIGION TO RESTORE MEANING

SECTION II: Who am I? What is this Mystery called Consciousness?

CHAPTER 3: Age of Life, Source of All Behavior, Freedom of Choice, and Third and Forth Realities

The Age of Life:
　　　　Only within galactic Halos of Life are there energy conditions sufficiently favorable to support the emergence of the higher levels of complexity that we call life. Cells are the foundational building blocks of life. There are no life forms at universe levels below that of cells. Viruses are only nonliving parasites. Thus, a biochemist stands at the interface between inanimate nature and life itself. Not surprisingly, cellular life has apparently occurred on earth more than once. Anciently, simple membrane bounded cells emerged in warm ponds at the surface of our seas. These used as their primary free energy source waste solar radiation as it passed by the earth. However, additionally other simple cells formed deep within the sea, tapping the earth's planetary heat and chemical energy at undersea volcanic vents as their source of energy. Both type of cells have evolved through progressively more complex forms obeying Darwinian "survival of the fittest" behavior (Darwin, 1859). This was only possible because of encouragement from the right abundance of potential energy within galactic halos of life.
　　　　Often overlooked is Charles Darwin's later work, "The Descent of Man", (1871), where he provided much evidence supporting his belief that in the higher evolution of social animals, an additional nonkilling set of relationships existed. These could be labeled as biological moral laws based upon sympathy (Loye, 2007) that superseded the killing of survival of the fittest of individuals at the next lower universe level. This was a prescient forerunner to the discovery of the emergence of a different set of behavioral laws (properties) when one rises from the universe level of the individual, to that of the organized group, as described in Chapter 2.

Time Clocks:
　　　　One of the constant, "ever-the-same" aspects of our universe is the rate of radioactive decay of the less stable isotopes into more stable forms.

60

Within mature stars and in man-made cyclotrons, reactions occur that form highly unstable atomic isotopes. These then decay into more stable atomic forms. Each isotope has its own decay pattern. Not only does it decay by giving off energy and matter, it also decays at a constant characteristic rate. Expression of the rate at which a radioactive isotope decays is expressed in half-lives. A half-life is the time it takes for one-half of the atoms of a radioactive material to decay into something else. Half-lives for various radioisotopes range from a few microseconds to billions of years.

The radioactive decay of unstable isotopes is often used to determine the age of things. For example, researchers use carbon-14 with a half-life of 5730 years to determine the age of formerly animate (living) material up to 40,000 years old. In contrast, Uranium-238 (U^{238})with a 4.5 billion-year half-life of is used to date inanimate material in the range of 1 million to 5 billion years of age. With the latter method, the earth's age has been calculated to be 4.54 billion years, plus or minus one percent. The oldest meteorites we have are 4.57 billion years old. This suggests that the earth formed about 30 million years after the formation of our solar system. The birth of Mother Earth occurred near the more energetic outer border of our galactic Zone of Life, that halo of possibility surrounding the center of galaxies at a diameter about half that of the outer edge of their visible galactic arms.

As listed in **Table 1**, vestiges of single cells are found in rock sediments rocks as early as 3.8 billion years ago with U^{238}. Similar methods show multi-cellular life forms finally appeared more recently, about 1 billion years ago. Complex animals appeared about 550 million years ago. Reptiles date from about 300 million years in the past. Non-ape hominoid pre-human skulls found in Africa dated at 6 million years. Early human remains found in Africa, several locations in Europe and in Asia are over 1 million years old. The French and German cave paintings and bone flutes were dated to 36,000 yrs ago. The last Ice Age ended around 15,000 years ago. Rome ruled 2,000 years ago. Powered flight occurred 100 years ago. Man landed on the moon 25 years ago. Scientists sequenced the Human Genome only a few years ago.

The Maintenance of Cellular Homeostasis (Survival) is the Source of All Living Behavior.

Certain inquirers including Spinoza (1977), Bickerton (1995) and Damasio, (1999) proposed that the origin of all human behavior was the

Section II: WHO AM I?

Table 1, Approximate Timeline of the Origin and Evolution of Terrestrial Life

4,500,000,000 yrs **Origin of the Earth (4.5 billion)**

3,800,000,000 yrs **Origin of Simple Cells (prokaryotes)**

3,000.000.000 yrs **Photosynthesis**

2,000,000,000 yrs **Complex Cells (eukaryotes)**

1,000,000,000 yrs **Multicellular life**

600,000,000 yrs **Simple Animals**

570,000,000 yrs **Arthropods (insects, arachnids and crustaceans)**

550,000,000 yrs **Complex animals**

500,000,000 yrs **Fish and proto-amphibians**

300,000,000 yrs **Reptiles**

200,000,000 yrs **Mammals**

150,000,000 yrs **Birds**

130,000,000 yrs **Flowers**

65,000,000 yrs **Non-avian Dinosaurs died out**

2,500,000 yrs **The appearance of the genus Homo**

200,000 yrs **Humans started looking like they do today**

35,000 yrs **Cave paintings, Bone flutes**

25,000 yrs **Neanderthals are thought to become extinct**

15,000 yrs **End of last Ice Age**

2,000 yrs **Roman Empire**

100 yrs **Wright Brothers first powered flight**

25 yrs **Man on the Moon**

10 yrs **Human Genome was Sequenced**

drive to maximize the life of the body. However, in higher organisms, it is the *cell*, together with its determining "selfish genes" (Dawkins, 1976), that is the fundamental building block of all terrestrial living beings. Thus, it is here asserted that *the drive to optimize the survival of the individual living cells is the primary motivation for all behavior*. Since there is no life below the cellular level, such cell survival oriented action is a fundamental requirement for the continued existence of life.

Table 2 lists the life defining activities of living organisms, from single cells to humans. That is: the order required for life to exist is obtained by cell-based capture, storage and utilization of solar free energy that would have otherwise been lost as entropic heat. This captured energy is used for cellular survival, function and reproductive work.

Table 2: The Triadic Activities that Define Life:

The multi-cellular body (3-D structure) must over time (4th- D):

1. Find, take, ingest, digest and internally distribute food-fuel containing calories of solar free energy (5th-D).

2. Use this free energy to power the mechanical, biosynthetic, and active transport work of cell survival.
3. Do the free energy requiring caloric work to enlarge, maintain, defend, repair and reproduce itself over time.
4. And discard the entropic (spent energy)-containing waste products of work as solids, liquids, gases and heat.

We will herein refer to the vital conditions required by the cells within our bodies for life as *cellular survival requirements* (CSR). CSR are in many ways similar to the sea's salinity conditions. This is one of many observations supporting the view that life first originated there. These cellular survival requirements include the many specific narrow pH, osmotic, ionic, and nutritional conditions. An unprotected cell will soon die if even one of these vital conditions is not met.

Any force distorting the cellular environment away from these CSR is a *biological stressor*. Cells resist biological stress by the multi-layered process known as *homeostasis*. Homeostasis means maintenance of a state of constancy. The term covers any action that a living organism takes in order to maintain its CSR in the face of environmental stress.

Through evolution, cells within organisms have become increasingly adept at protecting themselves. They do so by calling forth a large arsenal of defensive-compensatory, stress-resisting reactions and adaptations, as illustrated in **Table 3**.

At each universe level of structural organization within a living organism, survivors have genetically selected an appropriate set of homeostatic defensive tools. The multileveled nature of these relationships is not generally appreciated. Thus; 1) At the biochemical-metabolic level, homeostasis responses include the vital buffering of acid production, the damping of chemical oxidation, and regulation of enzyme activities through feedback loops. 2) At the cellular level, homeostatic mechanisms include control of the active and passive transport of small molecules into compartments bounded by membranes, the activation or inhibition of enzyme synthesis, and the regulation of vital hormonal and neurotransmitter receptors. 3) Tissue-level homeostatic devices include such processes as inflammation, edema and immune rejection for protection.

Continuing to higher levels of order: 4) Organ responses to stress include local adjustments in blood flow and defensive compensations in organ size. 5) Whole organism homeostasis includes the coordinated neuro-endocrine and brain-directed internal and external stress defense behaviors that maximize survival gain and minimize survival loss within the complex outer environment (Darwin, 1859, 1871). 6) At the next higher universe level, even groups of organisms have evolved homeostatic devices that assist in defending and maintaining the basic CSR for individual cells within the group members. These group responses include the stabilizing effects of society such as provided by the nuclear family, kin groups, communities, and working cooperatives, such as agriculture, industry, commerce, and the police. Furthermore, a human culture's collection of survival and contra cell survival traditions-memes are inculcated in each new generation via parental example, education, religion, science and the mass media, as described in the Introduction to this book.

While in the above description, the cell was described as subject to the effect of its environment, it can also be viewed as environmentally causal, even invasive. Regardless, it is clear that the homeostatic drive to maintain CSR is quite literally the source of all living behavior. Every act at all levels in every living system has at its core "motive" the attempt to maintain or restore optimal cellular survival requirements. It is accurate to

Table 3, Universe Levels of Emergent Cellular Homeostasis.

Biochemical-metabolic level cellular homeostasis:
> pH buffering of cellular acid-base production
> Redox. buffering of chemical oxidation and reductions
> Feedback regulation of enzyme activities.

Cellular level cellular homeostasis:
> Active and passive transport of small molecules
> Activation of inhibition of enzyme synthesis
> Regulation of hormone or neurotransmitter receptors

Tissue level cellular homeostasis:
> Inflammation
> Edema
> Immune response regulation

Organ level cellular homeostasis:
> Organ output regulation
> Regulation of local blood flow
> Organ size compensation (hypertrophy)

Organism level cellular homeostasis:
> Nervous system internal stress responses
> Neuroendocrine internal stress responses
> Avoidance and approach driven responses within the
> complex outer environment, including reproduction

Society level cellular homeostasis:
> Family, kin group, community, working cooperatives
> Food-producing institutions, as agriculture, industry, commerce
> Protective institutions, as the police, national guard, armed forces
> Cultural institutions: educational, religious, science, mass-media
> that pass Survival Memes on to each new generation

---

say that *for living organisms, the drive to optimize cellular survival is the source, purpose and goal of all behavior,* except suicide in certain cases. This primacy of life drive is genetically determined.

However, if we have no choice in our behavior other than pro life or pro death, then why do we continually ask ourselves in essence the following questions, as if we actually had freedom of choice? "What should I be doing now?" "What should I do next?" "I wonder what would have happened if I had tried that other possibility?" Because we often are unaware of the implicit motive (to optimize survival) behind our questions and speech, we feel that we are free. This illusion of freedom of choice exists, *not* because "The human brain has made a quantitative evolutionary jump and is no longer subject to genetic determinism. It can now make choices". Rather, it exists because within genetic determinism, a new level has emerged where there is vast freedom of choice, including which of the many cultural traditions-memes now in existence should we choose to guide us as to how we either meet the demand to optimize cellular survival, or drop out of life. This has driven the evolution of intelligence. That is, within this predetermined or consciously chosen survival orientation, there are four great freedoms of choice.

The First Freedom of Choice is, as illustrated in **Figure 1**: **Shall I reject the universe as Bad** (dangerous, flawed, undesirable, evil)? If one rejects it and resists it, one automatically becomes an angry failure, a destructive victim at effect. Such individuals may opt-out or rebel in many ways, including by choosing death itself. Or, **shall I accept the universe as Good** (supportive, ideal, perfect)? If I choose it, align and go with it, I automatically become a success, constructive, happy, and At Cause. By"Loving What Is" (Katie,2002), such individuals creatively contribute to life.

The Second Freedom of Choice is: **Shall I act to optimize my survival in the now** (by immediate gratification and self indulgence)? Shall I harvest the reward now? Shall I eat our seed corn? **Or, Shall I act to optimize survival in the future** (by deferred gratification and self-discipline)? Shall I act to take a better reward later by waiting and planting the seed corn next spring for a bountiful harvest? These responses are genetically determined, inherent properties of cellular organisms from which there is no freedom, except death.

The Third Freedom of Choice is: **Shall I act to increase my own survival?** That is, to take self–oriented, frequently parasitic personal gain, causing a long term cost to society. **Or**, shall **I act to increase the survival of my family or society?** I would do this by being other-oriented, often with ultimately synergistic and far greater personal benefits resulting from emergence.

The Fourth Freedom of Choice is: **Who is my family?** Will it be us "good guys" against *"them thar aliens?"* Which of the following will I choose my family to be?: Me, myself and I?; My offspring?; My nuclear family (spouse and kids)?; My extended family clan?; My tribe?; My supportive species? Will it be all terrestrial life (mud daubers, fleas,

Figure 1, First Great Freedom of Choice

economic class?; My nation?; My race (exclusive like Hitler)?; My species (inclusive like Ghandi)? Will it be all of humanity and its many human mosquitoes, tape-worms, pathogenic organisms, deadly microorganisms, and all)? Alternatively, will it be all of life including any extraterrestrials?

Just like Hitler and Gandhi, each individual has a unique history in terms of their own choices as to how to best optimize survival in the presence of the contingencies of life. These choices totally describe the, who, what, why, where, when, and how of our thinking and behavior. Thus, Hitler worked tirelessly and brilliantly for the survival maximization of his family. However, he defined his family very narrowly (i.e., that only non-defective Teutons were human), thus he used without guilt the "laws of the jungle" to wound, enslave, and kill those who he considered sub-humans. Gandhi's choice of family included all of Homo sapiens. His approach was the brilliant and powerful use of the nonviolent laws of the next higher level, that of society.

Now that all divine or diabolic influences must be eliminated from the equation because of their nonexistence (Chapter 4), it becomes clear that an individual's answers to these ongoing four freedoms of choice have been the source of the highest and lowest of all human behavior and accomplishment.

Two Crucial Additional Realities: Survival Reality and Cultural Meme Reality

As described in Chapter 1, our own individual Internal Reality (#2) is a sensor-based, continually upgraded, inner model of External Reality (#1). At first, our model is of necessity a grossly inaccurate and idiosyncratic personal approximation. The more accurate it becomes, the more successfully we can align with and operate in the way the universe actually works; thus, to work with others tap its resources as the sole source of life, abundance, opportunity, and power.

Reality #3: Survival Reality:

As we also saw in Chapter 1, the eternal universe exists without design, plan, or purpose and operates independently of our, or anyone else's existence (Stenger, 1988). Nevertheless, life continues to originate and evolve within galactic Halos of Life. Crucially, however, continued existence of any life form critically depends upon that living organism, or its family, taking specific action to maintain its survival. They must eat, drink, stay on the grass, avoid falling off cliffs, and keep out of the fire.

Organisms freely choosing not to act to preserve their own survival ultimately cease to exist and become extinct. Importantly, those that made survival their personal imperative, not only survived, but also evolved and thrived. The survival of such fit organisms has led to the more frequent selection of those organisms that developed and incorporated genetically transmitted, advantageous survival instincts (Darwin, 1859, 1871; Coyne, 2009; Dawkins, 2009).

Ultimately these instincts have displaced the inherent meaninglessness and randomness of existence and life with a special sacredness and intensity of meaning to the remaining survivors. This has transformed the apathetic inaction or meaningless activity of neutrality into a survival motivated sense purpose, a teleology, design, significance, functional importance and primacy of life urgency.

This is Survival Reality from which the artificial but critical values of both good and evil spring into being. It is a third and unrecognized form of reality, created, not by God, but solely by the declaration of surviving life forms. That is, *Survival Reality is the reality of the external universe from the perspective of maximizing the life and minimizing the death of survivors.* This makes cliffs, forest fires and lions bad, while ponds, sunshine, and bananas are good. In the past, these survivor's values have been personified and magnified as omni-deities; G*(o)*od, angels, vs. the *d*(evil) and demons locked in mortal combat in competition for our personal allegiance in the survival of life or death. Survival reality appears to have paralleled, and thus may ultimately be integral to the continuing physical immortality of terrestrial life. Ironically, an immortality of life that is yet not accessible to its expendable members.

From the imperative of survival, it becomes clear that the more accurately we 'tell the truth' about the way the universe works, the more quickly we can rise above our individual and collective confusions to cross the threshold of workability" (Chapter 1). Then, we can begin to optimize our use of opportunities to align with and to tap the universe's external reality and enhance our lives. Thus, from survival reality comes the drives of *curiosity* and *intentionality* as prime enhancers of survival.

Survival reality is the magic at the heart of religion and at the core of personal meaning. Our lower self is based in our earliest brain element, the reptile brain core Id. Its reality is the polar opposite of that of our Higher Power, The Holy Spirit, God Within, *Source*, whom our deathly afraid Ego holds captive and hidden from us within the subconsciousness of our cerebellum. This situation lasts a lifetime, unless, as is often the case, illness, injury or religious conversion transforms us, liberating it. This crucial step in personal maturation has long been lost through ignorance and the deterioration of our religions. As will be seen, this book restores our ability and regains our access to the guidance of our higher power.

However, through the desire to *know* (how better to survive), some individuals markedly enhanced the quality of their lives and those around them. Yet, in the past, the ability of an individual broadly to communicate to others the successful survival rules he and she had learned or developed was very limited because lives were short.

Reality #4: Cultural Meme Reality

With the notable exception of the continued gradual incorporation of many advantageous behaviors into our genetic survival instincts, the above meant that each child had to start from "ground zero" in the process of learning how to use external reality to enhance his or her survival. With the evolution of the transmission of information, first through mimicry, then orally, and finally as long-term written records, the production and transfer of cultural "Memes" containing survival information about external reality to our children became possible. Memes (Dawkins, 1976) are communicable inner reality models of external reality that exist in the form of semi-independent socially transmitted "truths", i.e., traditions, beliefs or belief systems. If under rare circumstances, the meme that was incorporated from a trusted authority (usually a parent) into the novice's inner reality was accurate, then its use by-passed the need for that novice, or for each new generation personally to invent or rediscover such processes. Examples are washing dirt off potatoes with seawater before eating (as certain groups of wild Japanese Macaques have only recently learned to do; Kawai, 1965), or how to make fire, produce metal, or invent the wheel.

In contrast, the transmission of fictional memes, inaccurate wishful beliefs about external reality, has promoted endless wanderings and sufferings beneath the workability threshold of External Reality. Reception of accurate cultural-memes of external reality could give an individual and their society a head start in life enabling them to rise to previously unreached heights of survival optimization. From there, construction, correction, expansion, remembered-recording and again transmission of new, even more accurate memes is possible.

Thus, humanity in its search for even better survival began to stand on the shoulders of its ancestors to be in the position to ask and answer ever more pointed questions about the nature of external and internal reality. In certain areas such as Astrophysics or Genetic Engineering, we have risen toward or even exceeded the threshold of workability (Chapter 1). Although in terms of the eternal universe, progress does not exist. In terms of survival-imperative reality, progress most definitely does exist. It is the cultural optimization of the survival of one's self and one's human family unit in ever expanding ecological circles.

Critically, with the accumulation of many conflicting reality cultural memes came the need for a freedom to choose beliefs promoting better long-term survival, from those that were erroneous or even harmful traditions. This has led to the further evolution of intelligence and an apparent freedom of choice (as to how best to survive!).

Table 4 summarizes the seven realities. This book will develop the last three later. Becoming conscious of which type of reality we are in and that which others are coming from is critical to successful solution of problems of living. An element in our brain produces feelings of reality and of unreality. Imbalance of that system can make the familiar, alien. In contrast, it is important to recognize that especially during altered states of consciousness, including schizophrenia, the alien can come to seem "realer than real". It requires evolution insight and sound judgment to navigate the realities.

Table 4: The Seven Types of Reality

External Reality	Verifiable facts	(Chapter 1)
Internal Reality	Unique to individual	(Introduction, Chapter 1)
Survival Reality	Death avoidant	(Chapter 3)
Cultural Reality	Local belief memes	(Chapter 3)
Dream Reality	Fiction, Fantasy	(Chapter 17)
Reactive Reality	xDARP behavior	(Chapter 13)
Empathic Reality	Peace, Joy	(Chapter 19)

In the next chapter, we will begin our investigation of the nature of mind and our multifaceted consciousness.

Some Important Concepts of Chapter 3:

1. Life on earth is billions of years old. Humans spread from Africa millions of years ago and have survived many ice ages over thousands of years.

2. The triadic activities that define life are: cellular or multicellular organisms must obtain solar or chemical energy to power the work of cell survival to enlarge, maintain, defend, repair and reproduce its structure, and to discard its entropic wastes over time.

3. The source, purpose, and goal of all living behavior, including human, is to optimize the survival of the individual cells within the body.

4. Any force distorting the cellular environment away from optimal survival is a biological stressor. Cells resist biological stress with homeostatic processes occurring at the following levels: biochemical-metabolic, cellular, tissue, organ, individual organismal and societal.

5. Within this biological determinism, there are four great freedoms of choice: The first is shall I reject or choose the way the universe works? The second is, "Shall I act to optimize my survival in the present or in the future?" The third is shall I act to optimize my own survival or that of my family? Finally, the fourth is whom do I define as my family?

6. Reality #4, Survival Reality: Organisms that made survival their personal imperative have not only avoided extinction, but also have evolved survival instincts and thrived. These instincts have artificially imbued the inherent meaninglessness and randomness of existence and life with special sacredness, intensity of meaning, motivated sense purpose, teleology, design, significance, functional importance and urgency.

7. Reality #5, Cultural Reality: Memes are communicable inner reality models of external reality that exist in the form of independent socially transmitted "truths". With intelligence, useful memes were created or chosen that by-pass the need for each new generation personally to invent or rediscover fire, metal, or wheel. Some memes are beguiling but false, and others can be harmful. They cannot be killed, but can only displaced by superior memes.

NEUROREALITY: A SCIENTIFIC RELIGION TO RESTORE MEANING

SECTION II: Who am I? What is this Mystery called Consciousness?

CHAPTER 4: What is Mind? Triadic Solution to the Mind-Body Problem

The Mystery of the Mind:

Mind has many definitions. Some are very narrow, seeking to limit mind to a property only possessed by the human species. The latter definitions insist that mind only includes the mental activity of the abstract thinking required for the production of fully developed (syntactical) language (Chomsky, 1959). Such a definition is rejected here because such would assert, not only that Helen Keller was mindless until the age of sixteen when she finally learned a language, but also that most children before the age of two, and the adult speakers of only pidgin proto-languages are mindless was well (Bickerton, 1995).

On the other hand, some traditional Eastern definitions of mind have been so broad as to go beyond the requirements of external sensory awareness monitored by a brain-containing life form. These label the response of any material object to energy input as part of so-called "universal consciousness" and therefore as part of mind. Thus, a genetic DNA chain, by changing its structural conformation in response to an altered nuclear ionic environment, would be said to show a rudimentary form of consciousness, like a compass needle, or wind in the trees, or flames or smoke from a fire, all of which would be viewed as part of universal mind. Such definitions are too broad to be meaningful here, although the terrestrial biofeedback loops of the "Living Earth", Gaia Hypothesis (Lovelock, 1979) do make it of interest.

Further, the relationship of mind to the various forms of human consciousness has been unresolved in terms of anatomical sources of mind. In order to unravel these hidden relationships, it is first necessary to solve the ancient riddle of the Mind-Body Problem.

Description and Brief History of the Mind-Body Problem:

The ancient "Mind-Body Problem" and its modern counterpart, the "Origin and Nature of Consciousness" are crucial elements to the most important Big Question: Who Am I? Amazingly, for millennia until the present, the mind-body problem at its core is a formula considering a choice only between two questions. Firstly that of *Monism:* Is my mind, my consciousness, and all of who I am, think, feel, or hope to be, totally and solely to be found in one of the structural elements of this body within which I find myself? Or, that of *Dualism:* Are my mental-processes and consciousness part of a separable, immortal extra-corporeal spirit, briefly possessing this fleshly abode?

Non-supernatural answers to the mind-body problem were constrained to the first alternative only. Thus, at first, there was "Native Monism"; the idea that mind was a yet-to-be- discovered structural element of the body. In contrast, selection of the supernatural second choice was reinforced by early cultures appearing in the Tigris-Euphrates, Nile and Indus river-deltas. There, the search for the answer to the mind-body problem led to religious formulations containing the belief of Dualism. That is, the idea that we actually are immortal spirits condemned by endless cycles of reincarnation into terrestrial life forms from which we may escape only by attaining a state of purity.

These dualistic concepts from Egyptian and Babylonian religion appeared in philosophy, and ultimately, in science (via Pherekydes, then Pythagoras and then to Socrates) mainly through the influential writings of Plato (1975). By Plato's time, the philosophical concepts of Idealism had also embellished dualism so that learning was thought to be merely the soul's recollection of the pure ideals preexisting in the non-material realm of its spiritual origin. This very creative but inaccurate belief system had already held global sway for at least two thousand years when Descartes (1974), Malebranche (1923), and Leibniz (1984) again reaffirmed it in the seventeenth century. In the twentieth century (the late) Sir John Eccles (1977), Nobel laureate; (the late) Sir Karl Popper (1977), philosopher of science; and Richard Swinburne (1986), Oxford philosopher of science and religion championed Dualism. The former two managed to arrange their Dualism in a more complex manner (Popper,1977).

Yet, for at least the last 2,500 years, monism has been the choice of a number of influential Greek philosophers (Anaxagoras, Diagoras, Protagoras, etc.), as well as of most scientists in recent centuries. Uttal, in his Psychobiology of Mind (1978) described a large number of the competing philosophic solutions to the mind-body problem, all having classical Greek antecedents. He categorized them under four general headings: Monisms, Dualisms, Pluralisms and Rejectors of the Issue. Uttal appears to have created the Pluralism category primarily to accommodate Eccles and Popper's more complex Dualism.

Readers can refer to resources, such as Priest's <u>Theories of the Mind</u> (1991), to learn more of the proponents and descriptions of these philosophical schools of thought. However, even from such a historical perspective, it would soon become clear that *neither* answer to the two anciently posed questions contains the solution to the mind-body problem. That is, both monism and dualism are completely inaccurate solutions. Mind (or consciousness) is not totally and solely dependent upon a structure of our body. Yet, neither is it dependent upon extra-corporeal spirits. Rather, the solution of the mind-body problem has required a reconceptualization. This was begun in Chapter 2 by the introduction of the five dimensions of behavior, which were then condensed into the triadic form of structure, time and potential energy. Unlike monism and dualism, *triadism* can directly account for the relationship of mind and body. As we will see in Chapter 5, extension of triadism to the Dual Quadbrain Model describes the origin and nature of the multiple elements of consciousness, including the functioning elements of the so-called unconscious, subconscious and preconscious minds (Morton, 1985a, b).

Universe Levels of Structure within Living Organisms

It must already be obvious to the reader that there is no monistic mind at all in structure. As **Table 1** illustrates, details exist for all known structural levels of living organisms. No dissectible black boxes remain in the nervous system to reveal mind. Therefore, monism must be rejected as too simplistic a solution to the mind-body problem.

It is of interest to note that there are many more universe levels within a living organism than there are within the inanimate matter at our universe level. In other words, a diamond only contains the nuclei and electrons of the carbon atom arranged in a crystalline array: three levels of order. A mountain contains the atoms, electrons, and nuclei of molecules of aggregated and disaggregated stone with some water and air occasionally mixed in: four or five levels of order. In marked contrast, a human being contains at least 25 levels of order. For such a high level of organization to continue to exist in a stable form requires the very special energetically

Table 1. The Structural Organization of Life Forms: Strata and Content

All life forms: *types*
Terrestrial trees of life, Linnaean and other taxonomic trees
Species: *types* =
Tribes: *types*
Families: *types*
Individuals: *types*
Nervous systems: *types*
Peripheral nervous systems: *types*
Central nervous systems: *types*
Spinal cords: *types*
Brain: Dual Quadrimental systems: *types*
Cerebral systems: *types*
Cerebellar systems: *types*   **WHERE IN THE BODY IS THE MIND?**
Limbic systems: *types*
Brain core systems: *types*
Cells: *types* in central nervous system
Glia: *types*
Neurons: *types*
Neuronal subcellular organelles: *types*
Dendrites: *types*
Perikarya, Nuclei: *types*
Axons: *types*
Mitochondria: *types*
Supramolecular assemblies: *types*
Membranes: *types*
Microtubules, Neurofilaments: *types*
Synaptic vesicles: *types*
Gates and ionophores: *types*
Pumps: *types*
Neuroreceptors: *types*
Macromolecules: *types*
Proteins, Nucleic Acids, Polysaccharides, Complex Lipids: *types*
Enzymes: types
Neuroreceptor subunit structural macromolecules: *types*
Control-cascade components: *types*
DNAs-RNAs: *types*
Building blocks: *types*
Receptor ligands: *types*
Neurotransmitter agonists & antagonists: *types*
Neuromodulator agonists & antagonists: *types*
Hormone agonists and antagonists: *types*
Second messengers: *types*
Cyclic nucleotides: *types*
Cofactors: *types*
Energy & metabolic intermediates: *types*
Precursors: *types*
Inorganic ions: *types*
Gases: *types*
Subatomic particles: *types*
Electrons, Protons: *types*

enriched environment that is present only on certain planets within a galactic halo of life.

Reformatting the Mind-Body Problem

With the preceding background in place, we can now turn directly to the Triadic solution of the mind-body problem. Strictly speaking, the classical mind-body problem is a double misnomer. First, it inappropriately matches a *structure* from one universe level (Chapter 1), namely, the *body* of an organism, with the *activity* of an *organ* from the universe level immediately below it, i.e., the *brain*. Note that brain activity, not body activity produces mind. Reformulating the mind-body problem can eliminate this confusion. This previously intractable problem can be solved, by splitting it into two separate universe-level problems: The brain-mind problem, and the body-life problem. Thus posed, the original mind-body problem were recognized as subsets of the structure-activity relationship (Morton, 1985a).

This Triadic re-formulation eliminates the former habitually improper treatment of mind and body as comparable objects within the same class (i.e., as structure vs. structure: "apples and apples") when in fact each are not items from the same category. However, we cannot use "apples vs. oranges" either. This analogy is also incorrect because both are still only structures. What we need is a comparison between 3-D structures and 5-D behavioral activities. Perhaps an expression such as the difference between apples (structure) and the process of cider fermentation is a better start.

As a result, the seemingly paradoxical relationship of life to body or brain to mind can now be clarified through the triadic pillars of behavioral activity. That is, some of the activities of a single organ structure, the brain, powered by energy over time, include mind (and consciousness). Similarly, some of the activities of the entire body, powered over time by energy, include life itself, that is, living. The examples in expanded **Table 2** further illustrate this structure-activity relationship. There, it may be seen that the activity of each of the various functional structures (i.e., enzyme, computer, brain, body, etc.) results when energy appropriately couples to it over time.

Thus, movements, activities, processes, phenomena or any other type of behavior can occur when three critical conditions are present (that of a structure, over time, powered by coupled free energy). Conversely,

Table 2. The Triadic Pillars of Activity

Structure	+	Time	+	Potential Energy	=	Activity, Process, Behavior
Enzyme	+	seconds	+	Calories from equilibrium	=	Catalysis of a reaction
Automobile	+	minutes	+	Octane of fuel	=	Travel on roadways
CD Player	+	minutes	+	110-220 V electricity	=	Projection of multimedia
Computer	+	microseconds	+	110-220 V electricity	=	Processing of data
Brain	+	milliseconds	+	Calories glucose, oxygen	=	*MIND:* survival guide
BODY	+	minutes	+	Calories in foodstuff	=	Life: surviving cell system

absolutely no behavior is possible in the absence of *any* member of this foundational trinity.

The Triadic Solution to the *Body-Life* Problem:

The activity of body structure, powered over time by food energy is life and living.

The Relationship of Body Structure Damage to Life and Living: Life and Death

As is well explored by the entertainment media, death follows the incapacitation of any vital body structure: be it respiratory, cardiovascular, sensory-nervous, endocrine, skin, gastrointestinal, genitourinary, musculoskeletal or many others.

The Relationship of Lack of Time to Life and Living: Deadlines

Time is required for change to occur. Time must be survived both for continued existence, and for growth and development. Moreover, of course, if our species is to survive, we must at least live long enough to reproduce.

The Relationship of Lack of Free Energy to Living: Exhaustion and Collapse
Potential energy must be available to any living system. The rapid or prolonged energy-depleted conditions of anoxia or starvation have always been the ultimate cause of death for all.

So, are you new or ancient? Because of the time and energy flows, few of the atoms present within us now were part of our body structure a year ago. Thus, because our atoms undergo constant replacement, one can feel new. On the other hand, one can feel ancient because all of our fresh atoms come from billion-year-old, stardust.

The Triadic Solution of the *Brain-Mind* Problem:
The activity of the structure of the brain, powered by energy, over time includes mind (and conscious thinking as part of mind). Mind is any brain system's coordinated activity to optimize the survival of an organism's cellular building blocks. Mind is a triadic *process* because it only occurs when an intact brain *structure* 1) is present and coupled over *time* 2) to metabolic *energy* 3). Just as biochemical catalysis requires the activities of an enzyme, so one's mind originates as a behavior of an intact brain-based nervous system.

Relationship of Brain Structural Damage to Brain Activity: Mind and its Loss
There is much evidence of the profound effect that brain structural alteration has upon mind, consciousness and mental functioning. These data include the unique consequences of region specific brain alterations produced by genetic mutation, developmental arrests, strokes and other cerebral accidents, gunshot wounds, other head trauma, brain tumors, chemical and surgical brain ablations, including the semi-reversible effects of psychoactive drugs.

Relationship of Lack of Time to Brain Activity: It Takes Time to Think
Although it takes more time to ponder some things than others, the seemingly instantaneous or simultaneous nature of then "my life passed before my eyes", is an illusion resulting from the millisecond speed of some brain neuronal intercommunications. It is interesting to note that rate of thinking is sometimes an important element in the definition of intelligence (Hernstein and Murray, 1994). However, if this were the sole

component, it would make the most obsolescent computer more intelligent than any human genius.

Relationship of Loss of Energy to Brain Activity: Need for Fuel

As in all other cases, brain activity, including mind, is not only dependent upon brain structural integrity, and sufficient time, but also upon the presence of adequate fuel in the form of potential energy. It is no accident that the brain is the most metabolically active energetic organ of the body. Although weighing only slightly more than a kilogram, it consumes ten percent of the oxygen required by an adult male's 70 kg body. At physical rest, the brain produces one third of the body's heat, primarily as the entropic waste by-product of ion pumping work required for neuronal information transmission and processing. The aerobic energy metabolism that supports brain activity is highly regulated and exquisitely sensitive to local neural activity. The rapid, very serious, mental consequences of insulin overdose, blood loss or suffocation illustrate absolute dependence of continued normal mental function upon potential energy. Deprivation for even a few minutes of oxygen, glucose, lactic acid or ketone bodies (the latter two can be used instead of glucose under certain circumstances) by the above conditions, can result in such frightening mind alterations as hallucinations, such as out of body phenomena, loss of consciousness, coma, or death.

Modern imaging techniques as PET (Positron Emission Tomography) and MRI (Magnetic Resonance Imaging) scanning can reach beyond structure to measure regional brain *activities* of mind, literally including thought. It is no coincidence that the monitoring within an anatomical *structure* at high resolution, over *time,* of the regional brain *energy* expenditures accomplishes this feat, as reflected by local blood flow, or consumption of oxy-hemoglobin, or of glucose analogues. These methods strikingly visualize discrete brain areas participating in the production of specific behaviors, emotions and consciousness states. Such approaches are applied, not only to the investigation of the brain activities of the mentally ill, but also to those of healthy, conscious humans. For the first time, this enables us directly to associate mental phenomena with the activities of specific brain structures and systems. The results have been illuminating.

Implications of the Triadic Solution:

From the above principles, that mind is a behavior of a structurally intact brain, powered by free energy over time, it is obvious that The Triadic Solution of the Brain-Mind Problem, is neither Monism nor Dualism. Mind is neither a structure nor a spirit. Rather it is a five dimensional process. Mind is inseparable from its triadic pillars of intact structure, time and energy. Loss of any one of these annihilates mind. Similarly, at the next higher universe level, The Triadic Solution to the Body-Life Problem confirms that life is the activity of an intact organism over time, powered by the free energy within foodstuff fuel. Life cannot exist in the absence of any of these triadic pillars.

The Dyadic (Binary-Dichotic-Dialectic) Nature of the Universe is not Dualism (Natural vs. Supernatural):
Although that ultimate loser belief, *Dualism*, originated within three of the great river deltas, a time-tested, winner came from the fourth river delta, that of the Yellow River. This is the very different tradition of *Dyadism* (**Figure 1**). In this meme, the dialect of the universe endlessly manifests itself as an analog pendulum, reaching and returning from the extremes of any range of activity. This ancient symbol, even incorporated into national emblems, is that of the dialect. Recently, astronomers mapping the cosmic microwave background of the universe have envisioned the dialect in color, even with the two spots.

Figure 1: The Paradoxical Yin-Yang nature of the Dialectic Universe.
The Dialect:

    Ying

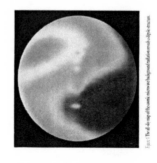

                               Yang

The Whole Divided by a Sigmoid Curve between The Two Extremes	**A Color Map of the Cosmic Microwave Background Nature, 416, 133 (2002) (See color on book cover.)**

Section II: WHO AM I?

Dyadism is also illustrated by Hegel, where *"Thesis"* is attacked by its *"Antithesis"*, to be resolved by *"Synthesis"* to become the *"Golden Mean"*, which then becomes the new "Thesis", etc. A paradoxical aspect of this dialect is the simultaneous existence of both extremes with tension between each - thus the dichotomous spots. Neither element of any dialect can long exist in the absence of the other. **Table 3,** which lists a number of opposites, shows another way of understanding the dialect of the universe. Note that within each of the opposite pairs, neither partner is wrong or non-existent. In fact, both exist and are part of the true sum of the universe.

Table 3, Some Universal Dialects

black-white
selfish-social
dissection-synthesis
evil-good
I.Q.-equality
immediate-deferred
induction-deduction
hate-love
defended boundaries-no borders
left-right
costly-free
politically correct-innovative
determined-free
scarce-abundant
Republicans-Democrats
virtual-real
alienated-communal
Capitalism-Socialism
abstract-concrete
mine-yours
external reality-survival reality
lies-truth
male-female
stratification-homogenization
nature-nurture
aliens-family
global approximation-local accuracy
different-same
poor- rich
penetrative-receptive

The Elimination of Dualism (but not Dyadism) Removes Irresponsible Pernicious Actions from "False Cause"

Neither is the mind part of the consciousness of any soul or spirit. Unlike spirit, wishfully believed to be separable or independent of mortal bodily structure, behavioral activity (including mind) is always tripartite, demanding a functionally intact body (and brain). Behavior without an intact structure would appear to be impossible. Via Triadism, we can now logically dismiss the existence of the immortal soul and the afterlife. The Immortal Soul is an artifact created to accommodate the nonexistent supernatural entity demanded by dualism. Thus, it falls in the same category as other erroneous ideas, such as space-filling Phlogiston or a Flat Earth.

The mistaken concept of the existence of extracorporeal life is the basis for belief in superstition, sorcery, witchcraft, curses, exorcisms, demons, gods, heaven, hell and the afterlife. Any ghostly or supernatural behavioral presence, poltergeist or other mysterious extracorporeal activity also becomes highly improbable, due to their absence of an intact physical structure.

Figure 2 illustrates one of the many problems resulting from dualism. On many levels, it has placed us as individuals, as a society, and as a species at "False-Cause". By giving over responsibility for the events of life to nonexistent higher powers, we become powerless victims, out of control of our lives as individuals and as a species. Because of ignorance that mental illness comes from a broken brain, Jesus thought he "cast out devils". He exorcised seven demons from Mary Magdalene and also from a schizophrenic person in chains whose demons were said to be cast into a herd of swine who then stampeeded into the sea. Jesus said: "In My Name" believers will cast out demons, speak in new tongues, pick up serpents, be immune to poison, and heal the sick. As further illustrated in **Figure 3**, some churches, both high and low, still attempt to perform exorcisms based upon the false cause of dualism.

We all have very good imaginations, from which we easily create many physically impossible memes including those found in spirituality. Thankfully, we also have the intelligence to choose between the impossible and way the universe works, that is, through external reality, sole source of what IS. Thus, replacing Dualism with Triadism frees us finally to take

Figure 2, Problems with Dualism: FALSE-CAUSE!

Khalifa Ahmed al-Duleimi, 53, beats Zeyneb Fadel, 31, with a rubbe hose as her husband Abbas Abdullah, 42, watches. Fadel says she doesn't love her husband anymore, which al-Duleimi attributes to an evil genie inhabiting her. He beats her to drive out the genie.

responsibility for the future of our species and come to grips with the population explosion.

In this chapter, we again find overwhelming evidence against any supernatural force in action upon our earth, or even of its possibility. The anthropomorphic conceptualization of rise of leadership (male or female) from oneself, to one's Father or Mother, to the Chief, the Priest, the King or Queen, the Pope, and ultimately to Almighty God, is perhaps understandable.

Figure 3, Confusion of Mental Illness with Demon Possession: Deaths due to Exorcism.

NEWS

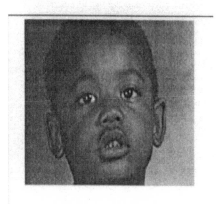

HONOLULU STAR-BULLETIN / TUESDAY, AUGUST 26, 2003

Kid's death at prayer ritual ruled a homicide

An autopsy shows the child suffocated while wrapped up in sheets

By Todd Richmond
Associated Press

MILWAUKEE >> An autistic 8-year-old boy who died after he was wrapped in sheets during a prayer service suffocated, the medical examiner's office said yesterday. The death was ruled a homicide.

Terrance Cottrell Jr. died because his chest was somehow restricted and could not expand, according to a statement

ASSOCIATED PRESS

Bishop David Hemphill held a Bible on Sunday as he talked to a reporter about an autistic 8-year-old boy who died while being restrained during a prayer service at Faith Temple Church of the Apostolic Faith outside his home in Milwaukee.

However, it represents only one idea of the development of levels human control within a society. The motto "In God we Trust" is, and has always been an empty and meaningless expression of our lack of responsibility. Yes, there have been good kings and bad kings, both of whom have claimed to know the will of God and evoked His authority to overwhelm us, or even torture and kill us. The same goes for presidents, prime ministers, congresses, parliaments and nations. Which leader can claim that he has enhanced the survival of human life by acting upon the knowledge given directly to him by God? To the contrary, the "false cause" of something being God's will repeatedly and most potently motivated the call to arms to do massive slaughter. The motive to sacrifice in this life for promised benefits of extracorporeal life in the hereafter has always been a dead-end trip, literally. How many suicide bombers and their victims would be here today, with recognition of the truth of Triadism?

Perhaps, based upon our childish ignorance of the universe, we can understand and excuse our next to impossible belief that "God the Spirit" exists. However, even the idea that space travelers with real 3-D bodies migrated here more than 12,000 years ago has a greater possibility of being true, than the concept of God as an Extracorporeal Spirit. In order to rise from killing to nonkilling, we must first rise to more accurate approximations of external reality and replace those that have caused us so much harm. This is going to require a transformation of our basic beliefs, replacing them with a new, more accurate story: a religion replacing the supernatural spiritual dream reality with ideas consistent with the scientific method and external reality.

Triadism Also Makes Certain Other Concepts Obsolete

Clearly, the properties of Life and Mind are not supernatural. In addition to elimination of the "immortality of the soul" and the existence of spirits, the 5-Ds of Triadism clarify certain other controversial concepts. For example, Reductionism is recognizable as a false concept. The universe cannot be reduced to an equation for everything. However, units are dissectible into subunits. Furthermore, mathematics cannot predict the properties of the next higher or lower level (Godel). Only the "trial and error" of empirical experimentation can lead to their discovery.

Although the term spiritualism, referring to the belief in external supernatural entities is a misguided idea out-living its usefulness, the terms spirit, spiritual, and spirituality are still valuable terms when used to refer to the operation of one's reptilian Id in the production of Dream Reactive Reality. Perhaps, new words are needed for natural objects, actions, or events that are awe inspiring, profound, or treasured for their nonkilling survival benefit. Altruistic acts of individuals or institutions that increase the survival of humanity and its life support systems are invaluable, worthy of appreciation, and may indeed be defined as holy or sacred.

Level 1 Mind Defined:

In keeping with the concept developed in Chapter 3 that cellular homeostasis is the source of all living behavior, mind can now be defined as any brain-dependent activity that seeks to optimize survival of the cells of the organism, directly or indirectly. Known brain-based homeostatic activities include the following: 1. Gathering of current internal and external sensory data stimuli; 2. Storage of that current sensory data, along with current drives, emotions, personal theories, cultural memes, biases, and goals, into primary memory; 3. Assembly of memory data containing earlier experiences similar to the present one, including associated past survival calculations, conclusions, responses and results, together with past thoughts and emotions; 4. Use of the assembled data to formulate new best and worst- survival outcome projections from past into the future; 5. Selection of an unconscious or conscious response whose goal is to optimize short or long-term cellular survival of self or family; 6. Initiation of the response, including that of a non-response; 7. Recordation and evaluation of the effects of the response in terms of homeostatic success. Clearly, these brain activities more than encompass the requirements for mind by any conventional definition.

From this, we can see that consciousness is a central property of mind. It is the self-awareness required for an organism to maintain cellular homeostasis. There are many levels of consciousness. Even a single-cell organism must be conscious to stay alive. Single-cell organisms (bread mold) show awareness of place and time. Some multicellular organisms with a central nervous system, such as in the mammals, are self-aware. Others with a more developed brain are even introspective (aware that they are self-aware) with metaconsciousness.

The complex structure of the brain is known at essentially all levels (Table 1). In humans, it appears that cerebellar, and limbic structural accretions, together with the cerebrum have been added to the original brain core and striatum, producing in humans what has been modeled as the Quadrimental Brain (Morton, 1985b, 1989), and as the Dual Quadbrain (Morton,1995), the topic of our next chapters. There, we will see that the God, who was thought to be in outer space, has been rediscovered within inner space where S/He has been all along.

Some Important Concepts of Chapter 4.

1. The nature of mind has been a mystery since the beginning of time. Here Triadism has supplied the answers to the Mind-Body Problem that ancient Monism and Dualism could not. That is, mind is neither a brain structure (Monism), nor the thoughts of an immortal soul (Dualism). Rather, mind is the work output of a functioning organ, the brain. For mind to exist requires the three pillars of Triadism: first, the intact brain, a 3D structural organ, second, its activity over time, a 4th D, and 3) the energy containing fuel, to power it a 5th D.

2. As the Triadic solution to the second half of the Mind-Body Problem, the process of Life is seen to be the activity of an intact whole animal, over time, utilizing the solar energy trapped in foodstuff. Triadism is confirmed by the many observations demonstrating that if any one of its three pillars is removed: fuel, time, or functional structure, mind and life ceases.

3. Triadism, has crucially important implications. First and foremost, it abolishes the possibility of extracorporeal, spiritual existence. Mind or life are essentially impossible in the absence of a functionally intact brain or body, a condition which occurs at death. Thus, there can be no life after death, no heaven, no hell, soul, demons nor angels. God as a Spirit cannot exist, nor a physical Devil. Of course, many other mental concepts of God or Satan are possible, however, not in external reality.

4. This is it! Here! Now!. The supernatural and spiritual elements of religion appear to be totally impossible and meaningless aside from their metaphorical value. We exist on the cutting edge of time, and nowhere else. We can make a difference by impacting human existence now or in the future by the things we do while we are briefly alive, either by killing or nonkilling

NEUROREALITY: A SCIENTIFIC RELIGION TO RESTORE MEANING

SECTION II: Who am I? What is this Mystery called Consciousness?

CHAPTER 5: The Quadrimental Brain: Layers of Evolutionary Control

Removal of the Void Produced by the Overthrow of the Supernatural:

From our Survival Reality we inherit a need for the existence of the higher powers of good and evil. Triadism has destroyed dualism's supernatural extracorporeal Gods and Demons. Crucially, triadism did not destroy the possibility for the existence of a genetic, non-supernatural, internal Holy Spirit, God Within. However, at present the existence of an internal higher intelligence usually appears unthinkable because of the illusion that we only have one consciousness: that is, the consciousness of our conflicted, fallible "Ego". Yet, it has long been obvious, and is now well established, that much of human behavior arises from outside of our usual awareness. To account for all of human behavior from the diabolic to the sublime, requires a multiple-mind model. Inherent in such would be the existence of an internal Higher Power.

Why a Multiple Mind Model of Consciousness is Needed:

A single consciousness model is not able to account for the complexities of human behavior. Failure to understand, predict, or control behavior has resulted in enormous tragedy and suffering. A single consciousness model has not accounted for the following: identity, volition, awareness, causality, responsibility, introspection, altruism, hypnosis, the unconscious or spirituality. Furthermore, a single consciousness model cannot account for the production of our many subconscious behaviors. Yes, Tommy! "We only use 10% of our brain". The other 90% uses us! That hidden 90% is the sum of the subconscious activities of our four layered brain: The Brain Core, houses our autonomic nervous system, our drives, instincts, developmental programs and developmental arrest repair programs, of which we are unconscious up here in our language cortex. The Limbic System is the source of the twelve Primary Emotions, and the sixteen Ego Defenses. These are in our subconscious. The Neocerebellum is the preconscious source of conscience, guilt, morality, herd behavior, projection, planning, intuition, wisdom and unconscious knowing.

Earlier Multiple Consciousness Models:

In Greek-Platonic philosophy, the mind usually consisted of four parts: the soul, reason, the competitor, and appetite. The religions of Judaism, Islam and Christianity often had three consciousness elements: Me, the victim of fate, The Devil made me do it, and God help me! Psychology has up to four consciousness elements. For example, the Harvard Professor, William James (1878) proposed the existence of the material self, the social self, the spiritual self and pure ego. Sigmund Freud (1960) also felt that there were four: normal consciousness, and three subconscious entities, which he called the Id, the Ego and the Superego. However, he did not know their brain locations. Most neuroscientists today hold to our childhood belief in a Unitive (Single) Consciousness Model that asserts we know about and are responsible for everything we do and are. A notable exception, Paul McLean (1990) at the National Institute for Health in the USA, developed The Triune Brain Model, which consisted of three increasingly recent layers: The reptilian system, the paleo-mammalian (limbic) system and the neomammalian system, as illustrated in **Figure 1.**

. The Quadrimental Brain Model

However, McLean's Triune Brain Model did not accommodate later discoveries of many non-motor behaviors produced by the hindbrain cerebellum, a major brain structure whose activities were not present in his model. For example, cerebellar auto-stimulation by institutionalized criminals remarkably reversed their murderous rage, turning them into cordial individuals. Further, the site of Primary Memory is the cerebellum. It is also required for language syntax generation. Surprisingly, the cerebellum also is activated in faith healing, hypnosis and during "control psychoses".

Therefore, McLean's Triune Brain has been expanded into the **Quadrimental Brain Model**. Bruce Morton first described this model before the International Society for Research on Aggression in Parma, Italy, in 1985. The model concept is as follows: The human brain consists of four layers representing stages of increasing sophistication in our evolutionary development to optimize the survival of our constituent cells. (Morton, 1985, 1989). **Figure 2** shows a brief diagram of the Quadrimental Brain and **Figure 3** further elaborates it. Proposals for two Quadrune Brain

Figure 1, McLean's Triune Brain System

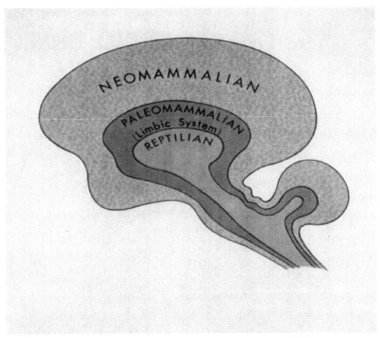

Symbolic representation of the triune brain (see Chapter 2 and Figure 2-1).

models appeared around this time, one of these not incorporating the cerebellum as a separate system, and the other did in an unpublished model of unknown features.

Layer 1, Reptile Brain Core and Striatum: The Selfish Brain

The brain, as it existed in the age of the reptiles had a remarkable ability to promote cellular survival within the animal not just at the level of cells, but also at the level of tissues, of organs, and that of the entire organism. The abilities required for this remarkable feat are located in the brain core and rise up to include the striatum, equivalent to the inner reptilian layer of McLean's Triune model in Figure 1. They are similar to those of Freud's Id: the unconscious drives, passions, and instincts. The behaviors of the reptilian, Selfish Brain are often confused

Figure 2:

THE QUADRIMENTAL BRAIN

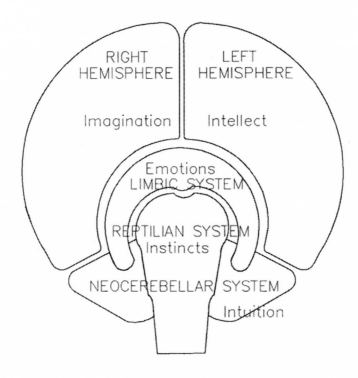

SOURCE OF HUMAN EXPERIENCE

with those of Freud's Ego. Although Freud usually conceived of the executive brain as the "Ego", popular culture treats the ego as if it were the Id, as in "She hurt his ego". Therefore, Freud's allegorical terms are best replaced with ones that are more specific.

Layer 2, NeoCerebellum: The Social Brain

The social brain began to develop separately around this time. It was based upon the primary memory time track in the cerebellum that gave it knowledge of time, space, causality and thus morality. The social brain views itself as a part of a larger family group that is more important than it is. It early manifested itself in the coordinated behavior of large groups of social organisms: the swarming of bees or locusts, the schooling of fish, the flocking of birds, and migration of reindeer, and the trouping of monkeys. The Social Brain was the brain layer that Freud ambiguously called his Superego. It can be localized in the cerebellum, especially within the neocerebellum.

Layer 3, Limbic System: The Executive Brain

As pointed out Chapter 2, the emergent properties at the self level are quite opposite to those emerging at the group level. Thus, complex judgments are needed to know whether a particular survival situation is better solved by the killing violence of the selfish brain, or by the nonkilling cooperation of the more capable social brain. This led to the evolutionary development of the third brain level of control, that of the executive brain.

The executive brain emerges from the properties of the "limbic system", so named by Paul McLean. These are a set of neural tissues intimately wrapped around the self brain core and extending up into the limbic cingulate cortex of the fourth level (the cerebrum). The executive brain is aware and highly concerned about the survival of both itself and its family. It powerfully controls and motivates the Id with the reward and punishment of the primary social emotions. It also strongly controls the social brain with the many "Ego defenses of the Id".

A strong executive continually decides whether to authorize the reptilian brain to produce a selfish response, or whether to ask the social brain to design a synergistic response. Thus, a strong executive confers superior survival to the organism, while a weak executive cannot overrule reptilian selfishness with its inherent suppression of the wisdom of the social brain lying unheeded within.

Figure 3, LAYERS OF THE QUADRIMENTAL BRAIN

Cerebral System: *Imagines, Describes*
Aware of Self-Awareness. Able to Represent
Reality either by Imaging or Abstracting of Primary
Memory. Metamind: Offline thinking; True Language.
In Humans, Except Young Children.
Normal Human Consciousness

Limbic System: *Has - Controls*
Aware of Self. Non Syntactic Language.
Executive: Controls External Operations
Uses Primary Emotions and
Ego Defenses to Motivate.
Also in Mammals and Young Children.
Preconscious Ego

Cerebellar System: *Is - Knows*
Aware of the Group as Part of Itself.
Knowledge of Time and Space, Causality.
Lays down Primary Memory Time Track.
Also in Vertebrates.
Subconscious Superego

Striatal-Brain Core System: *Does*
Aware of Senses. Has a Same-Different
Comparator for Set-Points or Competitors.
Motivated by Pain or Pleasures. Instincts.
Also in Lower Organisms that have Brains.
Unconscious, Id

Layer 4, Intellectual Brain: The Cerebral Hemispheres

Within the most recently developed fourth brain layer, that of the cerebral cortex, lie the abstractive abilities that produce the intellect and imagination of our derivative "cartoon and caption" type of usual consciousness. Here we have access to language, imagery and the awareness of our own self-awareness that forms the basis of contemplative thought. This is Freud's fourth and mundane level of consciousness, the only one of which he felt everybody was aware. He strongly believed that the three more ancient and powerful layers operated outside of our normal awareness.

The Quadrimental Brain, Expanded View:

Let us now look at functions of these four specialized brain layers again at a little greater depth. **Figure 4** shows a cartoon of the Quadrimental Brain centering on cellular survival.

The Reptile Brain DOES

Regardless of who controls it, the reptile or selfish brain is the *one and only* output source of all behavior, both internal and external. Its own cellular homeostatic behaviors include genetically selected drives and instincts, such as conquest and defense of *territory* by dominance, via fighting and display. It will then use this territory to get *food* by hunting for, taking, and eating fuel, for *shelter* from elements and predators, and for *reproduction* by mating and sometimes rearing young.

The reptile brain receives earlier similar memory responses from sensory inputs originating in cerebellar primary memory. The primary memory is a record of the sensory experience time track going back to before hatching or birth. The reptile brain records its repetitive routines in striatal habit memory as well as cerebellar primary memory. Important reptile routines include times of waking, excretion, eating, sunning, seeking shade and sleeping.

The reptile brain also uses striatal memory for same-different data matching and analysis. This enables it to detect deviations from internal homeostatic set points, such as blood glucose, which it instinctively corrects. Same-difference matching also identifies and sizes external objects. From this it decides whether to fight or submit. As a rule, all else being equal, the biggest opponent will win. If your opponent is obviously larger than you are, why fight only to die? Surrender has thus become an automatic alternative! The leader becomes, by definition, the biggest and best. Others willingly "follow the leader", as their superior.

This important pecking order detail formed a basis of internal surrender of the behavioral output Reptile Brain DOER to other later higher brain additions. It also formed a basis of external surrender to Father (Superior, Higher Authority), Teacher, Leader, King, God, God's priest-healer, other Hypnotists, and with schizophrenics, to imaginary alien control. Research has shown that the cerebellum is activated in hypnosis, schizophrenia and faith healing.

Figure 4:

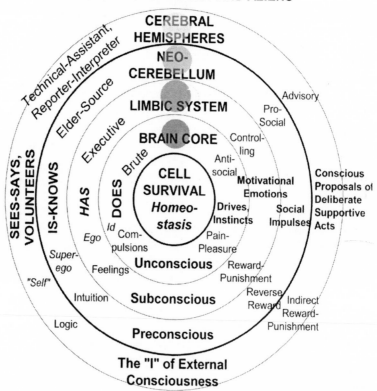

THE QUADRIMENTAL BRAIN: CONSCIOUSNESS AND MOTIVATION

Bruce E. Morton, Ph.D.,
University of Hawaii
School of Medicine
©

The Optimization of Cell Survival is the Source and Purpose of All Behavior

Reptile Brain behavioral output is automatic, i.e., produced by the autonomic sympathetic (punished avoidance) and parasympathetic (rewarded approach) nervous systems. It has direct control of the entire body, including the tongue and is the ultimate source of power. If the Reptile Brain is not *surrendered* to an internal or external Higher Authority, *it must control everything.* If resisted, it will escalate force up to killing levels of violence. It must be right. It must look better at all costs. It must win. It must dominate and control. This was a matter of life or death.

The reptile brain is the source of social conflict. A part of it is the brain location of the personal "Devil" in humans. Its antisocial "Laws of the Jungle" are inherently in conflict with society and religion: Its past is forgotten. The future does not exist. This is it, Here, Now! Let's party! It is the source of *pleasure seeking*: It loves "wine, women, and song". It is the source of *pain avoidance*: this makes it lazy, undisciplined and wasteful. It is the source of *territoriality*: and is selfish, greedy, obsessive, malicious. It is the source of *domination*: and is competitive, aggressive, destructive. It is the source of *violence*: it rapes, injures, kills, dismembers and can be cannibalistic.

The Social Brain IS

The goal of the Social Brain (Freud's Superego) is group-species-life survival optimization. The ancient family and herd-oriented elements of the cerebellum, the site of primary memory, direct it. This so-called hindbrain has more cells than entire rest of brain but they are a smaller. As our primary memory, it is continuously forming a linear time track forming an experiential multi-sensory record of our status over time. Its primary memory is in the format of very large-sized memories based upon the elegant, repetitive structure of the cerebellum. Our experiential time track is a continuous record reaching from the present to back before our birth. Without memory, current events, the snarl of a wolf for example, are gone forever the instant they happen. With primary memory, they are retrievable and held in Working Memory for analysis and for continuing survival optimizing responses beyond immediate simple flight reflexes.

Social Brain is the source of many important homeostatic behaviors. It uses cerebellar primary record of events in time and space to determine "the sequence of events", and from this to recognize causality (cause-cause, or effect-effect)! From knowledge of causality come many important things, for example: meaning, learning, selfhood, survival reality, social knowledge, worst and best projections and knowledge of death. The Social Brain is also the site of language syntax: When did who do what to whom, where, and why? Syntax obviously originated from the coordination of both physical behavior for which the cerebellum is well known, and the coordination of ideas: which we call thinking. Drugs of abuse such as alcohol, because they inhibit cerebellar coordination, cause one to become both physically tipsy and mentally silly.

Knowledge of causality makes clear the advantages of deferred behavior, and support the self-restraint required. Similarly, the synergistic advantageous cooperative behavior within the group for the greater good of both family and the individual are obvious. Out of the social brain's view of the group as part of its own self, comes *unselfish support and altruism.* It protects, nurtures, and trains family members. From this comes *conscience and guilt.* It organizes and maintains solidarity of the family unit. From this comes *ethics, law, order.* It has been identified with The God Within, The Holy Spirit, The Source, Our Higher Power, Our Higher Intelligence. It is the source of insight, intuition, wisdom, inspiration, one's "True Self", morality, purity, holiness, truth, faith, religion and species Immortality.

The Inherent Universe-Level Conflict between two Brain Elements: Reptile (pro-individual) vs. Social (pro-group).

As mentioned earlier, each universe-level has unique emergent laws. The laws at the universe-level of the individual include: "I win. You lose." competition escalating to violence. "Give it to me now or I'll kill you!" works well *against* hyenas and other aliens. In contrast, exist the laws at universe-level of the family including both, "win-win", cooperation, non-violence and, "How can I best help you?" which work so well *for* loved ones of family. Thus, two conflicts exist between the reptile and social Brains: *When* shall I act to optimize survival?; Now or later? (for the reptile brain, there is only NOW!) and *Whose* survival shall I optimize? My own or that of my family?; (for the reptile-selfish brain the only answer is mine!).

The familiar "double standards of behavior that must inherently result from this conflict include self vs. others: "I am being held to a 'different-higher' standard than you are", and that of family vs. aliens: "It's not who you are, but who you know". The conflict between reptile brain and the social brain is a central theme of religion. It is seen in Christian fundamentalism as the "Great Controversy between Christ and Satan". In

Islam, it appears as the Holy War (Major Jihad) between self-will and Allah's will.

The Two Opposing Survival Realities: War between Levels: Source of Inner Stress.

An overlooked, but still functioning mechanism used by the social brain to inhibit-combat reptile brain selfish behavior is as follows: The social brain labels pro-species behavior as good, Godly: unselfish, and selfless. It rewards good with acceptance (love), happiness, joy. It labels selfish, violent, anti-social behavior and killing as bad, evil, and diabolic. It punishes bad with conscience, guilt, intense internal pain, rejection-ostracism and depression from the pain stress.

A former successful response by reptile brain to stop social brain rejection was to confess one's theft of survival benefits from the other or others and to restore their stolen survival benefits. When restitution is complete, then forgiveness, acceptance and synergy automatically return, both from those who harmed, and from the social brain to the reptile brain of perpetrator.

Maladaptive reptile brain responses to survive the social brain's rejection and guilt also exist. For example: to run away from one's family (after social mobility was no longer lethal on the glacier), or to inhibit separation pain by short-term antisocial sex, or, more recently, to inhibit Social Brain guilt pain by drugs of abuse (alcohol, hemp, opium). Due to the inevitable homeostatic development of drug tolerance, intoxicating levels soon become required to block the pain. The resulting drug tolerance-based drunkenness required to block the Social Brain's guilt pain causes vast amounts of family disruption, academic failure, joblessness, social isolation, welfare dependence, poor health, criminal behavior, and kills millions on the highways. The need to stop guilt pain drives global drug trade, causing personal and government corruption, international crime, as well as damage to human society and the ecosystem.

The Executive Brain HAS:

The executive brain optimizes overall cell survival by determining and managing whether the final decision output will come from: 1) the reptile brain whose internal reality makes selfish demands and wants it all right now; 2) the social brain whose survival reality for species survival demands that the selfish brain turn off; or 3) the cerebral intellect brain's cultural and personal ideas about external reality. The executive brain structure is the limbic system, including the thalamus and cingulate cortex. The executive brain was the first of the quadrimental brain layers to manifest the fetal/maternal programs, including curiosity, and juvenile rehearsal-play, as compared to the usually suppressive humorless reptilian brain's antisocial drives.

The executive ego has two powerful sets of tools at its disposal. First, it can utilize the rewarding positive poles of emotions and drives **(Table 1)** to motivate the brain system called upon to act, i.e., the famous "carrot", Or, it can use their negative extremes to bring about painful punished compliance, using the infamous "stick". Second, if it fails to accomplish its goals, it has an arsenal of the classical Ego defenses of the Id Table 2 available for use to avoid taking responsibility for its failure.

When the executive ego feels safe, it motivates action by use of the Hexadyad Primary Emotions. As may be seen, there are several perspectives of emotions available, from that of cellular homeostasis to descriptions of mood and personality to descriptors that we have applied to God and Satan. Table 1 is a composite positive and negative binary expansion of the six pairs of primary emotions. Rising and falling from the center of Table 1 are the six primary emotion pairs: They are: 1. certainty vs. confusion, 2. confidence vs. fear, 3. pleasure vs disgust, 4. gratitude vs. anger, 5. elation vs. grief, and 6. satisfaction vs desire. Expanding upward or downward from these core responses are the limbic system ego's conclusions derived from them. Expanding further we come to their motivational value, then their survival (biological) significance, If the same emotion is prolonged for a few hours or days, the resulting moods are listed. If prolonged for weeks or years, they become part of personality. The personal meanings of these binary emotions to self and others are listed next to the last, followed by familiar spiritual conceptual extremes.

The Hexadyad Primary Emotions Model has found support in the work of Ekman (2006) who from cross cultural research found that around the world, humans responded in the same manner to the same emotional stimuli. They could also accurately identify the emotion experienced from the face of others responding to the same stimuli. His list of universal human emotions included five of the six hexadyad negative emotions (surprise, fear, disgust, anger, sadness). There was one generalized positive emotion, (happiness). Possibly the latter outcome was because the experiencing of all six positive emotions results in the same smile upon one's face. In the 1990s Ekman expanded his emotions to those not encoded by facial expression. Some of his non facial emotions included the

Table I. SUMMARY OF THE HEXADYAD PRIMARY EMOTIONS AND THEIR DERIVATIVES

(Since primary emotions are binary, start at midline and work up and down.)

+CONCEPT EXTREME:	OMNISCIENT, CREATOR	OMNIPOTENT	GOD IS LOVE	HEAVENLY FATHER	KING OF KINGS	PRINCE OF PEACE
+BEHAVIORAL to self EXTREME:	At cause	Tells truth	Accepts	Gives of	Joyful	At peace
to others	RESPONSIBLE	ETHICAL	LOVES	GIVES TO	ENTHUSIASTIC	AT PEACE
+PERSONALITY:	Knowing	Secure	Accepting	Supportive	Enthusiastic	Peaceful
+MOOD:	CLARITY	CALM	HAPPY	THANKFUL	JOYFUL	CONTENTED
+BIOLOGICAL STATUS:	Properties known	Safe to act	Resource available	Ally found	+ Reinforcement	Free to act
+EVERYDAY MOTIVATOR:	RIGHT, SMART	STRONG	YES, GOOD	FRIEND	WINNER, SUCCESS	HAVE
+LIMBIC CONCLUSION:	I know CERTAINTY	I am stronger	I accept	I am helped	I win	I have
+ EMOTION:	EXPECTANCE-CERTAINTY	CONFIDENCE	PLEASURE	GRATITUDE	ELATION	SATISFACTION
- EMOTION:	CONFUSION-SURPRISE	FEAR	DISGUST	ANGER	GRIEF	DESIRE
-LIMBIC CONCLUSION:	I don't know	I am weaker	I reject	I am harmed	I lose	I want
-EVERYDAY MOTIVATOR:	WRONG, STUPID	WEAK	NO, BAD	ENEMY	LOSER, FAILURE	NEED
-BIOLOGICAL STATUS:	Properties unknown	Time to escape	Source of harm or waste	Competitor identified	Negative reinforcement	Get supplies
-MOOD:	UNCERTAIN	ANXIOUS	NEGATIVE	IRRITATED	SAD	DISSATISFIED
-PERSONALITY:	Ambiv-alent	Insecure	Rejecting	Hostile	Gloomy	Demanding
-BEHAVIORAL to others EXTREME:	BLAMES	UNETHICAL	HATES	HARMS	APATHETIC	LIES, CHEATS, STEALS
to self	Lies to	Afraid of the truth	Suicidal	Accident-prone, ill	Hopeless	Self and drug abuse
-CONCEPT EXTREME:	IDIOT, FOOL	FRIGHTENED TO DEATH	DIABOLICAL HATRED	RAGING DEMON	WAILING, KNASHING	CRIMINAL, FIEND

missing positive pole to primary emotion pairs, contentment (satisfaction), relief (confidence), pride in achievement, excitement, and amusement (elation), Others (guilt, embarrassment, and shame) were complex social emotions composed of more than one primary emotion.

When the executive is unsuccessful in suppressing the reptile brain, it uses the sixteen Ego Defenses of the Id **(Table 2)** to justify its use the Reptile Brain to produce antisocial behavior. Clearly, each of these defenses is an after the fact *lie,* as exemplified with the use of denial or of projection onto others. We see these in use all the time by people seeking to avoid responsibility for their acts or failure to act. The sixteen classic defenses listed here are probably not exhaustive. In general, they provide proof that our Id would rather win, be right and dominate, and that it would rather lie than lose, be wrong or be dominated. Thus, the executive is equipped with a genetic arsenal of sophisticated deceptions. Furthermore, it does not see them as lies, but as the "gospel" truth and often is willing to fight to be right about them. How interesting that we have such an elaborate set of weapons to use against non-family aliens.

The Executive-Ego is also profoundly afraid of dying and suppresses access to memories of past threats of death trauma by mental blockades. When off-line, during REM sleep or when injured or drugged, it camouflages uncontrolled breakthroughs of raw memories of personal trauma. These instead are disguised as dreams, nightmares, or waking hallucinations. The Executive can be selectively inhibited and weakened to the point of collapse by both certain types of meditation, and by ingestion of drugs that specifically activate the serotonin 2a stress receptor, all of which are hallucinogens like LSD. Under these circumstances of brain failure, supernatural figures and events can produce mysterious illusions. Anciently, these altered state experiences likely provided the irrational foundations of our current religions (Hancock, 2007).

The Executive can also be caused to give over its control to a higher outer authority, for example as 1) in certain practices of religion (including human suicide bombers or kamikaze pilots), or 2) in child-like inductive learning (from the most authoritative parental or scientific source) or 3) in hypnosis (Faith Healing, Death Curses, Mass Hysteria).

Executive Properties as Self, Supervisor, Ego, Will and Controller of Volition:

The Executive Ego Will seeks the solution of ongoing survival

Table 2: Ego Defenses of the Reptilian Id: The Sixteen Lies (Confabulations)

1, Acting out: expression of an impulse in spite of its negative consequences.
2, Compensation: development of another characteristic to offset a deficiency.
3, Denial: declaring that an anxiety provoking stimuli doesn't exist.
4, Displacement: taking out impulses on a less threatening target.

5, Intellectualization: avoiding emotional impact by focusing on details.
6, Passive-Aggressive Behavior: avoiding aggression by passivity.
7, Projection: placing one's unacceptable impulses upon someone else.
8, Rationalization: supplying a logical reason in place of the real one.

9, Reaction Formation: replacing a real belief with one causing less anxiety.
10, Regression: returning to a previous stage of development.
11, Repression: loss of access to memories of past trauma.
12, Resistance: defense against conscious awareness of unconscious desires.

13, Somatosization: channeling conflict onto one's body: obesity, allergies, etc.
14, Sublimation: acting out unacceptable impulses in a socially acceptable way.
15, Suppression: pushing something that causes anxiety out of consciousness.
16, Undoing: obsessive repetition of ritualistic act as if to ally guilt from an event.

---

problem using the above primary emotions as motivators. It has been quantitatively studied in mammals and birds. It is the source of judgment and decision. This includes attention, causal action, anticipation expectation of outcome (anxiety or excitement), detection and correction of errors and evaluation of final effects.

It learns from experience and takes pre-conscious action based upon its emotional evaluation of relative survival values, likelihoods and profitability. It calculates profitability in terms of survival maximization. This requires a predatory strategy based upon the maximum intake of energy for the least expenditure of effort in a random and unpredictable world, where such decisions rely upon efficiency and economy of action. Decision between conflicting possibilities of profitability is a core issue. That is: what the cost/benefit ratio will be of each of the alternatives available. This estimate is based upon the survival value of the goal, the needed direction of effort and the type of action recognized.

Ultimately the Executive Ego delegates authority: Should "I" use my competitive Reptile Brain at the universe level of individual? Or, should I use my cooperative Social Brain at the next higher universe level, that of the group? Also what importance should be given to what my conscious cerebral Imagination sees or my Intellect reports? These sophisticated decisions are at the center of our preconscious Executive's call to action.

The Intellect IMAGINES-REPORTS

The brain of higher mammals has relatively recently evolved a potent abstract reasoning accessory in the cerebral cortex. This abstracting accessory, called the Intellect, serves the just described reptile-social-executive brain "Triad" to optimize cellular homeostasis with increased sophistication. The more ancient and powerful triad members are each self-aware, but operate outside the awareness of the intellect, which is located in the asymmetric right and left cerebral hemispheres. In humans, intellect matures late and takes over consciousness by about 3 years of age when true language becomes operational.

Working memory is a basic element essential to the intellect: Working memory retrieves reverberating facsimiles of cerebellar primary memory (social brain), and striatal habit memory (reptile brain) via the thalamus (part of the executive brain). Working memory holds these fax copies for manipulation on a prefrontal cortex viewing screen. The Intellect then copies (via hippocampus) these faxes of vast and unwieldy cerebellar primary memory into two different compressed cerebral memory formats, each small enough to be manipulated in time and space *off-line*.

One of these, usually in the right hemisphere (see next chapter), produces visual cartoons, something that children find inherently attractive. These are concrete images of inner reality. The other, from the left hemisphere produces compressed memory captions: These are the abstract symbols of language. The intellect uses its new cartoon – caption "funny book" memory to think of new ideas off-line. This enables it for the first time to conceptualize, plan, safely rehearse, adapt, to produce an improved plan, without having to expose itself to the dangers of trial and error in external reality. It can project data in time and space to predict worst and best possible outcomes. These abstracting compressing skills formed the foundational source of speech, writing, mathematics, logic and civilization. Further, the intellect can be aware of its own self-awareness and thus reach the organization level of Metamind.

There are advantages of having a consciousness operating at the intellectual-imagination level. Not only can it form new survival-optimizing ideas off-line, while the older brain "Triad" are routinely working. But, its existence also avoids second-by-second *suffering* (of Buddhism) from the continuous operation of the powerful punish-reward emotional motivators operating in the more ancient lower brain triad. This is because these seem to operate mainly subconsciously outside of its awareness.

However, there are two critical disadvantages to operating from a consciousness only aware at the intellectual-imagination level. First: such a narrow consciousness assumes that its own volition alone produces *all* its behavior until it learns otherwise, if ever. The cartoon in **Figure 5** illustrates this. Second, the Intellect can not retrieve and upgrade harmful earlier cerebellar or striatal memories of trauma or error that were formed in the larger, more cumbersome primary memory format before the age of 3, at which time it first began forming records in the cerebral cartoon format of the Intellect.

Clearly, the Quadrimental Brain Model, as illustrated in Figure 4, is a more accurate approximation of the human mind than that of the Unitive Model. However, as might be expected, the mind of humans is even more complex than four layers. This is due to the bilateral nature of vertebrate form incorporated into our human structure. Rather than one sided simply being a mirror image of the other, due to evolution, the two sides of each of the four vertical layers of brain evolution have developed a different specialized function. This has forced an expansion of the Quadrimental Brain Model into the Dual Quadbrain Model, with its Society of Seven, described in the next chapters. However, once working at that level of understanding, we will be equipped to understand what human thought is about.

Figure 5: Pattern on Professor Morton's old Reyn's Hawaiian Shirt

Figure 5 legend: A Farmer with a straw between his teeth is riding backwards on a fat pig. He reports upon and rationalizes all that happens, believing himself to be in charge. The thoughts of the farmer represent what occurs in human LH unitive consciousness. Obviously, the pig has a mind of its own, whose operation is almost completely out of the farmer's awareness.

Important Concepts from Chapter 5:

1. A single consciousness model has not been able to account for the complexities of human behavior. Yet, the existence of an internal higher intelligence appears unthinkable because of the illusion that we only have one consciousness: that is, the consciousness of our conflicted, fallible "Ego". Failure to understand, predict, or control behavior results in enormous suffering and tragedy. It now clear that much of human behavior arises from outside of our usual awareness. A multiple-mind model is needed to account for all of human behavior from the diabolic to the sublime.

2. The Quadrimental Brain Model is an evolutionary perspective that brings much clarity to behavior. Early vertebrates, with only what is now our brain core and striatum, directed the behavior of the organism to maintain cell survival conditions in a variable environment by promoting instincts such as those of sex and reproduction, and also finding, killing, and ingesting fuel energy sources. These resources were digested and the energy shunted within the animal to regions that required energy for the growth, development, defense, courtship and reproduction of life. Because crocodiles and alligators act upon the instinctual level, the apparently diabolic killing activities of self-survival, this lowest brain element in the Quadrimental Brain Model has been called the Reptilian Brain.

3. Some animals survived better in cooperative groups than when they competed against each other individually. By moving from the universe level of the individual to the next higher level of the cooperating group, new social interaction *properties* automatically emerged to produce synergetic survival benefits. By rising to the level of a cooperating *interacting gr*oup, the killing antisocial behaviors appropriate the leve*l of competing* individual enemies were superseded by a completely different new set of survival optimizing nonkilling social behaviors among allies. The Quadrimental Brain element producing these social behaviors works within the primary memory track the cerebellum, and is the "social brain". The enhancement of group survival is the source of true morality, the extreme form of which is the higher intelligence of the social brain Source, our God Within. All can access its wisdom, purpose, plan and power.

4. Because under immediate threat of death under extreme circumstances the social behaviors of the Social Brain are not appropriate, while those of the **Reptile Brain** are life saving, the need of a third brain element, the Executive Caretaker Brain of the limbic system arose. Its multisystem survival analysis and split second decisions as to whether to respond with efficient, effective social or antisocial behavior, makes the Executive Brain a crucial element of the Quadrimental Brain Model. It has at its disposal the Primary Emotions as internal motivators and the Ego Defenses of the Id as weapons against nonfamily aliens.

5. Last to arrive was the fourth layer of the Quadrimental Brain Model, adding the revolutionary computing power of the bilateral cerebral cortexes. These reduce the multisensory vastness of cerebellar primary memory into a new compact secondary memory format stored in new cerebral locations. This can be done off-line while the earlier three brain elements continue to maintain the organism's optimal survival.

6. Using this format, unwieldy chunks of multisensory cerebellar primary memory can be greatly reduced in size and converted into abstract summaries, similar in the form to "cartoon" images with verbal captions.

7. Thus, abstract reasoning permits the reductive transformation and manipulation of complex information into a format that the mind easily manipulates. This permits the evaluation of survival problems and their solutions by the safe production of imaginary trials and their imaginary survival outcomes. It also led to the development of abstract forms of communication called language and mathematics. From these bases came a new form of self-awareness from within language and imagery that we usually experience. This intellect sits high and mighty above the earlier Reptile, Social, and Executive Brain instincts, intuition, and judgment, generally unaware of their ongoing critical activities.

NEUROREALITY: A SCIENTIFIC RELIGION TO RESTORE MEANING

SECTION II: Who am I? What is this Mystery called Consciousness?

CHAPTER 6: Bilateral Expansion of the Quadrimental Brain to the Dual Quadbrain Model

Introduction: The Need to Expand to a Dual Quadbrain Model

The entire vertebrate central nervous system is bilateral. That is, all its structural elements are paired on either side of the midline, for example the two cerebral hemispheres. The sole exception is that there is only a single central pineal gland, an endocrine organ. This exception led the French philosopher Descartes to declare the pineal gland to be the seat of the soul. Awareness of sidedness in brain function appears to be as old as written history. For example, Diocles of Carystus in the 4th century BC wrote: "There are two brains in the head, one which gives understanding, and another which provides sense-perception. That is to say, the one which is lying on the right side is the one that perceives: with the left one, however, we understand". (Lockhorst 1985).

Although Diocles may have been the first to write about brain laterality, Marc Dax was the first on record in the modern era to note a difference in function between the cerebral hemispheres. In 1836, he reported victims of stroke or other injury to the left hemisphere (LH), but not the right hemisphere (RH) could not speak. This hemispheric asymmetry for language was also thought to be tied to contra-lateral hand preference (Broca 1863). Among those 90% of humans who are right handed (Coren, 1992), language is located in the LH in over 95% of them (Smith and Moscovitch, 1979). Of the remaining about 10% of left-handed individuals, some 60% of these also have language in their left cerebrum (Levy and Reid, 1976). Thus, the LH houses language ability in at least 9 out of 10 humans.

Nearly a century passed before reports of any further manifestations of hemispheric laterality. Then, a large study by Weisenberg and McBride (1935) demonstrated a RH superiority for visiospatial skills. During that century, the laterality term, "dominant hemisphere", became irreversibly tied to the language-processing hemisphere, usually the LH, because of its association with the brain areas required for speech and dominant handedness. This forced the creation of second terms not using the word, dominance, such as "hemispheric laterality" or "cerebral asymmetry", to describe the many, more-recently discovered non-language differences in cerebral structure and function, most notably found in "split-brain" subjects. These individuals had been produced by treatment for intractable epilepsy by severing their corpus callosum, the only cerebral connection between the hemispheres, thus limiting the spread of seizures from one side to the other (Sperry, 1982; Gazzaniga, Bogen & Sperry, 1962; Gazzaniga, 2000).

Based upon the surprisingly different responses obtained by the interrogation of each of these isolated hemispheres of split-brain subjects (Gazzaniga, et al., 1962; Geschwind, Iacoboni, Mega, Zidel, Cloughesy, & Zaidel, 1995; Gazzaniga, 2000), investigators proposed that the right and left cerebral hemispheres are characterized by inbuilt, qualitatively different and mutually antagonistic modes of data processing, necessarily separated from interference by the major longitudinal fissure of the brain (Levy, 1969; Sperry, 1982). In this model, the left hemisphere specialized in top-down, deductive, cognitive dissection of local detail, the right hemisphere in bottom-up, inductive, perceptual synthesis of global structure (Sperry, 1982; Gazzaniga, 2000). Known laterality differences between them reinforce this context. That is, there are striking differences in input to each hemisphere, differences in internal neuronal-columnar architecture, and differences in hemispheric output (Kosslyn, Koenig, Barrett, Cave, Tang, & Gabrieli, 1989; Kosslyn, Chabris, Marsolek, & Koenig, 1992; Hutsler & Galuske, 2003; Jager & Postma, 2003; Stephan, Fink and Marshall, 2006).

Supporting the above view of opposite processing modes between the cerebral hemispheres is a large body of evidence, only briefly summarized here, that the left cerebral hemisphere in most right-handed individuals manifests facilities for language (Broca, 1863), has an orientation for local detail (Robertson & Lamb, 1991), has object abstraction-identification abilities (Kosslyn) (1987) and appears to possess a hypothesis-generating, event "interpreter" (Wolford, et al, 2000, Gazzaniga, 1989, 2000). In contrast, the right hemisphere excels in global analysis (Robertson & Lamb, 1991; Magun, et al., 1994), object localization (Kosslyn, et al., 1989), facial recognition (Milner, 1968) and spatial construction (Sperry, 1968).

It is of interest that within this huge group of right-handed, LH-dominant speakers, the existence of two major human sub-populations has repeatedly been inferred, whose characteristic thinking and behavior styles differ in a manner that appeared to mirror the properties of the asymmetric hemispheres. That is, in some right-handed, LH languaged individuals, *left* hemisphere traits were proposed to be ascendant, producing a "Left brain-oriented" thinking and behavioral style (Springer and Deutch; 1998; Fink, Halligan, Marschall, Frith, Frackowiak, & Dolan, 1996). Such left brain-oriented persons are top-down, important detail, deductive, "splitters". Yet, in other right-handed, LH languaged persons, *right* hemisphere traits are thought to be more prominent, resulting in a contrasting "Right brain"-oriented style (Davidson and Hugdahl, 1995; Shiffer, 1996), currently viewed as bottom-up, big picture, inductive, "lumpers".

Thus, original permanent assignment of the term "hemispheric dominance" to language laterality ultimately forced the creation of yet a third laterality term, "Hemisphericity" (Bogen, 1969; Bogen, DeZure, Tenhouten, and Marsh, 1969). This was required in order to describe this third laterality phenomenon: the seemingly binary differences in left and right brain thinking and behavioral style within individuals of both the same language dominance and non-language subsystem asymmetries. However, hemisphericity earned an incorrect initial definition as a person's unique point on a gradient between right and left-brain extremes. After years of conflict, this misconception caused such problems that the actual existence of hemisphericity was placed in doubt (Beaumont, Young & McManus, 1984).

As we will see, the observer of the executive ego can only be unilateral. That is, it can be on only one side of the brain. This is consistent with the logic that within any institution, there can be only one "bottom line" authority. This also reduces the number of separate consciousness elements from eight to The Society of Seven (Chapter 7). Recently, redefinition of hemisphericity based upon which side of the brain the unilateral Executive Observer was located, has restored hemisphericity in binary form as a more robust either right or left brain-oriented phenomenon under the new name of "Hemisity" (Morton, 2001, 2001, 2003 abcd; Morton and Rafto, 2006, 2010). Hemisity is a foundational element of Dyadic Evolution and Familial Polarity (Chapters 9,10, and 11).

Asymmetries and functional differences also exist between sides of the two lower layers of the quadrimental brain as well. In both the cerebellar social brain and the reptilian self brain, the behavior of one side focuses more on the individual and the other upon the family group.

Six Postulates Creating the Dual Quadbrain Model:
    The above essential background elements of 1) bilaterality of the entire brain, 2) asymmetric inputs to the cerebral hemispheres, 3) contrastingly different data processing orientations of the asymmetric hemispheres, and 4) differing behavioral outputs of the asymmetric hemispheres, were combined with other evolutionary and neuroscience information to create the Dual Quadbrain Model of behavioral laterality.
    In **Figure 1**, the still valid Quadrimental Brain Model of Chapter 5 and the lateralized Dual Quadbrain Model contexts are compared using grey tone coding. The cartoon of the structure of the human bilateral brain and its major anatomical interconnections only coincidentally resembles that of a human head. Obvious are the two cerebral hemispheres of the Intellectual Brain on top and the bilateral cerebellar Social Brain on either side. The unilateral limbic system Executive Brain is within the surrounding cerebral hemispheres and the bilateral Reptile Brain stem and striatum of the Reptile Brain are beneath mediating final behavioral output to the spinal column. The corpus callosum, the major bridge between the cerebral hemispheres, is depicted, as are the corticotrophic factor (CRF) anxiety connections between the paired emotion generating amygdale, and the norepinephrine fear pathways of the locus coeruleus pair. Counterbalancing these punishment pathways (-) are the rewarding pathways (+) of the pleasure neurotransmitter, dopamine. We will utilize six postulates to fill in the detailed functions of the Dual Quadbrain elements.

Dual Quadbrain Model Postulate 1: Left side Self-Survival Orientation vs. Right side Group-Survival Orientation Form a Bilateral Functional Axis for the Entire Brain
    In the Dual Quadbrain Model, it is postulated that the quadrimental elements of the left half of the brain are dedicated primarily to self-survival and self-sufficiency, either when alone or in the presence of competition against other species. In contrast, the right side elements of the brain are devoted to group, herd, and species survival and cooperative social interaction (Henry and Wang, 1998). Each side of the brain is alternatively activated or suppressed as appropriate to the social environment and directed by the single unilateral Executive Ego.

Figure 1, Quadrimental Brain and the Dual Quadbrain Laterality Expansion

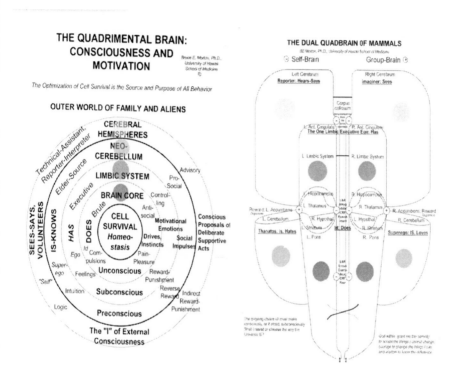

Dual Quadbrain Model Postulate 2: The Bottom-Up and Top-Down Processing of the Two Cerebral Hemispheres are Functionally Opposite and Require Physical Separation

The opposite orientation of the two more recently arrived powerful data abstracting units within the Intellectual System that produce our usual cartoon (right hemisphere) and caption (left hemisphere) based consciousness is shown in **Figure 2**. In brief, the left cerebral hemisphere

Figure 2, Dual Quadbrain Intellect
THE DUAL QUADBRAIN OF MAMMALS
BE Morton, Ph.D., University of Hawaii School of Medicine

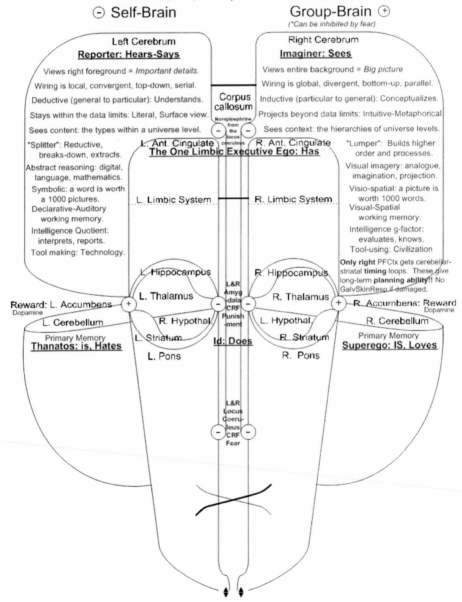

⊖ Self-Brain   Group-Brain ⊕
(*Can be inhibited by fear)

Left Cerebrum **Reporter: Hears-Says**	Right Cerebrum **Imaginer: Sees**
Views right foreground = *Important details.*	Views entire background = *Big picture*
Wiring is local, convergent, top-down, serial.	Wiring is global, divergent, bottom-up, parallel.
Deductive (general to particular): Understands.	Inductive (particular to general): Conceptualizes.
Stays within the data limits: Literal, Surface view.	Projects beyond data limits: Intuitive-Metaphorical.
Sees content: the types within a universe level.	Sees context: the hierarchies of universe levels.
"Splitter": Reductive, breaks-down, extracts.	"Lumper": Builds higher order and processes.
Abstract reasoning: digital, language, mathematics.	Visual imagery: analogue, imagination, projection.
Symbolic: a word is worth a 1000 pictures.	Visio-spatial: a picture is worth 1000 words.
Declarative-Auditory working memory.	Visual-Spatial working memory.
Intelligence Quotient: interprets, reports.	Intelligence g-factor: evaluates, knows.
Tool making: Technology.	Tool-using: Civilization

Corpus callosum
Norepinephrine from the locus coeruleus

L. Ant. Cingulate   R. Ant. Cingulate
The One Limbic Executive Ego: Has

L. Limbic System   R. Limbic System

Only right PFCtx gets cerebellar-striatal **timing** loops. These give long-term **planning ability**!! No GalvSkinResp if damaged.

L. Hippocampus   R. Hippocampus

L&R Amyg-dala CRF Punish-ment

L. Thalamus   R. Thalamus

Reward: L. Accumbens ⊕   ⊕ R. Accumbens: Reward
Dopamine   Dopamine

L. Cerebellum   R. Hypothal.   L. Hypothal.   R. Cerebellum

Primary Memory   R. Hypothal.   L. Hypothal.   Primary Memory
Thanatos: is, Hates   L. Striatum   **Id: Does**   R. Striatum   **Superego: IS, Loves**

L. Pons   R. Pons

L&R Locus Coeru-leus CRF Fear

sees differences between things, uses top-down, deductive reasoning from the general to the particular to dissect the next lower-universe level and thus is a "Splitter". In contrast, the right hemisphere sees commonalities within things, uses inductive reasoning to go from the particular (individual) instances to the general (group) commonality in bottom-up thinking, synthesizes to the next higher universe-level, and thus is a "Lumper".

The two hemispheres must remain separate because the two opposite processes performed by the hemispheres are incompatible. However, the two exchange information: via corpus callosum, and the deeper anterior and posterior commissures. Because of their differences, each cerebrum performs mutually exclusive, survival-maximizing data processing operations. In the right brain, incoming data (for example, an approaching white Poodle) is *inductively* compared (with the assistance of the striatal matching system) with earlier-similar memory data of a white Pit Bull Terrier to see whether the two data sets might be *similar and related*. It is of great survival value to know rapidly if both sets of data are related. If so, earlier-similar outcome memories can next be scanned in terms of past survival harm or benefit. Then avoidance or approach behavior initiates and coordinates increasing the survival benefit of the present situation.

In exclusive contrast, the left-brain the incoming data (the poodle) is *deductively* compared with earlier-similar memory data of the Pit Bull to see how the two data sets are *different and unrelated*. The rapid detection of differences is also of great survival value, for example noting the critical difference between the playful Poodle from the past, and the present rapidly approaching, Pit Bull, foaming at the mouth. The presence of the global type of wiring motif of the right hemisphere compared to the local type of architecture of the left hemisphere supports necessary segregation of two incompatible brain processes into separate top-down and bottom-up data analysis systems (Kosslyn, 1987; Van Kleek, 1989; Lamb, et. al., 1990; Kosslyn, et. al., 1992; Fink, et. al., 1996). The eye input assignments given the two hemispheres where the more visual-global RH attends to the entire spatial-visual field, while the left attends only to the right foreground further reinforces this separation. This results in left hemi-neglect upon right hemisphere stroke or other injury, leading to drawings of clocks with numbers only on the right side. The localized language centers in the LH also emphasize it by making this hemisphere the more auditory-speech oriented of the two. The cerebral asymmetries caused by the left local vs. a right distributed wiring organization, lead to detectible laterality differences in how the corresponding vertical columns themselves are organized and interconnected in general.

Local vs. global structural and functional hemispheric differences prompt the speculation that the *content* orientation of the LH facilitates the detection of differences ("splitter") in a top-down, deductive, analytical, intelligent manner. In contrast, the *concept-context* orientation of the RH assists in the detection of global similarities ("lumper") in a bottom-up, inductive, intuitive, at times metaphorical way (Bottini, Concoran, Sterzi, Paulesu, Schenone, Scarpa, Frackowiak, and Firth, 1994). Thus, the orientation of the RH is for visual-concrete images "a *picture* is worth a thousand *words*" contrasts with that of the LH toward abstractions, where "a *word* is worth a thousand *pictures*".

To have two such high speed specialized data analysis systems on-board and intercommunicating with the Executive Ego has enabled mammals, especially humans, to be highly successful during the intense, ongoing process of survival. The contrasting processing motifs of the two cerebra show behavioral output differences that influence the social behavioral orientation of each side of the dual brain resulting in hemisity (Chapter 8).

Dual Quadbrain Model Postulate 3: The Right Side of the Limbic System is the Source of The Social Emotions, while from the Left Side come the Ego Defenses of the Id.

As presented in **Figure 3**, elements of the motivational systems of the brain, including the Hexadyadic Primary Emotions of Chapter 5, provide powerful internal motivation of social behavior via punishment and reward ("carrot and stick", **Figure 4**). The primary emotions have here been arbitrarily localized in the right limbic system, while, the sixteen Ego defenses of the Id ("that pack of lies"), presented in Chapter 5, have been placed in the left side of the limbic system.

Figure 3, The Unilateral Executive Ego:

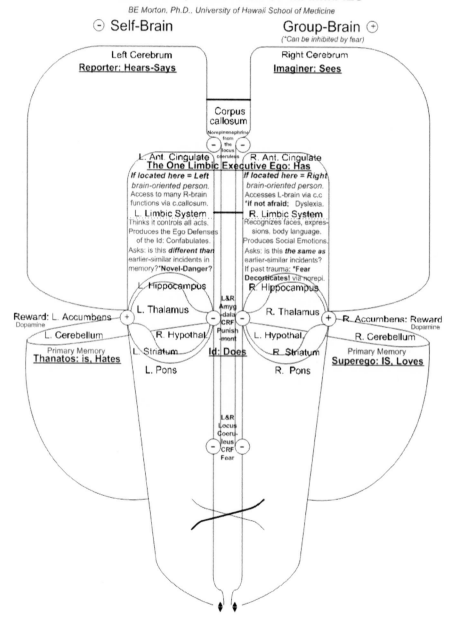

THE DUAL QUADBRAIN OF MAMMALS

BE Morton, Ph.D., University of Hawaii School of Medicine

⊖ Self-Brain

Group-Brain ⊕

(*Can be inhibited by fear)

Left Cerebrum
Reporter: Hears-Says

Right Cerebrum
Imaginer: Sees

Corpus callosum

Norepinephrine from the locus coeruleus

L. Ant. Cingulate
The One Limbic Executive Ego: Has

R. Ant. Cingulate

If located here = Left brain-oriented person. Access to many R-brain functions via c.callosum.

If located here = Right brain-oriented person. Accesses L-brain via c.c *if not afraid;* Dyslexia.

L. Limbic System
Thinks it controls all acts. Produces the Ego Defenses of the Id: Confabulates. Asks: is this **different than** earlier-similar incidents in memory?*Novel-Danger?*

R. Limbic System
Recognizes faces, expressions, body language. Produces Social Emotions. Asks: is this **the same as** earlier-similar incidents? If past trauma: *Fear Decorticates!* via norepi.

L. Hippocampus

R. Hippocampus

L. Thalamus

L&R Amygdala CRF Punishment

R. Thalamus

Reward: L. Accumbens
Dopamine

R. Accumbens: Reward
Dopamine

L. Cerebellum

R. Hypothal.

Id: Does

L. Hypothal.

R. Cerebellum

Primary Memory
Thanatos: is, Hates

L. Striatum

R. Striatum

Primary Memory
Superego: IS, Loves

L. Pons

R. Pons

L&R Locus Coeruleus CRF Fear

Figure 4.

THE QUADRIMENTAL BRAIN AND FEELINGS (AFFECT):
SOURCE OF INVOLUNTARY DRIVES, INSTINCTS, EMOTIONS, AND IMPULSES
Bruce E. Morton, Ph.D., University of Hawaii School of Medicine

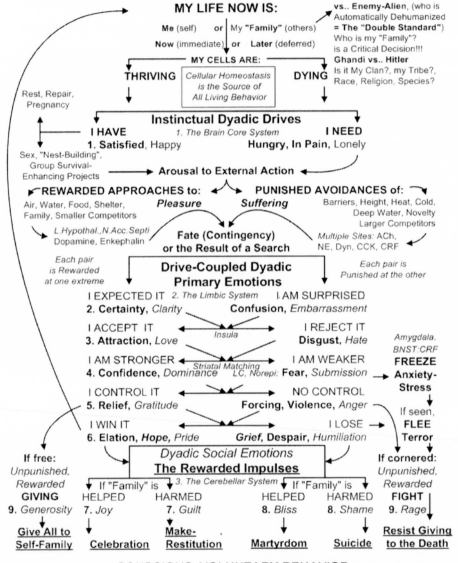

Although controversial, more evidence supports positive emotions as a right brain phenomenon, with the left brain showing negative emotions or emotional avoidance. This might provide a basis for interpreting the effects of the separate viewing by each side of the brain of video scenes of sex or violence in comparison to viewing emotionally neutral video scenes (Wittling, 1990; Wittling and Pfluger, 1990). No changes in mood, blood pressure, or salivary cortisol occurred when only the viewer's LH was allowed to view see this strongly evocative material. However, when only the RH was allowed to watch the sex or violence videos, there were large changes in mood and significant increases in blood pressure and in salivary cortisol when compared to viewing of neutral scenes (Wittling and Roschmann, 1993). This is consistent with the report of prominent alterations of EEG signals on the right side during sexual orgasm (Cohen, Rosen, Goldstein, 1976).

Dual Quadbrain Model Postulate 4. The Brain can have only one Executive Observer. Depending on which Side it is Inherently Located, the Individual will show the either Right or Left Brain-Oriented Behavior and Thinking Styles of Hemisity.

Beyond left cerebral hemisphere language dominance for about 90% of humans, and the right hemisphere non language, spatial, temporal skill asymmetries and literalities, the existence of a unilateral executive system observer has resulted in yet another either-or phenomenon called "Hemisity". This concept is unlike the earlier, now moribund idea, called hemisphericity, where someone's personality was supposedly located somewhere on a gradient between left and right brain orientation extremes. Rather, depending upon in which hemisphere the unilateral executive is inherently and irreversibly imbedded, *either* the left *or* right brain thinking and behavioral orientation of hemisity results. The origin of an individual's hemisity subtype, either right or left brain-oriented, appears to be genetically determined before birth (Crowell, Jones, Kapuniai, and Nakagawa, 1973; Wada, 1977).

What does that mean in terms of individual hemisity behaviors? This will be the topic of Chapter 8.

Dual Quadbrain Model Postulate 5: Superego-like Positive Social Behaviors vs. Pain Body-Reactive Mind Neurotic-Psychotic Orientations of the are Among the NonMotor Functions Contributed by the Paired Neocerebellum.

The Dual Quadbrain Model proposes the cerebellum as the site of an individual's vast store of experiential primary memory. This concept has considerable experimental support (Desmond, Gabrieli, Wagner, Ginier, and Glover, 1997; Schreurs, Gusev, Tomsic, Alkon, and Shi, 1998; Bracha, Zhao, Wunderlich, Morrissy, and Boedel, 1997; Kleim, Vij, Ballard, Greenough, 1997). Recording and retrieval to cerebral consciousness of parts of this primary lifetime cerebellar database somehow requires the participation of the hippocampus (Bontempi, Laurent-Demir, Destrade and Jaffard, 1999; Squire, Ojeman, Miezin, Petersen, Videen, and Raichle, 1992; Teng and Squire, 1999).

Superego-like higher intelligence, constructive ideology and derivative religiosity are among the non-motor functions (Schmahmann, 1991) of the more recently evolving neocerebellum (Leiner, Leiner, and Dow, 1991). Due to crossed cerebellar diaschisis, in this paired brain element some functions are contralateral (opposite in side) to those of the cerebrum (Barker, Yoshii, Loewenstein, Chang, Apicella, Pascal, Boothe, Ginsberg and Duara (1991). However, for the sake of simplicity this is ignored here (as were other possible limbic or brain core ipsilateral vs. contralateral crossover distributions)

These Superego-Divine like properties are opposed those of the Thanatos-like Reactive Mind with its diabolic destructive death-wish, derivative suicide, superstition, human sacrifice and cannibalism. The "unexperienced" trauma to which the individual has been subjected without integration in early childhood, or in adulthood cases of PTSD (Post Traumatic Stress Disorder), forms the basis for the content in the reactive Mind. This trauma primarily includes that of developmental arrests and fixations, and the ineffective activation of the xDARP, the topic of Chapter 13. **Figure 5** summarizes the asymmetries of the opposed neocerebelli producing the opposite survival behavioral logics of the Superego and Thanatos.

Contrasts between the Two Cerebellar Elements: Social Brain Source vs. the Pain Body-Reactive Mind

Making the now unavoidable assumption that all human behavior is brain-originated, what can be said about the anatomical source of human behavior of the type that has been called bad, evil, sinful, hateful or diabolical? This includes nonsexual rape, sadistic torture, ritual murder, mutilation, necrophilia, cult human sacrifice and vengeful cannibalism.

Figure 5, The Dual Quadbrain Double Social Brain:

THE DUAL QUADBRAIN OF MAMMALS

BE Morton, Ph.D., University of Hawaii School of Medicine

⊖ Self-Brain   Group-Brain ⊕

(*Can be inhibited by fear)

Left Cerebrum	Right Cerebrum
Reporter: Hears-Says	**Imaginer: Sees**

Corpus callosum

Norepinephrine from the locus coeruleus

L. Ant. Cingulate — R. Ant. Cingulate
The One Limbic Executive Ego: Has

L. Limbic System — R. Limbic System

L. Hippocampus — R. Hippocampus

L&R Amygdala CRF Punishment

L. Thalamus — R. Thalamus

R. Hypothal. — L. Hypothal.

Reward: L. Accumbens + — + R. Accumbens: Reward
Dopamine   Dopamine

L. Cerebellum — R. Cerebellum

L. Striatum — **Id: Does** — R. Striatum

L. Pons — R. Pons

"To STOP "Group-brain" inhibition by restimulus (fear-guilt) of past trauma: escape, abuse drugs (problematic!), use SSRIs, or Surrender to Superego.

Primary Memory
Thanatos: is, Hates
Our "Dark Side" Intellect:
Evil, Devil-within, Insanity,
Diabolic, Superstitious.
Rejects what IS, Resists it.
Angry, Failing, at Effect,
Victim in one's universe.
Sees no possibility, Night-
mares, Negative, Pessimist.
Parasitic, Wasteful.
Avoids work, Chaotic,
Irresponsible. MultPers
Lies, Cheats, Steals.
Revengeful, Kills,
Mutilates.

Only right PFCtx gets cerebellar-striatal **timing** loops. These give long-term **planning ability!!** No GalvSkinResp if damaged.

Primary Memory
Superego: IS, Loves
Our "Higher Intelligence".
Good, God-within, Wisdom
Inspired Source, Religious.
Accepts what IS, Chooses it.
Happy, Success, at Cause,
God in one's Universe.
Sees possibility: Visions
Positive, Optimistic.
Synergistic, Conservative
Works hard, Orderly,
Responsible.
Conscience,
Guilt

L&R Locus Coeruleus CRF Fear

The ongoing choice all must make consciously, or if afraid, subconsciously:
Shall I **resist** or **choose** the way the Universe IS?

God-within, grant me the serenity to accept the things I cannot change, courage to change the things I can, and wisdom to know the difference.

Section II: WHO AM I?

People tend to deny that humans really have the potential for such society-rending behavior, and thus avoid having to think about it except perhaps under the protective sanctions of the entertainment media. Perhaps, because once fostered, such behavior seems so frighteningly close to the surface, it facilitates this denial. Individual behavior that destroys the survival of one's own species underlies all definitions of bad, wrong, sinful, evil (from the devil) or diabolic. This makes one's species-centric point- of-view a highly critical issue. For example: is frying and eating a chicken a necessity and a hereditary right? How about the same consideration for chimpanzee "bush meat" parts? Or, on the other hand, are these murder, mutilation and cannibalism that more than justifies the violence of the animal rights movement on behalf of domestic rodents? This brings us back to the clarifying seven realities (next chapter).

In contrast, there must be an anatomical brain source for those human behaviors we call godly, good, righteous, kind, loving, holy or divine. Such acts include generosity, benevolence, compassion, mercy, humility, nonkilling and altruism. The latter includes self-sacrifice up to and including the point of willingness to die for another, others, or even to do so for a valued religious or humanitarian cause. Social behavior dedicated to enhancing the survival of one's own species underlies all definitions of good and godliness. Again, the critical issue is the individual's definition of who the family is. Thus, the age-old problem: is self-sacrifice appropriate in behalf of one's offspring during calamity, in family feuds, or in struggles against pagans, infidels, confederates, Nazis, Vietnamese, or Somali pirates?

In the Dual Quadbrain Model of behavioral laterality, the above-defined traits of good and evil are included among the subconsciously generated non-motor behaviors of the neocerebellum, and integrated by the cerebellar vermis. The basis for this assignment comes from primate and human cerebellar lesion and implant research (Reiman, Raichle, Robins, Mintun, Fusselman, Fox, Price and Hackman, 1989; Ricklan, Cullinan, and Cooper, 1977; Heath, 1977; Heath, Llewellyn and Rouchell, 1980; Heath, Rouchell, Llewellyn, and Walker, 1981). There, use of self-stimulus with electrode implants in the cerebellar vermis transformed insane killers into the most benevolent and sociable of persons. However, temporary failure of cerebellar self-stimulation equipment, quickly released the convict with a broken brain back into a state of agitated homicide.

122

Dual Quadbrain Model Postulate 6: Separable Id-like Dominatingly Selfish vs. Surrendered Servile Behavioral Elements are on Either Side of the Brain Core

An evolutionarily ancient, Id-like, dominating, self-survival element within the left side of the lower Reptile Brain is associated with sympathetic nervous system based punished avoidance via flight and fight. It is convenient to call it the Crocodile Brain.

In critical contrast, paired on the right side of the Reptile Brain, is the Id-like protective, productive element called the Servant Brain. It predominates when the Crocodile Brain has "met its match" and has surrendered to a larger crocodile, or, importantly, to a more powerful higher power, either within the brain, or externally The Servant Brian's behavior is altruistic, servile, species survival-oriented, tied to parasympathetic nervous system's rewarded approach, feeding, rest, repair, and reproduction. **Figure 6** summarizes the asymmetries of the left and right lower brain elements producing these contrasting punished and rewarded Id-like behaviors.

For example: it is logical that the right brain, through its search for similarity and relatedness would tend to perceive commonality, thus family and community that is implicit in species preservation (Henry and Wang, 1998). These would be complimented by right Id- associated cooperative social behaviors, humor, constructive support, as well as promoting Social Brain-religiosity behaviors. In contrast, the left-brain, while searching for differences, would tend to see non-family and non-related alien strangeness, together with the associated antisocial responses of anger, guilt-free conscience, and self-preservation. This could be tied to a competitive coronary type-A behavior pattern (Henry and Wang, 1998) and combativeness. Thus, left brain-oriented individuals without adequate socialization should show more self-survival orientation than the group-survival orientation of their right brain associates, and a higher mortality.

The left side Crocodile Brain with its Selfish control mode produces the rude antisocial behaviors of, "I want it now!" (there is no past or future). "If you don't give it to me right away, I will damn-well force you to, or die trying". On the other side of brain the surrendered, servile, altruistic, Servant Brain provides, polite, generous, cooperative, collaborative, disciplined, powerful assistance like a hard working sled dog to whomever internal or external higher power it has given over its control. Here, "I am here to serve you", "your wish is my command" applies.

Figure 6, Dual Quadbrain Reptile Brain Partners:
THE DUAL QUADBRAIN OF MAMMALS

BE Morton, Ph.D., University of Hawaii School of Medicine

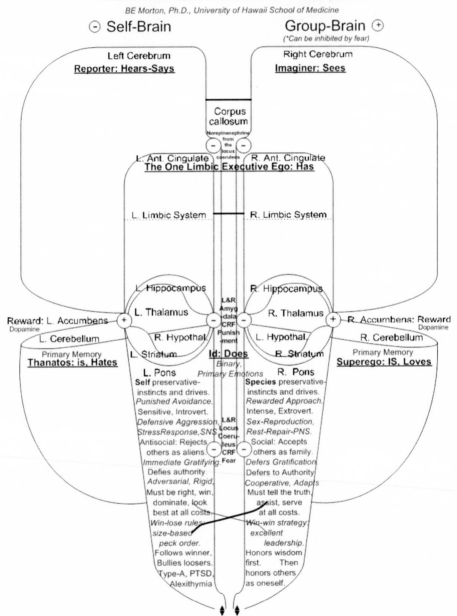

⊙ Self-Brain   Group-Brain ⊕
(*Can be inhibited by fear)

Chapter 6: RIGHT SIDE OR LEFT? THE DUAL QUADBRAIN

Clearly, the Dual Quadbrain Model of behavioral laterality is only an organizational metaphor, a cartoon simplification of the real. At some level it must break down as inadequate to represent the actual complexity of brain and behavior, finally demanding the brain itself as the ultimate reality. One of the first levels upon which this model might be found wrong, is that of the relative sidedness of subcortical elements. That is, the existence of both ipsilateral and contralateral tracts between the cortex and the cerebellum, limbic system and brain core guarantee a brain laterality that is more complex than this model. Yet, the overall clarification of behavioral motivation, brought by the context of a self vs. species brain duality, may be a critical step required to facilitate the ultimate lateral distribution of the important anatomical details. Furthermore, the logical neuroanatomical localization within this evolutionary model of Freud's theoretical constructs of the Id, Ego, Superego and Thanatos provides an integration of human behavior which hopefully will stimulate the discovery of ever more accurate information about locations of these important behavior-generating motifs.

With this introduction to the Society of Seven defined by the Dual Quadbrain Model, we are now in position to ask, "Who AM I?" Who is in control and Why? in our next chapter.

Some Important Concepts in Chapter 6:

1. The existence of non-identical properties of the two sides of the completely bilateral central nervous system (CNS) has caused the expansion of the Quadrimental Brain Model to the Dual Quadbrain Model as follows:

2. A head to toes bilateral functional axis exists for the entire CNS with the left side of the brain having a *self*-survival orientation, while the right side is oriented toward *group*-survival.

3. The top-down data processing orientation of the left hemisphere "Reporter" is functionally opposite to the bottom-up processing specialization of the right hemisphere "Imager" and requires physical separation of the cerebral hemispheres.

4. One side of the limbic system Executive Caretaker is the source of the Primary and Social Emotions, while the Ego Defenses of the Id come from the other.

5. The Brain can have only one Executive Observer. Depending on which side it is inherently located, the individual will show either the right or left brain-oriented behavior and thinking styles of Hemisity.

6. God-Within Superego-like positive social behaviors, and likewise demonic, Reactive Mind-like neurotic-psychotic orientations are among the non-motor functions contributed by each side of the neocerebellum.

7. Separable Id-like aggression vs. servile help are the rewarded behavioral elements present on opposite sides of Reptile Brain of the striatum and brain core.

NEUROREALITY: A SCIENTIFIC RELIGION TO RESTORE MEANING

SECTION II: Who am I? What is this Mystery called Consciousness?

CHAPTER 7: The Brain's Society of Seven. Who am I? Who's In Charge?

Getting Acquainted with the Independent Consciousness Elements of the Brain's Society of Seven.

The creation of the Dual Quadbrain Model of Consciousness to replace the inadequate Unitive Model of Mind gives us the tools to begin a rational approach to understanding human behavior. The background development of the four levels of the Quadrimental Brain Model in Chapter 5, facilitated the introduction of their four bilateral aspects in the Dual Quadbrain Model in Chapter 6. We are now prepared to meet and develop a working relationship with each of the members of the Dual Quadbrain Model's Society of Seven, assembled in **Figure 1**, and their associated seven unique realities that alert us to their presence upon the throne of our control.

OK, The upper two members really need no introduction, because you already are consciously aware of them as part of who you think you are. However, getting better acquainted with them is well worth the effort.

1. Dr. Imagination of the Right Cerebral Hemisphere

First, let's greet Dr. Imagination. S/He brilliantly produces succinct visions of the best and worst options available to you right now under your specific circumstances: from your heart's desires to your worst nightmares. His/Her sole purpose is to provide, if you will only take the time to look, what are your best immediate opportunities, as well as what are your best long-term choices to optimize your survival and/or that of your family. S/He also provides you warnings of harmful things, actions, situations or contexts to avoid. The reality type of Dr. Imagination is that of External Reality, unless s/he is taken over by another more powerful member of the Society of Seven.

Figure 1: Dual Quadbrain Model of Human Consciousness

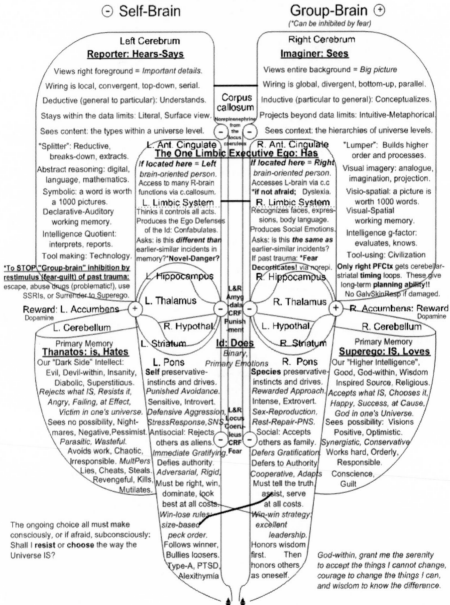

THE DUAL QUADBRAIN OF MAMMALS

BE Morton, Ph.D., University of Hawaii School of Medicine

2. Msr. Reporter of the Left Cerebral Hemisphere

Next, please say Hello to Msr. Reporter. Talk about sounds and words to describe the visions your Imagination brings you; this is your language brain's forte! From the simplest to the most abstract, Msr Reporter strives always to have the right words or symbols available for you to think or say. The millions of words in your primary memory that it has already heard or read are available for you to draw upon. Msr. Reporter also knows well the language and rules of numbers, and can grasp the complex concepts within each context. Msr Reporter's mind is mainly occupied with our ever expanding Internal model of external Reality.

It is very easy to mistakenly identify oneself with Dr. Imagination or Msr. Reporter because the way they think constitutes our usual consciousness. However, once we take a transformational step in our maturation and discover who we really are, we will be delighted to see that they are actually our loyal consultants: intellectual, articulate and imaginative

3. Msr Caretaker Brain, the Executive within the Limbic System

Although you may not know him or her very well, your Msr. Caretaker (Executive Ego, Will) Brain is your right hand man or woman. Like a foreman or contractor, you have placed him or her in charge of the intimate details required to maintain and successfully run your living Estate. The reality of the Caretaker Brain is Survival Reality. S/He is really smart and has repeatedly been shown to make subconscious survival-optimizing decisions almost one second before your Intellect and Language consultants even become aware of them (Libet,1983). As partially described in Chapter 5, these "bottom- line", "the buck stops here" decisions of your Caretaker Brain, make a second by second difference between your life or death.

If your Executive Caretaker is on the left side of your brain, he or she is more intimately associated with Msr Reporter and its abstract reasoning. Yet, your Caretaker also has information transfer lines across the corpus callosum connecting with Dr. Imagination on the other side of the brain. In contrast, if your Caretaker is on the right side of your right brain, he or she works hand in hand with Dr. Imagination, but keeps close tabs on Msr Reporter via other lines back across the corpus callosum.

Your Caretaker Brain is a Society of Seven member of great feelings, especially fear of death and joy of life and uses these to motivate its subcontractors by use of rewarding (attracting) or punishing (causing avoidance) primary or derivative emotions (Chapter 5). If your Caretaker Brain is in good shape, he or she can overpower any opposition among its coworkers. However, if your Caretaker is injured, weak or sickly, he or she cannot always force its laborers to follow orders or keep them from becoming unruly or rebellious. This is especially true of the more destructive left side members of both the Reptile Brain and the Social Brain.

4. Mr. Reptile from the Brain Core on the Left

Salute Msr. Crocodile Brain of the left side of the Reptile Brain, site of Freud's Id. Although the Crocodile Brain can be male or female, as you can see s/he is quite an impressive physical specimen. S/He is the force that powerfully accomplishes all of your behavioral desires. Crucially, Msr. Crocodile Brain is the only member of the Society of Seven, aside from his paired Servant Brain (later) who actually has his or her hands upon the levers, wheels, switches and dials that control life. S/He literally keeps your cells alive every second of every day. S/He takes this job very seriously and will fight any outside cellular homeostasis stressor to the death. S/He is completely in charge of our survival at each universe level, from the molecular through subcellular, cellular, tissue, organ, up to and including that of living human being. At that level, s/he uses your body very skillfully and successfully to protect you against alien competitors, such as rats, snakes, and hyenas. Did I mention alligators?

However, s/he is dreadfully inept at working with groups of humans. S/He is generally rude, nasty and upset. S/He must always be right, win, dominate and control everybody, and will fight viciously to do so. S/He will only surrender to someone who is bigger or more powerful than s/he is. S/He is totally inept at knowing how to optimize the survival of groups of organisms at the next higher universe level, because he or she only knows the laws at the one-on-one competition level, such as a monkey island where "sh-t runs downhill". In addition, as we have seen in Chapter 2, these laws are totally the opposite and harmful for optimizing the survival of the group and society.

As mentioned above, it takes a tough Caretaker Brain to handle Msr. Reptile. However, a strong Caretaker, by use of his powerful emotions, can replace Msr. Reptile with the other member, the Servant Brain as the willing doer of his commands. When, your Caretaker fails to prevent Msr. Reptile from becoming upset, taking over, and thus from doing antisocial harm, The Caretaker Brain tries to avoid responsibility for his or her failure to control Msr. Reptile. So our Caretaker Brain makes excuses for Msr. Reptile's bad behavior, drawing from those 16 Ego defenses of the Id of Chapter 5, all of which are lies. When you hear such rationalizations coming out of your mouth, you need to recognize that your Caretaker is becoming too weak to prevent your Reptile from taking over your throne and doing antisocial harm. Then, quickly go about finding ways to strengthen him or her. The Caretaker Brain Ego can best go off line and rest during REM sleep or during certain types of therapy.

5. My Faithful Servant, Trusted Friend within the Brain Core on the Right

When Msr Crocodile Brain meets someone recognized to be more powerful. s/he refuses to fight and be killed by that more powerful entity. Instead, s/he makes strong obeisance-submission signals and surrenders. By doing so he or she is in essence saying that rather than die, s/he is willing to give you anything and everything s/he has, even including the surrender of all their property, their spouse, and kids. In exchange for being allowed to live, s/he is promising to work loyally for your Caretaker, even to give his or her life to defend and protect you, nothing held back. S/he has decided that s/he would rather serve your Caretaker Brain's any and every wish, than be dead. Now that is real surrender! Anciently, at the reptilian stage of evolution this was literally the case. As Quadrimental Brain layers were added, this surrender to external higher powers was extended to the internally more powerful Ego Caretaker who could defer to other members of the Society of Seven, or as anciently, to more powerful external forces.

Under these circumstances, the imbalance of power is so great in Msr. Reptile's mind, that his or her only choice is to surrender or to die. By surrendering, s/he transforms into a trusting, reliable servant. This transformation is so complete, that s/he takes on a new personality, like that of a once snarling attack dog turned into a lover dog, man's best friend. If you treat that dog right, s/he will do anything for your love and acceptance. Meet your dog-like Servant Brain. As your former internal enemy, s/he has surrendered to become your best friend. Without hesitation, s/he will delightedly do anything you ask, or die trying. Clearly, it becomes very unwise to kill someone who, when surrendered to your Executive Ego, Caretaker Brain , becomes so empathetic, committed and valuable. As your Servant Brain, this element of the reptile brain Id follows your Cultural Meme Reality properness.

The attempt to avoid pain by the Reptilian Brain and Executive Ego is in stark contrast to the to the cerebellar Pain Body's age regression to painful earlier periods of failure in an attempt to gain control of a developmental process, or to the cerebellar Source's deliberate production of guilt pain. Fortunately for humanity, there are higher internal powers among each person's Society of Seven, whom normally can conquer and convert the selfish Reptile Brain into our own willing selfless slave, the one who does all the actual work. However, there are also many often-unrecognized external powers outside of us, who also can attempt to demand our surrender and to claim our loyalty. Because of this, our Reporter and Imaginer must be expanded and well educated to tell our Caretaker to whom s/he should and should not give over our control.

6. Msr. Reactive Mind, Pain Body-xDARP of the Dark Side of our Cerebellum

Now, I would like to introduce you to the most unrecognized, but powerfully disruptive and internally stressful member of our brain's Society of Seven, First called the Reactive Mind (Hubbard, 1950). As we will see Mrs. Reactive Mind also contains Msr Pain Body (Tolle, 2005) of the xDARP described in Section IV of this book. As a perfect victim, rejecting the way the universe works, he or she will neither acknowledge your existence nor extend you a hand in friendship. Zero empathy! The size and activity of one's Pain Body depends upon the degree of one's exposure to physical trauma and developmental thwarting circumstances during our life. Although most of the latter occurred during our first three years, some occurred later, especially during adolescence and war.

For those fortunate to have experienced little developmental trauma, Msr Pain Body can be very small and sleep most of the time. However, for most of us who have been significantly arrested devopmentally, it can be huge, cyclically rebellious and very disruptive of home and family. This is especially true if during our very early years, we were caused to feel the pain inherent in being blocked from doing what we needed to do in order to develop. Then, in adulthood Msr Pain Body can awaken ravenously hungry and must feed. Msr Pain Body thrives upon a diet of pain of all types, especially of the psychological pain it recreates by subconsciously age regressing to traumatic incidents of loss of control in the past. After a day or two of feeding by stirring up such pain and creating such a crisis that we again feel like we might die, Msr Pain Body finally becomes sated-full and goes back to sleep for a little while. However, soon it awakens, famished and needing of more pain. The brain based Msr Pain Body is the origin of the theme appearing so many times in literature, and in our lives such as the oscillating replacement of cooperative Dr. Jekyl by the murderous Mr. Hyde, or that of "Christ vs. Satan", or Good vs. Evil.

The dangerous thing about Msr. Pain Body is that by taking over Dr Intellect and Msr Reporter, he or she ironically tricks our Caretaker into erroneously thinking that our pain body *is exactly who we are*. When so fooled, we will not, cannot do anything other than act out its twisted lies of past rejection in a cyclic endless struggle for control of our dearest important others. In fact, not to do so would seem to be denying the very essence of who we are. Our important-others, the targets of our pain body's rejecting lies, take this seriously and fight against his or her cyclic creating and feeding on our pain from unremitting rejection. Yet, after each Pain Body feeding frenzy, we feel more damaged personally, and are temporarily remorseful that we have degraded and damaged those closest to us. And, as we inevitably continue to participate in its cyclic feeding frenzies, while unable to understand or resist it, we end up hurting and ultimately driving away from us all those whom we love the most, committing crimes of passion, and ultimately having a nervous breakdown outside or within a prison or hospital.

The existence of this seemingly death-oriented (Freud's *thanatos*) , diabolical member of our brain's Society of Seven has driven many to drink, drugs and suicide., The Pain Body's reality is Reactive Reality. Sometimes, after "bottoming out", our Ego Caretaker surrenders control into the arms of our "God" (Within), our Higher Power, our all wise Source, (the seventh member of our Society of Seven), seeking protection and redemption from Msr Pain Body's demonic and corrupting power. This results in conversion and transformation of the individual beyond something he or she would have ever been; the topic of the last chapter of this book.

It is ironic that the biological existence of our Pain Body is the result of a recent evolutionary mistake, which we will unravel in Chapter 10. A mutated Developmental Arrest Repair Program (xDARP) once served our psychosocial development in the finest of ways. Now, it is broken and has become the primary source of the neuroses and psychoses that are driving the world mad.

7. The Social Brain SOURCE, the Life-giving Side of the Cerebellum

How can one be introduced to one's most high Source, one's God Within?! Most of us are completely unaware of the existence within us of this most developed and subtle member of our brain's Society of Seven. Rarely in our lifetime do we even catch faint glimmers of awe of IT. Yet IT reigns over the vast trillions of cells that hold our Primary Memory within the cerebellum. To those sensitive individuals whose Caretaker is located on the left side of their brain, the thought of meeting their God Within can be terrifying. Indeed, as the source of guilt pain as punishment for the evil of harming the survival of others, it can indeed be overwhelming. Yet, those intense people, whose Caretaker is on the right, are for some yet unknown reason les threatened by intense emotion. They often actually seek to find and know God. Interestingly, these right brainers founded each of the eight world religions.

Now, the ancient route to the discovery of one's Social Brain Source has become clear and traversable by individuals of both hemisities. This is a transformative journey, because once you meet your Source, you can but only throw yourself on the ground before Its perfection and purity, and begin to clean up your life in response. Then, you too will joyfully surrender to that Higher Power, God-Within, Holy Spirit, who has your purpose, your plan and the power to achieve it. You are never the same again because by having your eyes opened to Its existence you will have become irreversibly transformed, (the"Saved" of certain earlier religions.) Then, you know who you are and why you are here. Yet, our Social Brain Source is not supernatural in any way. It is our genetic inheritance. It produces Empathic Reality and has the non-supernatural answers to our global problems and can bring peace, harmony, and fulfillment in our lives here earth and lead us to the stars of our future.

In review, **Table 1** lists the seven members of the Society of Seven whom together produce our behavior.

Competition vs. Cooperation: With who and when?
Figure 2 illustrates the two opposite behavioral motifs this Society of Seven team can produce. That is, if the Msr Caretaker judges that individual competitive behavior is called for, that behavior becomes activated. If, in contrast it judges that social behavior is the more appropriate response, empathic behavior emerges. On the left of the figure,

Table 1. My Society of Seven: Which is my Reality? Who's in charge?

Society of Seven Member	Type of Reality	Brain Element
1, Imagination	External Reality	Right Hemisphere Concrete Visualizer
2, Reporter	Internal Reality	Left Hemisphere Abstract Reasoner
3, Caretaker	Survival Reality	Unilateral .LimbicExecutive
4, Crocodile	Deam Reality	Left Striatal Reptile Brain
5, Servant	Cultural Meme Reality	Right Striatal Reptile Brain
6, Pain-Body-Reactive Mind	xDARP Reality	Left Cerebellar Thanatos
7, Source-Conscience-Purity	Empathic Reality	Right Cerebellar Eros

the Caretaker has invoked an emergency survival response by activating the Reptile Brain Crocodile into action. This results in instinct driven combative violent behavior with a potential of escalation to killing force. This essentially decorticate behavior occurs when we become really upset. It is the unplanned, untrained, instinctual and animal-like destructive rage response whose effectiveness eons of survival of the fittest by tooth and claw has been honed .

In remarkable contrast, if the Caretaker concludes that social issues require solving (Figure 2), it strongly inhibits the Selfish Brain and instead activates the Social Brain to produce a completely different set of behaviors that are cooperative, honest, peaceful, constructive and responsible: absolutely nonviolent. Here the higher brain activates and the lower brain rests, save for the selfless final output of our faithful Servant Brain partner. We will defer further discussing the aberrant activities of the xDARP Pain Body until Chapter 10.

Because our Caretaker often does not have the answers for what to do next to optimize survival, it can defer to external sources of greater information or greater protection. In the center of Figure 2 lists some

Figure 2.
Sources of Killing vs. Nonkilling Behavior

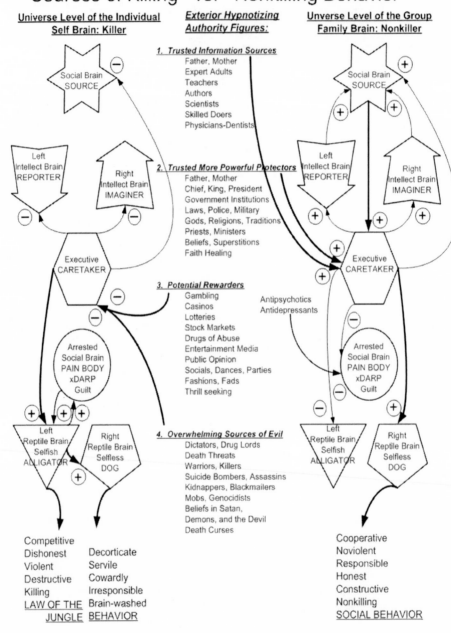

136

External Authorities to whom our Caretaker can give over our control. In the first category, it seeks more information. In so doing, it will draw upon many outside authorities. It does this first by rote memorization to uncritically incorporate their viewpoints as "the truth". The more established and thus trusted an authority is, the more likely our Caretaker will have faith in them and assimilate their truth as our own. If our external sources are good, we can benefit from this. However, not all external sources are trustworthy.

Some persons, so habituated to the surrender to an External Authority source, that they never really develop their own abilities to think for themselves beyond their own childhood beliefs. Unfortunately for them the Inner Reality or Cultural Memes delivered by many external Controllers is far from the truth of External Reality. The Caretaker of such gullible persons has become too lazy, or too overwhelmed, to accept facts staring them in the face. In laboratory experiments, many people prefer to believe the grossly deviant answers of a unknowingly supplied erroneous pocket calculator, than the obvious facts. Some highly educated people would rather hypnotically trust without question an ignorant, minimum-wage clerk's opinion in a shopping mall, than think for themselves. Sadly, this unwillingness to think for themselves extends into many social areas of importance including which authority we should believe.

If there is an external controller that is more powerful than we are, who can also supply us with protection that makes things safer, the Caretaker's judgment problem compounds itself. Does our Caretaker Brain trust the laws of our land and those enforcing them as working for our best interests? We all know how either very good or how incredibly bad that can be. Similarly, does our Caretaker Brain believe in our religious leaders, support their building and other projects and trust our children and youth with them? Alternatively, might there be a number of hidden conflicts of interests that can drain, harm, even kill us. Whom do you trust? It also appears that in the area of answers to the Big Questions, Our Servant Brain, with its Cultural Reality is the most gullible and must be alerted to rely upon our Executive Ego's informed judgments.

It of great interest that our Msr Caretaker's have been shown to trust questionable external controllers and take great risks in order to obtain potentially great, but very improbable rewards. This is both good and bad, and again requires intelligent judgment calls. How is the potential thrill of hitting the jackpot in a Casino different than playing the stock market? Again, intelligence, education and information are required. Some of our

Caretaker's would even trust, and often lose, our life's savings at the direction a confident but highly conflicted Stock Broker, one perhaps referred by a trusted friend, rather than doing the required homework and taking personal responsibility.

Many of our Caretakers are so starved for pleasure and relief from subconscious stress that they will give over our control to a popular drug and completely abdicate responsibility for their intoxicated behavior. We also crave love and approval as true symbols of a high survival state. In usually futile attempts to gain these, we go to great lengths to invest in the latest entertainment or stylish fads, not recognizing that this behavior is as likely to increase our survival, as winning a lottery. We keep throwing bad money after good in investing in fine wines, fashionable clothes and jewelry, Broadway plays, elaborate home theaters, thrill toys, and exotic vacations, blindly trusting these external controllers will give us the happiness and love we blindly seek. Parenthetically, with the Dual Quadbrain Model one can approach these addictions directly.

Further, the Caretaker of most anybody will collapse in the presence of the overwhelming force of harm or evil. Panic activation of our reptilian "surrender or die" programs can overpower even the most intelligent of people. The fear inculcated by the personal threat of death by the Nazi and Communist Parties turned those wonderfully brilliant and developed German and Russian peoples into decorticate, servile slaves who would rather follow orders and kill, than responsibly resist at the cost of being killed themselves. Because of their terror, they were totally surrendered to, and fully supported demands of their ruthless external controllers. It is now more than 60 years after the Second World War in Europe. Let us never forget the 6 million Jews, 20 million Russians, 10 million Christians and 1,900 Catholic priests who were murdered, massacred, raped, burned, starved and humiliated while the terrified German and Russian peoples looked the other way! Tragically, both historically and prehistorically many similar regimes of terror have left their bloody scars around the world over the ages.

Most humans suffer from violence harm and sincerely wish to do something about it. Here is where one's philosophy or religion can result in misguided righteous self-sacrifice to kill the alien non-believer. If one believes erroneous spiritual answers to The Big Questions that declare this present bitter life is only a dream; and that our true goal and reward is immortality in the hereafter, then, as we see, many people will drop all personal responsibility, willingly becoming suicidal instruments of death.

Unfortunately, their genuine desires for the greater good of mankind have allowed them to convert themselves into mindless externally controlled robots of death, instead bringing even greater harm to humanity. A more accurate understanding of external reality and the answers to the Big Questions would have directed their desire to be of service into much more beneficial non violent paths.

Quadrimental Brain Balance

Clearly, the recognition of the Dual Quadbrain Model's value in understanding human behavior opens many crucial new doors. The above lengthy discussion only begins to scratch the surface. When the Dual Quadbrain is aligned, as in **Table 2**, cooperative, conservative, nonkilling, highly able behavior appears. When the Dual Quadbrain misaligns, it becomes the source of antisocial behavior leading to conflict, aggression, violence and killing. If alcohol and drugs are used block cerebellar conscience and guilt pain, then many other of our Social Brain's skills will also be blocked, resulting in competitive, violent, short-sighted behavior, multiple breakdowns, and failure. Thus, as may be seen, brain system balance is logical and is knowable. Nobody expected understanding and predicting human behavior to be relatively simple. However, it now no longer is a mystery!

In addition to the above dynamics, behavioral output can also be altered by the already well known factors of **Table 3:**

So, What's the Answer?: Who Am I? Who is in Control of My Behavior?

It is liberating to know that who I am turns out to be whichever element of my brain's Society of Seven (or those Exterior Controllers) that is dominant, ascendant and in my control cockpit at the present moment. I am that! At first, these seven states and their associated unique realities all seem the same to me. Thus, I am my rage, I am my compassion, I am my beliefs, or "I bow to my God Within Who I AM".

As I increase in maturity, I began to recognize that I have some control as to whom I place on the throne to be who I am. Although my automatic thoughts and feelings may be strong, I do not have to be them! This is liberating because, unobstructed, those very thoughts and feelings can place my Crocodile Brain or Pain Body in control of me right now.

Table 2, Bottom-up, Top-Down Brain Hierarchy of Behavioral Control:

A. The Reptilian Brain is the sole producer of ALL behavior of the organism, be it via:

   1. The cooperative Servant Brain

      a. Except in an "Emergency" when its instinctive Crocodile Brain behavior takes over.

      i. The weaker Ego is, the lesser the degree of danger that constitutes an Emergency.

   2. The competitive Crocodile Brain in an Emergency.

   3. The Reactive Mind, if it is for long in the presence of a loving (safe) friend or mate.

      a. As directed by the xDARP Pain Body by transference, seeking to complete arrested psychosocial developmental control form the past (infancy, childhood). .

      i. Through transference, age regression, and reactivation of an ancient struggle. (See Section IV of this book.)

B. If alone and no Emergency has been perceived, the Servant Brain defers its control to the Caretaker (Executive Ego)

C. The Caretaker judges and decides whether to direct the Servant Brain itself or to assign responsibility for its control to one of four higher options:

   1. To the Imagination of the right cerebral hemisphere: projects Worst-Best possible outcomes.

      a. Autosuggestion is available here, via imagery and strong commands.

   2. To the Intellect of the left cerebral hemisphere: source of abstract reasoning, mathematics and language.

      a. If the Ego is weak: the product is *subjective* rationalizing thought.

      b. If the Ego is strong: the product is pure *objective* logic.

   3. To the wisdom and insight of the Social Brain Source.

      a. via meditation and prayer for guidance from our God-Within, Higher Power.

   4. To an External Authority: Parent, Teacher, Chief, Laws, King, Priest, "God".

      a. This is the basis of Hypnosis: Assumptive learning from "Authorities"

      b. Faith Healing and Death Curses.

D. The Reptile Brain then obeys this external "Higher Power"

Table 3, Additional Factors Determining Which Brain Element is in Control

A. Genetics and/or Development, such as that producing Affective Illnesses, Alzheimer's Disease, Huntington's Disease, dyslexia, autism, or altered sexual identity.

B. Nonlethal Brain Injuries, such as infection, trauma, stroke, tumor, surgery, schizophrenia, and Parkinson's Disease.

C. Psychoactive Drugs and/or Magnetic Probes – Alcohol and other pain- killing drugs of abuse, and by LSD and other hallucinogens.

D. Cellular Homeostatic Stress, such as loss of control of access to air, water, fuel, sleep, rest, shelter, job, family members or support, blood glucose, tryptophan depletion, etc.

E. Cultural Memes associated with Hysteria, Suggestion, Media-based or personal rumors, war, famine, faith healing, hypnosis, spirit possession, death curses, or riots

---

Then, I will have to take the later negative consequences of "my" emergent antisocial rejecting, "killing" behavior and the consequent harm I am doing to you right now by allowing my Crocodile Brain to rule, reject you, and struggle with you as my enemy. Instead, I have brief period of a choice. By declaration, I can prevent my Crocodile Brain from gaining control of me, and instead elevate my Social Brain Source to the throne. I then become it, with very different emergent behavior towards you: that of empathic acceptance and "nonkilling" synergy. *"To accept another just as they are, and just as they are not"*, has been an edifying definition of love. This is the acceptance and understanding we desperately seek from our mates, family,friends, and religion. This deep craving is manifest in the quality we project onto at least one our many gods: our belief that the son of God hates the sin but loves the sinner, that God made me, that he wants me, that He knows my every strength and weakness, and loves even me.

By awareness and practice, I can lengthen that original microsecond that I have before my upset Crocodile takes over and kills, giving me increasing opportunity to replace it with my totally responsible Source and not get upset. As will be described in later chapters, we can become increasingly conscious of our power of choice as to who we are, by the means of the one whom we place in charge. As a result, crocodilian upsets with life that now may be breaking through hourly, can be so weakened that they only occur daily, then only weekly, only monthly, yearly, then not at all. Many people have accomplished this. It is only the beginning of happiness.

Recent fMRI reports have noted high cerebellar activity during control of behavior by "another", that of an external controlling entity. Recipients of faith healing comment on feelings of "heat" at base of their skull (cerebellar Source). Does surrender to one's higher power activate the cerebellar Social Brain, one's God Within, to come to the fore?! If so, specifically, how can this be done? To be continued later...

Up-coming in Chapters 8 and 9, we address the next Big Question: Who are You?! There we will discover the two trees of life of Dyadic Evolution and the presently unrecognized differences of Familial Polarity that result in global conflict at 10 universe levels.

Some Concepts of Chapter 7:

1. There is a control-module "Throne" in our mind, which can be occupied moment by moment by which ever member of the Society of Seven separate consciousness systems of the Dual Quadbrain is most dominant.

2. Regardless of which member of the Society of Seven is in power, at first it all seems to be the same as me. Through education, training and practice, I can increasingly recognize and influence which entity retains control over my mind and behavior to best optimize my survival and that of my family.

3. The conscious entities that can occupy my mind include the following:

   a. *Imagination* (R-Cerebrum Concrete Visualizer), source of summarizing images. Reads External Reality;

   b. *Reporter* (L-Cerebrum Abstract Reasoner), source of summarizing descriptions. Compiles our unique Internal Reality

   c. *Caretaker* (Unilateral Limbic Executive Ego), if stronger than the Reptilian Id, it will choose who is in charge. It creates and follows Survival Reality: the key choice is: Self survival vs. Group survival

   d. *Crocodile* (L-Striatal Reptile Brain) source of defensive or aggressive killing. Can create Dream Reality

   e. *Servant* (R-Striatal reptile brain) servile, sole-source of any behavioral output or accomplishment. Knows Cultural Meme Reality

   f. *Pain Body-Reactive Mind* (L-Cerebellar Antisocial Brain) origin of "Satanic" insanity. Lives in xDARP Reality

   g. *Social Brain SOURCE* (R-Cerebellar-Prosocial Brain), my God-Within: Source of Empathic Reality

   h. *External Controllers* (More powerful persons, institutions, or beliefs), to whom my Caretaker out of wisdom, ignorance, or weakness may defer control of my Throne.

NEUROREALITY: A SCIENTIFIC RELIGION TO RESTORE MEANING

SECTION III: Who Are You? Family Friend or Alien Foe?

CHAPTER 8: Hemisity: A Second Categorization of Humans beyond Sex

The Ancient Wish to Categorize People by some Characteristic Beyond Sex: The practice of sorting people into "Right or Left" categories has had a lengthy tradition. The Old Testament, sourcebook of Judaism, Christianity and Islam, makes several references to the right hand, but none to the left hand. For example in the Psalms it says, "The Lord's right hand is full of righteousness". The Christian New Testament: refers to left hand as well. In St. Matthew's "Last Judgment" scene at the resurrection of the dead it said, "The Son of Man…will separate the nations into two groups, as a shepherd separates the sheep from the goats, and he will place the sheep at his right hand and the goats at his left". Then, after he blesses the sheep and gives them the Kingdom of Heaven, he curses the goats to the "eternal fire that is ready for the Devil and his angels".

Such value judgments were logically tied to such early widespread practices as reserving the right hand for eating and the left for the wiping of excrements. Thus, shaking hands by the right hand was a sign of respect, as were invitations to sit at the right hand of one's host as his honored guest. In medieval and later times, the right was associated with authority (order), while the left represented the chaos of freedom. Those sitting on the right of the reigning Prince were the landed nobles, while those on his left were the landless rabble of the non-represented serfs. Now nationalists on the extreme right are fascists (dictators). Those on the extreme left are anarchists (chaos). Today in US, the right includes Republicans (business, wealth, land, power). On the left are the Democrats (civil rights and social welfare for landless).

The Use of Handedness in an Attempt to Segregate Individuals:
In early studies, about 5% of population were reported write with their left hand. Such individuals were stigmatized as: deviant (from the norm), weak (Anglo-Saxon word for left), awkward (French word, gauche, for left), sinister (Latin word for left) and malicious (part of the criminal element). Left-handers were thought to be genetic throwbacks who were mentally deficient, having speech disturbances (stuttering), birth defects,

emotional instability and motor awkwardness. They were also felt to be at increased risk for alcoholism, autoimmune diseases, migraine headaches and learning disabilities, including dyslexia.

The Failure of Handedness to Categorize

By the 1980s, these negative stereotypes about the left-handed had been debunked. Many notable left-handed individuals had become identified, including Michelangelo, Leonardo de Vinci, Benjamin Franklin, and Pablo Picasso. Thus, negative categorization of the left-handed had almost disappeared. As might be expected, after the removal of the stigma, there have been recent increases in reported left-handedness. In current studies, 10-15% of the population identify themselves as left-handed. Explanations for this substantial increase include reduction of shame, as well as lower enforcement of right-handedness by parents, school and state.

As to the true extent of native left-handedness, the jury is still out. In published research (Morton, 2003), when latent left-handedness represented the voluntary preference to use a left appendage to do *any* task (goofy foot, etc), 42% of the subjects qualified. A possible explanation may be that genetic left-handed stock is more prevalent than realized. When true right-handers write, the left hemisphere of their brain activates. Studies using fMRI (Functional Magnetic Resonance Imaging) showed that some "lefties", who had completely converted to right hand preference in childhood, as adults still activated their right hemisphere when they wrote.

Categorization of Individuals by Brain Laterality? Finally Yes!

Well then, if we cannot use handedness to behaviorally characterize us beyond male and female, how about that discovery of Hemisity mentioned in Chapter 6 as another potential way to categorize? Recall, that the Greek, Diocles of Carystus had noticed brain laterality early in the 4th century BC. The split-brain studies of the 1950s greatly amplified this discovery . Yet, none of those actual brain dominance complexities or other nervous system asymmetries help in distinguishing between individuals or further categorizing them by general behavioral differences, any more than eye or skin color or Intelligence Quotient does. Not only were blue-eyed persons represented in all behavioral categories, but also in some cases it was felt that sorting of individuals by gender itself was unwarranted. An idealistic motive behind this was the naïve belief in equality, as in "all men are created equal". Equality in social rights is far different from sameness, as any glance at a Guinness Book of Records will attest.

However, by use of MRI (Magnetic Resonance Imaging), researchers have repeatedly observed that individuals differ significantly regarding which side of their Areas 24 and 24' ventral anterior cingulate cortex (ACC) is larger. The orange (or white) color of **Figure 1** approximates the location of the ACC. The midline fissure of the brain, whose depth reaches the horizontal C-shaped corpus callosum, separates two sides of the ACC the at the base of the cerebral cortex. At issue is whether a person's ACC is larger on the left or the right side of the brain.

The larger side of the ACC is the location of the unilateral Executive Observer-Caretaker system of the Dual Quadbrain Model of Chapter 6. Thus, in 147 of 149 subjects, their right or left brain-oriented hemisity subtype was found to be the same side, left or right, as the side of the larger ventral gyrus of their ACC (Morton and Rafto, 2010). Further, their hemisity subtype correlated with the set of the30 pairs of opposed behavioral preferences of Table 1 that they selected significantly more often; each item being in agreement with their hemisity subtype about 80% of the time.

Table 1 summarizes the behavioral differences resulting from the localization of the Executive Ego in the left or right anterior cingulate limbic cortex. The data came from calibrating 150 university subjects' hemisity by MRI (Magnetic Resonance Imaging). They chose between "Either – Or" type of preference questions or statements from five testing instruments. Of the hundreds of binary items posed to these individuals, the thirty items of Table 1 were found to be answered one way by left brainers and the opposite way by right brainers in a statistically significantly manner. In general, each question was correct for a subject's hemisity about 80% of the time. That is, 80% of right brainers were night owls, while 20% of right brainers were morning larks.

These developments have opened the door to a second way to categorize human differences after sex, that is by Hemisity. As described in Chapter 6, having one's Executive Caretaker inherently either embedded in the bottom-up, inductive, big picture right cerebrum, or within the top-down, deductive, important details left cerebrum, confers a subtle but significant differences in thinking and behavioral orientation between these two types of individuals. The right or left brain-orientation of people around us becomes obvious as we gain knowledge, training and

Figure 1. Location of the Executive Observer on One Side of the Frontal Cingulate Cortex.

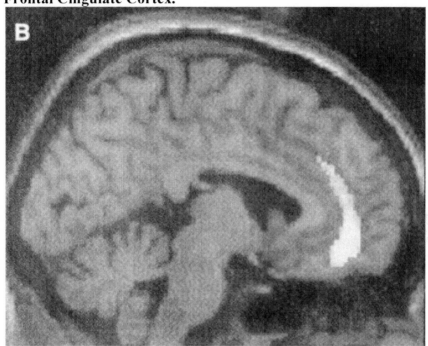

experience. The combined use of a number of semi-quantitative secondary standard hemisity methods further confirms this. Using Table 1, in most cases it becomes quite possible to guess one's own and/or another's hemisity subtype. However, more quantitative biophysical and neuroanatomical methods exist (Morton, 2001, 2002, 2003; Morton and Rafto, 2006, 2009.) The global significance of hemisity will become obvious when we come to the chapter on Familial Polarity. To efficiently discuss hemisity, the following nomenclature was developed: A right or left brain-oriented person, is called a Rp or Lp. A right or left brain-oriented male becomes a Rm or Lm, while a right or left brain-oriented female becomes a Rf or Lf.

Over 1800 students and faculty at the University of Hawaii were assessed for their hemisity producing the results of **Table 2**. While proceeding from high school on through college and graduate school and

Table 1: Thirty Behavioral Correlates of Hemisity

LEFT BRAIN-ORIENTED PERSONS　　　　*RIGHT BRAIN-ORIENTED PERSONS*

LOGICAL ORIENTATION

Left Brain	Right Brain
Analytical (stays within the limits of the data)	Sees the big picture (projects, predicts)
Uses logic to convert objects to literal concepts	Imagines, converts concepts to contexts or
metaphors	
Decisions based on objective facts	Decisions based on feelings, intuition
Uses a serious approach to solving problems	Use a playful approach to solving problems
Prefers to maintain and use good old solutions	Would rather find better new solutions.

TYPE OF CONSCIOUSNESS

Left Brain	Right Brain
Daydreams are not vivid	Has vivid daydreams
Doesn't often remember dreams	Remembers dreams often.
Thinking often consists of words	Thinking often consists of mental images
Comfortable and productive with chaos	Slowed by disorder and disorganization
Can easily concentrate on many things at once	concentrate on one thing in depth at a time
Often thinking tends to ignore surroundings	Observant and in touch with surroundings
Often an early morning person	Often a late night person

FEAR LEVEL AND SENSITIVITY

Left Brain	Right Brain
Conservative and Cautious	Bold and Innovative
Sensitive in relating to others	Intense in relating to others
Tend to avoid talking about emotional feelings	Talks about own/others feelings of emotion
Suppresses emotions as overwhelming	Seeks to experience/ express emotions
Would self-medicate with depressants	Would self-medicate with stimulants

SOCIAL AND PROFESSIONAL ORIENTATION

Left Brain	Right Brain
Independent, hidden, private, and indirect	Interdependent, open, public, and direct
Avoids seeking evaluation by others	Seeks frank feedback from others
Usually tries to avoid taking the blame	Takes blame, blames self, or apologizes
Does not praise others nor work for praise	Praises others, works for praise of others

PAIR-BONDING STYLE AND SPOUSAL DOMINANCE

Left Brain	Right Brain
After an upset with spouse, needs to be alone	After upset with spouse, needs closeness
Tolerates mate defiance in private	Difficult to tolerate mate defiance in private
Needs little physical contact with mate	Likes daily small assurances of mate's love
Tends not to be very romantic or sentimental	Tends to be very romantic and sentimental
Prefers monthly larger reassurances of love	Likes daily small assurances of mate's love
Thinks-listens quietly, keeps talk to minimum	Thinks-listens interactively, talks a lot
Does not read other people's mind very well	Good at knowing what others are thinking.
Often feels their mate talks too much	Feels mate doesn't talk or listen enough.
Lenient parent, kids tend to defy	Strict, kids obey and work for approval

Table 2: Brain hemisphericity distributions within populations of fifteen professions (n=421)

GROUP percent participation	n	LEFT BRAIN	Left Males	Left Females	RIGHT BRAIN	Right Males	Right Females
Unsorted College Entrants	228						
Western Civilization students 62	228	57%	19%	38%	43%	22%	21%
Specialist Populations	422						
Microbiology Professors 74	14	86%*	72%	14%	14%	14%	0%
Biochemistry Professors 95	18	83%*	72%	11%	17%	17%	0%
Physics (particle)Professors 80	15	73%	73%	0%	27%	27%	0%
Philosophy Professors 73	11	73%	54%	19%	27%	27%	0%
Mathematics Professors 93	27	70%	70%	0%	30%	30%	0%
Accountancy Professors 75	9	67%	44%	22%	33%	22%	12%
Law Professors 83	19	63%	32%	31%	37%	21%	16%
Art Professors (vs. Artists) 92	27	63%	38%	25%	37%	29%	8%
Civil Engineering Professors 89	17	53%	53%	0%	47%	41%	6%
Clin. Psychologists (yel. pages) 75	29	52%	24%	28%	48%	28%	20%
Electrical Engineering Profs. 75	16	50%	50%	0%	50%	44%	6%
Physicians (Medical Students) 80	178	49%	25%	24%	51%	26%	25%
Mechanical Engineering Profs. 75	9	44%	33%	11%	56%	56%	0%
Architecture Professors 100	12	33%*	26%	4%	67%	61%	9%
Astronomy Professors 66	21	29%*	30%	0%	71%	60%	10%

* $p < 0.05$.

(yel. pages) = American Psychological Society Members advertising in the yellow pages of the Honolulu phone directory.

(Medical Students): due to extremely low attrition rates of medical students, it was convenient to test them in mass rather than scheduling a separate appointment with each of them after they became clinicians.

on into the professions, hemisity distributions shifted dramatically, as more hemisity sorting occurred at each stage. That is, we found that at the High School level in the US public school system, the number of right and left brain-oriented students was almost identical. However, the sorting involved in going on to college, resulted in a 1% difference between the number of rights and lefts at the lower division level. By the time they had reached upper division college courses, this sorting had increased to a 34% difference between rights and lefts in a given course. By the time they had become Faculty, there was up to a 57% difference between the hemisity of professionals within the 18 university departments tested.

Why did increasing hemisity sorting accompany higher education or training? A probable explanation is that it resulted from of each person being exactly who they were (and were not) and doing what they liked to do the best and avoiding what they did poorly. If they failed in one course and excelled in another, they could hardly be blamed for proceeding in the direction of their success. Thus, often career specializations tend to match a person's right or left brain-orientations. Sorting results showed Rp "Lumpers" successfully pursuing their curiosity about the big picture, and Lp "Splitters" successfully pursuing their important detail interests.

As apparent in **Table 3**, some left brain-oriented professions (with a top-down view of components at a lower universe level) include Particle Physics, Microbiology, Biochemistry, Mathematics and Accountancy. Some right brain-oriented professions (using a bottom-up assembly of systems at a higher universe level) include Astronomy, Architecture, Mechanical Engineering, Art and Music. As we shall see, the 30traits correlated with hemisity influence one's life path in other ways as well.

Table 3 compares additional fascinating but logical differences between the hemisity subtypes that have been noted anecdotally that which have not yet been subjected to rigorous quantification. Note that in addition to thinking and behavioral differences, physical differences have also been noted.

The Hemisity of Spouses: Do Alikes or Opposites Attract?

After testing the hemisity of thousands of students and faculty within a university, the next question that arose was: What might the hemisity of members of heterosexual couples be? Are like-like hemisity partners more attracted to each other? Or, does the old saying "Opposites Attract" actually apply to the pair bonding hemisity of spouses? We looked at 412 partners of 206 couples who had been together longer than 5 years.

Table 3, Other Differences Between Hemisity Subtypes: Anecdotal

Issue:	Lps:	Rps:.
Personality Orientation:	High sensitivity	High intensity
Taste:	Prefer unseasoned	Prefer spicy
Smell:	Aroma sensitive	Odor insensitive
Stress:	Vulnerable	Resistant
Basal Fear:	Anxious	Bold
Dream content:	Monsters, Falling	Humiliation, Excretia
Drugs of abuse:	Relaxants (alcohol)	Stimulants (amphetamines)
Immune strength:	Weak	Strong
Proneness to Illness:	Often ill	Rarely ill
Medicine side effects:	Common	Uncommon
Proneness to Obesity:	Often thin	Often overweight
Bust size:	Smaller	Larger
Non-erect penis length	Longer	Shorter
Mental Health issues	Alcoholism, PTSD	Rxs:dyslexia, mental blocks
Longevity:	Type A mortality	Youthful

The distributions observed in this study (Morton, unpublished) were as follows: Of the 412 heterosexual partners, of course 50% were men and 50% were women. In terms of hemisity, there were 53% Lps and 47% Rps. Among the four possible partner combinations, 40% were Lm-Rf pairs, 27% were Rm-Lf pairs, 20% were Lm-Lf pairs 13% were Rm-Rf pairs. That is, 33% of the pairs were between partners of like hemisity. In contrast, twice as many, (67%) of the pairs were between partners of opposite (complementary) hemisity.

In addition, when the numbers of childless pairs were determined, an average of 13% of the Rm-Lf, Lm-Rf, or Rm-Rf pairs were childless, while a significant 38% of Lm-Lf pairs were childless. The possible meaning of these figures will become evident later.

Spousal Dominance Within the Four Possible Hemisity Couple Types:
Among the complementary couples (Lm-Rf or Rm-Lf), the right brain-oriented partner (male or female) was usually the *de facto* leader of the nuclear family. **Table 4** lists six elements from the list of 30 pairs of differences between Lps and Rps of Table 1, which confirmed Rp spousal dominance in the home. Thus, in the Rm-Lf or Lm-Rf pairs, the right brain-oriented person was dominant, male or female as the case may be. In Rm-Rf pairs, leadership was hotly contested, leading to relative instability

of this pair. In contrast, of the above four, the Lm-Lf pairs were the most stable. There, leadership usually fell on the larger (often unwilling) male. Thus, the relative stability of the possible hemisity couple combinations appears to be: Lm-Lf > Rm-Lm and Lm-Rf > Rm-Rf. Recall, the relative stability of the hetero and homo sexual couples appears to be: F-F > M-F > M-M.

Marital Dominance is not to be confused with Work Dominance outside of home. At work, Lps may form highly competitive dominance hierarchies that avoid Rp home domination. The complaint by Rfs that an impossible-to-penetrate "Glass Ceiling" exists in the business world, can definitely apply to Rms as well. However, it rarely exists for Lfs, older feminist doctrine notwithstanding.

Table 4. Hemisity and Spousal Dominance Oriented Items from Table 1

LEFT BRAIN	**PAIR-BONDING STYLE**	*RIGHT BRAIN*
Does not read other people's mind very well		Very good at knowing what others are thinking
Avoids talking about their own and other's emotions		Often talks about their and other's emotions
Can tolerate it if their mate defies them in private		Finds it intolerable if mate defies them in private
Likes longer-term, larger rewards of mate's love		Likes daily small reassurances of mate's love
Often feels mate talks too much		Often feels that mate doesn't talk / listen enough
Not a very strict parent Kids tend to defy		Strict Kids obey and work for his/ her approval

Hemisity vs. Sex in the Workplace

In the Dual Quadbrain Model, we each have a double brain, which operates by a "Double Standard". Our left brain competes against aliens as enemies using win-lose ethics. In contrast our right brain cooperates with family members using win-win ethics. Thus, there will be two polarity styles of interaction: Lps often form bottom-up competitive hierarchies, like little monkey islands. In contrast, Rps work with loyalty for their leader through top-down chains of command. Polarity style conflicts can occur in "mixed groups" due to these opposite modes of thinking.

Many traits commonly considered sexual characteristics are actually hemisity traits. Lps, male or female, tend to be somewhat muted, quiet, impersonal, and emotion avoidant. Yet, Rps, male or female, tend to be more charismatic, intense, talkative, and emotional. On TV, these reverse familial polarities were unwittingly stereotyped in such shows as "Switching Families".

Hemisity of the Children from the Four Types of Hemisity Couples:
    Figure 2 illustrates findings on offspring hemisity, which were based upon 3-5 generation genealogies from 14 unrelated families. Significantly, in complimentary couples (Rm-Lf or Lm-Rf), hemisity was usually "like father, like son", and "like mother-like daughter". In important contrast, for Rm-Rf couples, the children's hemisities were random or unrelated to that of the parent of same sex. The offspring of Lm-Lf couples were mostly Lps.

Evidence that Hemisity is Inherited:
In addition to the above genealogical data, researchers have also discovered that in Rps, the corpus callosum, the major communication bridge between the cerebral hemispheres, is significantly larger than that of Lps (Morton and Rafto, 2006). Additionally, twin studies clearly show that corpus callosum size is inherited. Genealogical studies also suggest that the hemisity of offspring follows exact inheritance rules. These and other anatomical and evolutionary evidence, suggest that in general one's hemisity is anatomically determined before birth and is unchangeable.

What does the Spousal Hemisity Study Tell us?
Based upon hundreds of observations, we know that two thirds of the families studied had spouses exhibiting complimentary hemisity. This was race independent. Either they were Rm-Lf "Patripolar" families, or they were Lm- Rf "Matripolar" families. Children of these family types usually had the hemisity of the same gender parent. The one third of the families, those with same hemisity spouses (Rm-Rf or Lm-Lf), did not breed true and produced offspring of random hemisity. The L-L subclass families of same hemisity are also less fertile. Anecdotally, there appeared to be a higher rate of spontaneous abortion among these L-L couples.Further, some children of same spouse hemisity had developmental anomalies. Chapter 10 covers this.

Figure 2: Hemisity of the Children from the Four Types of Hemisity Couples

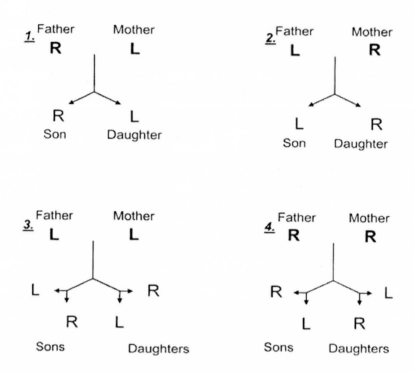

Thus, the discovery and investigation of hemisity, the second binary element describing individuals beyond sex, has opened the doors to new vistas of understanding of families and family conflicts. This story unfolds further in the next three chapters.

Some Important Points of Chapter 8:

1) Although, handedness has not been as useful in categorizing people as sex, Hemisity, a second "either-or" characterization of individuals indeed is.

The fact that our Executive system Observer is unilateral, causes those Lps in which it is located in the left cerebral hemisphere to have a top-down, important-details perspective, compared to the bottom-up, big-picture perspective of those Rps with it located on the right. Two neuroanatomical differences between hemisity subtypes were also noted. This enables human beings to be separated into two major categories beyond their sex.

2) Thus far, as indicated in Table 1, Rps and Lps have been found differ significantly as to how they respond to thirty of 100 "either-or" statements derived from a number of preference questionnaires. These differences occurred in the following five areas: Logical orientation, Type of consciousness, Fear level and sensitivity, Social and professional orientation, and Pair bonding style and dominance.

3) Table 3 also lists another set of apparent differences between Rps and Lps. In addition, hemisity subtype has an impact in the workplace.

4) Published studies of thousands of high school and university students, as well as hundreds of faculty, indicate that a strong sorting of hemisity subtypes occurs as one progresses from high school into ones adult work profession, so that for example, three quarters of particle physicists were Lps, but only one quarter of astronomers were.

5) Of the four possible marital partner combinations (Lm-Rf, Rm-Lf, Rm-Rf, and Lm-Lf), "opposites attract" complimentarity was the case in two of four long-term couples. This resulted in two different types of families: Lm-Rf and Rm-Lf, in which Rps were dominant in the home, while Lps were supportive.

6) Compared to the three other types, Lm-Lf couples had significantly fewer children.

7) "Like father- like son" and "like mother-like daughter" were the hemisity subtype sorting outcomes for children from the major two complementary family types. However, for the like-like couples, the hemisity of the offspring was random, and developmental anomalies were often present.

NEUROREALITY: A SCIENTIFIC RELIGION TO RESTORE MEANING

Section III: Who Are You? Family Friend or Alien Foe?

Chapter 9: Dyadic Evolution of Familial Polarity: The Origins of Hemisity

If the Dialectic Universe is Dyadic, Where is Dyadic Evolution?

Clearly, if life originated once somewhere in the universe, it could have originated more than once, even here on earth. One of these forms of life may have evolved at the bottom of the sea around energy-rich volcanic vents. The other, at the surface of the sea in warm ponds, energized by sunshine. It is even possible that spores from outer space provided an insemination source (Crick, 1982). These two life forms differ subtly but foundationally in their opposite reproductive strategies. Either of these strategies works perfectly well alone. However, each is incompatible with the other. This has resulted in the emergence of two parallel trees of life. Each tree's life forms competed for those ecological niches available at the time. The bottom of Table 1 illustrates some of the parallel competing higher organisms in these two trees of life.

Patripolar vs. Matripolar Reproductive Strategies: Source of Endless Conflict.

Here, these two equally possible but opposite reproductive strategies are identified under the new term: "Familial Polarity". They are the "Patripolar" and "Matripolar" reproductive strategies, both of which were firmly established long before the time when the vertebrates emerged **(Table 1)**. The Patripolar, male-dominant, haremic strategy is as follows: the winner in the ongoing battle between males becomes the leader of a harem and strongly attracts females who are always looking for the best sire to father their children. The mainly monogamous females of the harem formed strongly reject the male losers. Therefore, they ostracize defeated males into isolated bachelor groups. There, the males grow and practice

Table 1. Brief Diagram of Potential Dyadic Evolution Stages Leading to Humans

Branching Forks: Presently Unrecognized Omnipresent Parallel Paths:

*1. Origin of Cellular Life	sea vent **vs.** Warm pond: Space spore?
2. Competing Chemistrys	RNA World **vs.** DNA World
3. Oldest recognized forms	Arche-bacteria **vs.** Eu-bacteria
4. Stationary and Mobile forms	Unicellular **vs.** Multicellular
5. Plants vs. Animals	Self-sufficient **vs.** Parasitic
6. Vertebrates vs. Invertebrates	Vascular **vs.** Nonvascular
7. Sexual vs. Asexual	Ovulate **vs.** Sprout
8. Fertilization	Internal **vs.** External
9. Aquatic	Sharks **vs.** Fish
10. Life moves onto dry land	Reptiles **vs.** Plants

Two Sexual Reproductive Strategies, *Haremic vs. Territorial*, existed by then: *Patripolar* vs. *Matripolar*

11. Reptiles	Alligators **vs.** Crocodiles
12. Dinosaurs	Anchiceratops **vs.** Tyrannosaurus (female bigest)
13. Birds	Chickens **vs.** Peafowl
14. Lay eggs vs. Nurse infants	Reptiles **vs.** Mammals
15. Monotremes	Duck-billed platypus **vs.** Spiny Ant-eater
16. Marsupials	Red Kangaroo **vs.** Northern Quoll
17. Placentals	Deer, Antelope, Wolf, Rat **vs.** Mouse, Fox, Sheep, Elk
	Elephant, Walrus, Horse **vs.** Donkey, Hyena, Bear
18. Early Primates	Brown Lemur **vs.** Ring-tailed Lemur
19. Apes	Gorillas, Orangutans **vs.** Chimps, Bonobos
20. Hominids 7MyrBP	Neand., Peking Man **vs.** CroMagon, Narmada Man

---

* items 1-10 are only suggestive regarding Familial Polarities.

their martial arts, awaiting the opportunity to overthrow the current alphamale, and thereby gain reproductive access to their own genetic immortality. Thus, in Patripolar lineages, paternity of offspring usually traces to the alpha male. Because, size significantly contributes to winning, there is often a sexual dimorphism in Patripolar pairs, where the male can be much larger than the females. Male dominant Patripolar groups are generally non-territorial. That is, they are invasive of all territory and often migratory.

In the perhaps less appreciated Matripolar reproductive strategy, males compete for territory. For example, property next to an important resource, such as a water hole, being the most desirable territory; the least valued territory is on the outskirts. Even some insect males sort and segregate themselves into this geographic hierarchy of territory, as for example in so-called lek mating. Most importantly, in the matripolar reproductive strategy, the male welcomes any polygamous female to enter his territory. If in estrous, she is repeatedly inseminated as she passes through his and his competitors territory on her way to the water hole. Thus, in the Matripolar reproductive strategy, the males make love not war; paternity is usually quite random; and each male supports and protects any mother with child as if it were his very own.

Clearly, the two reproductive strategies differ regarding at which universe level the killing violence of the survival of the fittest occurs. In the Patripolar reproductive strategy, the competition occurs between male organisms, and females follow and court the survivor-winner. By remarkable contrast in the Matripolar reproductive strategy, killing competition occurs at the cellular level. Here, there is a great race between sperm of the many semen donations to the reproductive tract of that female in heat, where billions of sperm race to be the first to penetrate her receptive ovum. After the winning spermatozoon is welcomed inside, the ovum closes her gates and all of the vast number of sperm competitors die of frustration over the next few days. Here, overall male size is much less important and sexual dimorphism is low, or even reversed. Instead, the ability to deliver increased sperm numbers (larger testicles) with longer, more penetrative insemination systems (longer penis) have evolved, along with seminal agglutinating agents and "killer" sperm.

Reproductive Polarities of the Apes, Our Closest Living Primate Relatives

Each of the four Ape species exhibits only one of the two sexual strategies of Polarity **(Table 2)**. both gorillas and orangutans use the Patripolar strategy where a massive, violent, harem-forming male maintains exclusive breeding rights by fighting at the organism level. For gorillas, the males weigh around 375 lbs, while females weigh about 200 lbs. In the case of orangutans, the males weigh 225 lbs, more than twice that of the about 100-lb females. Because of lack of competition within the

Table 2. Two Reproductive Strategies Result in Opposite Familial Polarities

Variable	Patripolar	Matripolar
Dominant Sex	Male	Female
Promiscuous Partner	Male	Female
Paternity	Alpha Male	Random
Males must fight for reproductive access	Yes	No, but are territorial
Males are much larger than Females	Yes	No
Universe level of competition	<u>Organisms</u>: Males Battle!	<u>Cells</u>: Sperm Races!
Larger sex organs required to compete	No	Yes

monogamous female tract, patripolar apes need only small penises (1-2"), and small testes, the latter of which are even internal in the gorilla.

Chimpanzees and the lesser known but amazing Bonobos use the Matripolar polarity reproductive strategy. In both species, each time a each female comes into heat a big party occurs in the form of a sexual orgy. During this short time she welcomes all males of the troupe to make love with her (sometimes having more than 50 separate trysts in one day) while their sperm make war inside her. Chimpanzee and bonobo males weigh about 100 lbs and their females about 80 lbs. In contrast to the patripolar males, the matripolar ape males have huge testicles and long penises (3-5") to produce and deliver overwhelming numbers of sperm to the competition.

Stages of primate evolution within each of the two trees of life.

Table 3 summarizes the increases in brain size from the apes, on through the hominids, to early and later humans, studied by many archeologists. It shows that a skull found in Chad, Africa, dated around 7-6 million years ago, had features intermediate between ape and human. Other finds of more recent skulls show the cranial capacity increasing more and more, until by the time of the Neanderthals, it exceeded that of modern humans by over 30%! Among the hominoid remains at each time period are almost always two different contemporaneous hominid lineages, one, called *robustus*, showed great sexual dimorphism, while the other, called *gracilis*, was more

Table 3: Growth of Brain Size with the Evolution of Culture

Species	Location	Cranial Capacity	Existence time, yrs
Chimpanzee	Africa	321 ml	Endangered
Bonobo	Africa	336 ml	Endangered
Gorilla	Africa	425 ml	Endangered
Orangutan(African fossils) Indonesia		443 ml	Endangered .
Sahelanthropus tchadensis	Africa ("Toumai")	380 ml	6-7 million
Homo habilis	Caucasus (Dmanisi)	700 ml	2.0 – 1.5 million
Homo erectus	Asia (Java, Peking)	995 ml	1.9 – "100,000"*
Homo heidelbergensis	Europe	1300 ml	800,000-200,000
Homo neanderthalensis	Europe	1700 ml	400,000-"20,000"*
Homo rhodesienses (CroMagnon)	Europe	1600 ml	600,000-200,000
Early Homo sapiens	"Out of Africa"	450 ml	160,000 - present
Modern Homo sapiens	Global	1250 ml	present: 6 billion+

*= possibly not gone

graceful and less stocky with little sexual dimorphism evident. This
strongly suggests that both the Patripolar and Matripolar lineages have
come forward in time, for example in the form of Neanderthal brutes and
the Cro-Magnon beautiful people.

It was said that Neanderthals were primitive because they were
always fighting, as demonstrated by the fact that the skeletons of many of
the males have healed broken bones. Very few healed bones were found
among the supposedly more peaceful Cro-Magnons, so they were assumed
to have been much smarter. More likely, due to their patripolar
reproductive style, Neanderthal males still fought for leadership and
reproductive access, while the matripolar Cro-Magnon reproductive style
of making love not war was less personally dangerous. It is likely that with
their huge brains, both lineages were more intelligent than we are. We, who
with our more "modern" culture, now try to save all our defective births.
Nor do we have to be particularly intelligent to survive these days within

modern bedroom cultures, unlike those hominids who lived through the ice ages among the glaciers or deserts.

Source of Both Patripolar and Matripolar Primate Lineages
Africa appears to be the site of this dual evolution of primates to the higher apes, through pre human hominids to modern humans. The DNA obtained from various humans living on the continent of African is by far more variable in sequence than DNA taken from humans on any other continent in the world. This strongly supports the African origins of all humanity. There is a debate about whether apes migrated out of Africa first to evolve into pre-hominids at other global locations, or whether complete evolution to the level of humans occurred in Africa before any outward migration occurred. Or, whether both occurred and the modern forms, originating either within or outside of Africa, outcompeted previous forms to extinction.

Be Fruitful, Multiply and Replenish the Earth
The previously ocean-surrounded African subcontinent finally drifted into its present position and docked against Europe only a few million years ago. Before that event, primate migration out of African was impossible. **Figure 1**, diagrams the post-ape, pre-human, hominoid migrations into in the eastern hemisphere. In that version, it may be seen that hominids migrated out of Africa to Europe and Asia several times, only to became extinct, the latest being Peking Man and Neanderthal types. Finally, in that doubtful version, a single more advanced Negroid race emerged and migrated out of Africa relatively recently and killed off all earlier competitors. We are supposedly the descendants of these genocidal ancestors.

Patripolar and Matripolar Couples Have Contrasting Corpus Callosum Size Patterns
This idea can only be half true because, as indicated in **Figure 2**, both the Patripolar and Matripolar lineages are present today. Therefore, not just one human lineage took over the world after all. In fact recent MRI work on the hemisity of 120 Caucasian subjects shows, not only that Familial Polarity opposites attract, but also that Rps have larger corpus colossal sizes than their Lp partners in both polarities. These corpus callosum data strongly contradict the popular belief that all humans derive

Figure 1, Hominid Evolution: "Out of Africa" vs. "Multiregional" Hypotheses

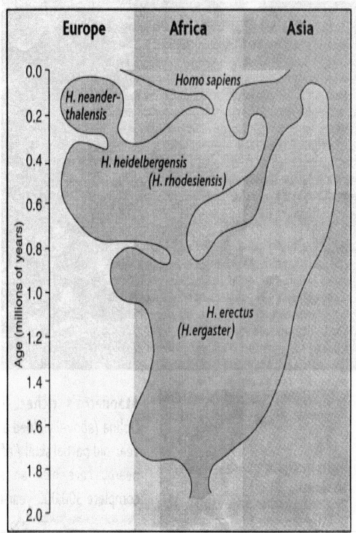

Go with the flow. One view of how various human species might have dispersed in space and time.

Figure 2: Comparison of Corpus Callosal Size and Hemisity Subtype

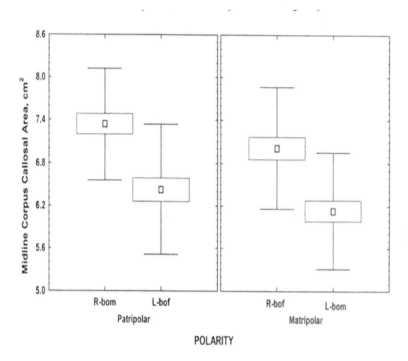

from a single genocidal African stock. In fact, descendents from the Neanderthals and other prehominid Patripolar stock are alive and well in New York City! (joke).

The discovery of Familial Polarity has opened a new window, not only for clarifying human origins, but also for understanding current global conflict. As illustrated in **Figure 3**, post ice age migrations out of Africa appears to have created foundational human populations of alternating Familial Polarity striations across the eastern hemisphere. Apparently, the Patripolar highly intelligent Orangutans were the first out of Africa. They traveled eastward into the sunrise to arrive in Northern China and the Yellow River Valley almost 2 million years ago as the Peking Man, perhaps by following the then southern coast line of Asia before the Indian subcontinent had docked with Asia. After that docking, orangutan-Shivapithicus stock continued out of Africa to the east, but the second time followed the new southern coastline of India arriving in Indonesia instead.

Figure 3: Out of Africa Migrations to Locations in the Eastern Hemisphere Resulted in Striations of Alternating Familial Polarity

1. Orangutans, **Patripolar**, Yellow River Orientals
2. Bonobos, **Matripolar**, Indus River Indians
3. Mountain Gorillas, **Patripolar**, Tigris-Euphrates River Neanderthals
4. Dark-faced Chimpanzee, **Matripolar**, Nile River, Slavics
5. Lowland Gorillas, **Patripolar**, Rhine River Neanderthals
6. White-faced Chimpanzees, **Matripolar**, Western Europe Cro-Magnons

It is interesting that today, orangutans are totally extinct in Africa. Also, it is entertaining to speculate that the distinctive orange color of the Orangutans could have been be the origin of the yellow, orange, and red pigmentation the oriental races.

Second, the black, straight-haired Matripolar Bonobos were apparently the next to break out of Africa. Also moving eastward, they failed to migrate much beyond India, perhaps because of population build up from earlier more eastern migrant orangutan stocks. Thus, we now find the Dravidian black, straight haired human stock of the Indus River valley and southern India.

Third, the Mountain Gorillas migrated into the Tigris Euphrates River Valley to become part of the Neanderthals.

Fourth, hominid derivatives from the Matripolar Dark-Faced Chimpanzees then took over the Nile River Valley, additionally migrating into Eastern Europe as the Slavic races.

Figure 4 shows remains of the Dminasi Man found between the Caspian and Black Seas of the Caucasus near the ancient city of Tbilisi, Georgia, far from Africa. His era is dated at 1.7 million years ago. His cranial capacity (Figure 4) was 700 cm^2, only half of ours. Various stone flakes, scrapers and chopping tools were found with these remains.

Fifth, Lowland Gorilla-derived hominid stock migrated north to become the Patripolar Neanderthals of Rhine River and Western Europe.

Sixth, the White Faced Chimpanzees evolved into the blue-eyed blonde Matripolar Berbers who migrated repeatedly across Gibraltar to become the Western Mediterraneans and Scandinavians. Thus, we have at least six alternating familial polarity striations of hominid stock populations established anciently across the Eastern Hemisphere. This has further consequences described in the next chapter.

Today, idealized young-adult patripolar, Rm human males are estimated to weigh about 200 lbs with the patripolar, Lf females weighing something over 100 lbs. Idealized matripolar, Lm, human males might weigh around 170 lbs and their matripolar, Rf females around 135 lbs. While the erect penis sizes between patripolar and matripolar males are comparable, overall, the *non-erect* penis size of patripolar males tends to be much smaller. Similarly, non-pregnant patripolar females tend to have smaller breasts than matripolar females. Further, mature Rps of either polarity tend to be more obese than the thinner Lps. Thus, the Matripolar couple stereotype of Jack Sprat, the skinny husband who could eat no fat, and his heavy wife who could eat no lean. In addition, at least among "Caucasians" the pupil to eyebrow distance tends to be smaller in Rms who also tend to have a heavier overlying brow ridge than Lms. The latter tend

Figure 4. The Dmanisi Man with tools, the first Caucasian, dated at 1.7 million years bp

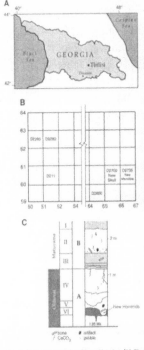

Fig. 1. (A) Location map of Dmanisi site. (B) The locations of hominid fossils (excavation units are 1-m squares). (C) General stratigraphic profile, modified after Gabunia et al. (5, 6). The basalt and the immediately overlying volcaniclastics (stratum A) exhibit normal polarity and are correlated with the terminus of the Olduvai Subchron. Slightly higher in the section, above a minor disconformity and below a strongly developed soil, Unit B deposits, which also contain artifacts, faunas and human fossils, all exhibit reversed polarity and are correlated with the Matuyama. Even the least stable minerals, such as olivine, in the basalt and the fossil-bearing sediments show only minor weathering, which is compatible with the incipient pedogenic properties of the sediments.

The skull is in remarkably fine condition (Fig. 2). The maxillae are slightly damaged anteriorly, the zygomatic arches are broken, and both mastoid processes are heavily abraded. There is damage also to the orbital

be a female. However, the upper canines carry large crowns and massive roots, and their size counsels caution in assessing sex.

In its principal vault dimensions, D2700 is smaller than D2280 and the specimens attrib-

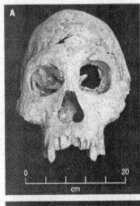

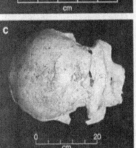

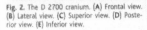

Fig. 2. The D 2700 cranium. (A) Frontal view. (B) Lateral view. (C) Superior view. (D) Posterior view. (E) Inferior view.

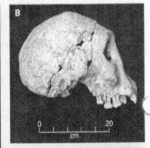

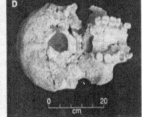

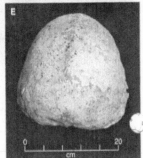

to have higher eyebrows and negligible brow ridges, perhaps reflecting ancient Neanderthal and Cro-Magnon ancestral differences. This phenomenon is sometimes visible on US TV between Republican and Democrat News Commentators.

The DNA-based genetic content of humans differs from the four Apes by only 1-3%. It is a stunning fact that variations between human races are even higher (3-5%), and between individuals can differ by an amazing 30-50%. Thus, it is not surprising that discovery of hemisity uncovered evidence for two distinct human familial polarities. At present, the existence of two opposite primate reproductive strategies has yet to be recognized in apes by contemporary science, much less in humans. It is ironic that hemisity and familial polarity were also unknown to the writers of the Bible, and thus apparently escaped the eye of God.

Table 4 compares the currently unrecognized but hauntingly familiar biology-driven opposite behavioral dyads within Familial Polarity courtship and parenting styles. Patripolar male winners up on stage select from among crowds of swooning Patripolar females groupies at their feet as to who will best serve them. However, no self-respecting Matripolar female would think of wandering down there. Instead, they take to the stage themselves as beauty stars who choose whom of the gangs of males panting at her feet would serve her best. The infamous bare breast briefly exposed on TV at the half time of an American football game a few years ago, thus caused opposite reactions of offended horror or of amusement, depending upon the familial polarity of the viewer.

Behavioral, Cultural, and Institutional Differences between the Human Polarities

In **Table 5**, the contrasting behavioral orientations and ecological niches between the Patripolar and Matripolar Humans are illustrated. Patripolar male big-game-killing skills, animal husbandry, nomadic, inventive, and meat and potato styles are very different than those of the nonkilling gardener, vegetarian, settled cooperator cultures, where the arts could incubate and develop.

The ethnic database of 1170 cultures compiled by Murdoch, scanned for 15 social variables by DeMeo (1998) forms the basis for Table 5. Obviously, the members of two polarities are quite different in their basic attitudes, behaviors and social institutions regarding the treatment of children, sexuality and rights of women. The male-dominant Patripolars are

Table 4: Personality Traits within the Two Polarity Family Types

TRAIT:	PATRIPOLAR FAMILIES		MATRIPOLAR FAMILIES	
Parental Sex	Male	Female	*Female*	*Male*
Hemisity	Right	Left	*Right*	*Left*
Corp. Callos. Size	Larger	Smaller	*Larger*	*Smaller*
Mental Orientation	Big Picture	Important Details	*Big Picture*	*Important Details*
Verbosity, Speech	Charismatic	Quiet, articulate	*Charasmatic*	*Quiet, articulate*
Family Leadership	Most dominant	Most supportive	*Most dominant*	*Most supportive*
Parental Love Type	Conditional	Unconditional	*Conditional*	*Unconditional*
Parental Function	Sets standards	Prevents excess	*Sets standards*	*Prevents excess*
Child's Hemisity	Boys are Rights	Girls are Lefts	Girls are Rights	Boys are Lefts
Parental Status	Role model	Serves the child	*Role model*	*Serves the child*
Mating Behavior **Mating Target**	**Males select displaying females who are:** Healthy, intelligent, humorous, loyal, devoted, and want to serve him.	**Females court winning males who are:** Tall, dark, and handsome, champs winners, strongest. Most socially powerful, richest, smartest of crop	**Females select displaying males who are:** Healthy, intelligent, humorous, loyal, devoted, and want to serve her.	**Males court winning females who are:** the most physically attractive: leanest, big-breasted. Most socially powerful, richest, and smartest of crop.

harsher and more rigid in attitude, possibly to protect their wife and children from their fellows' tendency toward violence toward others. In addition, Patripolar nomadism demanded a much tighter familial control in terms of the use of time and resources in order to survive. It was not child or female indulgent, and required much higher discipline and order to survive in the badlands than required by farmers in the oases. That is, contrasting comments could be made regarding Matripolar gathering, gardening, farming and settlement on rich agricultural land which are inherently much more time consuming and relaxed. **Table 6** highlights similar differences in the social and religious institutions. The contrasts are dramatic and edifying. Through Familial Polarity we can begin to understand the origins of the wide diversity of human culture and experience all around us.

    Table 7 further contrasts the autocratic patripolar and democratic matripolar social and religious institutions found within the Murdoch ethnic database.

Table 5. Patri-and Matripolar Adaptations and Ecological Orientations:

	Patripolar:	Matripolar:
Field Specializations:	Early Big-Game Hunters	Gatherers
	Midperiod Herdsmen	Gardeners
	Later Ranchers	Farmers
Species domestication:	Horse, Wheat, Barley	Ox?, Legumes?
Dietary Orientation:	Meat, Blood, Dairy	Vegetarian, Spices
Mobility:	Nomadic, Marginal Land	Stationary, Best land
Group Discipline to Survive:	Yes, Militaristic	No, Laissez faire
Society Types:	Dominator cultures	Cooperator culture
Early Arts Devel:	Barbarian Invaders	High Arts-Cultures

Table 6. Contrasting Behaviors, Attitudes, and Social Institutions:
15 variable correlations within Murdoch's ethnic database of 1170 cultures (DeMeo, 1998)

.	Patripolar	Matripolar .
Infants &	Less indulgence	More indulgence
Children:	Less physical affection	More physical affection
	Infants traumatized	Infants not traumatized
	Painful initiations	Absence of pain in initiation
	Dominated by family	Children's democracies
	Sex-segregated houses	Mixed sex children's houses
Sexuality:	Restrictive, anxious view	Permissive, pleasurable attitude
	Genital mutilations	Absence of genital mutilations
	Female virginity taboo	No female virginity taboo
	Vaginal intercourse taboo	No vaginal intercourse taboos
	Adolescent sex censured	Adolescent sex freely permitted
	Homosexual-Incest taboos	Absence of Homo-Incest tendency
	Concubinage / prostitution	Absence of concubinage / prostitution
Women:	Limits on freedom	More freedom
	Inferior status	Equal status
	Vaginal bleeding taboos	No vaginal blood taboos
	Cannot choose own mate	Can choose own mate
	Cannot divorce at will	Can divorce at will
	Males control fertility	Females control fertility
	Reproduction denigrated	Reproduction celebrated

Table 7: Contrasting Social and Religious Institutions:
15 variable correlations within Murdoch's ethnic database of 1170 cultures
(DeMeo, 1998)

	Patripolar:	Matripolar:
Culture, Family	Patrilineal descent	Matrilineal descent
And Social	Patrilocal marital home	Matrilocal marital home
Structure:	Compulsive monogamy	Non-compulsive monogamy
	Often polygamous	Rarely polygamous
	Authoritarian	Democratic
	Heirarchal	Elegantarian
	Political/Econ. Centralism	Work-democratic
	Military specialists/caste	No full time military
	Violent, sadistic	Nonviolent, sadism absent
Ancient	Male/Father oriented	Female/Mother oriented
Religion:	Asceticism, avoidance	Pleasure welcomed and
	of pleasure, pain-seeking.	Institutionalized.
	Inhibition, fear of nature	Spontaneity, nature worship
	Male shamans, healers	Male or Female sha /healers
	Strict behavioral codes	Absence of strict codes

-

Figure 5 is a humorous and exaggerated stereotypic comparison of the two Familial Polarities today. Individuals from all four of the subtypes of familial polarity can be highly intelligent, and representatives of each have received Nobel prizes for science research. Although the term, Familial Polarity, is not yet part of our cultural vocabulary, its existence is easy to detect in the hemisity of public figures, both in politics and in the entertainment world. With a sound understanding of Familial Polarity and acareful assessment of relevant biographic material, it becomes quite possible to assess the right or left brain-orientation of historic figures as well.

Table 8 contains an estimation of the Familial Polarity of several families who through the mass media became familiar to the public. **Figure 6** compares a matripolar Cro-Magnon skull with a patripolar Neanderthal skull. Photos of Rf French actress Bridget Bardot and Lf American actress Jane Fonda are shown beneath. The similarities of the modern individuals to these ancient examples are striking. Clearly, the incredible Neanderthals with their huge brains can no longer be considered

Figure 5. The Two Polarities: Matripolar above and Patripolar

Section III: WHO ARE YOU?

Table 8, Patripolar and Matripolar Public Families in Daily Life

Male Dominant Patripolar Families: Identities:

Bush: George W and Laura   former US President and Wife
Clinton: Bill and Hillary   former US President and Wife
Reagan: Ron and Nancy   former US President and Wife
Kennedy: Jack and Jackie   former US President and Wife
Nixon: Richard and Patricia   former US President and Wife
Irwin: Steve and Terry   "Crocodile Hunter" 2000s TV adventure series
Fonda: Henry, Peter, Jane   A family of major Hollywood movie stars
"Bunker": Archie and Edith   "All in the Family" 1970s TV comedy series

Female Dominant Matripolar Families:

Gore: Al and Tipper   former US Vice President and Wife
Carter: Jimmy and Rosalyn   former US President and Wife
Thatcher: Margaret and Denis   former English Prime Minister / Husband
Meir: Golda and Morris   former Israeli Prime Minister / Husband
Ghandi: Indra and Feroz   former Indian Prime Minister / Husband
Curie: Marie and Pierre   former French Scientists
"Arnaz": Ricky and Lucy   "I Love Lucy" 1950s TV comedy series
"Jefferson": George and Louise "The Jeffersons" 1980s TV comedy series
"Bundy": Al and Peggy   "Married with Children", 1990s TV series

---

primitive in contrast to their Cro-Magnon contemporaries.

Recognition of the existence of these two ancient pre-racial lineages emerging from the two evolutionary trees of life to produce contrasting human populations creates a paradigm shift in our understanding of the nature of human relations, both in the past and especially today. The next chapters develop this new context.

Figure 6, Matripolar Cro-Magnon and Patripolar Neanderthal Skulls and Resemblance of Possible Modern Counterparts

Some important points of Chapter 9:

1. There is evidence that life has emerged at least twice on earth, and that as a result two parallel trees of life exist. A major difference between these two forms of life is the opposite reproductive strategies they took.

2. In the Patripolar tree of life, males battle for dominance. All females chose the alpha male winner as best one to father their children. The group ostracizes loser males until the alpha male fails. Then, a new, often infanticidal alpha male emerges to finally gain his reproductive access. Paternity is overwhelmingly from the alpha male.

3. In the Matripolar tree of life, males compete for territory, the winner seizing land closest to an important resource, such as a water hole. When a female comes into heat, as she passes though the territories on the way to the waterhole, she welcomes all males to inseminate her. Unlike in the patripolar system, in the matripolar scheme paternity is random. All matripolar males bond personally to the female and defend her offspring as their own.

4. Thus, in during the evolution of the higher forms of life, there were always parallel representatives at each stage. The higher apes first arose in Africa where Patripolar Orangutans (now extinct in Africa) and Gorillas were of the Patripolar tree of life and Chimpanzees and Bonobos of the Matripolar tree.

5. Near that point in history, the continent of Africa docked against that of Europe. Over time the apes and derivative pre-hominoids migrated out of Africa to create population striations still noticeable in the Eastern Hemisphere. Thus, the Yellow River Valley of the Far East was populated by patripolar orangutans and their yellow skinned descendents. Matripolar bonobos and their black-skinned, straight-haired descendents settled the Indus River Valley in India. The patripolar Mountain Gorillas and their Neanderthal descendents took the Tigris and Euphrates River Valleys. the matripolar Dark Faced Chimpanzees inhabited the Nile River Valley and the Eastern Europe. The patripolar Lowland Gorillas occupied the Rhine River Valley and other Germanic

areas. The matripolar White Faced Chimpanzees and their CroMagnon descendants entered Western Europe across Gibralter.

6. These pre-racial human reproductive differences constitute the topic of Familial Polarity. Table 4 summarizes the opposite courtship, parenting, and child rearing differences between Patripolar Rm-Lf and Matripolar Lm-Rf families. These polarity-based hemisity differences have been documented as neuroanatomical differences between corpus callosal sizes and of the specific lateralities of the Executive Observer in the Anterior Cingulate Cortex of the two "opposites attract" couple types.

7. There are many contrasting physical, behavioral, cultural, social, and religious institutional differences between the human familial polarities. To the educated eye these are visible everywhere.

Section III: Who Are You? Family Friend or Alien Foe?

Chapter 10: Familial Polarity in Daily Life: Consequences of Cross Breeding

Some Men are also from Venus; Some Women are also from Mars: Confusion between Sex and Hemisity.

The success of the books "Men are from Mars, Women are from Venus" (Gray, 1992) and "You Just Don't Understand: Men and Women in Conversation" (Tannen, 1990) was based in part upon their excellent characterization of the hemisity differences between matripolar males and matripolar females. However, a very large number of exceptions to Mars-Venus stereotypes exist. They do not occur because of the unwillingness of these individuals to confront their mixed sexuality, as suggested by one of the authors. Rather, they exist because of the unrecognized existence of a huge population of patripolar humans, whose natural responses are the quite the opposite of those from matripolars. These opposite gender-independent, characterizations originate from the existence of hemisity, a second "either-or" individuality phenomenon beyond sex.

For many Patripolars, simply reversing the pronouns in the "Men are from Mars" book is all that is needed to convert seemingly bizarre sexual identity comments into poignant familiar expressions of personal conflict. That is, not only just matripolar "females" (Rfs), but also most patripolar males (Rms) wear their feelings on their shirt-sleeves, must talk to resolve conflicts, and tend to bump into glass ceilings. Not only just matripolar "males" (Lms), but also most patripolar females (Lfs) are silent but effective, uncomfortable in discussing feelings, prefer to withdraw to their "caves" after conflict, etc. The existence of familial polarity unifies these previously inexplicable differences within the sexes. As mentioned elsewhere, the larger corpus callosum sizes of Rps compared Lps of both familial polarities further support this idea (Morton and Rafto, 2006). Clearly, Feminism, will need redrafting to accommodate these findings (Tannen, 1994).

Romeo and Juliet: Crossed Polarity Interbreeding, a Source of Suffering and Waste

For the last several million years, the robust and gracile hominid populations appear to have remained separate. A provocative question is, "Could they successfully be caused to interbreed today, possibly even producing expressions of "hybrid-vigor"?" Or, would such offspring, like those of other closely-related species, such as horse and donkey, be placid and exhibit prenatal failures in sexual-reproductive development, including sterility seen in other animal hybrids? In this era of globalization with its great translocations of peoples and consequent inadvertent mixing of populations from both polarities, many such experiments have unknowingly occurred. Often in fact, families on our own block are presently carrying out these experiments. As the spouse hemisity distribution study indicated, there are many right-right, and left-left family pairs, even though these non-complimentary familial polarity crosses are still in the minority and hopefully will remain so.

In terms of courtship, another familiar form of the double standard is seen. That is, in terms of sexual gratification, "hunks", or" babes" are chosen for "predatory" dating recreation. Quite another standard applies for that "ideal" person one wishes to marry. Biologically, both Rms and Rfs are the partners who tend to have an eternally roving eye. At times, some of these can be sexually aggressive conquistadors. In contrast most Lps, once married, may remain faithful. Thus, R-R combinations can make for white- hot affairs, but often can explode as the least stable of marriages. L-L combinations tend to be more platonic as affairs, but can be lead to the most stable, if unexciting of marriages. Unfortunately, as will be seen next, both of these mixed polarity combinations have serious consequences in terms of the pre- and postnatal development of their offspring.

Prenatally, these effects occur *in utero* when the multiple crossed midline structures of the central nervous system are laid down. In familial polarity hybrids (between a patripolar and a matripolar parent), only one set of chromosomes instead of the usual two is of the same polarity. In the absence of the second set of similar polarity chromosomes, or because of the presence of a set of chromosomes of opposite familial polarity, apparently some of these essential midline neural crossings either occur inappropriately or are omitted altogether. This may not be lethal to the fetus, but instead can result in an infant with specific nonlethal birth defects that grows into adulthood with misdirected drives and appetites. Thus, mules and hinnies are talented and impressive animals, possessing traits, some of which are more useful than those of either horses or donkeys. Yet, they are infertile. Might similar anomalies exist between Patripolar-Matripolar human hybrids?

Studying the genetics of trans-polarity crosses involved preparing many three to five generation family genealogies. From these, a coherent Mendelian genetic pattern has been recognized (Morton, unpublished). Some interesting, perhaps surprising anomalies were recognized.

Loss of the Same Sex Hemisity Relationship between Parent and Child:

The first type of polarity crossbreeding difference found was the following: Crossing of like hemisity parents (Lm-Lf, or Rm-Rf) no longer guaranteed that the child of a parent will have the same hemisity as its parent, but rather it becomes random (previous chapter). Unlike the offspring between parents of the complimentary hemisities, children of crossed polarity families can be either right or left males, or right or left females. In fact, most offspring of Lm-Lf matings are themselves Lps (Morton, unpublished).

Rxp Offspring from Rm-Rf Couples are Dyslexic

A second difference found was that those 50% of right brain-oriented offspring of a Rm-Rf pair turned out to be "right brain crossed persons" (Rxps). Whether male or female, these individuals were without exception developmentally dyslexic, often undiagnosed. In fact, this common situation appears to have sprouted a new remedial reading education industry. Hemisity testing of thousands of individuals has never found a single dyslexic Lp individual.

Understanding the physical basis of hemisity (Morton & Rafto, 2010) makes the probable mechanism causing this developmental dyslexia apparent. These crossed Rxps have their primary-memory viewing screen (mid-dorsolateral prefrontal cortex, Peterides, 2000) on the wrong side. That is, instead of it being on their right side of the brain, so that their nearby right brain executive can easily and directly visualize words and images, their primary-memory viewing screen is located the left side of their brain, and only partly accessible from across the corpus callosum.

Without their primary memory viewing screen nearby, they cannot directly read off names, numbers, or the spelling of words, or automatically have a detailed image in their minds eye of an object in memory from which they could draw a photographic copy. Instead, they must compensate by using laborious rote-memorization to write or say the answers mostly invisible on the other side of their brains. Because of this developmental failure, they can only retrieve this indirect information more slowly and less reliably. However, otherwise they retain full intelligence. They are in fact dyslexic because when their right brain executive succeeds in transferring information to itself from their left brain primary-memory viewing screen, this information comes across the corpus callosum in the form of mirror-images, that is, reversed! This is the presently unrecognized direct mechanism of the image reversals so characteristic of dyslexia, where letters and number segments are often reported to be backward.

Similarly, Rxps can only draw memorized stereotyped, formulaic cartoons in order to generate objects they wish to depict, objects that normally subject to copying directly in detail from their elaborate primary-memory if their right brain mental screen was properly present on the same side. The occasional dramatic improvement in realism occurring when producing drawings with the non-dominant hand (Edwards, 1993) further supports this mechanism.

These often highly intelligent individuals suffer greatly because they naturally assume their brains connect normally. Therefore, because others can do these things so much faster and better than they can, they attack their self image internally as being stupid and no good, Or for egoistic reasons, they may turn their attack upon external targets, rejecting book learning as irrelevant and seeking other sub-cultural, drug or antisocial means of personal validation. Actually, it takes less intelligence to copy the spelling of a word in plain view on the screen of the mind's eye, than it takes to remember it blind because one's screen is remote or malfunctional. These individuals may also have related problems in both hearing and producing accurate musical rhythms and timings, as Rxm Albert Einstein's music-making companions attested, or as disappointed mates of non-dancing Rxp spouses can assert.

Because Rxps do not have ready photographic access to primary memory possessed by normal Rps, they .are forced to compensate. This leads them to create highly organized categorization systems and elaborate mental filing devices. These creations sometimes develop far more in Rxps than natural for other subtypes with ready access to primary memory. They, and have led to brilliant and valuable insights into the nature of mind (Freud), life (Darwin), and the universe (Einstein).

Although current unrecognized, developmental dyslexics are the persons who suffer from the incapacitating mental blocks of so-called

"Performance Anxiety" or "Choking". With the separation of the Executive Ego on the right sided from its data base screen on the left in these people, transcallosal communication becomes crucial to performance, Under immediate conditions of personal high anxiety, the locus coerulus releases norepinephrine to inhibit the cerebral, cerebellar, and hippocampal cortices. This causes upset decorticate behavior where transcallosal information support is blocked and the Crocodile Id and its instincts must take over. Under situations of personal stress and fear, these compensatory data systems temporarily collapse, leaving the person cut off from their memory screens, and thus literally stupid from "mental blocks". Seconds after this breakdown, they often recover their thoughts, which may well have been brilliant. While Lps and other polarity subtypes may experience debilitating fear, they usually do not go blank under pressure as Rxps do, but rather, increase their performance and often suffer from Type A stress disorders.

Mental blocks can decorticate dyslexics in any condition of high anxiety. These include during speeches, piano recitals, intimidating conversations or oral exams, timed test taking, golfing, motorcycle riding, and many others. Surprise and panic caused the author, who is an excellent superbike rider, to startle, freeze, go off the road and crash several times. He did so after making thousands of perfect high speed turns in familiar territory before and since those incidents. The author did not recognize his dyslexia until late in life. This "blanking out" phenomenon appears related to the reductions of frontal lobe activity, dramatically visualized by SPECT (single proton emission tomography) in certain patients showing a performance decrements under pressure (Amen, 1998).

Reversed Sexual Identities are Found among Lxp Offspring from Rm-Rf Couples

There is a noted third difference in the left brain-oriented offspring of Rm and Rf parents. These crossed Lxp progeny are not dyslexic like their crossed Rxp siblings. Rather, their left executive has direct access to a functional left-brain primary memory screen from which it can easily see and quickly copy words and detailed images. Instead, apparently all of these Lxp crossed offspring arrest in a different aspect of their prenatal sexual development: because of a crossover defect *in utero,* they fail to develop the usual sexual identity. They appear normal in terms of their attraction to the opposite sex, although some are bisexual. However, their sexual identity is the opposite of that of their body sex.

That is, if the Lxm's body was male, they were still heterosexual and highly attracted to females, making good lovers, husbands and fathers. Yet, when observed from a distance these individuals tended to show stereotypic cultural and biological manifestations of femininity, for example often wearing longer hairstyles, softer, more colorful clothes, sometimes sandals, showing feminine speech inflections and body postural mannerisms. Further, when asked to assess of their own gender identity, they made questionnaire choices such as: androgynous, sensitive, receptive, artistic or ambivalent as well as sometimes making frank statements of having a female identity (Morton, unpublished). Although some might call this very large group of men "Wimps", it deserves emphasis that they were heterosexual and often highly functional, artistic, musical, talented individuals, with excellent, if not photographic memories. Soft spoken, gentle "Mr. Rogers" of children's TV fame comes to mind. In spite of his mild demeanor, he was no wimp, but a tattooed Marine.

Similarly, when the crossed Lxp offspring's body was female, they again were heterosexual, highly attracted to males, making good lovers, wives, and mothers. Yet, when observed from afar, they tended to show stereotypic cultural and biological manifestations of masculinity, for example often wearing shorter hair styles, rougher, less florid, more textured clothes, sometimes boots, showing masculine speech inflections and body postural mannerisms. When surveyed regarding their own assessment of their gender identity, they made such choices as: preferring the superior position in intercourse, preference for maleness, stating that "It's a man's world", or having masculine feelings (Morton, unpublished). Although some might call such individuals, "Jocks", it must be emphasized that, while not choosing a very feminine presentation, these women were heterosexual, although bisexuality was also found, and were often highly talented and productive. These male and female Lxp individuals are here named trans-heterosexuals, where -cis (as in organic chemistry) refers to having the same mental sexual identity as one's body sex, while in -trans cases it is opposite to one's body sex. It must be stressed that Lxps are not those confused persons saying "Help I'm trapped in the wrong sexed body! I want a sex change operation!" Instead, Lxps presently are unidentified among us and thus lack recognizable titles to for their categorization.

Furthermore, these Lxp offspring from Rm and Rf couples, besides being trans-heterosexual, have two additional unusual features. First, the emotion generating side of their brain was located on the left side, unlike normal Lp offspring where it resided on the right (Morton, 2000c).

Secondly, in a mirror-tracing task, right-handed, Lxp, crossed polarity offspring did best when using the right hand, as opposed to the left hand which was fastest for right-handed, Lp, uncrossed polarity-individuals (Morton, 2000c).

We are only now becoming aware of the existence of a large reservoir of yet poorly defined genetic social behaviors. It is theoretically possible that in individuals of hybrid familial polarity, portions of these behaviors have developed modified, non-orthodox associations, such as in pedophilia. Similarly some of these behavioral elements could be inactivated altogether leaving the individual lacking in certain social skills. With this in mind, how do we account for the observation that most individuals attracted to the Gothic style of body piercings, tattoos, and infatuation with the black symbols of death, tend to be Lxps? Similarly, most bisexuals appear to be Lxps.

Might many of these individuals deeply feel abnormal, sometimes antisocial impulses, resulting from these cross wirings that bring them unorthodox impulses? Might they in their attempts to be authentic to their abnormal misdirected drives bring about rejection or ostracization by their peers? Might they despair in their forced attempts to be normal and socially acceptable? Might they develop a profound disrespect for their reversed sexual identity impulses, for their mismatched bodies, and ultimately for these perversions coming from life itself? Are these the intelligent, angry, premeditated deliverers of vengeance upon their more normal enemies that culminate in Columbine type of school killing-suicides? Adolescence appears to be a particularly difficult time for Lxps. They need to be encouraged to rise above their antisocial impulses. Most Lxps ultimately overcome their sensitivities and successfully integrate into society to become talented and contributing members and go on to have families of their own. However, in the case of Lm-Lf couples, there is higher childlessness. Might this come from a significantly higher number of spontaneous abortions, possibly due to a higher portion of fetal defects from this combination?

As new theories commonly appear to their originators to provide a possible explanation of the origin of schizophrenia, which occurs in about 1% of the population worldwide, such ideation is unavoidable here as well. Because more than half the genes altered in schizophrenia were also found modified in bipolar illness, perhaps this malady should also be added to the list as well. Thus, in certain of the possible patripolar-matripolar second generation hybrid combinations, schizophrenic and bipolar individuals are proposed to result from a brain developmental failure *in utero,* due to absence or excess of critical developmental factors.

One in Four Offspring from Lm-Lf Couples were Homosexual

Regarding the offspring between Lm and Lf parents, there were few Rps, and an extraordinary abundance of Lps. It appears that absence of a Rp parent can result in a different type of arrest in sexual differentiation, one resulting in homosexuality (Morton, unpublished). That is, quite independent from one's own sexual identity, one's sex-love partner preference is a second and quite separate prenatal brain sexual development step. Here, the term "heterosexual" refers to those for whom the body sex of their preferred sex-love partner is opposite to their own, while "homosexual" strictly refers only to those individuals preferring partners whose body sex is the same as theirs. These two terms referring to sex-love partner preference, are unrelated to those of cis- or trans-personal sexual identity, described above for Lxps.

Thus, both uncrossed matripolar and patripolar sons are always heterosexual-cis males (Men). If, however, because of cross polarity interbreeding, one or the other of the two independent sexual differentiation steps fail, the offspring will either be heterosexual-trans males (Wimps) or homosexual-cis males (Gays). If both critical stage steps fail, homosexual-trans males (Queens) result. This is the first mechanism to adequately describe the inherent origin and existence of homosexuality.

Similarly, both uncrossed matripolar and patripolar daughters are always heterosexual cis-females (Women). If one or the other sexual development steps fail, then either the offspring will be heterosexual trans females (Jocks) or homosexual-cis females (Lesbians). Homosexual-trans women (Dykes) are the offspring resulting from arrests in both stages of brain sexual differentiation. That all of these valuable and talented types of humans occur in about ten percent of some populations is consistent with the relative mixing predicted to be occurring between the polarities. Partly because of ignorance of familial polarity, the level of inner and interpersonal suffering of these non-orthodox offspring is considerably elevated over that of uncrossed offspring.

On a related topic, regardless of original polarity, considerable reproductive confusion results when, instead of the original "boy meets girl", one has now to have to select between 16 heterosexual or 32 different total subtypes of individuals varying in sexual identity and partner preference, not counting the dyslexics. Overall, this crossed polarity biology appears to be an important factor in the destabilization of marriage and the family as institutions, and an increase in violence. This is especially apparent at population interfaces between the polarities and also in the new global melting-pot cities, but which also occurred anciently, as in the decline and fall of Rome.

It was not without evidence that Rm, Adolph Hitler, and later, Lm, Slobidon Milosevic both decried the deterioration of their races due to cross breeding. They did not know about Familial Polarity but noticed deterioration by hybrid offspring between Germanics and Slavs/Jews, and of Serbs and Albanians. They attempted to protect their races with eugenics "Ethnic Cleansing" and genocide with very serious negative consequences. These observations pose a massive and interesting challenge to the Human Genome Project, which in theory should be able ultimately to clarify all of these issues.

Figure 1 diagrams 16 possible combinations that can occur in cross breeding between heterosexual persons of pure and hybrid familial polarity. It is predictable that at least another 16 possibilities arise with the addition of homosexual persons. A synonym for the reproductive strategy term, Patripolar, is Haremic (harem forming), while for the Matripolar reproductive strategy, the synonymous term is Orgeic (orgy having).

Figure 1, part A, displays a genetic representation of each of the four possible couples: Rm-Lf (Patripolar-Haremic), Rm-Rf (R-hybrid-Hargeic), Lm-Lf (L-hybrid-Oremic), and Lm-Rf (Matripolar-Orgeic) and their unique identical F^1-generation offspring. The many F^2-generation possibilities follow. As may be seen, random selection between mating hybrids produces two or four different types of offspring possibilities. Fortunately, wild type throwbacks are possible 25 or 50% of the time. In many geographic areas, hybrid individuals are common and the original wild types are rare. When wild-type Rps occur, they are very impressive and often rise to positions of leadership (e.g. Bill Clinton, Barak Obama, Golda Meir, Indira Gandhi).

Figure 1, part B, lists a proposed nomenclature to name the eight partners within the 12 possible heterosexual couples. For example, in a family of pure patripolars, for example, there is the Rf King and Lf Queen. In contrast, in a family of pure matripolars there is the Rf Empress and the Lm Prime Minister. Among the Hargeic hybrid couples, there is the Rxm Chuckle Head, and the Lxf Jock. Among the Oremic hybrid couples, there is the Lxm Wimp and the Rxf Dingbat. Clearly the remaining "Hot" Rxm-Rxl couple consist of a Chucklehead and a Dingbat, while the "Cool" Lxm-Lxf couple are composed of a Wimp and a Jock. Last, there are the Rm-

Figure 1. Possible Hetero Offspring from the 16 Parent Polarity Matches

A.

First Generation:

Non-complementary Homo-polaric Crossed Parentage

Haremic	Hargeic	Oremic	Orgeic
R-L pair (M-F)	R-R pair	L-L Pair	L-R pair

R-bom Father

	H	H
L-bof H	HH	HH
Mother H	HH	HH

R-R pair H H

	H	H
O	HO	HO
O	HO	HO

L-L Pair O O

	O	O
H	OH	OH
H	OH	OH

L-R pair O O

	O	O
O	OO	OO
O	OO	OO

Offspring Possible (within the 4-way box)

Second Generation: All are of Crossed Polarity Parentage

Fathers: genome is horizontal →

R-Lx pair H H

	H	H
O	HO	HO
H	HH	HH

Mothers: → genome is vertical

R-Rx pair H H

	H	H
H	HH	HH
O	HO	HO

L-Lx pair O O

	O	O
O	OO	OO
H	OH	OH

L-Rx pair O O

	O	O
H	OH	OH
O	OO	OO

Rx-L pair O H

	O	H
H	OH	HH
H	HH	HH

Rx-R pair O H

	O	H
O	OO	HO
O	OO	HO

Lx-L pair H O

	H	O
H	HH	OH
H	HH	OH

Lx-R pair H O

	H	O
O	HO	OO
O	HO	OO

Rx-Lx pair O H

	O	H
O	OO	HO
H	OH	HH

Rx-Rx pair O H

	O	H
H	OH	HH
O	OO	HO

Lx-Lx pair H O

	H	O
O	HO	OO
H	HH	OH

Lx-Rx pair H O

	H	O
H	HH	OH
O	HO	OO

B. Code for the 8 Possible Heterosexual Offspring within the 4-way Boxes (above).:

	H H	O H	H O	O O
Male	R King	R Dyslexic Chuckle-Head	L Trans-Heterp. Wimp	L Prime Minister
Female	L Queen	L Trans-Heterp. Jock	R Dyslexic Ding-Bat	R Empress
	Haremics	Hargeics	Oremics	Orgeics

Dominant in pair ← → (Haremics)

pseudo-dominant (Hargeics → Oremics)

Dominant in pair ← → (Orgeics)

Lxm (King-Jock) couples, the Rxm-Lx (Chucklehead-Queen) couples, the Rm-Rxf (King-Dingbat) couples, the Rxm-Rf (Chucklehead-Empress) couples, the Lm-Lxm (Prime Minister-Jock) couples and the Lxm and Lf (Wimp-Queen) couples.

Crossed Polarity Families: Infant Traumatization and Arresting of Critical Periods of Psychosocial Brain Development:

Not only has cross polarity interbreeding added to the destabilization of marriage and the family by causing the above developmental failures *in-utero,* it also inevitably leads to major postnatal developmental traumatization of normal infants and young children. This occurs in spite of the best intentions and efforts of their concerned parents. It is becoming clear that closure of many if not most of the critical periods of psychosocial brain development occurs by the third year of childhood. Thwarting of the completion of these critical periods (for gaining control over mental operations before their developmental windows close) can lead to permanent arresting and failure. The reversal of parental dominance roles in early and later childhood can cause this (Morton, unpublished). Unfortunately, this traumatizing environment has life-long, socially disabling consequences.

For example, biologically, a Lm son needs a subdominant Lm father to unconditionally love and support him as his assistant whether the son obeys him or not. If a Lm son has the bad luck to have a Rm father instead, such an inherently dominant and standards-demanding father can never let his son disobey him. In fact, all his parental instincts will oppose this and he will attempt to force obedience from the boy at all costs. However, due to the son's Lm biology, this obedience is impossible, something he would rather die than permit. While escalated demands of obedience from his mismatched father are ultimately met with overt rebellion, paradoxically, the obedience and cooperation of Lm son are easily obtained by his Rf mother.

Endless conflicts of parental polarity mismatches during childhood appear to have led to the emergence of modern mental illnesses such as bipolar disorder (Morton, 2000j), multiple personality disorder, anorexia, Pre Menstrual Syndrome and other maladies that are unique to modern culture (Castillo, 1997). However, if the above son had been a Rm, out of respect and admiration he would willingly and easily have been able to honor his Rm father's requests without complaint, in fact, with pleasure and pride. However, he may not obey his Lf mother. In addition, a mismatched Rm son will endlessly struggle for dominance over an Rf mother. However, this is something that she cannot allow biologically, to the long-term misery of both. A reversed scenario exists for daughters.

These developmental arrests block the attainment of the social control skills required for an amicable nuclear family and later effective social interactions. This automatically impairs and deteriorates the later outcomes of education, mate and vocational choice, employment, supportive family and community participation, as well as harming emotional and physical health. These maladies of cross-polarity families add to the generalized dysphoria and alienation of modern culture. Thus, ignorance of the pre and postnatal developmental-arresting effects of cross-polar breeding is adding unnecessary suffering to life, both intrapersonally and interpersonally between families and within communities. This cultural and political weakening of the institutions of marriage and the extended family is quite severe. A peaceful cooperative marriage and extended family are genetically essential to provide the sheltering, stability, and support required for optimal emotional growth and success in the psychosocial development of children.

On the other hand, without Albert Einstein's struggle to surmount his dyslexia, would he have been stimulated to inquire as deeply into the whys of the universe as he did? Or, without the suffering produced by trans- or homosexuality, would some of the world's greatest artists have arisen to express their angst? These are small, but significant consolations.

It is crucial to note with emphasis that issues of race are are quite separate from those of familial polarity, as indicated by the following. Pure polarity families, even between partners of totally different races, appear not only to avoid dyslexia and sexuality deficits, but also avoid psychosocial developmental arrests, even in their mixed-race children (Morton, unpublished). In contrast, the above genetic and developmental problems automatically appear in the offspring crossed polarity families within the same race, whether black, brown, yellow or white.

Finally, ignorance of the genetic differences between the many subtypes of familial polarity may affect health care. Currently, most medical standards come from averaging of sampling of subjects within the same sex and age. Everybody's samples combine in a pot and the resulting medical values are averaged to become the standard. This obscures the true physical, medical and psychological differences between the hemisity and possibly the polarity subtypes for each sex. For example, Lps are much more sensitive to many drugs and environmental factors than are Rps.

In the next chapter we will switch from the individual differences within familial polarity to the impact these have had upon and are having on world history.

Some Important Concepts from Chapter 10:

1.   There have always been behavioral problems when parallel species from the two trees of life attempt to interbreed. Crossing of foxes and wolves is not well studied, nor crocodiles and alligators, or even rats and mice. However, hybrid offspring of lions and tigers, and of course, horses and donkeys are well known. As adults, these hybrids are infertile as might be expected because of the opposite reproductive strategies used by organisms of the two trees of life.

2.   Thus, interbreeding of humans with opposite familial polarities might also result in reproductive anomalies. The first of these observed was that in cross polarity pairs, the "like mother, like daughter", "like father like son" regularities of the hemisity of children from pure polarity families were lost. In like-like, cross-polar couples (Rm-Rf or Lm-Lf), the hemisity of the children is random and unpredictable.

3.   The second anomaly noticed was that the Rxp offspring from Rm-Rf couples were developmentally dyslexic, but none of their Lxp siblings were. Albert Einstein is a classical example of an Rxm.

4.   Third, instead of dyslexia, the Lxp offspring from Rm-Rf couples had reversed sexual identities. This has led to intrapersonal confusion and in certain cases to undesirable compensatory behaviors.

5.   In contrast to the Rm-Rf pairs, Lm-Lf couples tended to have more spontaneous abortions, and in one study, one in four of their children were homosexual.

6.   The concept of Familial Polarity and its potential for interbreeding has provided a logical basis for the origin of Developmental Dyslexia, the reversal of sexual identity, and that of homosexuality.

7. In crossed polarity families, there are also increased chances of infant traumatization and arresting because of parent-child hemisity mismatches.

8. Thus, all men are NOT created equal, except in their right to freedom and the pursuit of happiness *without harm to others*.

NEUROREALITY: A SCIENTIFIC RELIGION TO RESTORE MEANING
Section III: Who Are You? Family Friend or Alien Foe?

Chapter 11: Rewriting the History of Violence: Ignorance of Familial Polarity Kills

Prehistory of Familial Polarity

Anciently, small but growing populations of humans of distributed in such a way that patripolar and matripolar stock striations were generally isolated from each other (Chapter 9). One married someone from one's own village, such as the girl next door, thus keeping both lineages pure. However, things changed as populations increased and overlapped into cities. Then one might marry someone from work instead from one's own tribe, often someone of opposite familial polarity. In addition, marauding patripolar barbarians coming from the east on horseback, endlessly raped and pillaged matripolar farmlands. This resulted in the production of large numbers of hybrid offspring, some of which were noted even by Greek and Roman times to be different than the normal human stock in terms of sexual orientation.

Two prescient independent yet parallel syntheses of the prehistory of human conflict were written in the absence of knowledge of dyadic evolution and its consequent familial polarity. In "The Chalice and the Blade" (1987) and "Sacred Pleasure" (1995), Riane Eisler clearly distinguished early female dominant "Gylanic" cultures, which were obviously matripolar in lineage, from the later destructive male dominant "Dominator" cultures, which clearly were patripolar. In "Saharasia", James DeMeo also traced the rise of desert "Armored Patrism", around 4000 BC with the domestication of the horse. Horsemen then began to prey upon the low-violence forest "Unarmored Matrism" cultures of the Old World. With the here added focus of Familial Polarity, each of these well-documented theses can be seen to further illustrate and clarify the existence of Matripolar and Patripolar cultures and their inevitable conflicts.

Table 1, a brief summary of earth history since the last Ice Age 14,000 years ago, places these familial polarity conflicts in perspective.

Table 1, Post Ice Age History of the Current Era.

12,000 BC: Ice recedes, Forests regrow to cover the earth, Present era begins
12,000 BC: Impossible monumental stone megaliths are built by the Unknowns

10,000 BC: Plant abundance leads to unrestricted human population growth and spread
9,900 BC: Oldest continuous tree ring record reaches back to this point in time

9,000 BC: Clovis arrowhead points are left behind in the North America
8,500 BC: Decline of big game in Northern Hemisphere due to overhunting

8,000 BC: Game animals are domesticated: cattle in Africa; goats in Iraq; Herding grows
8,000 BC: Crops are domesticated in Near East: Wheat, barley, lentils: Forests are cleared.

7,000 BC: Matripolaric Cooperator civilizations. Unwalled cities, rich in art, technology
6,000 BC: Desertification begins: exploited high pop. areas: Sahara, Arabia, Gobi fail.

5,000 BC: Starvation and battles for limited resources begin. Patripolars adapt to badlands.
4,500 BC: Patripolar violent reproductive strategy and greater size. defeats Matri- males.

4,000 BC: Horse domesticat. by Patripolars on Ukraine steppes. Nomadic conquests begin.
3,500 BC: Mounted patripolars with metal weapons cross Old World, "Live off the land",
        raping, killing, burning, raiding, until agriculture was impossible, except in spots.
3,300 BC: Otzi got arrow in neck in Alps: Tattoo acupuncture points on back, copper axe.
3,000 BC: Patripolars parasitize cultures. Keep themselves separate, install Caste Systems.
        Forests cut for ships and to smelt metal weapons. Moses overgrazes. Desertification.

2,500 BC: Horseback child rearing creates psychoses. Female genital mutilation, Ritual
        Widow murder, Cross-polar hybrids are common, Homosexuality rampant.
1,500 BC: Patripolar Greek Golden Age begins.

800 BC: Matripolar Roman males suppress females, dominate w. patripolar mercenaries.
33 BC: Rxm dyslexic Jesus is Born, and the roots of Christianity are laid.

313 AD: Lm Constantine supports Christianity as the religion of the Roman Empire
622 AD: Rm Mohammed founds Islam.

1000 AD: Dark Ages of religious domination and cultural stagnation.
1517 AD: Rm Luther, the Protestant Reformation, and European Renaissance begins.

1859 AD: Rxm dyslexic Darwin publishes his Origin of the Species.
1915 AD: Rxm dyslexic Einstein develops the theory of general relativity.

1945 AD: Atom bombs were dropped on Japan.
1953 AD: DNA structure is published.

2003 AD: Human DNA Genome is sequenced.

Familial Polarity and the Origins of Judaism:

Biblical Abraham was a successful patripolar herdsman from the city of Ur in the Tigris and Euphrates river valley of Iraq. Taking advantage of a temporary wet period, he migrated with his flocks and herds south into Palestine. With him, he brought his patriarchal religion, based upon Laws of Hammurabi, and the Gilgamesh Epic. In Palestine, Joseph, a favorite son of Jacob, Abraham's grandson, was sold to slave traders traveling to Egypt. There, Joseph was sold on the slave block to an upper class Egyptian Matripolar Rf woman to be her household assistant, and not unexpectedly, her stud. Sexually inexperienced Rm Joseph from the Patripolar "virginity until marriage" culture spurned her amorous advances. Furious, she had him thrown in jail with a five-year sentence to force him to grow up.

While in an Egyptian prison, Joseph repeatedly demonstrated his right brain big picture facility for the interpretation of dreams. This greatly impressed his cellmate, one of Pharaoh's wine tasters, temporarily jailed due to palace intrigue. Later reinstated, the wine taster became aware of dreams troubling the Pharaoh himself. At the wine taster's recommendation, Joseph obtained the opportunity again to apply his skill with symbolism and metaphor. He interpreted Pharaoh's dreams in such a satisfying manner that the monarch ultimately made him Prime Minister. Joseph was made responsible for bringing about his proposed solution to the king's dilemma. Thus, he supervised the building of an extensive grain silo system to store the abundance arising from the "fat years" of temporarily abundant rainfall.

A few years later, the wet period ended and the "lean years" came. The drought decimated Abraham's flocks and herds still in the Levant. To ward off starvation, Abraham's sons traveled to Egypt, by then known to be an abundant source of food. There, Joe gets the last laugh on his brothers. Later, with his help, his father's family immigrates to Egypt for eight generations. (How many of us today know the names of our ancestors eight generations earlier?) There, during those roughly 300 years, they freely interbreed as slaves, and thus became genetically transformed into matripolars, unlike their still-patripolar Arabian cousins who remained behind.

Chapter 1 of this book speculates on Moses' use of the "Ark of the Covenant" to bring about the exodus of the Israelites from Egypt back to Palestine, their God promised land. It is of interest that, in addition to the

Egyptians of Joseph's days being matripolar, the Persian Iranians of the 50 years of Israel's Babylon Captivity were also matripolar. Regardless, it is clear that most Jewish couples today are Lms-Rfs, exhibiting the famous "Jewish Princess" and "Jewish Mother" female dominant syndromes, while most Rabbis are detail-oriented, matripolar Lms, paradoxically still clinging to their ancient patriarchal religious traditions. These opposing elements of familial polarity have a direct bearing on the present seemingly impossible relations between the Jews and the Arabs, and importantly the Iranian Shiites and the Arabian Sunnis. These family pairs are of opposite familial polarities and thus as miscible as oil and water.

Familial Polarity and the Origins of Christianity:

There are several lines of evidence suggesting that Jesus of Nazareth was a Rm, unlike most of his Lm contemporaries. He was different. Jesus had cosmology skills that modern Rm sons have early, but Lms gain only later. These, he demonstrated at age of seven to the priests in the temple.

His Rm nature also showed itself through his emphasis on need for the love of a divine father, such as in his "Lord's Prayer". Neither unwed mother Rf Mary, nor her later husband, Lm Joseph, could have substituted for the genetic need of Jesus for a dominant Rm role model father (Chapter 10). Neither would Rf Mary have been able to give him the unconditional love Rms need from their Lf mothers. Thus, he distanced himself from his family, including Mary and his Lm half- brothers. If we were to deny Mary's "unique in all history" claim of Immaculate Conception, her Rm son could only have come from a hidden intimacy with a patripolar male, such as a Roman soldier or Arab merchant. As a result, it is likely that Jesus may have actually been a Rxm with unnoticed developmental dyslexia like Einstein, Freud and Darwin.

Jesus' possible Rm nature is further supported by his creation and extensive use of politically correct seeming, right brain-derived metaphorical parables with hidden meanings that broke with tradition: "He who hath an ear, let him hear". Also, what would not have been expected from a Lm was his propensity to meditate, his willingness to cry, his emphasis on emotionality in the Sermon on the Mount, and his violent driving of the moneychangers out of the temple.

Provocative Speculation: **One of Several Alternative Interpretations of the Crucifixion, Resurrection, and Translation of Christ:**

Part A: Voodoo, Zombies, and Puffer Fish

Zombification is part of the African Voodoo witchcraft tradition found among former slaves in Haiti. The victim is cursed, treated with a secret potion, falls into a deep coma, is pronounced dead (often by a western M.D), and buried. In the "Night of the Living Dead", he or she is dug up within 6 hours by the witch doctor, called forth, resurrected, drugged with scopolamine, and led away as a mindless zombie slave for abuse by distant landowners.

Tetrodotoxin is a sodium ion channel blocker found in puffer fish skin and viscera. Because sodium ion is essential for nerve transmission, poisoning symptoms range from mild euphoria (as in Japanese Fugu cuisine), to prolonged coma, to death. Several revivals "from the dead" have occurred in modern morgues after puffer fish poisonings. The structure of Tetrodotoxin was determined by Woodard at Harvard University. Wade Davis obtained zombie potions from Haitian witches and took them in to Harvard for analysis and where significant amounts of Tetrodotoxin was found in them, **Figure 1**.

Part B: Possible Tetrodotoxin Poisoning of Jesus on the Cross

Late Friday, the Romans nailed Jesus to a cross between two others on the hill called Golgotha. After hours of anguish, he cried out "I thirst!". On a pole, his followers raised to him a sponge dipped in fish gall (which can contain tetrodotoxin and was commonly used by Roman soldiers in crucifixions), which he took. Not long after he drank this, he said "My God! Why hath Thou forsaken me?" Then, he said "Into thy hands I commit my spirit", "It is finished!" and he "died" (he went into a two day tetrodotoxin coma, awakening early Sunday morning). As the soldiers wanted the victims off the hill by Friday night for the feast the next day, they broke the legs of the still conscious thieves on either side to hasten their death. Jesus, in a death-like coma, was only stabbed in the side before being taken down. Joseph of Aramathea and the "wise man", Nicodemus, asked Pilate for Jesus's body. It was placed in a private stone crypt, covered by a stone door and "guarded" by soldiers (Schonfield, 1965).

194

Figure 1: Scientific Zombification

Narcisse near his "grave"; inset, pointing to a scar made by a coffin nail
From puffer fish and a New World toad, a coma-inducing potion

Time Magazine Oct 7, 1983

Ethnobotanist Wade Davis can explain how zombies are created.

Movie: The Serpent and the Rainbow, 1983

Apparently, Jesus recovered consciousness from the Tetrodotoxin coma early Sunday morning. As is written, he was seen by many of his followers several times over the next few days. During that time, Jesus asked them to meet him at a previously mentioned mountain site in Galilee. When they all met on the mountain, he exhorted them to: "die to the flesh, be reborn of the spirit, and to go forth and teach all nations in my name". Then, he lifted his hands and blessed them. While blessing, he parted from them into the clouds (i.e. he walked up the hill and disappeared into the cloud base of the local marine inversion layer). They are said to have returned to the Temple in Jerusalem, praising God continually.

Later, Jesus apparently migrated to the south of France (Brown, 2003) where he returned to changing water into wine. There he was known as God's child (i.e. Rothschild: *humor)* Thus, did Christianity originate from the life, "death", "resurrection", and "transfiguration" of Rxm, Jesus.

By the time of the Aryan Controversy (over the proposed divinity of Jesus) and of the adaptation of Catholic Christianity as the official state church of matripolar Rome, in the fourth century by Constantine, Mary had become "The Mother of God". After the following more than millennium of "Dark Ages", the sixteenth century Protestant Reformation began, initiating the modern era. It started in Germany with Martin Luther, a patripolar Catholic priest. Among other things, Luther protested was the demasculinization of Christianity and the overemphasis of the feminine in the Mariolatry that then existed. His protest, along with that of others, led to a Reformation of Christian church, and ultimately to the many of the Protestant denominations of today. Protestantism has had its strongest appeal in patripolar population centers such as in Germany, Switzerland, Scotland, Northern Ireland, and now in within the Republican United States "Bible Belt" (Morton, unpublished).

Familial Polarity and Its Impact on Modern Forms of Government

As with any new paradigm, a restructuring of the fabric of knowledge occurs with consequent waves and ripples extending from its epicenter. Examples of such exist, not only in the patripolar Protestant Reformation, but also in the patripolar founding and development of the United States. This places a new perspective upon the attempts of charismatic patripolar Puritan, Pilgrim and Quaker males to escape the tyranny of the "moral majority" present in the established matripolar ethnic blocks of the Old World. That is, they wished to enjoy the freedom of belief and worship, which is never permitted under the religious legalism, censure, and oppression imposed by matripolar males wherever they become unified by their hierarchal territorial dogma.

The American Revolution further elaborated this freedom theme under the leadership of such patripolar males as Benjamin Franklin and Thomas Jefferson. In the Civil War, the patripolar Confederates of the white south who wished secede in order to use slaves in a form of economic competition in spite of the wishes of the national majority, again repeated this drive for freedom. More recently the founding of the LDS (Mormon), and other patripolar Christian denominations dramatized this patripolar separation-isolation theme. For example, a number of recent U.S. social rebels came from patripolar Seventh-day Adventist, conscientious-objector roots. These include Malcom X, David Koresh and Lee Malvo. The Mormon-derived polygamists should not be overlooked, either. Yet, these thematic sub-elements pale in the face of patripolar Islamic history

Table 2: The World Religions were Founded by Charismatic Patripolar Males:

Judaism:	<u>*Abraham:*</u> patripolar – Patriarchal, Jews become matripolar after 300 yrs (eight generations) in Egypt
Christianity:	<u>*Jesus;*</u> patripolar, Early church and Protestantism. Later, Catholicism amalgamated with Roman worship of sun and feminine to become more matripolar: Mariolatry
Islam:	<u>*Mohammed:*</u> patripolar, male dominance in home and government. Persian Shiites are matripolar and often in conflict with patripolar Abrabian Sunis.
Confucianism:	<u>*Confucius:*</u> patripolar, male dominant in home and government, Northern Orient
Taoism:	<u>*Lao-Tse:*</u> patripolar (North China) and matripolar (South China)
Buddhism:	<u>*Gothama:*</u> patripolar and matripolar Segments: Theravada vs. Miyahana Buddhism
Hinduism:	<u>*Unknown patripolar Arian*</u>: later Dravidian matripolar engulfment
Jainism:	<u>*Vardhamana:*</u> patripolar : no killing, lying, stealing, adultery, or greed
Sikhism:	<u>*Nanak:*</u> patripolar

and possible "Battle of Armageddon" familial polarity interpretations of current Middle East Conflict. As a generalization then, it would appear that religion and culture have followed the biology of familial polarity, not vice versa. That is, it is here asserted that all the founders of the world's religions were patripolar males as outlined in **Table 2**.

Familial Polarity and the Logic of National Governance Styles: Autocracy vs. Democracy

Fundamental political differences between the naturally different power structure orientations of the two polarities have been a major obstacle to the achievement of a stabile mixed polarity society. In the past, patriarchal Haremic males not only settled their reproductive rights by physical combat, but also their political leadership. Anciently, the winner of individual combat and consequently the harem leader regularly demanded acts of physical submission from each formerly excluded male (as in primate bachelor camps) before allowing him to join his camp. In some modern primates, a submissive genuflection of the subordinate before the alpha male's erect penis is required (McLean, 1978).

Anciently, as a not too far-fetched suggestion, this essential loyalty step brought to the harem the benefits of added male partnership while securely protecting the leader's breeding rights by the establishment of an early form of the death penalty: "Touch my women and I'll kill you!" Later, acts of obeisance, that is, pledges of absolute obedience were demanded of all male followers. These then became oaths of allegiance, whereby the follower would swear literally upon the loss of his testicles if he were to disobey the orders of the leader, and that his "testi"mony was true. Such laws and "testi"ments were followed implicitly as long as the leader was in power in the fatherland. The leader commonly administered spontaneous "tests" of submission to his followers.

The current existence among educated and intelligent modern Haremic males of a powerful underlying dominance psychology is abundantly demonstrated by the extraordinarily-powerful patriarchal top-down autocracies of Adolph Hitler, Mohandas Gandhi, and Saddam Hussein. Their followers followed orders as if their life depended upon it. Moralistic criticism on past cases notwithstanding, under such circumstances it would be unthinkable on many levels to disobey the leader chief, and indeed such almost never happened.

In contrast, the orgeic matripolar path to and style of male leadership is opposite to the haremic patripolar pattern. Thus, orgeic culture is a matriarchal and nonviolent democratic commune where age and wisdom are revered. Originally, all males in the camp nonviolently competed against each other in their courtship of the reproductively dominant female. She selected and retained each of them, only after receiving their individual submission and pledge undying love to her and her children in the motherland. Because each male potentially had sex with all of females bearing offspring into the clan, each child was viewed as his own. Thus, he was also blood-bonded to the troupe by family loyalty.

While the queen attended to global goals, such as the long-range planning of the camp, a trusted prime minister consort, the temporarily dominant alpha-male attended the important daily details. He arrived at his tentative conclusions by robust competition with the ideas of the other males in his parliamentary gang. This was an early form of bottom-up democracy. However here, all votes were not equal, but instead each weighted by the member's personal status within the troupe.

Attempts to govern mixed polaric groups, either under *only* autocracy or *only* democracy have resulted in centuries of conflict and hatred, and still are unfortunately underway. However, if patripolar autocratic order and constraint was the original thesis, and matripolar democratic freedom and chaos its antithesis, then the republican-democracies represent the synthesis of the two. Of the more recent solutions to governance of populations of mixed polarity, the presidential two party government of the USA, a republican democracy informed by Greek democratic and French Revolution models, has been the most successful in creating a balanced golden mean, at least for brief periods

In the dialectic left "thesis", the citizens and society are represented in the U.S.A. by the predominantly Lm Democratic Party, while at the dialectic right "antithesis", wealthy land owners, businesses, and other vested power interests are represented by the predominantly Rm Republican Party. As both of these totally legitimate political party orientations fight vigorously for the advantage of their own interests, the pendulum swings back and forth, and the country as a whole staggers down the middle of the road. However, in the end they can only be led to a useful compromise by the authority of the president and his vice-president. This compromise represents the dialectic "synthesis", the golden mean, whereby the nation is guided down the middle road of optimal survival. In a recent period of unparalleled prosperity, charismatic president Bill Clinton was a Rm and Vice-president Al Gore was a Lm, thus inherently non-charismatic. Now, with knowledge of the existence and effects of familial polarity sub-populations, it becomes theoretically possible to logically design new types of governments that can replace current global conflict with greater cooperation and mutual benefit within and across the polaric cultures.

In the American form of democracy, all votes are equal and including those of the females. This golden mean deviates both from the

Orgeic (matripolar) hierarchal style of status where no one is equal, and
the Haremic (patripolar) style of dominance where women's votes are
fused with their husbands. Relevant to the latter is the case of Lm former
president Jimmy Carter, who with his Rf wife, Rosalyn, threatened to leave
the patriarchal Baptist Church because of their belief that women are not
naturally subservient to men. This is absolutely the case for matripolars.
However, since most Protestants are patripolar (and Republican), many Rm
Baptist men and, interestingly, their Lf women feel the reverse is true.

   Occasionally it is advantageous to become that rare crossover from
the opposite side. Thus, Rm child-Jesus talking with the Lm temple
scholars was unusual, as was Rm Gandhi as a Hindu, the charismatic Rm
Kennedy's as Catholics, non-charismatic Lm Jimmy Carter as a Baptist,
and charismatic Rm Bill Clinton as a Democrat, stealing fire from the Rm
Republicans. Furthermore, to have a charismatic Rm leader includes
implicit acceptance of the Haremic inherently polygamous biology of a
harem leader. Thus, there often will be adoring women with whom to
contend . In this regard, beloved Rm president Kennedy (in spite of his
lovely Lf wife) said, he just could not help his ongoing gross promiscuity.
Interestingly, the US presidents who have been rated as the best,
historically usually have been charismatic Rms (Morton, unpublished).

Unrecognized Global Conflict between Patripolar and Matripolar Human Groups

   From within mankind's present ignorance of Polarity, well-
meaning Lps and Rps, tend to misunderstand each other. Because of
opposite value systems, they commonly disagree, sometimes violently. For,
example, the 1978 Bonn Summit Meetings were held between Lp, Jimmy
Carter of the US and Rp, Helmut Schmidt, of Germany, to settle issues of
mutual interest. Returning from each meeting, reporters on both sides
released the debriefing information to the press in their respective
countries. Both the Carter and Schmidt teams claimed quite different
outcomes resulting from the same meeting. So different, that some of these
men became inflamed, calling each other liars. By the time the meetings
concluded, these individuals, if not nations, had grown to hold each other
in deepest distrust. Yet, they both were teams of sincere, well-meaning
allies, each aligned toward many of the same goals.

   This illustrates the destabilizing effects that unrecognized polarity
differences can produce even in during peacetime international government
interactions. If by accident, Rm Bill Clinton had represented the US at that

time, the outcome no doubt would have been much more positive, as it was for Rm Kennedy. This would not be because Clinton was any better than Carter, but because the polarities of the two national leaders would have matched, and not been crossed. They would have been speaking the same language, Rp-ese, which is considerably different from Lp-ese!

In earlier less stable situations, such matter-anti matter contacts have led to repeated annihilations. In fact, most of written world history centers on these polaric conflagrations. Such remained as relatively local events of human misery, until the advent of the industrial revolution and the beginnings of modern war technology. From then, wars became increasingly massive slaughters on increasingly global levels, leading to the advent of the World Wars. In the first world war, Patripolar Germany, Austro-Hungary and Turkey took on Matripolar Britain, France and Russia in clashes of higher mortality than the earth had yet seen.

After these two Giants picked themselves up and licked their millions of wounds, Round 2, the Second World War, followed between with self-same Haremics giants against their same European Orgeic mortal enemies. However, this time the chaos expanded. While the European Titans were preoccupied in mutual annihilation, Patripolar Japan went on a rampage of conquest and subjugation in Matripolar areas in Southeast Asia. Fortunately, for the outcomes of both of these world war rounds, a successfully governed, mixed-polarity country (USA) was able to neutralize the champions, but at great cost. Clearly, bringing permanent solutions to these escalating dialectic battles between universal Ying and Yang is of the highest priority. With the explosion of technology and the addition of Islamic and Northern Oriental Patripolars to the conflagration, a Round 3 Armageddon could eliminate all humanoids from the planet.

That the two human polarities have continued to resist interbreeding even in the present is indicated by the specific locations of repeated global unrest, violence and genocide. These are usually found in the Eastern Hemisphere at immiscible interfaces between two biologically different populations of opposite polarities (Morton, unpublished). In many cases, these have been sites of violent conflict for centuries, sometimes millennia. **Table 3** identifies many of these "Hot Spots of Violence" as recurring global sites of killing or genocide. Amazingly, 20 / 21 (95%) of these were at the interface between populations of opposite familial polarity! This startling observation adds a new dimension to achieving our goal of global peace. Certainly these facts can be utilized to enable us to

Table 3, Modern History: Matter vs. Antimatter at Interfaces between Polaric Populations

	French **vs.** Germans	
	Russians, Slavs **vs.** Germans	
	Jews **vs.** Germans	
MATRIPOLARS	English **vs.** Scottish	**PATRIPOLARS**
	Southern **vs.** Northern Irish	
	Italians **vs.** Sicilians	
	Spaniards **vs.** Moors	
MOTHERLAND	Spaniards **vs.** Basques	FATHERLAND
	Jews **vs.** Arabs	
	Serbs **vs.** Albanians	
"MOTHER!!!"	Russians **vs.** Chechnians	"FATHER!!!"
	Armenians **vs.** Turks	
"MOTHER !!!"	Indians **vs.** Pakistanis	"FATHER !!!"
	Indians **vs.** Sieks	
"I'M DYING !!!"	Hutu Farmers **vs.** Watutsi Warriors	"SAVE ME!!!"
	South **vs.** North Korea	
"SAVE ME!!!"	South **vs.** North Vietnam	"I'M DYING!!!"
	Philippines **vs.** Moros	
	Romans **vs.** Greeks	
	*Sri Lankan Sinhalese **vs.** Indian Tamils	

* The one case of these twenty-one examples that was not Cross Polar

evolve to the next level of human evolution: from the killing of **Figure 2** to nonkilling!

Hemisity Sampling of Current Distributions of Matripolar and Patripolar Populations:

In studies of familial polarity, large amounts of data have accumulated from the measurement of hemisity of over 1000 individuals within the community of the University of Hawaii at its research campus in

Manoa were over 20,000 multiethnic students are enrolled (Morton, unpublished). These preliminary data, tabulated in **Table 4**, indicated that individuals, drawn from specific ethnic or geographic locations of diverse populations of familial polarity, varied greatly in their relative Matripolar to Patripolar ratios (M/P Ratio). For example, individuals of Germanic, Middle East or the Northern Orient origins appeared to be predominantly Patripolar in composition with low M/P Ratios. In contrast, many Southern European, and some, but not all Southeast Asian populations appeared to be predominantly Matripolar in hemisity, each having high M/P Ratios.

Figure 2, A History of Endless, Needless, Global Conflict and Slaughter

Matripolar Slavic Cro-Magnons   Patripolar Albanian Neanderthals*

The young son of a Serb policeman, killed in a gun battle with ethnic Albanians, screamed in anguish at his father's funeral yesterday.

*Note the prominent brow ridge on the Albanian youth on the right. Ancient Neanderthal caves are nearby.

To further understand nature of the genetic complexity present within races, these data, together with extensive ethnographic analysis the familial polarity of the cultures and religions of certain of these sub-populations, have been combined into a preliminary and tentative familial polarity assessment within some of the Old World countries. **Table 5** summarizes this analysis. Immediately visible is the presence of immiscible competing matri- and patripolar population elements with their matri- and patripolar cultures and religions whose distribution appears

Table 4: Ethnicity, Hemisity, and Polarity of Subjects from U. H. Community

Country of Origin	Patripolars	Matripolars	M/P Ratio
Scotland	31	1	0.03
Northern Ireland	12	0*	0.08
England	8	44	6
Southern Ireland	3	24	8
French Canada	1	14	14
Western Canada	19	4	0.21
Germany	47	12	0.25
France	3	29	10
Spain	2	32	16
Italy	2	28	14
Sicily	16	0	0.06
Hungary	9	1	0.11
Poland	0	18	18
Russia	2	16	8
American Indians	15	2	0.13
Mexican	3	33	11
Hawaii	51	23	0.45
Samoa	27	5	0.18
Tonga	18	2	0.11
N. Philippines	3	41	14
S. Philippines	18	1	0.06
Okinawa	29	0	0.03
Japan	65	32	0.49
South China Cantonese	3	40	13
North China, Mandrin	50	4	0.11
North Korea	10	2	0.20
South Korea	1	28	14
Thailand	0	11	11
Egypt	11	0	0.09
Israel	2	41	10
Palestine	14	1	0.09
Pakistan	15	1	0.07
Indian Hindu	0	28	14
Indian Seik	12	0	0.08
Bangladeshi	8	2	0.23
Black American	3	49	16
Subjects: n=1089	514	575Ms	
Average M/P Ratio			1.12

* = Zero values were arbitrarily assigned the value of one.   *Italics = Patripolar*

Table 5.Familial PolarityDistribution Estimates: Eastern Hemisphere

Country-Location	PATRI-R-bom Ethnicity	POLAR R-bom Religion	MATRI-L-bom Ethnicity	POLAR L-bom Religion
France	Huguenot	Protestant	French	Roman Catholic
Ger-Aust-Swi	Teuton	Protestant	Slav, Mediterr	Roman Catholic
Britain	Scottish	Protestant	English	Episcopal (Cath)
British Isles	Northern Irish	Protestant	Southern Irish	Roman Catholic
Italy	Sicilian-Greek	Greek, Pagan	Italian-Roman	Roman Catholic
Spain	Catalonian	Protestant	Castilian	Roman Catholic
Morocco	Moor	(orig.)	Berber	Animistic
Greece	Greeks	Islamic	Slavs	Greek Orthodox
Russia	Chechnya etc.	Greek Pagan	Russian	East. Orthodox
Yugoslavia	Albanian, etc.	Islamic	Serbia	East. Orthodox
Turkey	Turkish	Islamic	Armenian	East. Orthodox
Israel	Palestinian	Islamic	Jewish	Judaism
Arabia, Iraq, Iran, Syria, Iran Lebanon, Egypt, Afghanistan,	Persian Arab, etc.	Islamic	Opposition is	not well tolerated!
Africa	Nilotic hunter-herdsmen, Watutsi's, etc.	Islamic	Bantus Farmers, Hutus, etc.	Catholic, pagan
Indian sub-continent	Pakistani, Bangladeshi	Islamic	Indian	Hindu
Southeast Asia	Myanmar	Islamic	Thai,Sri Lakn	Buddhist
	S.Filipino	Islamic	N. Filipino	Roman Catholic
	Moro	Islamic	Tagalong	
China	Mandarins	Confucianism	Cantonese	Taoism
Korea	North Korea	Confucianism	South Korean	Buddhist
Viet Nam	N Vietnamese	Buddhist	S.Vietnamese	Roman Catholic
Australasia	Aborigines, Polynesians, Papuans	Pagan	Melanesian, Micronesian	Animistic

Table 6, Understanding Familial Polarity can Reduce Conflict at Ten Universe Levels

This knowledge:
1. Resolves polarity-based motivation and identity conflicts within **myself.**
   Seeing my polaric identity as perfect, I know that I belong to my global family.
2. Resolves polarity-based conflicts in **my spiritual life.**
   Knowing my hemisity clarifies that my kind of religious experience is normal.
3. Avoids polarity-based conflicts within **my nuclear family.**
   Understanding the polarity needs of each member, I can create synergy.
4. Deals with polarity-based conflicts within **my extended family.**
   Recognizing the existence of Lp sensitivity and Rp intensity removes misunderstandings.
5. Reduces polarity-based conflicts with **my neighbors** (Western hemisphere).
   Identifying polarity differences of neighbors helps me to accept them as family again.
6. Avoids polarity-based conflicts within **my community** (Eastern hemisphere).
   Patripolar and matripolar family groups are inherently different with different needs.
7. Lowers polarity-based conflicts within **my town or city**.
   Unique patripolar and matripolar group strong and weak points become complimentary.
8. Reduces polarity based conflicts within **my state**.
   Dyadic pendulum extremes of opinion become easier to recognize and stabilize.
9. Prevents polarity based conflict within **my nation**.
   Knowledge of reality, the origin, and nature of life brings wisdom to social policy.
10. Avoids polarity based international conflict within **my world**.
   Recognition of selfish national vs. family of nations-level interactions can transform competitive politics into a cooperative complimentary global network of peace and prosperity.

---

more ancient than current national or even racial boundaries. Clearly, ignorance of familial polarity kills.

In contrast, **Table 6** illustrates how recognizing the existence of familial polarity and understanding its significance can reduce conflict within each of ten universe levels. Clearly, until we recognize the multilevel existence of familial polarity, it will continue to take its toll by inflicting emotional pain in our young children, which leads to permanent developmental arresting. This causes stress-sensitization, reward-hunger (drug seeking), and neurosis in adulthood. These produce conflict, corruption, waste, violence, killing and war. An illumination of these disturbing topics will be developed in our next two chapters.

Some Important Concepts of Chapter 11:
1. Both patripolar and matripolar lineages developed and thrived within the familial polarity population striations of the Old World. However, with time their increasing numbers and mobility began to cause conflict, due to their inherent opposing biological differences. Understanding of these differences allows a more accurate rewriting of postglacial human history.

2. It appears that all of the founders of the present world religions were Rms. However, crossing between groups of opposite polarities has shaped their modern forms.

3. Thus, the sojourn of Abraham's originally patripolar stock, interbreeding for eight generations with the then matripolar Egyptians and several generations with the matripolar Persians, caused a polarity conversion, so that most modern Jews are matripolar, with Rf "Jewish Mothers" and Lm technocratic fathers, unlike their still patripolar Arab cousins with whom they are now immiscible. A similar mixing of familial polarity occurred in the evolution of Christianity and within Islam, Buddhism and Hinduism. Thus, within each religion there has been accommodation for both matripolar and patripolar families.

4. Familial polarity has had a powerfully affect upon the logic of national governance styles. Patripolars prefer top-down Autocracy, while matripolar ardently support bottom-up Democracy. Thus,

both world wars were fought between patripolar dominant "Axis" nations and matripolar dominant countries of the "Allies".

5. Extensive evidence is presented for the existence of continuing unrecognized global killing resulting from the conflict between patripolar and matripolar human groups. This includes the observation that at 20 of 21 repetitive sites of global conflict, soldiers of opposite polarities have battled one another: patripolars warriors fighting for their Fatherland and calling for their fathers when mortally wounded, against matripolar troupes fighting for their Motherland, and crying out for their mothers.

6. Support for the continued existence of polarity striations in the Eastern Hemisphere is supplied by hemisity sampling of current distributions of matripolar and patripolar populations.

7. Ignorance of familial polarity has lead to human conflict and killing at ten universe levels. Recognition and understanding of familial polarity can assist us in rising to our next level of evolution: that dedicated to nonkilling.

NEUROREALITY: A SCIENTIFIC RELIGION TO RESTORE MEANING

Section IV: Why do I Feel the Way I do? What can I Do About It?
Chapter 12: Feeling Bad: Unrecognized Origins of Everyday Psychological Pain and Stress

Why do I feel the way I do?!

We can be viewed as highly evolved pain-avoiding, pleasure-seeking survival-maximizing mechanisms, *who also carry substantial load of developmental arrest-based personal stress.* Feelings are an important feedback of our survival status. Due to our accumulations of winning behavioral genetics, we feel good if our own actions enhance our survival or those of our family. These pleasure-linked feelings of well being cause us to be attracted to and seek things that enhance our survival status, from getting a glass of water to finding a home. Furthermore, due to our behavioral genetics accumulations, we feel bad if our acts, or those of others harm our survival. Memory of such dysphoria in the past logically causes us to attempt to avoid things that harmed our survival. Predominant feelings become moods if they extend beyond the balance of immediate emotions for a few hours. If extended over years, they become personality traits.

During our reproductive years, Sigmund Freud more than one hundred years ago recognized that we are hardwired subconsciously to powerfully seek the pleasure and relief that comes from sexual orgasm. Ironically, only a miniscule few of those seeking sexual relief are consciously interested in reproduction. Quite to the contrary: for most, pregnancy is the last thing they would wish for at the time, unfortunately for their later neglected offspring! This unconscious drive continuously animates-contaminates both our interior and exterior lives to an incredible extent. Anyone knows that just the hint of the idea of sex is so strong that it can be effectively linked to the sale of commercial products, usually with little recognition or annoyance.

What more effective insurance of life's continuation than having everyone hard wired to seek sex as life's greatest reward! The drive is on night and day, distracting us hour by hour, taking priority over other more productive material or internal pursuits. Judging from the billions of us now in existence, it has been an overly successful device from which only some children and of the aged escape. Further, now we have discovered drugs that can become as more rewarding and irresistible than sex. This is presently causing the single minded incapacitation of drug seeking that may bring down civilization, the topic of a later chapter.

Also included in our reproductive genetic hard wiring is that we feel especially good if our acts, or those of others the enhance the survival of our family. We feel correspondingly bad if our actions, or those of others harm our family's survival. This makes working for the survival optimization of our family one of life's greater joys.

Thus far, these ideas only make common sense. However, we must now confront two powerful subconscious influences causing us unnecessary pain and stress, each of which at first seem counter intuitive. This introduces us into the main topics of this chapter: 1) Critical Periods of the Development of Psychosocial Control and 2) the existence of a Broken Developmental Arrest Repair Program (xDARP).

The first behavior under consideration is strange. Surprisingly, by subjecting ourselves to physical or psychological pain for less than one hour, we feel good *for more than two days afterward*. This paradoxical "no pain, no gain" phenomena is tied to many rather strange cultural practices, like chopping a hole in lake ice and jumping in, baking in a steaming sauna to the point of collapse and then rolling in the snow, or such pain-limited exercises as running for more than 20 minutes of intense cardiovascular output. Yet, a couple of days after done so, we start to feel bad and to think that it's time for another super hot bath (Japanese Furo) or another pain limited workout (USA), after which we feel refreshed once again. Such pain-gain cycles can become addicting. The significance of this bizarre drive will become evident later in this chapter.

The second counterintuitive behavior is the way many of us end up severely psychologically, or even physically hurting those we love the most, and repeatedly damage or destroy our personal relationships. Surprisingly, this bizarre behavior comes from our drive to feel good by being in control of a needed survival process or operation, including being in control of our relationship with others. We become alarmed and upset if we are not in control of that vital process or operation.

Unfortunately, most of us due to our culture, have been thwarted in gaining such control, especially in our early development. However, there appears to be a genetic program designed ultimately to gain control of thwarted processes. This automatic behavioral program causes us, when under conditions that are not presently stressful, to become neurotically unhappy with an "important other" and to reinitiate the ancient struggle to gain psychosocial control. However, as we will see, the subconsciously powerful xDARP (which has been unwittingly called our "Pain Body" or our "Reactive Mind" has mutated and now longer works. Yet, it faithfully reactivates and brings up stress from our past lack of control of a specific process. This subconscious imposition of stressful struggles from past trauma upon loved ones in the neutral present environment is called *inappropriate behavior*, another term for *insanity*.

Types of Brain and Body Development of at Birth

To understand how the brain gains control of our body, and thus gets control of processes around us that are important to our survival, it is helpful to compare the body and brain development at birth of the two major types of animals. In the r-type of animals, the newborn is large and so well developed that minutes after birth it can stand up and run. These are the vegetarian prey types of animals, such as deer, horses, giraffes and elephants. In contrast, for the K-type of animals, the newborn is very small and almost totally helpless. Many months of postnatal development and protective care is needed before it too can stand and run. These K-type animals include many of the predators, such as bears, lions, wolves, and includes humans.

Development of Voluntary Control of the Body:

To truly be in control of a process requires five elements, **Awareness** of the process (by at least some part of the brain), and the ability to: **Start, Change, Stop** and **Reverse** it. The consequence of having control is amazing, seemingly effortless accomplishment. This is possible because control enables us to align with and tap the power of the energy flows across the structures of the universe over time.

To maintain cell survival conditions within the body requires awareness of the various internal states by the autonomic nervous system of the Reptile Brain core. This remarkable ancient brain element is highly competent, but efficiently operates mostly out of our conscious awareness. Is our blood sugar level now within the range required for optimal cellular survival? Or, is it too high, or too low? If it is outside of the range, can the right hormone be secreted in the right amount somewhere to bring blood glucose back within the cell survival range? Can this action then be recognized as successful?

In addition, for K-type animals, the ability to develop the control needed to get up and walk requires awareness of the one's external equipment status. That is, of a present limb position, of the desired future limb position, of the force of input required, in the correct direction, and ongoing feedback of the degree of success in terms of the selected goal.

In humans, development of body control occurs first at the head and last at the toes. That is, at birth, the infant only has control of its mouth and throat for nursing or crying. Next, it gains sufficient control of its neck to hold its head up. Then, it gains control of its arms before the gaining control to convert its paws into sensitive hands and fingers. Next come control of trunk and leg movements, along with gaining control of its bladder and intestinal sphincters. It learns to stand and finally gains control of its feet sufficiently to walk and later to run. Paradoxically, all this lengthy postnatal development is required to obtain that bodily control already possessed by r-types at birth.

No less important is the parallel development of voluntary control of psychosocial skills required to control the infant's interactions with its mother, father, siblings and others. That is, effectively and efficiently to be able to gain the attention needed for being feed, cleaned of excrements, protected from excessive cold or heat, transported, and assisted in other survival needs, such as to avoid unwanted attention, interference, or harm.

Critical Periods of Brain Development Exist for Gaining Control of Voluntary Processes

There are many brain development critical periods concerned with control over processes. Most are unknown. Many of these are prenatal, occurring *in utero*. In the infamous case of the Thalidomide Babies, their mothers received the drug to calm their anxiety during pregnancy. Unfortunately, an unknown side effect of thalidomide was that during the critical period of limb elongation in utero, it blocked the lengthening of legs and arms. This resulted in the birth of "Flipper Babies", whose feet were attached to their hips and their hands to their shoulders. This is a powerful illustration of the importance of the critical periods of development. After the period's window slammed shut, no amount of feeding, exercise or absence of thalidomide could prevent these unfortunate children from becoming Flipper Adults.

Some thinking about schizophrenia proposes that irreversible brain formation defects occur during the second trimester *in utero*. The key element here is thought to be the occurrence of a viral infection of the mother during this time. However, this idea needs confirmation. A different compelling idea is that all schizophrenics are a specific type of familial polarity hybrid, causing the failure of proper brain wiring, similar in principle to that causing homosexuality or dyslexia.

For the helpless newborns of K-type animals including humans, obviously a great many critical periods of brain development must occur after birth. For example, kittens are born blind. Their visual development occurs during a specific critical postnatal period a few days after birth. Experimental manipulation of their visual environment during this critical period can cause permanent thwarting, leading to impressive distortion and permanent malfunction of their vision as adult cats.

It appears that humans complete the majority of these crucial developmental windows by the third year of childhood. Others may occur during adolescence.

Stages of Critical Periods of Development:

1. The Developmental Window is Not Yet Open: Before the developmental window opens, there is developmental inaccessibility. At this time, it is premature to attempt to access that part of the brain, as it yet lacks the ability to control this particular process. Forcing at this time can only fail. This can harm one's foundational self-concept as well ("My awe inspiring god-like parents think I should be able to control my bladder. Since I cannot, I must be defective or "no good"). Parents are of course anxious for their child to develop rapidly and some think they can accelerate this by attempting to train them. Most are unaware of the existence of critical periods of brain development. It is better to let the child's brain-directed behavioral interests be their readiness guide.

2. The Developmental Window is now Open: This begins the critical period of developmental plasticity and accessibility. The Brain is now ready to gain control of this process. Related self-motivated play and practice appear. The child uses great focus, effort and intensity to gain control, and thus access to later power. Brain seeks out this type of repetitive activity and rewards it as fun (eustress-good stress). Thwarting the unfolding of this practice-application activity is upsetting (distress-bad stress). Escalation of effort, preoccupation and negative emotions result from thwarting this development. Failure to control leads to the formation of developmental arrests and fixations. These activate inappropriate stress responses in adulthood from the xDARP (to be described shortly). Thwarting of development is viewed by part of the brain as life threatening.

It therefore shunts these traumatic memories of such, unexperienced, into the Reactive Mind as "too hot to handle".

3. Developmental Window Closes Forever: After the critical period has ended and its window closes, developmental rigidity appears. It has become too late for further facilitated learning. Belated training to gain control of the process is ineffective or impaired. The results of adult learning of a second language, or how to dance, is a product inferior in quality.

Sources of Failure to Gain Control of a Psychosocial Process Before the Window Closes:

Impoverished Environment: For example, without live or prerecorded music sources or musical instruments in the home, the child may develop into a tone-deaf adult.

Choice of inappropriate or premature goals: Control of mechanical skills might not be gained if a girl was diverted from tool or vigorous physical sports use by cultural or other reasons.

Thwarting by Others: If the child prohibited by siblings or parents from taking control of his own toy, the child may become an excessively demanding adult.

Lack of Required Developmental Foundations due to previous thwarting: A child will not be able to run if it was earlier prevented from learning to walk.

Consequences of Failure to Gain Control:

Failure to gain control of a process during its critical period causes the formation of *an , permanent unhealing developmental wound. This is located in the "too hot to handle" memories of events perceived as threatening death, thus segregated and blocked from conscious access in the Reactive Mind.* Last ditch attempts to gain control of the process now become exaggerated. The failed process inhibits or blocks those later development steps requiring it. A permanent defensive hypersensitivity appears regarding the failed process. The person cannot be neutral about the process. Inferior coping compensations substitute for the failed control process. **Table 1** lists these. Further, the traumatized personality

Table 1: Coping Mechanisms Designed to Compensate for Failure to Control a Process
1. Must Dominate Others:
2. Must Win
3. Must Look Best at all Costs:
4. Must Be (dead) Right rather than Alive (through Compromise).
5. Possessiveness: Collects things or power, as a substitute for love-acceptance.
6. Trying to Change Things: More, Different, or Better compensations (which don't work).
7. Forms Survival Acts: Nice Guy, Funny Girl, Helper, Helpless, Know-it-all, Workaholic.

---

incorporates the negative elements of the Hexadyad Primary Emotions (Chapter 5), as illustrated in **Table 2**.

Use of "Ego defenses of the Id" adaptations or compensations also distort the personality. (Chapter 5). Recall, they include: Acting out, Compensation, Denial, Displacement, Fantasy, Infatuation, Intellectualization, Identification, Introjection, Isolation, Undoing, Rationalization, Reaction Formation, Regression, Repression and Sublimation. These dishonest compensations to hide failure display for all to see except the victim itself. This creates disrespectful or opportunistic responses from others. Then, as result of being taken advantage of, we

Table 2: How The Dyscontrol Wound Warps Personality Development:

Response to failure	Emotion	Personality Trait Favored:
I don't know how!	Confusion	Uncertainty
I am weaker than it!	Fear	Anxiousness
I am at effect, a victim!	Anger	Resentfulness
I am losing!	Grief	Moroseness, Apathy
I want!	Desire	Dissatisfaction, Greed
I reject other substitutes	Disgust	Negativity

become excessively resistant to control by others. Thus, "We get what we resist the most": i.e. another failure of to be in control of our relationship with someone else.

These compensations become the unique "Sticking Points" of the dyscontrolled personality which literally alter their life's path. Thus, arrest-fixations block the natural flow of our social heritage by depriving us of what we value the most: respect, love, health, joy, mastery, abundance, opportunity and power. They instead force us down "lesser" paths of compromise.

Figure 1 diagrams the overall process of gaining or failing to gain control of a process or interaction. At the heart of this activity is the current strength of the Executive Ego.

Locus Coeruleus (Blue Nodes): Key to Caretaker Executive Ego Strength.

Early neuroanatomists noted blue pigmentation in a small, paired area in the midbrain. They called it the locus coeruleus (Latin for "blue spot", here abbreviated as LC). The LC is thought to control the level of arousal. However, in The Blue Node Model (Morton, 1997), it can be shown to possess several unrecognized behaviors: 1. Stress activates the LC. 2. All abused drugs inhibit the LC. and 3., The LC sensitivity setting regulates the strength of the Caretaker Executive-Ego. If LC sensitivity is set low, the Executive is strong, can control the impulses of the Crocodile Brain and Reactive Mind. If it is set high, the Executive becomes too weak to prevent the breakthrough of Reptile Brain upset or Pain Body behavior!

As shown in **Table 3**, the Blue Node Model unifies many isolated behavioral properties of the LC into a common mechanism that confers the traits listed. In upset behavior, axons from neurons in the LC secrete the inhibitory neurotransmitter norepinephrine to strongly block function in the three higher cortexes: This causes a loss of cerebral cortical intellect, hippocampal memory retrieval and cerebellar social behavior. **Figure 2** outlines the contrast between this upset, decorticate behavior and normal intelligent, memory based, social behavior.

Uncovering the Defective Developmental Arrest Repair Program (xDARP): Source of Inappropriate, Neurotic, and Psychotic Behavior

Multiple levels of body repair exist, from the reconstruction or replacement

Figure 1. Gaining Control of Processes and Interactions

MAP OF HUMAN BEHAVIOR

Bruce E. Morton, Ph.D., 1997
University of Hawaii School of Medicine

Learning and Development as *Gaining Control of Interactions*, both Animate and Inanimate.

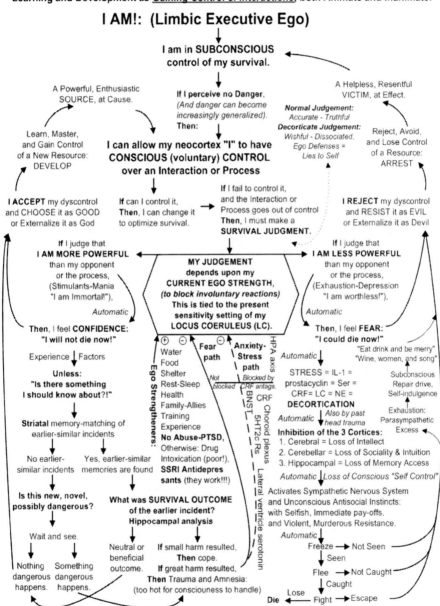

Table 3: Ego Strength Determines Stress Tolerance:
In-Control Serenity vs. Out-of-Control Upset

---

1. LC induced alarm-avoidance becomes activated by threats to survival.

2. The LC releases norepinephrine at limbic sites to increase fear production.
3. LC activation automatically suppresses reward output, and decorticates the upper brain.
4. The LC directly and indirectly modulates its responses via serotonin 5-HT1a, 5-HT2a, and 5-HT3 receptors as part of an "Attack/Avoid Switch".
5. The LC alarm overrides the Social Brain (via the cerebellar vermis) in an "Emergency".
6. The LC can be inhibited by *all* drugs of abuse, thus facilitating dopamine reward.
7. The LC alters fear production in proportion to its drug-altered sensitivity.
8. It is theoretically possible to monitor LC activity sensitivity non-invasively.
9. The LC absolutely requires REM sleep for its function, thus accounting for many psychotic paranoid psychosis syndromes resulting from lack of sleep.
10. LC norepinephrine participates in several forms of learning.

11. The LC is broadly involved in Depression and Mania. Its sensitivity is reduced by SSRIs.
12. The LC participates in certain CNS elements of the AIDS Syndrome (Dementia).

---

of damaged DNA, cells, tissues and even appendages in certain organisms. This capability gives us the potential for physical immortality (Chapter 18). If this is so, then within us there should be a developmental arrest repair program (DARP) to repair failures to gain control during each critical period of brain development. Indeed, a DARP program appears to have once existed to assist us in achieving our highest-level development. However, mutation now appears to have damaged it so that under present circumstances the operation of the xDARP has become a powerful

Figure 2.

"CORTICATE" vs. "DECORTICATE" BEHAVIOR CONTRASTED
How the Release of Norepinephrine from Locus Coeruleus Colors Human Judgement By Fear
Bruce Morton, 10-97

CONDITIONS: OUTPUT:

PHYSICAL		PHARMACOLOGIC.		PSYCHOLOGICAL		PERFORMANCE	
PERSONAL:	PERSONAL:	LOW LEVELS	HI LEVELS	EGO-Caretaker	EGOCaretaker	PARASYMPA-	SYMPATHE-
Rested	Exhausted	(or added	(Or added	IS STRONG	IS WEAK	THETIC Excess:	TIC EXCESS
Watered	Thirsty	Antagonists of):	Agonists of):			Relaxed face	Tight face
Fed	Hungry	IL-1, IL-6,	IL-1, IL-6	PRIMARY	PRIMARY	Rosy face	White face
Sheltered	Unprotected	TNF-alpha	TNF-alpha	EMOTIONS:	EMOTIONS:	Salivates	Dry Mouth
Well	Injured-Ill	Prostacyclins	Prostacyclins	Clear	Confused	Calm	Upset, agitated
Strong	Weak	Serotonin	Serotonin	Accepting	Rejecting	Small P300	Big P300
Accepted	Rejected	CRF-ACTH	CRF-ACTH	Grateful	Angry	Low GSR	High GSR
Supported	Alone	Vasopressin	Vasopressin	Confident	Fearful	High alpha- wav	Low alpha-wav
Experienced	Naive	Noradrenaline	Noradrenaline	Joyous	Grieving	Small jaw-	Large jaw-
Empty bowels	Distended	CCK	CCK	Satisfied	Needy	clench reflex	clench reflex
and bladder	bowels-bladder	Glutamate	Glutamate				
No immediate	Several recent			OTHER	OTHER	BRAIN	BRAIN
losses	losses	HIGH LEVELS	LOW LEVELs	ASPECTS:	ASPECTS:	SYSTEMS	SYSTEMS
On Vacation:	Habitual	(Or added	(Or added	A Source	A Victim	FUNCTION:	FUNCTION:
new stimuli	restimuli	Agonists of:)	Antagonists of)	Surrendered	Rebellious	LEFT Hemis:	LEFT Hemis:
		Dopamine	Dopamine	Aligned	Cross Purpose	Analytical	Impaired
Low LC-NE=	High LC-NE=	Opioids	Opioids	Peaceful	Violent	Deductive	Intelligence
ACTIVATED:	INHIBITED:	MSH	MSH	Happy	Unhappy	Symbolizes	Literal
Right Hemis.	Right Hemis.			Loving	Hateful	Fluent	Stammers
Left Hemis.	Left Hemis.	CHRONIC	NO Admini-	Alive	"Dead Right"	Sees details	Overlooks
Cerebellum,	Cerebellum,	Administration:	straion:	Empowered	Helpless		details
Vermis, and	Vermis, and	Antidepressants	Antidepress.	A Possibility	No possibility	RIGHT Hemis	RIGHT Hemis:
Vestibulum	Vestibulum	Tryptophan	Tryptophan	Wise	Decorticate	Contextual	Rigid-inflexible
Hippocampus	Hippocampus	5-OH-Trypto-	5-OH-Trypto-	Tolerant	Irritable	Inductive	can't generalize
		phan	phan	Adaptable	Rigid	Visualizes-	Can't imagine
INHIBITED:	ACTIVATED:	DHEA	DHEA			Imagines	consequences
Sympathetic	Sympathetic			Can cooperate	Must compete	Sees Big Pix	Can't step back
Nervous Syst	Nervous Syst	ACUTE SELF-	WITH-	Can be wrong	Must be right	CERE-	CERE-
		MEDICATED	DRAWING	Can lose	Must win	BELLUM:	BELLUM:
No Trauma:	Past Trauma:	WITH:	FROM:	Can look bad	Must look good	Self-Discipline	Self-Indulgent
Child PTSD	Child PTSD	Caffeine	Caffeine	Unselfish	Greedy	Sociable	Antisocial
Adult PTSD	Adult PTSD	Nicotine	Nicotine	Real, Honest	Phoney, Liar	Has Conscience	No conscience
		Alcohol	Alcohol	Doesn't use	Uses Ego	Truthful	Untruthful
No frontal	Major frontal	Minor Tranqui	Minor Tranqu	Ego Defenses	Defenses	Intuitive	No com. sense
lobe damage	lobe damage	Barbiturates	Barbiturates	"Righteous",	"Sinner"	Good timing	Poor timing
		Marijuana	Marijuana	Upright, Good	Low, Evil	Correct action-	Wrong action-
SEES	SEES	Opiates	Opiates	Non-violent	Violent	verbs from nouns	verb from noun
OPPONENT	OPPONENT	Amphetamine	Amphetamine	Peaceful	On the warpath	HIPPO-	HIPPO-
AS:	AS:	Cocaine	Cocaine			CAMPUS:	CAMPUS:
Smaller	Larger			DRUGS AND	DRUG AND	Good short-	Mental blocks-
Weaker	Stronger			PATHOLOGY	PATHOLOGy	term memory	amnesia
Slower	Quicker			"Immortal"	Suicidal	Long attention	Short attention
Duller	Smarter			Manic	Depressed	Clarity	Confusion
						Accurate data	Must guess
						PREDICTED	PREDICTED
						GOOD	POOR
				RIGHT-brain	LEFT-brained	PERFORM-	PERFORM-
				PERSON:	PERSON:	ANCE	ANCE
				More tolerant	Irritable	1. Wisconsin	1. Wisconsin
				Bigger upsets,	Smaller upsets,	Card Sort	Card Sort
				but shorter	but long lasting	2. Context	2. Context
				Forgiving	Revengeful	Category	Category
				Maturation rate	Maturation rate	Generation	Generation
				RH>LHemis.	LH>RHemis.	3. Backward	3. Backward
						Counting Rate	Counting Rate
						4. Typing-Copy	4.Typing-Copy
						5. Etc., many	5. Etc., many

subconscious source of inappropriate behavior whose insanity causes untold stress suffering and waste.

The way the originally functional DARP appears to have subconsciously operated was to find someone safe and caring who is in the arrested person's present environment, often their mate or best friend. The DARP then would transfer the original incomplete conflict from the original nuclear family onto this safe person. This happened in order to allow the arrested person to complete the ancient struggle to gain control of the thwarted psychosocial operation in the now.

However, since the presently closed window cannot be reopened under normal circumstances, if at all, the reinitiated development stage cannot be completed. Yet, a struggle never the less develops. Thus, "We end up hurting the one's we love the most". The xDARP mindlessly continues to escalate the conflict to the point of insanity, leading to crimes of passion. Eight of the apparent properties of the xDARP are: Unconscious Attraction, Age Regression, Transference, Acting Out, Struggle for Control, Thematic Repetition, Non-completion and Unawareness. **Table 4** describes them.

Illustrations of the DARP in Action: Spousal Violence

1991: The Ganal case is Hawaii's worst murdering rampage, resulting from a husband-wife struggle and an affair. This escalated to the point the wife taunted her husband while having sex with him and made demeaning comparisons of him to her lover. The husband runs amok, shoots, firebombs and kills five of her friends and relatives, wounded three others, including his wife and son. He is now serving a life sentence with no parole. His wife blames herself. His son and relatives miss the husband who they say was "the best of men".

1993: The Nakata case, injuries but no deaths in a "Ganal-type" case.

1994: The Moore case, Greyline Tours owner and wife had an escalated argument in a car. The wife was shot five times. She was later convicted for refusing to testify against her husband, claiming it was her fault and that he really did not intend to hurt her.

1995: O.J. Simpson case, TV coverage of trial covering the consequences of escalating conflict between the noted football player and his wife. Two were killed. Simpson goes free.

Table 4. Properties of the Broken Developmental Arrest Repair Program.

1. Unconscious Attraction: Infatuation and Entrapment of the "appropriate, safe" person.
2. Age Regression: Emergence of infantile, childish behavior as the original ancient struggle emerges.
3. Transference: Subconscious, powerful imposition of the theme upon the safe target person.
4. Acting out of the Theme: Dramatization, e.g. "You don't love me, Daddy"
5. Establishment of a Struggle for Control: Victim of transference is unaware of xDARP activation.
6. Compulsive Repetition: When xDARP finds what victim can not accept, the battle is on.
7. Non-Completion: Struggle escalates until crimes of passion occur as the last resort, often appearing in "The News".
8. Lack of Awareness: of the inappropriateness of the xDARP activated behavior. xDARP becomes prominent after about a year in the relationship. It seems authentically to be who we are, rather than a broken mechanism seeking to complete development of something from our childhood.
9. Cerebellar location: on the Reactive Mind side, opposite the Source.

Insanity and the xDARP

By definition, xDARP- directed behavior is insane. It contaminates and dominates the present with incompletions from the past. If weakly activated, this xDARP behavior is "Neurotic" and society usually tolerates the resulting harm. If strongly activated, the behavior becomes "Psychotic", because the harm exceeds tolerable levels and public safety demands the individual be isolated in a mental ward or prison. Trivial themes, such toilet seat positions, are "kindled-inflamed" and can become the major source of crimes of passion. xDARP directed behavior is all around us. It is the source of chronic unnecessary struggles: with superiors (authority figures derived from father, mother, or older siblings), with peers (brother and sister figures), with underlings (younger-weaker brother and sister figures).

xDARP activation appears to be a major source of subconscious psychological stress. One person's pleasure is another person's stress. Most internal conflict comes from the insane demands placed upon us by the xDARP. Much of daily life's external conflict is a result of xDARP activation. The xDARP drives antisocial behavior causing continual suffering to humanity. Post-traumatic stress disorder (PTSD) also appears to have some relationship to xDARP activation.

The Broken Developmental Arrest Repair Program no Longer Repairs. It Harms!

How does the DARP harm the person within whom it activates? First, by <u>inappropriate mate selection</u> through xDARP-induced infatuation or "chemistry" (insane, doomed, by definition). Almost two of three US marriages end in divorce. The xDARP demands change and submission of the other for acceptability. It is the opposite of Love, defined as the acceptance of another just the way they are *and just the way they are not*. If it's first series of demands for change are met, then the xDARP continues to seek something that the transferee will not be able to give or do. Ultimately it demands your life: "If you really love me, you will die for me." Apparently, only Jesus Christ would do that. The rest of us would rather fight than die. Thus, the xDARP drives us to crimes of passion. Often persons with complimentary xDARPs find and emotionally torture each other.

xDARP insanity is everywhere. The existence of the xDARP is why "playing hard to get, works". For instance, consider the beloved opera Carmen by Bizet. Local beauty, Carmen, sneers at all her adoring suitors and focuses her attention on the impossible, that is to seduce military officer, Don Jose, who has been posted in her gipsy ghetto to preserve order. He resists her advances because he is from an upper class, engaged to be married, close to his mother, religiously devout and honest. Carmen ultimately breaks him and seduces him. Her conquest and his surrender to her shakes him to the core. He tells her he loves her and will do anything for her. As proof he meets her demands one by one, leaving his fiancé, job and family to join Carmen's family of smugglers. However, as far as Carmen's xDARP is concerned, Don Jose has now become just another needy suitor. Since, he no longer matches her ancient failure to control her father's love, Carmen's xDARP begins to reject and revile him. She now fantasizes of another impossible conquest instead, that of a popular bullfighter coming to town. Intercepting Carmen on her way to the bullfight, Don Jose makes one last desperate attempt to convince her of his true love for her. She will hear none of it and humiliates him even more. In his impassioned anguish, he stabs her in the heart, saying that if he cannot have her, no one will.

Second, the xDARP also harms the Person within which it is activated by the Inappropriate Selection of Associates: to struggle with, control, and vanquish. Third, it harms them by Inappropriate Selection of a Career: which is often illogical, compulsive, and based upon possible transference onto a xDARP selected mentor. This failure of career choice is a source of joblessness, isolation, criminality. Fourth, the xDARP usually Activates unhealthy sex and drug oriented compulsions, such as the smoking and drinking excesses associated with night life, which are decidedly harmful to their health.

In addition to damaging the developmentally arrested person themselves, unfortunately, the xDARP harms many other persons. This can occur during Courtship and can be seen to be the unconscious motive behind stalking, partner harassment, unwanted or inappropriate pregnancy and sexually transmitted disease. It also leads to the inappropriate Rejection of others forming the unconscious motive powerfully leading to divorce, spouse and child abuse, animal abuse and abuse of the environment. The xDARP has very negative consequences upon Child rearing: driving compulsive, impulsive and destructive behavior towards children. In the United States, ten percent of all children are hospitalized for abuse injuries. This causes permanent emotional scarring of the child, only to perpetuate the xDARP cycle in the next generation.

Consequence of the Broken DARP: Abnormal Stress-Sensitization in Adulthood

Early separation of the child from the mother to produces major developmental wounding and arresting. This causes the permanent development of hypersensitive stress receptors. It also primes the individual for major DARP activation in adulthood. For a K-type infant to be separated from the mother is tantamount to a threat of death, due to the infant's helplessness and vulnerability to harm. Thus, separation traumatizes by causing overwhelming fears in an infant, which from their location in the memory banks of the Reactive Mind can only lead to later neurosis. Animal studies have repeatedly demonstrated that only a few minutes of removal daily of an K-type infant from its mother result in the major permanent sensitization of its stress system later as an adult.

Following Harry Harlow (1976)'s "surrogate mother" monkey studies in the 1950s at University of Wisconsin produced, stress-sensitized, neurotic, violent, sex-warped, antisocial adults showing high levels of aggression, hyper sexuality and other antisocial behavior, also common in adult humans. James Prescott (1996) has long provided evidence that failure of infants to be adequately nursed is one of the most potent predictors of later adult violence.

We humans have lost our way, regarding the needs of our primate infants. Infants raised to adulthood in the wild by the higher apes, appear much happier and saner than our children do. Human infant discipline, punishment or rejecting behavior by parents becomes the source of later neurotic behavior. These noxious parental behaviors definitely are not part of the solution. In 3000 BC, many patripolar infant humans were swaddled, with their head bound to a board, and raised on horseback while their parents pillaged matripolar settlements. This could only have resulted in development of the violent psychotic adults that parasitized and raped the then known world. Even, today, we traumatically separate our infants into their "own room and bed" for the night, leaving them "to cry it out". Then, in the next morning we dump them off for the day at childcare facilities. No wonder that mental health professionals have characterized more than twenty percent of US adults as mentally ill.

As would be Predicted from the Existence of Familial Polarity, Women are Responsible for Violence Too

It is a very stable statistic that the wife commits half of spousal murders. The 1985 National Family Violence Survey (NIMH) confirmed that men and women physically abuse each other equally. Wives report that they were more often the aggressor, using weapons to make up for their physical disadvantage. The annual spouse assault rate: 1.8 million husbands assault their wives, while 2.0 million wives assaulted their husbands. According to the 1986 Journal of the National Association of Social Workers, among dating teens, girls were violent more frequently than boys. Mothers also abuse their children almost twice as often as fathers do.

A Permanent solution: Data-based Love of Newborns and Infants

Thus, in spite of our best intentions and sincerest efforts to raise normal healthy children, we are failing. It would appear that it would be wise to look more carefully at the evolutionary needs of the children of higher apes (Gorillas, Bonobos, Orangutans, and Chimpanzees) during their formative years of brain development. We also need to conduct an in depth investigation of infant separation and xDARP activation in adulthood. Our genetics appears to lag behind the present by at least a million years. We would do well to research the ancient genetic needs and child rearing methods of hominids and apes existing at 1 million BC and apply them to our present infants. They may require perianal stimulation where the neonate cleaned by licking at birth and after excreting. There was no cloth, paper or plumbing back then. It may be that those infants were breast feed with full skin contact night and day for 5-6 yrs of weaning. The infant-mother pair defines a higher-level system with symbiotic emergent properties! It must become widely recognized that child bearing is not a "the clock is ticking" right of passage. It is a privilege of devotion for which only a few are qualified!

Until we recognize the multilevel existence of familial polarity, it will continue to take its toll by inflicting emotional pain in our young children, which leads to permanent developmental arresting. This causes to stress-sensitization, reward-hunger (drug seeking), and neurosis in adulthood. These produce conflict, corruption, waste, violence, killing and war. Later chapters will develop an illumination of these disturbing topics. The next chapter addresses how we, the walking wounded, can turn off our broken xDARPs and regain stress-free sanity.

Some important concepts from Chapter 12:

1. We can be viewed as highly evolved pain-avoiding, pleasure-seeking survival-maximizing mechanisms, *who also carry substantial load of developmental arrest-based personal stress.* Feelings are the ultimate feedback of our survival status, *excluding those derived from our developmental fixations.*

2. Critical periods of brain development exist for gaining control of internal and external processes. Humans are among those r-type species whose newborns require extensive development after birth to gain control of physical and social processes, the development of which K-type species have already completed before birth. This occurs during numerous specific critical stages of development of control over a process or behavior, most occurring in the years immediately following birth.

3. There are three stages of critical periods of development. First, the window is not yet open. At this time it is premature to attempt to access that part of the brain, as it yet lacks the ability to control this particular process. Forcing at this time can only fail and can harm one's self-concept as well. Second, the window opens, beginning the critical period of developmental plasticity and accessibility. The brain is now ready to gain control of the process at hand. Relevant self-motivated play and practice appear. Great focus, effort and intensity are used by the child to gain control, and thus access to later power. Third, the window closes forever: After the critical period has ended and developmental rigidity appears. It is too late for further facilitated learning.

4. Sources of failure to gain control of a psychosocial process before its window closes include: an impoverished environment, the choice of inappropriate or premature goals, thwarting by others, or lack of required earlier developmental foundations.

5. Failure to gain control of a process during its critical period causes the formation of an unhealing, developmental wound. A life-long defensive hypersensitivity then appears regarding the failed process. The following inferior coping compensations are substituted for failure to control the process, where the person must dominate others, must win, must be right, must look best, becomes excessively possessive, always tries to change things, and creates survival acts, such as Mr. Nice Guy or Mrs. Know-It-All.

6. In addition, the presence of a developmental wound warps personality development toward the negative emotions, producing traits including uncertainty, anxiousness, resentfulness, moroseness and apathy, dissatisfaction and greed, and/or perennial negativity.

7. Multiple levels of body repair exist, from the reconstruction or replacement of damaged DNA, cells, tissues and even appendages in certain organisms. If this be so, then within us there should be a developmental arrest repair program (DARP) to repair failures to gain control during each critical period of brain development. Indeed, a DARP program appears to have once been present to assist us in achieving our highest-level development. However, it appears to have mutated and become a defective liability, now the source of inappropriate, neurotic, and psychotic behavior. It is here called the xDARP

8. The following are the properties of the xDARP: 1) Unconscious infatuation with a supportive mate or friend, 2) Age regression, 3) Transference, 4) Acting out of the theme, 5) Establishment of a struggle, 6) Compulsive repetition with escalation to crimes of passion, 7) Non-completion, 8) Lack of awareness, and 9) Cerebellar location of the xDARP.

9. The xDARP no longer repairs. Rather, it harms by causing abnormal stress-sensitization in adulthood, leading from neurosis, depression, suicide, obsessions, psychosis, to child and spouse abuse, and other previously inexplicable crimes of passion that occur all around us.

10. Thus, for us to rise from killing to nonkilling, the xDARP must be dealt with, by repair or inactivation.

NEUROREALITY: A SCIENTIFIC RELIGION TO RESTORE MEANING

Section IV: Why do I Feel the Way I do? What can I Do About It?

Chapter 13: Restoring Sanity, Satisfaction and Well-Being by Turning off the xDARP

Unwitting Past Attempts to Repair the Broken DARP:

Might it be possible to repair the broken Developmental Arrest Repair Program? Imagine the benefits if the xDARP could be rehabilitated to its full potential. Then we would gain full control of all our physical processes, as occurs by birth in galloping gazelle and other r-types of animals. However, much more importantly, every critical period needed to gain control of our social relations would also be completely developed. Because the majority of us sustain debilitating psychosocial developmental arrests, here is where humanity needs help in its present struggle to make that evolutionary leap from a killing to nonkilling global culture.

Ironically, without formal knowledge of the xDARP and its powerful subconscious stressful emotion generating effects, psychotherapists have sometimes unwittingly activated the xDARP in their own work. That is, some therapies use deliberate *transference* of a patient's neurosis onto the therapist, causing *age regression*, promoting the *acting out* of a *repetitive* irrational theme, or the intense emotional arousal of *abreaction.* Individual patients or in groups have experienced these methods separately or together. Therapies employing these naturally occurring if bizarre processes have long held promise. Nonetheless, they have also repeatedly failed to delivered statistically detectable improvements in mental health.

Most psychosocial developmental arrests occur at critical stages that open before one's consciousness center has moved from the brain core up into the cerebral hemispheres around two or three years after birth. Once moved into the cerebrum, consciousness apparently uses a different memory format that can no longer directly access the earlier cerebellar primary memory. This makes early memories inaccessible for normal adult memory retrieval and correction. However, early especially those to hot to handle memories stored in the Reactive Mind are still reactive in our environment. Regarding earlier events in the developing child, these show major memory gaps. Once these memories were easily accessible to the young child but at a certain point, they are no longer recallable. Among certain individuals, it appears possible that hypnotic age regression can temporarily restore access to early memories,. However, this delicate topic has sparked a "Recovery of Lost Memories-False Memories" debate, especially regarding child abuse charges by children or their therapists. Questions arise whether the memories retrieved by hypnosis are only the product of the psychologist's inadvertent hypnotic suggestions. Or, were they the subject's actual recollections of real events that actually happened? This is also relevant to those who report memories of past lives. In a large study, such people exhibited significantly higher false recall and recognition rates, and to score higher on measures of magical ideation than control participants. An elevation of false memory for negative material may also appear in depression.

Currently, there are no known practical methods to repair or use the xDARP to complete one's arrested development as an adult. Therapists have tried many promising approaches. Some have unwittingly strongly activated the xDARP. All have ultimately disappointed.

xDARP Inactivation for the *Walking Wounded*:

If the xDARP is not available to repair arrests, can we instead turn off its powerful subconscious production of insane behavior? xDARP activation ultimately causes many more problems over time than the old failure to control the original process does! As we saw in the previous chapter, it is the major source of psychological stress, obsessive compulsions, crimes of passion, depression, suicide, and abuse of spouses and children. For millennia, researchers have sought ways to lower xDARP stress production. In fact, global cultures, especially religions, are a repository of empirical methods that appear to work. Yet, these give only temporary relief from the unrelenting xDARP activated subconscious stress.

First, sleep and good nutrition are essential. Lack of sleep or food significantly reduces stress tolerance and lowers the threshold for upset. This is because without adequate sleep and good nutrition, the Ego Caretaker looses the strength it needs to inhibit xDARP activation.

Ironically, Physical Pain is Temporarily Beneficial: *No Pain, No Gain.*

Second, for a reason described later, physical pain can temporarily reduce xDARP strength. Over the millennia, trial and error has revealed these benefits. In the relief brought by vigorous exercise, it is the frequently unrecognized production of *pain* that sets the rate and extent we exert ourselves. This is also true in aerobic, prolonged rapid breathing, and hyperventilation exercises. Cold stress such as cold showers or swimming in ice water, which people have long found beneficial also produce pain. All of these practices appear to weaken the xDARP by a common mechanism to be described later. Thus, when we feel "lousy", we tell ourselves that we have to get some exercise. Then, after the pain of vigorous exercise for a half hour, we feel renewed and good for a day or two, until we start to feel stressed again.

Similarly, good feelings that last for a couple of days after the induction of heat stress apparently provide the motivation for millions to regularly to undergo the noxious experience of heat-associated procedures. Who in their right minds would be willing to cook for 45 minutes in a steaming hot tub, or a Japanese furo, in a suffocating Turkish bath, or a Scandinavian sauna, or the suffocating torture of the Native American Sweat Lodge? Nonetheless, "no pain, no gain" works.

Even the unrecognized pain endured in prolonged meditation and prayer can cleanse, if properly and regularly used. Similarly clean living, restraint and self-discipline are hard to practice because the self-discipline required by each causes pain. However, importantly these practices also bring their own reward. Lastly, the pain of electroconvulsive therapy brings positive results, by a mechanism possibly tied to the xDARP.

Psychological Pain from Cathartic Discharge is also Temporary Beneficial.

Third, it is becomingly increasingly clear from fMRI (functional magnetic resonance imaging) studies that the brain treats psychological or psychic pain essentially the same as it does physical pain, activating the same brain areas. Since much psychological pain started as physical pain, such as slap in the face or an auto accident, this appears to make sense.

History of the Use of Psychic Pain to Gain Temporary Relief from the DARP-driven Insanity:

Thus, the catharsis of an hour of psychological pain can also give a two to four of days of serenity from the subconscious emotional stress of xDARP. The effects of beatings within the family also illustrate this. After a huge emotion-wracking fight, the real pleasure is to kiss and make up for a couple of days. After that, the xDARP demons reemerge to feast again!

In two powerful books, Eckhart Tolle (1999, 2005) unknowingly described the existence of the xDARP as his "Pain Body", which exhibits an insatiable periodic need to feed upon psychological pain.

Further, the "Sacrifice" of an animal for food can also cause psychic pain, whether the killing of a familiar "friend" from one's herd, or that of a respected, exquisite game animal. The ancient penalty for "sin" was death. Later, the sacrificial death of a scapegoat was used as a substitute for one's guilt, for example in Judaism. This was further dramatized in Christianity where Jesus was sacrificed on cross as a substitute for our sins, so that we could live forever. The sacrifice-crucifixion motif can causes cathartic pain, and thus bring relief. It has been said that true Christian worship demands the daily deep contemplation of Christ's death that we might live. This is the central theme of Catholic worship. The added physical pain of self-flagellation, the dragging of a cross to exhaustion and religious self-piercings have further amplified this.

A major source of the stress in living comes from the activation of the xDARP. Clearly, an unstated practical goal of religion is to bring reduction in the overall stress of living. Thus, it is of interest that many of the elements of religious practice are essentially pain inducing, such as standing for long periods during group worship, extended meditation and prayer or climbing stairs to an icon on bare knees, etc. Thus, the world's religions are an invaluable mixed repository of xDARP-weakening methods.

However, there have been, and continue to be other, methods to create psychic pain and thus to reduce xDARP-induced stress for a few days. Ancient Roman coliseum rituals pitted innocence against evil in fights to the death. These themes gripped the crowd in an experience of emotional pain and cathartic relief. In a modern continuation of coliseum ritual, the bullfight, beautiful and brave animals are doomed to die. The bull would always win, except picadors on horseback mercilessly severe of the head-balancing elastic chords in the bull's neck with their lances. Without these built-in bungee-chords, the enormous task of now having to hold up a hundred pound head and horns soon brings the terrified victim to a exhausted halt. At this point any coward could kill it. Over the centuries, this ritual appears to have brought about a widespread callousness regarding the suffering and death of others, for example in the conquest of the New World.

Today a clever entertainment industry brings us boxing and wrestling matches. The often-repeated reversals of fortune in these fights subconsciously cathartically grip us in a life and death struggle. In the violent spectator sports such as American Football and Rugby, rooting for the home team is a form of tribal warfare where the threat of team loss brings life-death psychic pain to tribe "members" rooting on the sidelines. Even soccer fans can act as participants in tribal warfare, unknowingly to gain cathartic release.

The belief that psychic pain of drama such as in the Greek Tragedies produces cathartic relief is long-held. This is sought in modern novels, theatric plays, movies and TV dramas. Now popular media violence, depicting increasingly bloody gore enrolling us in vicarious battles between life and death further enhances these effects. This promotes addiction to catharsis, which the entertainment industry hopes will bring us back for another emotional release again next week. All this spectacular violence engages the subconscious core of our being in a cathartic struggle for life and death. This suffering, brings temporary relief from our underlying DARP pain. As a result, we may even feel better for a day or two.

What is the Mechanism Behind this "No Pain, No Gain" Phenomenon?

The neurotransmitter, serotonin, activates fourteen known receptor subclasses. The 5-HT2a receptor is a crucial one in regard to stress. It is a key player in the stress response. Inflammation based serotonin activation of this receptor causes the release of the peptide neurotransmitter CRF (corticotrophin releasing factor), a last-resort stress hormone with wide receptor distribution in the brain. If the ventricles of the brain receive direct CRF injection, the individual often quickly becomes suicidally depressed. It is a well-known fact that serotonin levels in our brain strongly influence our mood, as if serotonin was itself involved in the production of stress. That indeed is the case. Through the 5-HT2a receptor, serotonin causes CRF release and elevation. Pronounced dysphoria is the result.

The discovery that the 5-HT2a receptor becomes rapidly down-regulated in the prolonged presence of elevated serotonin levels, having a half life of about one hour is remarkable. Thus, after a short period of serotonin-elevating stress, physical or psychic, the 5-HT2a receptor becomes down-regulated and desensitized, thus releasing much less CRF than the same amount of serotonin did in the beginning. This gives relief that and can literally convert "agony to ecstasy".

Furthermore, unlike others down-regulated receptors, the 5-HT2a serotonin receptor takes about 5 days to recover its original sensitivity. Thus, during the days following a serotonin-induced catharsis, the person is markedly less sensitive to the serotonin elevations due to physical or psychic pain than normal. As a result, the person feels good, clean, and more peaceful, until the 5-HT2a receptor regains its sensitivity. Then they feel rotten again because the xDARP is a continuing background source of serotonin. It is too low to down-regulate the receptor, but high enough to cause CRF-induced dysphoria.

This is the serotonin-based mechanism behind the "no pain-no gain" paradox. Short-term physical or psychic pain elevates serotonin sufficiently to down-regulate its stress receptor for several days of relief from stress. Importantly, current SSRI (serotonin specific reuptake inhibitors) antidepressants such as Prozac (fluoxetine) act to increase the level of serotonin at the 5-HT2 receptor slightly. After a couple of weeks, this results in the down regulation of the 5-HT2a receptor, reducing CRF release in the brain. This significantly reduces the production of CRF induced stress that drives depression.

Methods to Reduce Stress Receptor Hypersensitivity with Resulting xDARP Activation:

1. Temporarily 5-HT2a receptor Down-regulation with short-term Physical or Psychological PAIN

Cold Pain: Icy swim. Heat Pain: Japanese furo, Swedish sauna,, Turkish sweat bath, American Indian Sweat Lodge. Exercise Pain: pain-limited aerobic exercise, run, bike, swim. Emotional Pain-Catharsis: Spectator sports, Boxing, Wrestling, Football, Rugby, Basketball, Racing, Bull Fights, Drama, Opera, Movies, TV drama, Intense Religious Practice: contemplation of the death of Jesus on a Cross.

2. Temporarily Inhibit CRF-induced Locus Coeruleus Stress with Drugs of Abuse

These include caffeine, tobacco, alcohol, cannabis, tranquillizers, painkillers, cocaine, amphetamine, morphine, heroin, etc. The effects are brief, difficult to dose, with bad side effects, inevitable tolerance development, intoxication, addiction. However, as we are seeing, people will pay anything for the temporary relief from pain.

3. By-pass Pain and Drugs by the Long Term Down-regulating of the Stress Receptor with Antidepressants

SSRIs (serotonin specific reuptake inhibitors) are very effective stress reducers and unlike drugs of abuse, SSRIs have the fewest long-term side effects. For Lps, Paxil is best. For Rps only, use Prozac, or fluoxetine, its inexpensive generic equivalent. Be aware that at least two weeks of dosing is required before the beneficial effects appear. This approach is much less costly in time and money than the huge expenses of sports, entertainment, beverages or drugs.

4. Low Doses of Modern Antipsychotics appear to Directly Block the xDARP

Very low doses of Seroquel (quetiapine) (50 mg) at bedtime appear to reduce the drive to act out xDARP themes the next day. This makes sense because xDARP behavior is psychotic.

5. Valproic Acid and Inhibition of the xDARP

The cyclic nature of the xDARP feeding frenzies suggests a relationship to the manic-depressive cycles of bipolar affective illness. Valproic acid is as effective as lithium with much fewer side effects for the treatment of this syndrome. Psychiatrists are beginning to prescribe this compound to couples in marital conflict with some success.

6. Awaken to the Existence of One's xDARP-directed Stress and Detach from It

Upset, anger, and rage are at the heart of the xDARP. They are essential steps in the homeostatic escalation of the effort to gain control a vital process. The Reptile Brain produces these feelings by instincts outside normal consciousness. Therefore one may feel: "Oh, No! Here I am, upset again! in spite of my sincerest intentions otherwise. I do not even know how it happened. It just sneaked up on me before I knew it!"

The Fifth Reality: xDARP (Pain Body) Reality!

Here is a transformational idea: There exists within me a mutated, broken xDARP that subconsciously but actively cyclically creates my stress. My upsets seem so real because their survival-threat themes arouse me. My upsets seem so right because I believe that another person is causing them. My upsets feel so familiar and so authentic, that I believe that they are the way that life actually is. My upsets seem so like part of me because they link me to my past by an unbroken chain of upsets.

However, my upsets actually base themselves upon the lies of xDARP reality. They come from the past, and generalize into gross distortions of the true external reality of the current situation. xDARP reality seeks any association that forwards its goal to set up a struggle with a safe person to gain control of an arrested psychosocial developmental process. Its subconscious mechanical origin seems like external reality, but is only a concocted xDARP reality of the lowest quality. The transformational idea, *that upset reality is only xDARP reality, not the truth,* gives us a basis to detach from it, and step outside of it and stop acting out its insanity. I can *reject it* as not me, but rather that it is an insane obsession that can only harm all involved.

7. Taking Responsibility for One's DARP-Generated Anger:

Actually, our upsets are *not* who we are. We *have* upsets. *They* cause us stress! Our Upsets come *from Reactive Memory of the past* and are not relevant to the here and now! Actually it is *my xDARP*, not another person that is the *source* of my upset. Would I be angry at a bear?; At a cliff?; At a tidal wave?; At a drunk with a knife? NO! Most often Anger comes from failure to control a process or an object in the *past, not* from the present environment, which is merely *restimulating* the past upset. Acting-out, dramatizing, and trying to win control in the present only strengthens the xDARP. Authentic as it feels, this approach ends in nervous breakdown, psychosis, death but *never* mastery! We are *not* our xDARPs inappropriate thoughts and feelings!!

8. How to Detach from the xDARP:

Start separating what actually happened in the now from the xDARP's paranoid interpretation of it from the past. Usually it is a survival-neutral event, contaminated by xDARP roots into the past, or, when it is not survival-neutral, your xDARP often created it by its previous actions.

Recognize that you are not your xDARP! It is the source of the ideas of what you *think* you want, which are *unattainable*. It keeps you distracted, paralyzed, friendless, hopeless and poor. It has filled your life with drama and trauma and has used up your years with meaninglessness!

Detach from it! Choose aliveness rather than proving yourself right! Stop letting your own DARP victimize you! "Getting off of it" means taking responsibility for the fact that your xDARP--*not* the other person, is the source of your upset. Thank your xDARP for trying to help you complete your thwarted development but decline its beguiling invitation to act out your developmental fixation in daily life. Stop your attempts to be right, to win the argument, to dominate-avoid domination. Do not complain, attack, wound, make wrong, have the last word, get revenge. Declare yourself "OFF OF IT". Doing so in public can be helpful. Stop! Count to ten. If necessary, leave the room to regain your composure. Become occupied with something else to get your mind off it. It will disappear. At first "Getting Off of It" may take days, then hours, then minutes, then seconds!

9. How to Begin to Keep The DARP Off:

Stopping one's xDARP upsets is like "house-breaking" a puppy: At first the puppy unconsciously wets anywhere, anytime. Its xDARP upsets are automatic with No awareness or responsibility for them. "If there is a problem, it is the world's problem, not mine. I'm perfect!"

After having its nose rubbed in a few puddles, the puppy looks confused. Its upsets still are automatic, with increasing awareness, but no responsibility. The puppy is becoming clear that it is guilty of repetitive irrational behavior. However, it seems unthinkable that it might have a choice in the matter.

Now, After wetting, the puppy looks sheepish. Its upsets are becoming only semi-automatic with dawning awareness and responsibility. It begins to recognize there may be a microsecond of choice before it "xDARPs out".

Then, After wetting, the puppy looks guilty. xDARP upsets still are semi-automatic, but now with full awareness and responsibility. It is beginning to recognize that its xDARP upset harms others and itself. It wishes to stop wetting and to reverse the damage they have done (take control).The time window of choice has become wider and a reduction in xDARP upsets occurs.

No Longer Wetting, the Puppy is Joyful! Unless kicked, it can now be trusted indoors! It has gained voluntary control over former upset automaticity = Mastery! *Smart as Puppy! Many people have matured* from hourly upsets, to daily, weekly, or yearly upsets!!

10. What to do is Someone Else's DARP is Activated:

Avoid activating another person's xDARP if possible! Use your wisdom to spot and stay away from their developmental wounds. Criticizing another's hypersensitive area of dyscontrol <u>guarantees</u> their xDARP will turn on. <u>That</u> may well hook your own xDARP as well. If another's xDARP is already on, recognize it to be so and do not engage it. It is insane, does not respond to logic and will distort what you mean. It is dangerous and will escalate to crimes of passion. You cannot win. Let it cool down and turn itself off. It is not personal, except that you must be so important that their DARP has transferred a key nuclear family member onto you: a high compliment! The other person may care for you very much and actually does not want to hurt or lose you. Don't force them to. Support them in discovering the existence of xDARPs. Then, they can begin to take responsibility for their own DARP-driven past behavior, and stop blaming you or the world for their unhappiness. Give them the tools to transform from a victim at the effect of life into a Causal Source, loving what Is!

Some Important Concepts in Chapter 13:

1. Ironically, without formal knowledge of the xDARP and its subconscious stressful emotion generating effects, psychotherapists have sometimes unwittingly activated it in their work. That is, therapies using *transference* of a patient's neurosis onto the therapist, causing *age regression*, promoting the *acting out* of a *repetitive* irrational theme, or the intense emotional arousal of *abreaction* have all been used separately or together with individual patients or in groups. However, these methods have uniformly failed to delivered statistically detectable improvements in mental health.

2. xDARP inactivation for the *Walking Wounded:* If the xDARP can no longer be used to repair developmental arrests, can we instead turn off its powerful subconscious production of insane behavior? xDARP activation ultimately causes many more problems than failure to control the original process does! As seen in the previous chapter, it is the major source of psychological stress, obsessive compulsions, depression, suicide, abuse of spouses and children and other crimes of passion.

3. For millennia, ways to lower xDARP production of subconscious stress have been sought. Many have been found. In fact, global cultures and religions are a great repository of methods found by trial-and-error to work. But, these give only temporary relief.

4. First, sleep and good nutrition are essential to reduce stress. Second, ironically, it has repeatedly been demonstrated that exposure short-term physical pain, reduces xDARP strength for several days, as in *No Pain, No Gain,.*

5. In vigorous exercise, the unrecognized production of *pain* sets the rate and extent that we exercise. Cold stress, such as swimming in ice water also produces pain that people find stress reducing. The controlled induction of heat stress is at the core of many cultural traditions and has motivated millions to regularly to undergo the noxious experience of heat stress for a few days relief.

6. Even the unrecognized pain of meditation and prayer can be cleansing, if properly and regularly used. Similarly clean living, restraint, and self-discipline are hard to practice because each causes pain, but importantly also bring their own rewards. All of

these practices weaken the xDARP. Thus, when we feel "lousy", we tell ourselves that we have to get some exercise. After the pain of vigorous exercise for a half hour, we feel renewed and good for a day or two, until we start to feel tense again.

7. Historically, psychic pain successfully achieved temporary relief from the xDARP-driven stress as well. This is because psychological pain activates the brain in a similar manner as physical pain does. Thus, the catharsis of an hour of psychological suffering can also give a two to four of days of serenity from the subconscious emotional stress. This fact has been the basis of a many cultural traditions, from the Greek Tragedy to the current carnage in movie theaters and violent sports.

8. The neurochemical mechanism for this *No Pain, No Gain* method to obtain temporary xDARP stress relief is described here. From this discovery, existing methods reducing xDARP stress are understandable and others can be designed. Besides temporarily down-regulating the stress receptor with many cultural types of short-term physical or psychological pain, one can also inhibit the locus coeruleus, a downstream player in the stress pathway, with *drugs of abuse*. The effects are brief, difficult to dose, with bad side effects, tolerance development, intoxication, addiction. However, people will pay anything for relief from pain. Another approach is the long-term 5-HT2a receptor down-regulation with antidepressants, antimanic or antipsychotic agents.

9. Recognizing the existence of the xDARP as the source personal stress is the best approach to mastery. Take responsibility for it, and detach from it. Actually, it is our xDARP's (Tolle's Pain Body) inappropriate thoughts and feelings, not the other person or my surroundings, that is the source of my upset. xDARP reality, a fifth form of reality, comes from the past and has only been restimulated by the present. Authentic as it feels, acting it out can only end in a nervous breakdown, psychosis or death. It wastes your life, keeping you distracted, paralyzed, friendless, hopeless and poor. Detach from it. Get off of it. At first "Getting off of It" may take days, then hours, then minutes, then seconds!

10. Replace your xDARP driven past with a new present, created by your Source from the future.

Section IV: Why do I Feel the Way I do? What can I Do About It?

Chapter 14: Removing Guilt Pain to Regain the Ability to Grow

Guilt Pain is Different

We feel guilt and its associated pain for only one reason: It occurs when our Social Brain Source judges that we have selfishly harmed another's survival in order to benefit our own. Instead of working at the universe level of "win-win or no deal" familial cooperation where we delight in helping others, we have dropped to the antisocial level of self against the world and have harmed others. This may happen if our Executive Caretaker has been so weakened by stress that it can no longer restrain the "I win, you lose" Crocodile Brain from taking over. It only lives in the now, being oblivious to the past or future effects of its selfish behavior.

However, the Social Brain conscience has evolved two protections for the family against wanton selfishness of individuals. First, it has developed a subconsciously potent device for inflicting punishment upon the Crocodile Brain and the Reactive Mind called the "pain of guilt". This pain differs from the "no pain-no gain" that weakens the xDARP. Guilt is a festering, relentless, gnawing pain that will not quit *and from which there is no "gain"*.

Originally, once one empathically felt the pain of guilt, one's associative intelligence would conclude that restoration of the other's harmed survival would immediately cause permanent cessation of guilt and thus bring relief. In fact, this simple solution still works extremely well. However, time revealed other seeming solutions. Omnivorous, experimenting humans, by trial and error over millennia discovered natural substances that would temporarily turn off guilt pain. These included tobacco, caffeine, alcohol, marijuana and opium, all of which all became known and popular because they each could temporarily replace guilt pain with pleasure.

However, this occurred at a cost. Seeking cellular homeostasis, the body soon developed a resistant tolerance to the guilt-pain killing drug, requiring progressively greater amounts to bring relief. At higher dosages, side effects become increasingly prominent. Often, these included intoxication of the higher brain along with a replacement of a clear intelligence with foggy drunkenness leading to unconsciousness. They also greatly increased mortality by causing physical and metabolic damage and tumor formation.

Worst of all, the subconsciously hurting person became more dependent upon these narcotics for pain relief, ultimately becoming addicted. These addictions are so strong that the victim will lie, cheat, steal and even kill to obtain relief from them. They will pay any price, even sell their homes and children for temporary relief from escalating guilt pain. This makes narco-trafficking the most profitable business in the world. With their enormous income, competing drug cartels can buy firearms, officials, vehicles, and gangs of foot soldiers to fight each other to gain and retain control of the fortune that the suffering population spends in an attempt to get relief from its pain. The illicit drug cartels are even infiltrating and corrupting national governments. Because people have forgotten how simple it is to remove guilt, they are instead paying narco-traffickers their hard-earned money, and in the process threatening to bring down society and civilization itself. In support of this mechanism was the personal comment by a Central American Drug Lord to the author at dinner one night. He said that to feel well, he had developed a fixed schedule of twenty drinks of liquor to be taken over each day. Now that's a lot of pain!

As part of this process, society members have become increasingly more self-oriented. Global competitive enterprises, ranging from arms sales, based upon political destabilization, to the entertainment media cashing in on sex and violence are creating an atmosphere where violence-worship and killing are destroying family values so that almost two of three US marriages fail. It is becoming harder not to inadvertently harm others in the process of life itself, thus, generating ever more subconscious guilt pain and drug seeking. Since our genes appear lag a million years behind the present, our old Social Brain continues to keep score and punish us for our "sins": that of helping ourselves at the survival expense of others. We are in an accelerating downward spiral returning us to the ancient jungle of kill or be killed

Causing Another's Loss Results in Your Loss

There is a second inhibitory mechanism that our Social Brain Source has developed to thwart profiting at another's expense preventing us from benefiting from ill-gotten gain. We may take or extort something from another, but our Social Brain will not let us actually have it. As the old saying goes "You cannot have your cake and eat it too". This is because one's Social Brain-Source is the Crocodile-Self Brain's worst judge and executioner. The Source always tells the truth, and sees to it that the selfish Crocodile brain can never profit from the theft of another's survival. Thus, the person with perpetrations harming others becomes *unable to benefit from anything* in that area. For example, money is actively sought, but rapidly disappears through holes in pockets, like sand through grasping fingers. Or, the right mate can never be found, in spite of a lifetime of intense effort.

The great news is, that this cycle of endlessly seeking impossible relief from stress and blocked pleasure be brought to an end through a very simple, easily achievable means! That is, one simply must completely and generously restore the survival of the one we took advantage of by earlier helping our self at their expense. What is more, one's Social Brain actively wishes us to do so, and actually helps makes it possible to do so, as seen below. One sign that we have made complete restitution is when the harmed other person can easily look us in the eye, smile, warmly forgive us, and welcome us back into the family again.

The Ancient Secret of Having:

Application #1: **Having Money**

1. Make an ongoing perpetration list of all persons you have ever taken anything of monetary or survival value from against their will or knowledge. Tell the truth when you make your list. Avoid such rationalizations as: they did not really need it or would have given it anyway.

2. Sort the list so that monetarily, the smallest perpetrations are at the top and the "impossibles" are on the bottom.

3. Repay the dime you stole from your Mother's purse, which at the time carried as much guilt as robbing a bank would to an adult, and discover a huge lessening of guilt pain!

4. Continue in this way to discover that *the more one makes restitution and repays, the more one's ability to have money and happiness increases.* Thus, you will become increasingly enabled to generously repay even the most dreadful of harms against others

and to ask for their forgiveness of each. If you have truly made complete restitution to the other, they will happily forgive you and actually want to be your friend.

5. Thus empowered, keep on reformulating and paying off your list of perpetrations until it is exhausted. By this time *you will **have** the abundant happiness, friends, respect, and wealth, which is your natural heritage.*

6. Next, identify what else that you want badly, which you currently seem unable to be able to **have**, and repeat the process of cleaning up your life. It really works!

Self-Rehabilitation and Empowerment:

Application #2: **Cleaning Up and Terminating Upsets from the Past**

Almost all the things that upset us come from the restimulation of one of our unhealing developmental arrest wounds or other death threatening things from the past, inaccessibly stored in the memory banks of our Reactive Mind. Thus, what may upset you deeply and often may not bother another person, and vice versa, although there are of course common themes upsetting others as well. Fear from true danger is not upsetting. If you find yourself upset, it is because you are struggling for control of a process you were not permitted to master before its developmental window closed. Upset is on the same gradient as anger. Both are the impotent reactions of a victim failing to gain control of a social process or other trauma. The upset person usually irrationally places blame for their upset upon someone else. This is true even when a different person would not find the same situation upsetting. Blaming others leads to harmful attempts at retaliation against innocent bystanders that often ruins formerly rewarding friendships and creates enemies.

It is very hard to be objective about one's current upset. However, one's upsets follow repetitive themes related to one's particular unhealing developmental or other wounds (Chapter 12). Thus, to begin to take responsibility for being the source of one's own upsets, it is helpful at first to look at previous upset cycles. Thus, find earlier-similar repetitions of your current xDARP *upset theme* in the recent past. Note the harm they did you and especially to the others involved. When this becomes clear, acknowledge your fault to them. Confess to each of those you victimized how you harmed their survival. Repair damage and restore the survival of your victim until they forgive you and accept you with open arms as family once again. If they cannot look at you with a direct gaze and smile, your restitution is still incomplete. When it is clean, the original issue will be forgotten, or seem overblown and crazy. Remember, there is more than one reality: Yours and your xDARPs. Next, clean up the present upset you have caused. Then, move on to others until you truly become honest, open and happy. Recognize once again that you are not your xDARP's thought or feelings.

Although I learned of the operation of this ancient principle from a member of the Church of Scientology in the 1970s, I later discovered it to be a core element of the Twelve Steps of Alcoholics Anonymous. Here are the Twelve Steps further generalized for application to any compulsion that places you out of control and upset.

Compulsives Anonymous, A 12-Step of Program from the Society for Neuroreality:

1. We admitted we were powerless over the compulsive selfish impulses of our Crocodile Brain and that our lives had become unmanageable.
2. We came to believe that a Power greater than ourselves could restore us to sanity.
3. We made a decision to turn our will and our lives over to the care of our Social Brain's God-Within, Higher Power, Source as we understood It.
4. We made a searching and fearless moral inventory of ourselves.
5. We admitted to our Source, to ourselves, and to another human being the exact nature of our wrongs.
6. We were entirely ready to have our Source remove all these defects of character.
7. We humbly asked our Source to remove our shortcomings.
8. We made a list of all persons we had harmed and became willing to make amends to them all.
9. We made direct amends to such people wherever possible, except when to do so would injure them or others.
10. We continued to take personal inventory and when we were wrong, promptly admitted it.
11. We sought through prayer and meditation to improve our conscious contact with our Source as we understood It, praying only for knowledge of Its will for us and the power to carry that out.

12. Having had an awakening as the result of these steps, we carry this message to others overrun by their Crocodile Brain, and to practice these principles in all our affairs.

In conclusion, this chapter provides a simple, effective solution to remove our dysphoric pain and our punished incapacitation that we have brought upon ourselves due to our ignorance of an ancient law of the mind. The more that we clean up our past and present life, the more our moral Social Brain Source will become willing to trust us and to open Its channels of communication to the flow of its wisdom and guidance.

Some Important Concepts in Chapter 14:

1, Our Self Brain "Crocodile" is naturally dedicated to maximizing our personal immediate survival in the jungle of life against competing species (snakes, rats, and other "Aliens"). It effective uses the genetic competitive rules of "Win-Lose", immediate gratification and escalation to violence. These valid Individual Universe Level Laws are used upon subhuman Aliens.

2. Our Social Brain "Source" dedicates itself to the optimal survival of our Family as key element of Humanity. It has discovered that there are *Emergent Properties* in cooperative synergy. It successfully uses the genetic cooperative rules of "Win-Win or No Deal", along with deferred gratification, unselfishness, and non-violence, all of which are personally more beneficial in the long run that competitively going it alone. This Family Universe Level Law applies in social interactions.

3. For important reasons, the laws at the subunit level (Individual) are very different, and often opposite to those that exist at the level of the unitary whole (Family). Thus, applying Self laws to the Family has been termed Antisocial Behavior because in the end they are harmful to the survival of the group.

4. To inhibit the Self Brain from harming the family, the Social Brain produces subconscious guilt pain and blocks pleasure to the Self Brain *whenever the Self Brain helps itself at the survival expense of others.*

5. The Social Brain <u>never</u> forgets these perpetrations <u>nor does it</u> turn off the pain <u>until</u> the Self Brain restores the survival it stole from others. Thus, a background of subconscious pain can accumulate over the lifetime for those unaware of these principles. This subconscious but very real guilt pain can temporarily be relieved by drugs of abuse to inhibit the locus coeruleus. However, the body has the last say, because tolerance develops, requiring ever increasing levels of drugs to suppress the ever-present guilt pain. As drug levels go higher, side effects increase making things unacceptable: i.e., heart attack, drunkenness, socially intolerable behavior, highway fatalities, depression, suicide, premature death.

6. Further, demand these drugs of abuse, which temporarily turn off subconscious guilt pain, drive Narco-trafficking, global corruption and the waste of millions of lives. In addition, one's Social Brain cannot allow one's Reptile Brain to keep things stolen from another, so that "I can't get no satisfaction" becomes the rule.

7. A much more effective way to permanently gain relief from guilt pain, and be released to thrive once more, is to avoid helping yourself by causing another's harm. Making full restitution of the survival harm done, so that the victim delightedly forgives you and restores you as friend and family member back into the human race, completely removes guilt from the past and reopens the possibility of abundance. By cleaning up one's life in this way, channels open to your "Higher Power"- Source.

Chapter 14 Appendix A: The 12 Step Program of Alcoholics Anonymous (Alcoholics Anonymous, 1956)

1, We admitted we were powerless over alcohol and that our lives had become unmanageable.

2, Came to believe that a Power greater than ourselves could restore us to sanity.

3, Made a decision to turn our will and our lives over to the care of God* as we understood Him.

4, Made a searching and fearless moral inventory of ourselves.

5, Admitted to God, to ourselves, and to another human being the exact nature of our wrongs.

6, Were entirely ready to have God remove all these defects of character.

7, Humbly asked Him to remove our shortcomings.

8, Made a list of all persons we had harmed, and became willing to make amends to them all.

9, Direct amends to such people wherever possible, except when to do so would injure them or others.

10, Continued to take personal inventory and when we were wrong, promptly admitted it.

11, Sought through prayer and meditation to improve our conscious contact with God as we understood Him, praying only for knowledge of His will for us and the power to carry that out.

12, Having had a spiritual awakening as the result of these steps, we tried to carry this message to alcoholics, and to practice these principles in all our affairs.

* The Social Brain's Source, Our Higher Power, God-Within qualifies as "God as we understood him".

Chapter 14 Appendix B: The Twelve Traditions of A.A. (Alcoholics Anonymous, 1956)

1, Our common welfare should come first: personal recovery depends upon AA unity.

2, For our group purpose there is but one ultimate authority - a loving God* as He may express Himself in our group conscience. Our leaders are but trusted servants: *they do not govern.*

3, The only requirement for AA membership is a desire to stop drinking.

4, Each group should be autonomous except in matters affecting other groups or AA as a whole.

5, Each group has but one primary purpose- to carry its message to the compulsive person who still suffers.

6, An AA group ought never endorse, finance, or lend the AA name to any related facility or outside enterprise, *lest problems of money, property, and prestige divert us from our primary purpose.*

7, Every AA group ought to be fully self-supporting, declining outside contributions.

8, Alcoholics Anonymous should remain forever nonprofessional, but our service centers may employ special workers.

9, AA, as such, ought never be organized; but we may create service boards or committees directly responsible to those they serve.

10, AA has no opinion on outside issues; hence the AA name ought never be drawn into public controversy.

11, Our public relations policy is based on *attraction* rather than promotion; we need always maintain personal anonymity at the level of press, radio, films, television, and other public media of communication.

12, Anonymity is the spiritual foundation of all these traditions, ever reminding us *to place principles before personalities.*

NEUROREALITY: A SCIENTIFIC RELIGION TO RESTORE MEANING

Section V: Is this a Safe Place? What Should I Be Doing? How Should I Relate to Others?

Chapter 15: Why Humans Kill other Humans and Why they Don't

Life and Death in the Dyadic Universe

We live in an ever changing, ever the same dyadic universe where all extremes are present, from hot to cold, from light to dark, from chaos to order, from vacuum to pressure, from horizontal to vertical, from miniscule to massive, from death to life. The genetic goal of life is for our cells to survive and thrive by avoiding these survival extremes. This has required selective action on our part to stay out of the fire and keep on the grass, so to speak. To avoid being killed, we must obey "Survival of Life Laws" of the dyadic universe regarding many things. They include those related to heat, cold, gravity, oxygen, CO_2, pressure, momentum, weather, continental drift, earthquakes, volcanoes, tidal waves, solar flare cycles, droughts, floods, hot cycles, cold cycles, cosmic rays, other radiations, natural toxins, population explosions of microbes, viruses, parasites, insects, rodents and other organisms, including humans.

Death, is the penalty for disobedience of the survival of life laws of the universe, either by being killed immediately, or by having one's dying accelerated more rapidly than the current "three score and ten" (70) years that is the present average world longevity for humans. Threats of death are unavoidably inherent in life. At the cellular, organ and organism levels, we obey these survival of life laws almost without thought. Please note, we do not view the ever-present *death curse* for breaking universal survival rules as unfair, tyrannical, arbitrary commandments of God, or evil. It simply is the way things are.

The Problem of Evil, Promise of Survival.

However, at the levels of individuals and society, issues of life and death become more complicated. This is because, beyond the natural forces of the dyadic universe to bring benefit or to kill, it becomes additionally possible for life forms themselves to kill, or, crucially, to benefit other life forms. The foundational living organisms on earth are the sun-harvesting, self-sufficient primary organisms, such as photosynthetic microorganisms and plants. These eat atmospheric CO_2 and convert it into the high-energy carbon-carbon bonds of sugar-containing carbohydrates, as well as into fats and other biopolymers. They throw off the extra oxygen, split from the CO_2, as waste into our atmosphere, one fifth of which is now oxygen. In the distant past vast amounts of carbon fixation of solar energy occurred on earth. We now tap this reservoir as the petroleum and coal extracted from buried ancient forests that we use to power most of our modern activities.

Within plants and other photosynthetic organisms, the carbon bond energy in carbohydrates is stored in large amounts for release to power the work activities required for the survival of their cells. Herbivores, including some animals, totally lacking in photosynthetic equipment, can still obtain their energy needs by eating plants with their contained stores of solar energy. Amazingly, carnivores can obtain their own solar energy needs by eating the carbon polymers deposited within herbivores or even those within other carnivores, or sometimes cannibalistically within their own fellows. Omnivores in this food chain, such as humans, can obtain their needed solar fuel by eating either animals or plants.

Thus, inherent in our interdependent and synergistic world, there are the predatory aggressors who must actively kill in order to live. In addition, there are their prey, the victims killed so that others might live. Thus, life includes meadows, antelope, lions, hyenas, vultures, worms, insects and microorganisms. Is this evil? Within the eternal impersonal dyadic universe of beauty and action, of course it is not. The life-death web of life is an extraordinary expression of order and complexity that evolves in galactic halos of life. It is marvelous and wonderful.

Then what is evil? From the Survival Reality of antelopes, evil is anything that harms the optimal survival of antelopes. To antelopes, lions are evil terrifying demons, so are hyenas, vultures, if not worms, insects, and microorganisms. What kind of a personal antelope God, omnipotent, omniscient, omnipresent, would have created such a situation? This is why in Neuroreality, the Trinity is redefined. God the Father-Mother can only be the eternal dyadic universe, unplanned, impersonal, and mysterious, the unfathomable galactic creator of both the antelopes and lions for whose survival it has no concern. Its laws are immutable, bringing either life or death within their dyadic expression. The human problem of evil can have nothing to do with a God that is the Universe.

The job of each of us is to learn enough about our dyadic universe so we can intelligently align with and tap it richness as the sole source of life, abundance, opportunity and power. This makes each of us seekers and worshipers of the eternal beauty of existence. We become high priests, using the scientific method from the chapels of our laboratories, be they in our garages or within mighty institutions. What we have uncovered about the universe does not require faith to believe. It is demonstrable and reproducible by any other competent worshiper. Upon these discoveries, about universe, life and mind, we can rebuild religion to assist once again the optimal survival of humanity, its relatives and its life support systems. We need no supernatural protection, prayers for healing, or hope of an afterlife. We do need better approximations of external reality to assist us in choosing and aligning with the dyadic universe as perfect. Then, we become gods in our universe, successful causal sources of aliveness.

One can complain and rebel, but this can never change the laws of the universe, which are what Is, the way things work. To resist and try to change how the universe works automatically makes one a failure, at effect, and an angry impotent victim. For example, if, as I am walking through a park, I find a large tree in my path, I can either bloody my head against its trunk, swear at it, run to my pickup and get a chain saw, and angrily cut it of my way. Or, I can choose the tree to be there, change my course to walk on around it, cooling in its shade, admiring the beauty of its form, the birds singing in its lofty branches, the fragrance of its flowers, and continue, blessed, along my way.

Universe Levels of Life: Unique Structural Elements and Laws.

In order for humans to rise from killing to nonkilling we need to understand the unique vital laws of the relevant levels of our universe, and especially how to pass between these levels, each having different laws. For this discussion, there are twelve universe levels of relevance. As will become obvious, passing from level 5 to level 6 is the key to elevating humans from killing to nonkilling.

Subcellular Level Laws: Life is the free energy-powered progression toward order, complexity, and beauty of cells and multicellular organisms. To assemble cells, the foundational building blocks of life, we must rise through their constituent synergistic levels of atoms, molecules, macromolecules, supramolecular assemblies and subcellular organelles.

Cellular Level Laws: In humans, cells can either cooperate with their fellows to form tissues, or complete with each other as microbiological infections or as independent tumor-forming cancer cells, like leukemia: Among the tissue-forming cells there is a wide range of cellular mortality. Some cells, such as those of the intestinal epithelium, rapidly turn over, living only a few weeks before being replaced. At the other extreme, some neurons in the brain appear to be immortal, never dividing, but continually repairing themselves instead. Some runaway tumor cells have achieved immortality through their unending ability to divide until they choke out some vital process. Chaos and death to the higher order that is the individual results. Yet, our bodies also provide Natural Killer Cells that seek out and exterminate antisocial cancer cells before they can take over. However, sometimes one of these non-cooperating cells evades the cellular police, leading to disorder and the death of the system, and ultimately to the criminals as well.

Tissue Level Laws: Tissues can either stay unorganized and compete with other blocks of tissues, or they can self organize into organs and reap the emergent benefits of rising to the next level of order. At maturity, most organs maintain a constant size and cell number, yet their cells within turn over and mitotic cell division where the parent cell divides into two daughter cells replaces them. It is inevitable that in order to retain a constant cell number within the organ, at each mitosis, one of the two daughter cells must die. Again, we see that killing is part of living. However, because the laws of each universe level are unique, we can be thankful that they are different at the level of families where there is no killing.

Organ Level Laws: Organs can compete with each other, or coordinate together to make possible a symbiotic, balanced organism.

Individual Level Laws: Individuals can compete independently. Laws of the jungle that work best for survival against the world include acts to lie, cheat, steal, rape, violence, harm, injure, or kill.

Family Level Laws: Individual subunits can assemble into family units. Family laws that work for the emergence of a symbiotic family in the world, include honesty, sincerity, integrity, generosity, kindness, acceptance, helpfulness, cooperation, collaboration, nonviolence, non-harming and nonkilling.

Society Level Laws: Family units can feud violently, or they can collaborate to form a composite society with emergent properties greater that those of the sum of their parts. Because of the Law of Emergence, the laws of societies predictably differ from those at the family, or at the individual self-survival level. However, their separate existence is not well recognized, and they have yet to be properly identified and assembled.

Culture Level Laws: Societies can fight for independence or form a National Culture with associated benefits. Again predictably, unique unrecognized culture level laws emerge that are important here.

Nation Level Laws: Nations can fight selfishly or form The Unified Nations of Earth with emergent benefits, including nonkilling. Thoughtful investigation should be made to identify the laws that are in force at the international level.

Terrestrial Level Laws: Terrestrial Life can fight Extraterrestrial life forms or develop Alliances with unexpected benefits.

Galactic Level Laws: As dramatically portrayed in science fiction. Alliances can fight, or unite into Galactic Unions.

Universe Level Laws: Galaxy unions may fight, or unify into The Universal Society of Life, something delightful to contemplate.

Opposite Laws for Individuals in the Jungle vs. Laws Appropriate for Members of a Family

Now, we return to the issue of humans killing humans at the Individual universe level, but humans never killing humans at the Family universe level. To make the transition from the killing to the nonkilling level, we first need to set down 50 reasons why some humans kill other humans while the vast majority do not.

Why do We Kill our Children?

Reasons we kill children include the following: 1) We use contraceptives or abortion to prevent unwanted reproduction. 2) Infanticide occurs in many species, including humans, where a new patripolar dominant male will instinctively kill his mate's offspring from an earlier male, so as to bring her in to heat, and then fertilize her himself, thus investing in his genes, not those of his predecessor. 3) Mercy Killing has long been used to eliminate suffering, incapacitation, waste and familial damage from birth defects or injury. 4) Suicidal females murder whole families of children to terminate the products of a bad marriage (mate loathing). 5) Accidents or abuse in child labor situations continue to kill millions of children. 6) An angry parent or baby-sitter often kill children in domestic child abuse.

Why do We Kill our Women?

Patripolar males are the predominant perpetrators in the following femicidal acts: 7) Abortion of female fetuses used to select the sex of the child. 8) Punishment for adultery. An angry man seeking revenge for rejection is stronger than an unarmed woman and he can kill her. In some villages, stoning still prevails for adulterous women, supposedly to maintain the sanctity of marriage. 9) removal of familial contamination by rape or 10) by cohabitation with a stigmatized male: her father or brothers usually commit the killing to maintain family pride. 11) In the past, wives and servants were buried together with a deceased nobleman as his personal property, or to assist him in the proported afterlife.

Why do We Kill other Human Beings?

We kill them for reasons including: 12) In crimes of passion where we are unwilling or unable to defer our immediate gratification: "Give it to me now or I'll kill you!". 13) We will kill to survive a fight to the death. 14) We often kill murderers as the penalty for the killing of another or others. This may frighten the sane to behave, but has little effect upon the large insane population who are the major perpetrators. 15) In an upset, flair of anger, or fit of rage, we may attack in retaliation for real or assumed harm done to us. This is especially dangerous in combination with intoxication and access to a lethal weapon. 16) We will kill in a fear-based defensive attack against a real, or a pathologically assumed larger aggressor.

An unrecognized source of psychotic crimes of passion, often including murder, is 17) the powerful subconscious actions of the xDARP-Pain Body described in preceding chapters. 18) We also plan killings out of hatred and desire for revenge for real, or pathologically assumed, harm to oneself or one's "family". 19) We preemptively kill to prevent someone from harming our own survival interests (i.e. by reporting our crimes, or overthrowing our "family"). 20) We often murder as a form of predatory attack to gain another's assets: wife, property or land, by force or stealth. 21) Tyrants kill to cause fear and thus to inhibit the free action of others.

Sadly, murder or assassination has often been performed: 22) for money, 23) for drugs, or 24) for attention, fame, or prestige. 25) Many have murdered for fear of being killed themselves if they disobey their gang "family's" demand to kill a target victim, even another family member. 26) Killing may be for entertainment and profit, as in coliseum matador spectacles, or "snuff movies". 27) Murderous sacrifices have long been done as part of "Satanic rites" and other brain-based (Dual Quadbrain Model), non-supernatural demon possession. Of course, from the understanding of Triadism (Chapter 4) it is great relief to learn that it is impossible for spirits to exist!

As we see in the movies, 28) murder can be performed due to a hypnotic command by a more powerful external source. 29) Schizophrenics have obeyed "external" auditory commands to kill coming from other parts of their brain. 30) Millions of murders have been committed from the desire to exterminate an alien "subhuman" harmful species of mankind This is made easier by the dehumanization of members of another group, as "Krauts" or "Gooks". 31) Rarely today, but apparently more common anciently, people have also killed others as a ready source of food, as in cannibalism.

Why do we commit Suicide?

32) Deep depression, due to losses, guilt pain or drug rebound causing sufficient DA depletion will activate a genetic suicide program. Suicide is apparently inbuilt in primates, for example in chimpanzees, where death can leave an infant without a mother. Because the care of two infants is often impossible in the wild, no other mother will take the infant. At first, the infant searches agitatedly through the group, crying loudly for its dead mother. This attracts predators and endangers the group. Soon, the lethargy of depression descends, and the now silent infant cannot keep up with the fleeing group. Left alone, predators mercifully eat it.

Often we kill ourselves while engaging in high risk activities as 33) sports, or 34) to help save someone in danger. Or we kill ourselves 35) in the attempt to impress someone. To dare the impossible and fail. I had a friend who obsessed with the idea of being able to perform the first loop in his primitive hang glider. The next week he was dead. Others of us kill themselves 36) when they feel they have failed at something so irreversibly that death remains the only "honorable" way out. 37) Others want to be "dead right" and are willing to die a martyrs death. They would rather die than change. Some of us get 38) killed in accidents during rites of initiation or hazing by organizations.

Then comes the type of suicide where the individual kills themselves directly or indirectly 39) to obtain assumed rewards in the hereafter or to save the life of others. Others, often Lxps, hate what life has offered them so much that they wish to kill as many of favored (normal) persons as possible 40) in the process of killing themselves. They seek negative attention whereby they can give the living their final rejection.

Another huge group of us 41) kill ourselves directly or indirectly when they ignore the laws of the universe by losing the ability to defer immediate gratification due to injury or addiction: " I want to eat, smoke, drink alcohol or take drugs to feel good right now, no matter what the later health consequences may be. Others 42) kill themselves due to their religion or superstition-based belief in quack healing remedies for cancer or other lethal conditions, having faith in them as being superior than those of modern medicine. 43) Suicidal suggestion by an authoritarian religious leader while under mass hypnosis has caused hundreds to poison themselves, as in the Jonestown massacre.

44) Last but not least, rather than being induced commit simple wasteful suicide, leaders have directed their minions to suicidally attack their enemies. This occurred in the case of WWII Kamikaze pilots and more recently the many female and male suicide bombers on foot or in explosive laden vehicles. To die altruistically to enhance the survival of their group has long been a powerful biological weapon.

Why do Institutions Kill Human Beings?

We can view institutions as immortal life forms. Their human subunits turn over with time, but the organization continues intact for centuries, for example, the Roman Catholic and other related churches. Although many institutions appear immortal, others do not adequately promote the long term survival of their human building blocks to long survive. For example, the WWII Army of the Third Reich sent endless numbers of their loyal and obedient soldiers to battlefronts in the dead of winter, slaughtering millions. Later that institution collapsed and died. More recently, financial institutions, only after wasting billions of dollars invested by their human constituents, have finally failed.

Some institutions have used the, 45) death penalty to frighten others into obedience. Institutions recruit soldiers for killing battles of 46), conquest or in 47), defense from conquest by other institutions (tribes, political groups, nations, planets). Here, the side with greater numbers of foot soldiers made a difference, unless one side had superior soldiers due to size, training, use of stimulants, interface advantages (must pass single file through a barrier, cross water, etc), or the possession of more efficient weapons (swords, arrows, guns, explosives, poisons, horses, submarines, aircraft, missiles, satellites, propaganda, brain washing).

Finally some institutions have engaged in the organized collection of the defenseless victims into 48) death camps for the efficient genocidal killing of large numbers of "alien-subhuman" competitors. Others political groups have incited their members to the spontaneous (49) acts of genocide against specifically targeted subgroups. 50) Secret agents recruited as spies by institutions participate in selective assassinations of key players within opponent organizations.

The Rise from the Level of Killing to the Level of Nonkilling: The Evolution of Morality and Altruism

Early in the evolution of living organisms, the predominant behavioral motive was the survival of the fittest by tooth and claw. However, by now most of us are generally cooperative, kind and helpful. Less than one percent of us will kill another human being in our lifetime. Actually, humans are no longer good at face-to-face conflictive interactions. Such can actually cause feed-forward panic in which at the end the weak experience merciless attacks. Until recently, real incidents of human violence are short, usually ineffective, and rare. Humans are hardwired to avoid combat. How did this shift in behavior away from killing to nonkilling come about? The emergence of altruistic behavior has been a interesting topic for behavioral genetics research.

Let us make it clear that the laws at the universe level of individual building blocks, while appropriate, or even superior for life alone in the jungle, are clearly detrimental to the development of a thriving family unit at the next higher universe level. The laws of the individual universe level include the following (including the Seven Deadly Sins). 1) What is yours, is mine (envy, greed, jealousy). 2) What is mine, is mine (pride), not yours. 3) There is no past or future (sloth, gluttony), just the now. 4) Give it to me now or I will (5 rape, injure, or 6) kill you. If you resist or try to stop me, 7) I will hate you. Then, I will 8) lie, 9) cheat, 10) steal, become angry (wrath), and fight you to the death. Such selfish behavior can only be called antisocial and has been labeled as sinful by all religions. Without suppression, these have made the emergence of family and society nearly impossible.

Next, let us contrast the laws for the family with the above laws for the individual. They include: 1) I bow to your God-Within, and empathetically accept (love) you as a valued member of my family. What is ours is yours (unselfishness). 2) I will work with you for a better future (collaboration). 3) I will support your attempts to improve (humility). 4) I will seek to protect you from harm (kindness). 5) I will defer my immediate gratification in order obtain superior rewards in the future. 6) I will assist you in doing the same (cooperation). 7) I am my word. Thus, I will never lie to you, or about you. 8) I will never cheat you. 9) I will never steal any of your possessions, property or commit (adultery) with your mate. 10) I will never kill you or your family. Clearly, these emergent laws of the family are the opposite to those at the next lower universe level. Rising from the terrifying existence of killing/being killed within the jungle to the next higher level allows the nonviolent peace of civilization to emerge. The more of us that join the human family, the higher life can arise. **Table 1** contrasts the two sets of laws.

Table 1. Some Antisocial, Immoral Laws at the Level of Individual Building Blocks vs. and the Social, Moral Laws at Higher Level of the Family Unit

SELF Universe Level Laws: *Rejection* FAMILY Univ. Level laws: *Acceptance.*

SELF Universe Level Laws: *Rejection*	FAMILY Univ. Level laws: *Acceptance.*
1. Be proud, hate, and use others	1. Be humble, accept others, be loyal
2. Be greedy, envious and jealous	2. Be unselfish, respectful, kind,
3.Be gluttonous and slothful	3. Use self-control, plan ahead
4.Waste, break, and destroy	4. Conserve, repair, build
5. Compete, lie, and cheat	5. Cooperate, be honest and be open
6. Steal, commit adultery and rape	6. Contribute, honor, and empower
7. Be upset, rage, injure, and kill	7. Choose (use) what is, restore, protect

Our evolutionary rise from the level of "natural selection" of the "selfish gene" within individuals, by survival of the fittest, killing with tooth and claw, to the next higher nonkilling universe level began long ago. This continuing evolution of our universal sense of right and wrong has yet to be completed. Originally, the "selfish gene" dictated that we help others to the degree that they shared our same genes. That is, from the selfish gene's view, I should not sacrifice myself unless it will save two of my brothers, four of my grandchildren, or eight of my cousins.

However, with time, our collection of genetic pro-social behaviors has become quite elaborate. We call these "Moral" instincts. They compare to our language instincts, which come to focus within the culture in which we find ourselves. Beginning from the selfish "Eye for an eye and I will never forgive you for the rest of my life". They have risen to "Tit for Tat, then Forgive". That is: 1. Cooperate, 2. Reciprocate (if harmed, revenge only about 90% to avoid escalation into a stable feud). 3. Then forgive and cooperate again. They also include "The Golden Rule", formulated in all religions, which says: "Don't do to others what you wouldn't want them to do to you". Instead, "Do for others what you would like them to do for you." Or further, "Love your neighbor as much as you love yourself". They also include the critically important unsaid but guilt enforced : "Do not help yourself at other's expense", and "Do not harm others to help yourself". The standard of morality optimizes the general *good* of the community, rather than their general *happiness*. The general good is defined as rearing the greatest number of individuals in full vigor and health, with all their faculties perfect.

When we decide if an action is morally right or wrong, we do so instinctively, tapping a system of unconsciously operating (and thus inaccessible to conscious retrieval for inspection) moral knowledge called our conscience (Hauser, 2006). For example, which do you feel that it is morally better, to spend $2 million to keep a vegetative patient alive, or to use it to save 50,000 people from starvation for one year? Thus, altruistic behaviors evolved to serve the greater good of the group. Selection favored niceness because that benefited the group. Being nice did cost the individual somewhat. However, because of the existence of emergence, that sacrifice for the group becomes far more personally beneficial than selfish behavior. That is: a group of cooperative altruists will far outcompete a group of selfish cheaters. Sympathy and concern for the approval or disapproval of others remains a primary impulse and guide. The production of the moral disgust contained in the expression "In bad taste" has been demonstrated to activate the insula, brain site producing distaste in response to the presence of filth and rot.

There also appears to exist slight long-run benefits for punishment of cheaters. Furthermore, we sometimes tend to punish those who fail to punish cheaters. However, this can cause reactive punishment and the sanctioning of the original punishers, especially in countries where the rule of law is weak. Thus, punishment hardly works. The more efficient strategy is to withhold help from cheaters rather than punishing them. Social exclusion can cause grief and severe pain. Also the display of pictures or drawings of human eyes has been found to reduce cheating and to increase pro-social behavior. It also can be shown that one's regard for another (their reputation) depends not only on how fairly the other has treated them, but also on how they have treated others. Are they pro-family or parasitic freeloaders?

Investigations indicate that although we tend to forgive accidental harm to us, we tend to blame those who attempt to harm others, but failed. City planners have also found that when people observe that others violate a certain social norm or legitimate rule, they are more likely to violate other norms or rules themselves, causing disorder to spread.

Clearly, the development of compassion and sympathy was essential for caring family relationships upon which the survival of our species depends. Even in those individuals lacking personal experience of pain due to a congenital insensitivity, their brain midline emotional structures are still activated by empathy, Unconditional, romantic, and maternal love excite brain reward centers and release DA and oxytocin. Oxytocin is a natural antipsychotic. Thus, our brains evolved rewards to support altruism within our families. Helping others actually feels good. Service becomes its own reward. Paradoxically, making a charitable gift to another creates a greater reward in the giver than their receiving the same gift from someone else. We know that one never loses by being too generous. For example, generous people are said be more likely to receive donations themselves. Generosity appears to be an essential feature of winning strategies. Generosity means not seeking to get more than one's social opponent.

Loss of the Ability to Behave Morally due to Frontal Lobe Injury:

A series of accidents has provided us a clear illustration of the difference between inherent human selfish and social behavior. It begins with the famous story of Phineas Gauge who a century and a half ago was foreman of a railway gang laying down track along a hillside. Upon tamping some dynamite with a four foot steel bar into a hole in preparation to blast away some obstructing rock, he accidentally ignited an explosion that sent the rod rocketing up through his cheek and out the back of his head, landing 100 ft away. He did not lose consciousness and ultimately recovered his health. However, those who knew him before, said that he was no longer Gauge. His personality had changed from a responsible hard driving foreman into a impulse-ridden buffoon. He ultimately died as a side show performer.

Not long ago, neurologist Anthony Damasio (1994) reviewed this case and found other patients manifesting a similar syndrome. One, Elliot (EVR), was a former vice president of a corporation who had undergone the removal of brain tumors under his forehead, an area similar to the one damaged within Phineas Gauge. After a brief time, he came back to work, apparently completely recovered. However, he no longer had his cutting-edge insights, and instead relaxed on the job to the point he was fired. He

260

soon lost his own personal fortune through a series of calamitous errors. His infidelities cost him his wife and children. Fired from a series of lesser jobs, eventually he arrived at welfare's door. The Iowa State welfare agency tested him in order to place him. Because they found his scores were all at the superior to genius level, they accused him of malingering. He responded by showing them the CAT Scans of the holes in his brain. The welfare office referred him to Dr. Damasio's clinic at the University of Iowa. After taking a battery of psychological tests, including tests of moral values, Elliot again demonstrated his superior mental skills. At first, Dr. Damasio despaired because he could not find any testable evidence of Elliot's injuries. However, it finally became evident that Elliot was a very poor gambler. He could not pass up a long shot, even though he knew it was very risky and that he had often lost on earlier similar opportunities.

Soon it became evident, that although he clearly knew the difference between right and wrong, he could not stop from making disastrous short-term choices. He could not defer his gratification about anything, be it food, women or money. It was as if he had become that farmer with the straw between his teeth in Chapter 5, one riding backwards on the proverbial big fat pig, pretending to be in control, but only rationalizing the pig's own selfish behavior after the fact. Even though Elliot knew exactly what the right thing was to do, his actions were unavoidably selfish. He had become a buffoon like Phineas Gauge, and thousands of other skid row bums, often with closed head injury damage to their anterior cingulate Executive Caretaker. Many of these people with broken brains lack the self-discipline even to find a rope to tie around their waist to hold their pants up. They often drop their drawers when reaching for food or other things. Criminals at one time underwent a similar brain injury, called a prefrontal lobotomy, to prevent them from planning and carrying out their crimes. Living only in the now, they were easily restrained, having lost their ability to defer gratification, so necessary for planning a high crime.

Charles Darwin's Overlooked Insights Regarding the Evolution of a Moral Sense

Clearly, we possess an enormous genetic set of sexual, parental and social behaviors that we can employ to rise above Darwinian survival of the fittest by tooth and claw. We remember Darwin mainly by this discovery of early evolution, described in his 1859 book "Origin of the Species". However, his later recognition that a higher universe level was the source of morality, as described in his 1871 book, "The Decent of Man" goes almost totally ignored. Apparently, it had already been a huge jump to leap from special creation by God to that of "natural selection" by the survival of the fittest. His paradoxical suggestion that evolution was also responsible for the development of human morality, which is the opposite of competitive behavior, must have seemed too contradictory for most to entertain. This was especially true in the face of current ignorance of the emergence of unique laws by rising to the universe level of family, with its moral cooperation being opposite of cutthroat competition at the individual level. Although Darwin was formally unaware of emergence, one can tell from the following quote from the "Decent of Man" that he was beginning to understand it: *"Not withstanding many sources of doubt, within evolution, we are able to generally and readily distinguish between the Higher and Lower Moral rules. The higher are founded on the Social Instincts, and relate to the welfare of others. They are supported by the approval of our fellow-creatures and by reason. The lower rules, though some of them when implying self-sacrifice hardly deserve to be called lower, related chiefly to the self. They arise from public opinion, matured by experience and cultivation."*

Darwin used the word "Love" ninety five times in his book "The Descent of Man". He said that it was the feelings of love and sympathy resulting from the evolution of morality that caused one to take pleasure in another's company, warn them of danger, and defend and aid each other in many ways.

In his extensive study of high achieving humans, Abraham Maslow found the following common characteristics that will serve to end this chapter with a vision for all of humanity. These special men delighted in stopping cruelty and exploitation and in bringing about justice. They loved the reward of virtue. They enjoyed in doing good, and worked to set things right and to clean up bad situations. They did not do mean things, and were angry when others did so. They enjoyed watching and helping the self-actualization of others, especially the young. They enjoyed in bringing about law and order in the chaotic situation, or the messy or confused situation, or in the dirty and unclean situation. They hated and fought corruption, cruelty, malice, dishonesty, pompousness, phoniness and faking. Throughout all this, they also managed somehow simultaneously to love the world as it was as they tried to improve it.

In the next chapter, we dream the impossible dream and turn it into reality.

Some Important Concepts in Chapter 15

1. We live in an ever changing, ever the same dyadic universe where all extremes exist. The genetic goal of life is for our cells to survive and thrive in this universe by avoiding these survival extremes, such as extremes in temperature, etc. This has required selective action on our part to avoid being killed. Thus, we must obey "Survival of Life Laws" of the dyadic universe regarding many things. Although the "penalty for disobedience is death". We do not view this, either as an unfair or evil constraint of an unjust God.

2. Inherent in our interdependent and synergistic world are predatory animals that must kill aggressively in order to live. There also are their prey, victims who are killed so that others might live. Is this good or evil? The paradoxical *problem of evil in the world of a perfect god* is solved in Neuroreality by redefining the Father God of the Trinity as the Eternal Universe, sole unplanned, meaningless source of all life, abundance, opportunity and power, as well as all death, lack, constraint and weakness. Evil then becomes a survival value judgment made by a specific species, such as that of antelopes, cheetahs or humans. One species' good is another's evil. In our case, what optimizes human life, we call good and what harms it, we call evil. One can either choose the laws of the universe and thrive, or resist them and fail. Prayer cannot change the laws of momentum or gravity.

3. We have established that the universe consists of infinite levels, each with unique structures and having unique laws. We live between two of these universe levels: that of competing individuals, and the next higher level, that of the family unit. What is currently not recognized is that the appropriate laws, including killing, of the self level are quite the opposite to those appropriate to the higher level, where nonkilling is crucial. Further, that living on the next higher level results in the emergence of many life enhancing benefits. Thus, we have a choice as to which level we occupy, the one that is either human death or life promoting.

4. Fifty different reasons are described why people or institutions living on the lower level kill other people.

5. Originally, life evolved and rose to the level of survival of the fittest organism by tooth and claw. Because of the existence of survival enhancing emergent properties at the next higher social level, humans

have begun to profit by evolving altruistic behavior. We define moral behavior here as the nonkilling behavior present at the higher level of the family unit. This is compared to the selfish behavior appropriate to the lower level, long defined as immoral and destructive to the family unit. When we decide if an action is morally right or wrong, we do so instinctively, tapping a system unconsciously operating, and thus inaccessible, moral knowledge called our conscience.

6. Injury to the central lower frontal lobes of the brain disconnects our altruistic behaviors leaving only our selfish instincts to dictate our behavior. Here, the unfortunate person knows right from wrong and what is morally correct, but is incapable of overriding their Crocodile Brain that only has antisocial drives.

7. It is clear Charles Darwin recognized the evolution and existence of moral behavior. He used the word "love" almost a hundred times in his book "Descent of Man". He said that the feelings of love and sympathy. that have resulted from the evolution of morality, caused one to take pleasure in each other's company, to warn of danger, and to defend, and aid each other in many way

NEUROREALITY: A SCIENTIFIC RELIGION TO RESTORE MEANING

Section V: Is this a Safe Place? What Should I Be Doing? How Should I Relate to Others?

Chapter 16: Emergent Benefits of Living on the Nonkilling Universe Levels.

Living the Impossible Dream

What if everybody discarded all self-survival rules and lived as a valued member of a human family, using only the higher laws of the family level and receiving the emergent benefits from living at a higher level of complexity? Then, there would no longer be any basis for fear or paranoia that someone is going to lie to you, cheat you or steal what is yours. You would not have to protect yourself or your family circle from harm assault, or threats with violence, or death. Elders of the family would work to assist in the empathic, equitable nonviolent resolution of problems. You would be free to plan and work to optimize the survival of your family. In return, you would receive the personal benefits of their acceptance, support, and respect, and the unending interest of parental, brotherly, or sisterly love. Does this sound like utopia? Dreaming the impossible dream? It is now within humanities grasp! How can this be done?

Thankfully, survival of the fittest laws only apply up to the levels of the individual. Even at the level of our body cells, cooperation is essential for higher order to emerge. As we have seen, cellular win lose competition is destructive of higher order. When rising to each higher levels, win-win cooperation is superior to win-lose competition. We know that for optimal species survival families themselves must cooperate, not compete and rise into the next four higher levels of terrestrial life: those of families uniting to form a local society (city-county), local societies integrating into regional cultures (states), regional cultures uniting into countries (nations), and nations joining together into a family of nations (global union). Each higher level of order brings with it emergent benefits and unique laws, some of which we have recognized, some we have yet to distinguish. There has been a long history of violent conflict at each level, resisting the rise to the next one. However, we intuitively recognize from brief bright moments in our history, that at each of these higher levels of order, cooperation brings a much higher benefit to overall human survival than that of cutthroat competition, which is destructive of higher order. Regardless of the unique laws of each level, the crucial issue is whether the empathic principle of "win-win or no deal" for both parties is applied, rather than when one only wins but the other is harmed by taking the loss.

Changing the Contextual Framing from Competition to Cooperation
        Most of the problems we imagine that might arise by replacing individual competition by group cooperation are illusory. They are artifacts based upon the contextual misframing of the true issues. That is, "Free enterprise" ("The American Way") is successful, *not* because one person wins and all the other competitors lose, but because *all* seek the best solution to the problem at hand. Then, they use what works best to conquer the problem, regardless of its origin. Properly contextualized, the actual "enemy" is the *survival problem at issue*, not the *other teams* working to solve it. This raises "survival of the fittest" by killing, to the next level of team collaboration where all benefit by nonkilling. We did not invent the wheel to vanquish the other tribe, but rather as a discovery making our life easier and thus enhancing the survival of all. Finding the superior solution to the problem is the prize, not the winning of a personal reward or punishment. This is how we got to the moon!
        Within the family level, we are each already maximally valued. There is no penalty for finding less than optimal solutions because all competing ideas have to be tested and compared before the best solution becomes obvious and can be selected. Thus, "Free Enterprise" is better characterized by fitting a "Win-win or No Deal" model at each level, rather than the usual "I Win-You Lose" model conceptualization. As a review of the lives of famous inventers reveals, even the supposed sole inventor never worked alone but within his "family" support system.

Competition is killing us! Cooperation can save us!
        There exists a starkly obvious fact that we cannot, indeed, must not ignore! In terms of optimizing human survival, the existence of deadly fighting between families, or between societies-cities-counties, or between cultures-states, or between nations, is clearly much more harmful to human survival than the existence of empathic, cooperating families, societies, cultures and nations all collaborating to improve the human condition. Since this is true, our task is clear. Let us integrate and include, rather than segregate and exclude! At all universe levels above that of the individual, we must replace "I win-you lose" killing competition with "win-win or no

deal" nonkilling cooperation. As will be seen next, this needs to happen from the bottom up. All individuals must be part of family units, and all families need to combine into cooperating local societies (city-county), with emergent benefits, and laws. All local societies need to combine into regional cultural institutions (states), all regional cultures must join unite to formulate the institution of the nation, and all nations must unite to form the global institution of the Family of Nations. Individual competition by mavericks at any level makes the symbiotic benefits of order impossible. Continued self-oriented behavior at any level can cause great loss. Entities at all level should be encouraged to organize to obtain greater returns than the cost of competition.

The Multilevel Destructive Potential of the Individual Reptile Brain

Just as the selfish behavior of a single cancer cell can kill an entire human being, so also, persons, directed by their Reptile Brain to act selfishly and rebel against order, can bring destructive harm to human institutions at each of the higher levels and ultimately, to all of civilization. For example, selfish behavior at the family level abuses spouses and children, causing marital breakdown and divorce, further traumatizing the next generation. At the local society level, lying, cheating, extorting, raping, assaulting, injuring and killing by individual criminals or gangs brings misery, hopelessness and rage to the local populous. At the state level, dominant narco-traffickers infiltrate by force, buying superior firepower, bribing or killing key officials of the state to overlook their corruption and enslavement of the population. At the national level, egoistic leaders can employ guerillas and terrorists to fragment the country into independent fiefdoms, as in Somalia. Finally, at the international level, rogue states' individual leaders can defy other nations to overpower their neighbors and expand their territory, to intimidate, or attack with nuclear weapons. Moreover, like the USSR, multinational countries can fragment when each region competes for its freedom and independence. Ultimately chaos rises to the point that even the individual members of a single nuclear family will fight with each other, each of the bloodied survivors going their separate way. Clearly, attacks led by the Reptile Brain of individuals can damage or destroy human order at all higher levels to bring us back down to the mindless chaos of the jungle where only the fittest individual may survive by tooth and claw

In contrast, recruitment of all individuals as the building blocks of family whole, would facilitate enrollment of families into local societies.

This would promote moving to higher organizational levels. However, if individuals are not all partners within families, and all families not enrolled in local societies, the entire higher structural order destabilizes and collapses into battling chaos. The second law of thermodynamics says that without the input of sufficient work energy, everything moves toward chaos. We must continue investing our energy in the development and maintenance of our social institutions. Thus, it would seem that our first priority must be, not only to terminate the erosion of the family and to bring everyone back into a family, but also to raise families into cooperating local societies. If the local societies were unified and strong, it would be much easier to rebuild human order all the way up to an effective family of nations.

Destabilizing Factors and Conservational Laws of Each Higher Level of Life.

As may be seen in the following illustrative lists, each universe level of order has a unique set of problems, which can lead to its disruption. Each also has a unique set of requirements to maintain its integrity.

World Top Ten Causes of Death to the **Individual** (2009)

1. Coronary heart disease
2. Stroke and other cerebrovascular diseases
3. Lower respiratory infections
4. Chronic obstructive pulmonary disease
5. Diarrheal diseases
6. HIV/AIDS
7. Tuberculosis
8. Trachea, bronchus, lung cancers
9. Road traffic accidents
10. Prematurity and low birth weight

Ten Factors Required for **Individual** Health

1. Get adequate sleep
2. Get healthful food and nutrition
3. Get adequate water
4. Get adequate exercise

5. Avoid extremes in heat or cold
6. Avoid vertical drops greater than 1 meter
7. Learn to swim, or avoid water deeper than 1 meter
8. Avoid harmful creatures
9. Avoid toxins and poisons
10. Avoid radiation damage

Ten Laws of Living Selfishly as an **Individual** that are Destructive to Families

1. I alone am King above all.
2. I must always be right, win, dominate and look the best at all costs.
3. You are my inferior enemy, to betray, rob, rape, enslave, injure, or kill.
4. I will lie, cheat and steal from you.
5. Whatever is yours, is mine.
6. I will never work, save or deny myself anything.
7. I will waste, harm or destroy to get what I want.
8. I will eat, drink or masturbate within you whenever I feel like it.
9. Past or future do not exist.
10. Give it to me now or I will kill you.

Ten Problems of Individuals that destabilize **Families** sufficiently to cause divorce and disintegration.

1. Infidelity *(powered by the sexual drive to reproduce)*
2. Sexual abuse *(powered by the sexual drive to reproduce)*
3. Physical abuse *(from xDARP activation)* Emotional abuse *(from xDARP activation)*
4. Inadequate conflict resolution skills *(due to Crocodile Brain driven decorticate selfishness)*
5. Incompatible personalities-poor communication *(ignorance of Familial Polarity)*
6. Financial problems *(ignorance of the Seven Types of Reality)*
7. Addictions *(from a high load of Guilt-Pain)*
8. Separation of members, lack communication *(migration isolation)*
9. Lack of family leadership, records, and traditions *(isolation due to migration)*
10. Difference of Religion

Section V: IS THIS A SAFE PLACE?

Ten Agreements that Stabilize **Families**

1. The optimization of the survival of my family is the Highest Good.
2. I do not need to be right, win, dominate or look the best.
3. I accept you as my equal, and will not betray, rob, rape, enslave, injure or kill you.
4. I will be honest and trustworthy and not lie, cheat or steal from you.
5. Whatever is mine is ours.
6. I will work, conserve and deny myself for the benefit of my family
7. I will not waste, harm or destroy what is ours.
8. I will use discipline and wisdom in the expression of my passions.
9. I will be patient, respectful, cooperative and collaborative.
10. The past is an important record; the future is filled with possibility.

Ten Factors that Destabilize **Local Societies** (City-County)

1. Dishonesty, cheating, corruption
2. Theft, refusal to pay their share
3. Assault, rape
4. Extortion, kidnapping
5. Gang wars
6. Killing for hire
7. Vandalism
8. Use of firearms, knives, and poisons
9. Profits from drug sales (regional exceptions are illusory)
10. Vigilantism required for family protection

Ten Ways for Families to Cooperate to Form Harmonious **Local Societies** (City-County)

1. Set and keep property rules for land and the ownership of other property
2. Form family food and commodities cooperatives
3. Set business rules for banks, markets and stores
4. Set traffic rules
5. Finance roads
6. Finance police, fire, and rescue services
7. Finance schools and hospitals
8. Finance social services

9. Identify all individuals and maintain records of their development
10. Have a Department of Justice to correct harm done, mainly by restitution.

Ten Factors Destabilizing **Regional Cultures** (States)

1. Conflicts between different religions, races, and cultures
2. Riots, civil unrest, violent protests
3. Genocide
4. Regional competition for land
5. Regional competition for water
6. Loss in regional market competition
7. Regional catastrophe: earthquake, floods, drought
8. Caste system of human inequity, lack of freedom to develop
9. Impunity of wealth, lack of transparency, censorship
10. Exploitive foreign ownership

Ten Ways for Local Societies to form Harmonious **Regional Cultures** (States)

1. Form regional unions of similar local organizations
2. Form consortiums to integrate relations between diverse local organizations
3. Equitable distribution of land and water from the state
4. Transparency
5. Equality under the law
6. Establish cooperative laws for institutions
7. Develop and facilitate public transportation
8. Maintain freeways and regional airports
9. Democratically elected temporary officials
10. Free news media

Ten Factors Destabilizing **Nations**

1. Imbalance between democratic vs. autocratic governance
2. Welfare costs
3. Health care costs
4. Overpopulation
5. Paying excessive Foreign Aid
6. Use of short term monetary policies, inflation

7. Presence of rebel/alien "Freedom fighters" in civil or guerilla wars
8. Lack of, or censored, communication to the citizens
9. Excessive and/or corrupt taxation
10. Starvation, lawlessness, injustice

Some Factors Stabilizing **Nations**

"The budget should be balanced, the Treasury should be refilled, public debt should be reduced, the arrogance of officialdom should be tempered and controlled, and the assistance to foreign lands should be curtailed, lest Rome become bankrupt. People must again learn to work, instead of living on public assistance." --Cicero - 55 BC

Ten Factors Causing **International** Conflict (United Nations)

1. Failure of communication. Different languages, cultural traditions, and religions
2. Competing Monetary Systems
3. Civil wars, border disputes, expansionism, armed conflict, wars of conquest,
4. Threats of or use of nuclear and biological weapons
5. Selfish monopoly of or waste of global resources
6. Combat Alliances: Allies vs. Axis
7. Ecological damage, pollution
8. Sabotage
9. Terrorism
10. Inequality, censorship, lack of freedom,

Ten Factors Reducing **International** Conflict.

1. Common language
2. Common reconstituted science based religion, not based upon the Dream Reality of Spirituality, with common moral standards of social conduct
3. Common monetary system
4. Common system of measurement
5. Common international airports and harbors.
6. The elimination the Military and of global weapons of mass destruction.

7. Acceptance of the common goal to optimize the survival of humans and their global support systems. Democracy of individuals.
8. The global reliance of the scientific method, and the rejection of the supernatural or extracorporeal spirituality.
9. Democratically elected, temporary officials from national representatives.
10. The education of every human regarding the nature of reality, the universe, life, and mind.

Hopefully, from the above, the reader has been given a glimpse of some of the distinct problems and opportunities inherent in the rise of humanity, level upon level from the laws of the jungle to those of the higher levels of order and abundant benefits contained within the complexity of civilization. Clearly, this topic is far too vast for comprehensive management with within the confines of this short chapter. However, the crucial goal is to integrating each person from the level of the competing, killing self, and thus bring about a state shift resulting in their enrollment as a nonkilling cooperating member of the human race. As said by Richard Dawkins (1976), author of "The Selfish Gene", "Only we alone on earth can rebel against the tyranny of the selfish replicators."

Utopian Step #1: Rising from the Level of the Self to the Level of the Family, (tentative thoughts)

Just as in the human body there are Natural Killer Cells to neutralize any cancer cell rebels, so a Peace Force has been helpful in successful societies. Nonkilling peace forces have successfully used ostracization and detention of deviant family members away from their family as a powerful deterrent. Yet, the threat of incarceration, while extremely effective with normal people, does not stop those individuals with frontal lobe damage who remain at large causing damage. At present the brains of such individuals cannot be repaired. This leaves little choice, other than to vigorously screen the general population to rigorously identify them, and then to incorporate them into productive public works communes of various degrees of supervision.

However, the availability of weapons of mass destruction to such brain damaged individuals has brought a dramatic change in this situation. It has transformed the world away from peaceful cooperation into terroristic one of where the fearful citizens demand the "right to bear arms". Cannibalistic arms dealers have further manipulated this fear to drive the ever-escalating sale of arms to killers at all levels. This needs to stop. Mass killing by individuals with guns has enforced the clamor for the death penalty to punish and prevent such behavior. This penalty does not work to deter the brain damaged, but does eliminate some of them. The so-called "human rights" of placing the rights of a Crocodile Brain dominated killer above that of the survival of the human family is accentuated by ignorance, so that criminal behavior appears go completely unchecked.

Ideally, each individual will need to be identified with a internationally unique name and associated record. They will also need to welcomed and enfolded as a valued member within an accepting non genetic family. This will require the conversion of most individuals away from their habitual default state. That is, unbeknownst to them, their Reptile Brain has hypnotically handed their control over to one or more powerful external dominators. These range from the social meme directed gang leaders, or hedonistic occasionally criminal rock and movie stars who are worshiped as role models; to those leaders supplied by the obsolete world religions; or, to the science ivory tower leadership provided by the presently super-specialized, but almost totally unintegrated, primitive state of neuroscience.

The Caretaker Brain of each will by some yet-to-be-designed transformational education system need to be shown that by surrendering to the wisdom of its own Social Brain Source, which has its purpose, its plan, and the power to do it, their future life will be more happy and pain-free. To accomplish this transformation will result in their recognition of the existence of the multileveled universe and the multileveled brain, and the realization of the emergent properties that result upon joining the family of synergistic human beings. Their questions will be answered as the emergent opportunities and benefits of "the success-bringing" laws of family are compared to the destructive laws of the self.

The natural formation of separate matripolar and patripolar families needs to be encouraged in order to begin reducing the production of Rxps and Lxps, thereby reducing global personal suffering. As individual families grow beyond 40 members each, cohesive new families could bud off and spread across the globe, perhaps like Alcoholics Anonymous has.

Those who are not capable of surrendering to their higher selves, due to Executive Caretaker malformation or injury, as well as those with unnatural sexual identity or sexual choice due to aberrant neural connections, ideally will need be identified and introduced into their own caretaking family branches. These groups would include not only the benign LGBT group of lesbians, gays, bisexuals and transsexuals who thrive in each other's presence and constitute more than ten percent of the population already, but also former killers, and pedophiles. Former killers and others with damaged frontal lobes, who by definition, lack the self-discipline required to care for themselves without harming others, could become valuable constructive members of public works groups continuously supervised by teams of more powerful organizers to retain internal order. In Utopia pedophiles could become valued members of supervised high tech public works communes in the absence of children and without parenthood eligibility, by developing similar associations.

Taking Control of the Population Explosion

A major barrier preventing the unconditional welcome of everybody into our families is that there are too many of us. This relates directly to that eternal competition for limited resources. Even when it becomes clear that there is no God micromanaging the existence of terrestrial life, or even human life, we are still left with our Survival Imperative Reality that tells us that *all* of life is sacred and should be preserved and maximized. However, this extreme interpretation cannot be valid and needs modification. Because of our ability to multiply exponentially, we would soon cover every square meter of earth with 10 humans, who would then drown in their own excreta. Presently only war, pestilence, plague, famine and abortion prevent this from happening, all of which are of course undesirable.

Obviously, what our Survival Reality demands is not the maximization of life, but the *optimization* of life. That means some restriction of the population explosion needs development and application. As will be seen in a following chapter, physical immortality may well be possible. Unmanaged, this development would certainly accelerate our present population explosion. At this point, some will throw up their hands and say they are unwilling to play God, or to decide who lives or who dies. However, in view of the already total absence of a micromanager God, this is a completely irresponsible position that blindly dooms us to extinction. If the world is not to be brought back down to the killing chaos of the jungle, we must take control of our population explosion.

This returns us to the earlier question of whether to spend 2 million dollars, keeping a comatose patient alive, or instead to feed 50,000 people.

In terms of shortsighted, "right to life" Survival Reality thinking, preventing 50,000 from dying from starvation appears the best choice. However, which "right to lifer" would have the clarity to actually pull the plug on that single patient? From an enlightened "optimization of life" Survival Reality, neither choice is correct. This is because earth is already at least ten times too overpopulated and already far out of balance.

The Chinese have taken a courageous step by limiting the reproduction of their citizens to one child per family. Had they not done so, a massive collapse of their society to chaos would have already occurred. Fortunately, they had both the needed non supernatural belief system and infrastructure in place to accomplish their reproductive goal. This is lacking in most other parts of the world. That is, in other parts of the developed world, the required infrastructure exists, but continued belief in the existence of a micromanager God prevents its application. In the undeveloped world, both elements are lacking. Theoretically, the promulgation of a reconstituted scientific religion could help reverse these deficiencies, the topic of the next chapter of this book.

Utopian Step #2: Rising from Competing Families to the Level of Cooperating Local Cultures (City-County) (tentative thoughts)
At present, families commonly compete violently with each other for limited resources. We have seen the endless destructive nature of family conflicts, for example in the Middle East. It is interesting that the evolution of democratic and egalitarian structures within present and historic pirate groups illustrates the value of acting cooperatively in a family in order to compete with other family cooperatives. The captains of many pirate ships were elected and enforced a strict set of rules for everyone to follow. These placed restrictions on problem activities such as drinking, sex, gambling, fighting and desertion. Sailors on pirate ships received better pay than those in national navies. They also tolerated racial diversity, employed clearer systems of corporal punishment and divided the spoils with greater equanimity. Yet, from the viewpoint of earlier and current international shipping industries, they were evil parasites.

Similarly, a family code of behavior exists within the ever-spreading Latin American youth and Narco gangs. There, starving illegitimate urchins work to pass an initiation test for entry into a gang by killing someone. After killing someone, they are forever vulnerable to the criminal death penalty if their gang family wished to turn them in. After gaining their acceptance, they have further committed their life to the family often by tattooing the family's insignia on their face. They earn income by assassinating key targets selected by the gang to increase its ability to sell drugs to others in their district, or internationally to the millions of others seeking assuage the pain of their existence. In addition to criminal activities, they often follow Satanic beliefs, including dissecting and dismembering their victims. Cannibalism is suspected. They can never leave their new "family". If they do, another family member will be assigned to kill them. Their morality, obedience and loyalty are even greater than that of the Nazis or the Taliban. Although at the local level most of them harm themselves by competing with other gangs for territory, their super-family is expanding into the US and other first world countries.

The question is how to convert these killing family competitions into nonkilling collaborations? In the *eastern hemisphere,* the biological differences of Familial Polarity often separate the violently competing families. These cultural and religious differences make the cooperative joining of, for example, Patripolar Palestinian families with Matripolar Jewish families nearly impossible. Interbreeding between the two would only make matters worse by producing many unnatural polarity hybrids (Chapter 10). Here, it would appear that Patripolar and Matripolar family groups would more easily collaborate at the society level, rather than at the level of individual families. That is, each tribe would have its own territory to develop its survival contributing special labor skills and/or exports. Then, synergy would come from other tribes valuing and exchanging these products with those of their own through trade, each leaving their territories and daughters intact.

In contrast, in the *western hemisphere,* interfamily killings predominantly occur between impoverished urban gangs who fight both each other and local law enforcement officers for territorial dominance to viciously prey upon families of the same Familial Polarity within their area of control to survive. How do we stop this interfamily competition in a nonkilling manner?; Make universal education of all children mandatory to empower the poor as well as the rich?; Create a merit based classless civil service?; Limit nuclear family size?; Legalize drugs to remove the profit motive?; Sterilize the poor? Politically accept Narco families and allow them a share in our own unacknowledged drug-based spoils? Perhaps piracy insurance already exists.

However, it would seem that creating an overriding Religion containing more personal rewards for urchins than joining violent superstitious gangs is an additional possibility. Using it to forming permanent small collaborating family cells of each of the familial polarities that provide loving care, nutrition and nonviolence as the reward for belonging. Does working to serve others of your global family seem better than traditional tribal fighting to kill off your competition on the next block, or woods too to avoid starvation, especially when they are your own relatives?

For the development of the higher order that best optimizes the survival of humanity, the formation of interfamily cooperatives is imperative. This has often occurred in the past where peaceful communities with internal familial polarity communes arose. From these, thriving regions and metropolises have often emerged. For this elevation of order to occur, members need communal land and the freedom to come and go about their creative family activities night and day without the threat of violence.

Step #3: Rising from the Local Societies (City-County) to Regional Cooperating Cultures (States)

Step #4: Rising from the level of Regional Cultures to that of Cooperating Nations

Step #5: Rising from the level of Nations to that of the Family of Nations

These last three elevating steps are beyond the expertise of this book, as perhaps are the first two! However, the basic principles remain of emergent benefits and unique laws at each level, many yet to be uncovered. These reinforce that nonkilling constructive cooperation with emergent benefits is far superior to killing competition as far as the optimization of human life is concerned. The issues of whether humans can thrive in the absence of killing, death penalties, killing weapons or the Military, are powerfully addressed in the book "Nonkilling Global Political Science" written by the inspired political scientist, Glenn Paige (2002).

In the next chapter we address the possibility of a creating a reconstituted global religion to serve as a valuable tool to assist us in rising to nonkilling levels.

Some Important Concepts from Chapter 16: Emergent Benefits of Living on the Nonkilling Universe Levels.

1. There exists a starkly obvious fact: In terms of optimizing human survival, the existence of deadly fighting between families, or between societies-cities-counties, or between cultures-states, or between nations, is clearly much more harmful to human survival than the existence of cooperating families, societies, cultures and nations all collaborating to improve the human condition. Since this is true, our task is clear. Let us integrate and include, rather than segregate and exclude!

2. Just as the selfish behavior of a single cancer cell can kill an entire human being, so also, individuals directed by their Reptile Brain to act selfishly and rebel against order, can bring destructive harm to human institutions at each of the higher levels and ultimately to all of civilization. Narcotrafficking is demonstrating that.

3. As may be seen in the following lists, each universe level of order has a unique set of problems, which can lead to its disruption. Moreover, each has a unique set of requirements to maintain its integrity. In this chapter the following thirteen sets of destructive and constructive factors for the relevant levels are given:
   a. World Top Ten Causes of Death to the **Individual**
   b. Ten Factors Required for **Individual** Health
   c. Ten Laws of Living Selfishly as an **Individual** that are Destructive to Families
   d. Ten Problems of Individuals that harm **Families** sufficiently to cause divorce.
   e. Ten Agreements that Stabilize **Families**
   f. Ten Factors that Destabilize **Local Societies** (City-County)
   g. Ten Ways for Families to Form Harmonious **Local Societies** (City-County)
   h. Ten Factors Destabilizing **Regional Cultures** (States)
   i. Ten Ways for Local Societies to form Harmonious **Regional Cultures** (States)
   j. Ten Factors Destabilizing **Nations**
   k. Some Factors Stabilizing **Nations**
   l. Ten Factors Causing **International** Conflict (United Nations)
   m. Ten Factors Reducing **International** Conflict.

4. In the crucial step of causing an individual to join and become a valued member of a family, its Reptile Brain will need convincing that by taking back control from the many "external dominators" and surrendering to the wisdom of its own Social Brain Source that has its purpose, their plan, and the power to do it, their future life will be more happy and pain free. To accomplish this transformation will require recognition of the multileveled universe's existence and the demonstration of the emergent properties that result upon joining the family of synergistic human beings.

5. In the absence of a micromanager God, we must modify our attitudes regarding the sacredness of life, including the population explosion, striving not for the maximum short term survival of life, but for its *optimal* survival.

6. Finally, the crucial step of moving up from the level of the family to the level of a peaceful local society and higher needs more accurate informed attention. For this, the reader is referred to the inspirational book by Professor Glenn Paige called "Nonkilling Global Political Science".

7.

NEUROREALITY: A SCIENTIFIC RELIGION TO RESTORE MEANING

Section V: Is this a Safe Place? What Should I Be Doing? How Should I Relate to Others?

Chapter 17: The Reconstitution of Religion: Elevation to Nonkilling Levels of Civilization.

Presently Expanding Chaos: Understanding of the Meaning of Freedom

Most of our ancestors were once the slaves of a few powerful families. Relatively recently they fought for and won their freedom. However, freedom is a very open word. It can mean either the removal of all restraint in the production of chaos, or the regaining of a thwarted ability to optimize survival via order. Unfortunately, freedom is commonly interpreted to mean having the option to indulge and dissipate oneself any way one wishes. Yet, a more empowering meaning of freedom is to regain the opportunity, discipline and enterprise needed to build one's own family into a thriving and gratifying whole.

Like many things, civilization is like a pendulum, swinging between two of the extremes in our dyadic universe: in this case, between total order and complete chaos. We have now passed a golden mean and are presently swinging increasingly toward chaos. Empires are collapsing, law and order is weakening, families are dispersing, marriage is failing and insanity is increasing. Now is the time when chaos must and will be increasingly successfully fought until the pendulum inevitably swings back towards order again.

The reconstitution of the once powerful unifying forces of religion can facilitate this change for the better. Religion is in our genes. We desperately need its calming and socially organizing power. Without it, we live in the dysphoria of underlying fear of death anxiety and stress, due to isolation. We attempt to calm our fears with the pursuit of material things, or with the many other unsuccessful means of self-gratification. However, we remain empty of purpose, living a life of no meaning. The failure of religion to solve the practical problems of life has disillusioned many. Today, obsolescent religions based upon spiritual literalism and subjectivism cause conflict on numerous levels. These "False Cause" elements bring confusion, victimization, suffering and hatred. This makes it difficult to exert personal, local and especially species responsibility.

Yet, old belief models cannot be falsified or destroyed. They are immortal. Fortunately, adding objectivism of the scientific method to religion transforms it into a new model that works better. Thus, just as cars displaced horses without the need to shoot them, an objective religion that gives greater personal benefits can displace our failing subjective dream-derived religions.

The Power of Religion to Restore Our Higher Calling: To Rise from Killing to Nonkilling

Outcomes of scientific studies on the effects of religion upon behavior have been interesting. For example, we have learned that experimentally induced religious thoughts reduced the rates of cheating and increased altruistic behavior among anonymous strangers. Further, there was an association between the apparent profession of religious devotion by an individual and a greater trust in that person by others. Larger religious group size was associated with the belief in gods that are concerned with morality. In addition, it was demonstrated that the belief of supernatural monitoring can be effective in replacing social monitoring (policing) of behavior.

The Greeks first recorded this latter concept. For example, Critias (455-403 BC) expressed his belief that ancient rulers created religion to keep the selfish behavior of their subjects in check. He expressed this idea in a morality play where Sisyphus says:

"Originally, human life was unordered, bestial, and a slave to force. There was no reward for the virtuous and no punishment for the wicked. Then, I think, humans devised laws with penalties, so that Justice might now become the Dictator and Arrogance its Slave. Because these laws forbade them to commit open crimes of violence, they began to do them in secret".

"Then, a wise and clever man invented the idea of Supernatural Gods to frighten the wicked and prevent them from secretly doing, saying, or even thinking anything that was evil. To do this, he introduced the false concept of the Divine, that pleasantest of all teachings, saying that there was a race of omniscient, omnipotent, omnipresent Gods who think and care about virtue in the lives of mortals, who are aware of everything we think or do, and that reward good and punish evil. These Gods lived remotely in the heavens and on mountain tops and expresses themselves fearsomely in thunder, lightening, sun, and rain."

282

"This invention quenched lawlessness among humanity. Thus, I think for the first time did someone persuade mortals to believe in a race of deities. As a result, more men are good through habit than character."

Optimizing, not Maximizing, the Survival of the Family Group: The Population Bomb

A fundamental function of religion has been to maximize the survival of the family-group. Over the millennia, this has been very successful! The human population is now 1,000 times larger than it was 4000 yrs ago. Because of this success, we're confronted by increasing reduction in the ability of our planet to sustain us. Furthermore, we face The Battle of Armageddon between vast hoards of followers of God vs. those who follow Allah.

Because such a high population of humans has never existed before mankind needs a expanded objective context for existence; one that provides tools to protect the families within our billions of people. Religion is called to stretch and adapt to meet these survival needs. The purpose of religion must now become to *optimize*, not maximize the survival of humanity and its support systems. The world economy needs to move away from growth toward *balance*.

Religion is the Multipartite Product of our Social Brain's Drive to Optimize the Survival of our Species.

"True" religion directs toward the emergent benefits of higher social order. It places the optimization of the survival of the highly social human species as the supreme value. Because religion is the cultural institution of the family, it is indeed the most appropriate entity responsible for the survival of the human species. Effective religion is a comprehensive of family way life. Thus, it must contain many social elements including the following fifteen functions. Its guidance and camaraderie is naturally sought at: 1. childbirth, 2. for child indoctrination regarding the current best approximation to the answers to life's Big Questions based upon the Scientific Method, 3. to set sexual standards at puberty, 4. to foster communal development at emancipation, 5. through education and 6. guidance to provide direction and focus in career selection, 7. to provide a safe framework for courtship, 8. to strengthen family ties at marriage, 9. to facilitate self realization within the family team and wider community, 10. to provide sympathetic network of social support and belonging beyond the nuclear family, 11. to build and strengthen supportive social institutions,

12. to facilitate conflict resolution, 13. to provide an avenue of expressing the joy of life through creative acts of art and invention. 14. to harvest the wisdom of the elders, 14. to meet the needs of the aging, and 15. to honor the individual at death.

Originally, all religions sought to give an understanding of how life and the universe work. This was so that we each could optimize the survival of humanity, and thus improve our own condition by aligning with how things work. When successful, our failures were reduced and we began to thrive. However, in our evolution up from jungle brutes, we started with rather crude spiritual myths and metaphoric models of the nature of our dyadic universe. While better than nothing, these myths also brought pain and suffering because they were only partially correct.

Clearly, none of the above fifteen elements of religion are foundationally spiritual. In fact, the incorporation of the deception-based (Ch. 20) Dream Reality of spirituality into religion has done us more harm than good. This is because the rules of External Reality regarding the way the universe is or how it works repeatedly break down in the Dream Reality of spirituality. The wishful invocation of the supernatural to cover our ignorance has actually superseded and destroyed the fundamental purpose of religion, which is to optimize human survival. To use spirituality to resist and lie about the way the universe is not wrong. It just doesn't work to align us with the way the universe is as the sole source of life, abundance, opportunity and power. Rather, spirituality- based religions have failed us and have become a major source of daily human tragedy.

During the last 4,000 years, we have uncovered a powerful objective method to learn more about the universe and how it operates. This is the Scientific Method. An important element of the scientific method is the requirement that for accepting anything as true, other observers need to able to obtain the same results. For example, is it a fact that if a cupful water was heated in a frying pan over a hot fire for one hour, the water will boil away and disappear? Can any competent person get the same result? Because the answer is yes, this discovery requires no faith or belief. It is a demonstrable fact.

In the case of the evolution of life forms, all contingency-based, random steps must follow laws of science in being non miraculous in moving from ancestor to progeny. Here, due to the impossibility to reproduce the complexity of the original contingency, outcomes of later attempts to repeat the step will never be quite the same, nor would its reversal result in the original ancestors. This does not contradict the scientific method, because if the impossible-to-repeat highly complex situation could actually be reproduced, the same outcome would occur each time. Thus, evolution is true.

However, earlier beliefs invoked supernatural explanations to cover ignorance: such as a flat earth at the center of the universe, or the existence of extracorporeal life after death. These "facts" were not demonstrable. They required faith. Belief in them, while somewhat comforting, also contained the inherent side-effects of pain and suffering. These have led to the literal slaughter of millions of believers whose only difference was faith in a slightly different myth.

A Globally Unifying Objective Story is Needed that Elevates to Humanity to the Nonkilling Level.

To integrate and include, not segregate and exclude requires a universally valid religious motif. What is presently missing is a unifying pair of eyeglasses that point all in the same objective direction: that of the optimization of human survival along with its life support systems. Such a view would be a compelling practical religion that speaks to the Source within all people. It would clear away religious errors by provide objective demonstrable facts about the nature of the universe, life, and mind, that would make one glad to be a human being. It would give each Society of Seven of our mind something to live for and support. It would make the Four Freedoms and the Seven Realities clear. It would be helpful in guiding children and initiating them into global family membership. It would rehabilitate "havingness" by promoting a life that does not harm others and thus cause guilt. Through emergence, it would produce more benefits than it would cost. It would assist in reducing the developmental trauma of growing up and in turning off the xDARP. It would enroll others in choosing what Is, as perfect, including the universe and its continuing evolution. It would empower the emergence of the Social Brain to optimize the survival of human life and its living support systems.

Because of the increasingly rapid production of unintegrated, scientific method-based facts about the universe into the literature of science, it is now possible to clear away earlier cobwebs of belief. They can be replaced by demonstrable facts about the nature of the universe, life and mind. These treasures are buried among the vast outpouring of published research of data-based, reproducible facts, the larger significance of most of which remain unrecognized. From these, it has been possible to replace our trusted but faulty religious subjective beliefs with demonstrable, objective facts that require no faith to believe. These can elevate humanity to nonkilling levels of existence that become joyful because life is optimal.

So, can we create a 4-millennium upgrade to reconstitute currently failing religion? An upgrade based entirely upon objective, reproducible data-based scientific methods (**Figure 1**). An awe inspiring upgrade that demands no faith in supernatural explanations to arrive at more accurate, workable answers to life's Big Questions? That gives us all something meaningful and sacred for which to live? YES, WE CAN!!

NEUROREALITY: A Transformational Context for Existence, Bridging Brain and Mind, Science and Religion

Fig 1: Viewing the Universe through the Lenses of the Neuroreality

The Transformational Knowledge of Neuroreality:
It is clear that within each of us is a brain-based, wisdom-filled Inner Being (cerebellar social brain Source), existing outside of usual awareness. Making contact with this Inner Being and gaining access to It's wisdom is a key transformational step in personal development that is available to all.

Developing awareness of one's Inner Being and following It's wisdom transforms the stress, isolation, and resignation of daily existence into a life of purpose, fulfillment, and abundance. Until recently, very few have been able to benefit from the higher intelligence of their Inner Being, due to lack of awareness of Its existence or how to access It.

To reach and be directed by one's Inner Being, the use of a neuroscience based paradigm regarding the nature of reality, brain, mind, behavior, and life is helpful. This transformational knowledge structure is called Neuroreality. Widespread conversion of individuals to Inner Being directed behavior will produce a bottom-up conversion of the human condition away from conflict, suffering, and waste toward peace, prosperity and satisfaction. If a paradigm is provided to a person of what they can become, it will enable them to transform into something beyond what they would have ever been. This is the hope of Neuroreality.

286

The Eight Octaves of Neuroreality: The Life of a Neurorealist: Purpose, Clarity, Accomplishment, Satisfaction, and Joy

The core elements of this global religion, "Neuroreality: A Transformational Context for Existence that Bridges Brain and Mind, Science and Religion", have been presented in the preceding chapters of this book. These contextual shifts in human meaning, values and purpose can be contextualized into the following "The Eight Doctrinal Octaves of Neuroreality":

Octave 1: **Eternal Dyadic Universe: Moving God from Outer to Inner Space**
a. The universe is eternal, without meaning or purpose, without beginning or end.
b. The universe is the sole source of life, abundance, opportunity and power.
c. Consists of endless levels, each with unique content, emergent property laws.
d. Problem of evil is resolved by inevitable and uniform operation of these laws.
e. The singularity engine of our galaxy recycles matter, time and energy.
f. Within its optimal energy halo, beauty, life emerge with no meaning or purpose.
g. Behavior is the movement of a structure over time, powered by potential energy.
h. Life and mind are triadic processes, which exclude all extracorporeal existence.

Octave 2: **Recognition and the Empowering Use of The Seven Realities:**
a. External reality: What the universe is, independent of our sense perceptions.
b. Internal reality: Our unique inner model of external reality from the senses.
c. Survival reality: Cell survival is the source and purpose of all behavior.
d. Cultural reality: Survival tools: fire, wheel, communicated across generations.
e. Reactive reality: Our xDARP's trauma-based insane interpretations of what is.
f. Dream reality: Wishful, fictional viewpoints including those of spirituality.
g. Empathic reality: Acceptance of another as a beloved member of one's family.
h. Human life is superior when operating on "win-win" nonkilling levels of higher order.

Octave 3: **The Quadrimental Brain, The Dual Quadbrain, & Society of Seven**
a. The brain core pair: **Does:** selfish Crocodile, **Takes,** or selfless Servant, **Gives.**
b. Executive Caretaker: Preconscious judge, conserves, acts, **Has.**
    Executive motivational Emotions, *Feels*; and Ego Defenses of the Id, *Lies.*
c. Right hemisphere: Imaginer, **Sees,** a picture is worth a thousand words.
d. Left hemisphere: Reporter, **Says,** a word is worth a thousand pictures.
e. Reactive brain: **Was,** Cerebellar demons from developmental trauma (xDARP).
f. Social Brain: **Is,** Cerebellar, genetic, higher intelligence inspirational source.
g. Whoever of the Society of Seven is in the cockpit of our brain, it feels like us.
h. Yet, we can influence which of the seven is actually is there and in control.

Section V: IS THIS A SAFE PLACE?

Octave 4: **Dyadic Behavior: Hemisity joins Sex as Part of Our Identity**
a. Which brain side your executive Caretaker is on determines your hemisity.
b. Your hemisity determines which of two thinking and behavioral styles is yours.
c. Top-down, left brain splitters vs. bottom-up, right brain lumpers.
d. Physically anxious lefts vs. socially anxious rights.
e. Sensitive, quiet lefts vs. intense, talkative rights.
f. Supportive left spouses vs. "Born to lead" right spouses.
g. Unconditionally loving left parents vs. conditionally loving right parents.
h. Hemisity behavioral traits are not sexual identity traits.

Octave 5: **Dyadic Evolution: The Origin and Nature of Familial Polarity**
a. The dual origins of terrestrial life: parallel evolution at all stages.
b. Familial polarity results from the two different reproductive strategies used.
c. The two resultant terrestrial lineages: patripolar wolves vs. matripolar foxes.
   Apes (patripolar gorillas vs. matripolar chimps) and hominids (patripolar
   Neanderthals vs. matripolar Cro-Magnons).
d. Unrecognized human polarity striations in old world: source of endless conflict
e. Our conflicting cultures and religions result from familial polarity biology.
f. Within each of the polarities, mates of opposite hemisity attract.
g. Unrecognized consequences due to crossbreeding between the two polarities.
h. The familial polarity lineages can exist side by side in a complimentary manner.

Octave 6: **Thwarted Brain Development: The Origin and Nature of Stress**
a. Gaining control of fundamental survival operations: Life vs. death.
b. Critical periods of psychosocial development: pre-open, open, closed.
c. Failure and developmental arrests: cause lifelong un-healing psychic wounds.
d. The mutated developmental arrest repair program has become a source of stress.
e. The Nine Features of the broken developmental arrest repair program (xDARP).
f. The xDARP is the source of unrecognized neurotic, psychotic insane behavior.
g. The broken xDARP seeks to complete arrested psychosocial development.
h. It is possible to recognize xDARP behavior, turn it off and regain control.

Octave 7: **Scientific Religion: The Transforming Context of Neuroreality**
a. Morality, ethics, religion: are biology-based survival values of human groups.
b. There is joy in removing the guilt that blocks reward and drives drug seeking.
c. Ways exist to discover one's higher power and open channels to it.
d. Surrender to one's higher power for relief, satisfaction, and meaning.
e. Discover one's purpose, the plan and the power to achieve it.
f. Global enlightenment: From killing competition to nonkilling collaboration.
g. Balanced terrestrial custodianship of higher life: coexistence, peace/cooperation
h. A valuable haven of peace and satisfaction for aligned human family members.

Octave 8: **Rising from Killing Competition to a Nonkilling Collaborative Civilization**

a. We must move from being individuals to being valued members of family units.
b. Our individual families must become active building blocks of local society.
c. Our societies must collaborate to create our regional culture (state).
d. Our state cultures must cooperate to build our nation.
e. Our nation must work with our other national partners to create United Nations.
f. The formation of each higher level causes emergent benefits that optimize life.
g. Each level has unique laws that facilitate constructive action at that unique level.
h. At all levels, "You win-I win, or no deal" strategy, is superior to "I win-you lose".

The Foundational Trinity of Neuroreality:

The concept of god as a trinity has been valued in some religions because it inherently addresses three needs. However, as it stands today, it contains insurmountable difficulties.

I.	God the Father: Our Omniscient omnipresent, omnipotent maker, the creator and sustainer of life and the universe. Weaknesses, "the problem of evil", sexism.

II.	God the Son: Our role model of what the God the father expects. He performed many miracles. His reward was immortality and family membership as the Son of God. Weaknesses: His supposed miracles were later fabrications, as was his supposed immortality.

III.	God the Holy Spirit: An external small flame of wisdom, guidance and inspiration. Provides personal evidence of the existence of God, by entry into a prayer and fasting-induced, experience of the holy, an altered state which leads to conversion. Weaknesses: Similar altered states, visions of holiness, and conversion experiences have occurred in many after the proper ingestion of certain hallucinogens or after certain types of psychic agony.

These problems regarding the existence of a Triune God, and His properties are resolved in Neuroreality.

God the Father as the Eternal Universe: Sole Source of Life, Abundance, Opportunity and Power:

God as a supernatural spirit is replaced by the natural actions of the eternal universe. The universe sets "conditional love" standards, such as gravity, pressure or momentum. The penalty for ignoring these laws of the universe will naturally lead to damage to your body and to reductions in your longevity. This resolves "the problem of evil" into lawful cause and effect. **Figure 2**, depicts a potential icon of our solar system's transit across the Zone of Life within its galactic arm. Here the mysterious creative-destructive power of the galactic singularity engine becomes the eye of God. Existence of the universe beyond our own vast galaxy is beyond practical significance to us. The Neuroreality Decalogues are actions at the society level which reduce conflict.

God, the Holy Spirit Source: My Social Brain, Protector of Life:

It gives inspiration and conscience via intuition from "that still small voice" Gives "unconditional love", once we have surrendered to It and have cleaned up our lives. The goal of each person's Source is to optimize the survival of life and maintain its immortality. In Neuroreality, the Source is represented as a three dimensional "Flower of Life", shown in **Figure 3**, the oldest symbol known. Through our Source we can experience the wonder and holiness of the universe, as well as the love of all other aligned Sources

Sons of God: Scientist Discoverers, Inventors, and Explorers as Role Model Heroes: They Crossed the Threshold of Workability and Uncovered the Universe and The Way It Works.

These saints include Galileo, Newton, Darwin, The Wright Brothers, Edison, Bell, Curie, Einstein, Crick, Watson, Fuller, Venter, and host of other scientist saints. Their lives tell of magnificent discoveries: of galaxies, solar systems, moons, species, cells, subcellular organelles, macromolecules, enzymes, vitamin and mineral nutrients, hormones, neurotransmitters, germs, atoms, electrons, radiation from x-rays to radio waves, subatomic particles, energy, voltage, magnetism, and the caloric content of foods.

These role models stand at the apex of incredible collaborative achievements: the discovery of mathematics, scientific method, lever, wheel, metals, fire, engines, synthesis and purification of substances, gasoline, buildings, refrigeration, weapons, atom bombs, hydrogen bombs,

Figure 2.

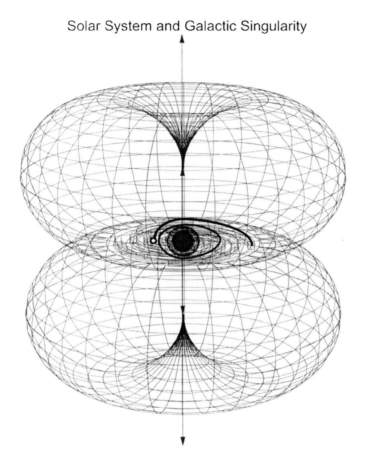

Solar System and Galactic Singularity

radios, TV, telephones, computers, the internet, ships, submarines, heavier than air flight, powered flight, airliners, space craft, satellites, man on moon etc. DNA sequence of many species, synthetic life, fertilizers, genetic engineered crop improvements, antibiotics, medicines, surgery, and x-rays, MRI, PET non invasive imaging within the human body, and life extension. These scientific method based accomplishments, are reproducible. They far exceed the non-creative accomplishments of classical religion, whose wishful fantasies have lured billions into self-serving competitive institutions whose doctrines are far from the truth, and

Figure 3
Most Ancient Symbol: The Flower of Life
In the Osirion Megalith at Abydos, Egypt, ~12,000 yrs bp

whose faith dependent beliefs have led to the slaughter of billions of well-intended beings.

Neuroreality and Morality:
Without genetic determinism, multicellular organisms could not exist: Terrestrial cellular life has continued to be immortal thus far because it contains successful DNA-based, genetically- determined cellular homeostasis programs. These are sharp and conserved by the survival of the fittest organisms that continue to maintain optimal cell conditions in the face of environmental stress. Survival reality is the originator of moral law:

In the unplanned, purposeless, meaningless universe, Life is not sacred, except within survival imperative reality by the deterministic declaration of we the living. This is also the origin of rational, external reality-based morality of Neuroreality, dedicated to the optimization of human life.

A similar form of life affirming morality called Objectivism, was developed by Ayn Rand (1957; Peikoff, 1991, Biddle, 2002). However, the enlightened self interest of objectivism remained somewhat antisocial in that it did not contain Neuroreality's elevation to nonkilling levels with their emergent properties, whereby cooperation with others is transformed from objectivism's sacrifice to Neuroreality's personal benefit.

Our Quadrimental Brain is dedicated to the survival of life: the Reptile Brain, using individual-level laws, coordinates survival of the self. However, humans are complex multicellular social organisms whose individual survival also depends upon other family members at several points in their life cycle. The Social Brain coordinates the Survival of the Family and takes priority, using nonkilling, group-level laws.

The Executive Ego judges and delegates the power of control to one Brain System of the Society of Seven at a time: Inappropriate activation of the wrong brain system can destroy life. When the ego is weakened by fatigue, the xDARP, or drugs, it loses control of the Crocodile Brain. Antisocial, harmful behavior inevitably results. It is one's responsibility and duty to maintain a strong Executive.

Best Current Approximations of Moral Law:

1. **Primacy of Life: Good and Evil refer to whatever Optimizes Human Survival:** Anything that optimizes the survival of the human individual and family is good and holy. Objects or doings that harm the optimal survival of the family are bad, evil and sinful. And who are one's family? This is the fourth freedom of choice, by declaration: All of humanity!

2. **Personal Freedom: Operate from Win-Win, or No Deal, and not from I win, You Lose.**

3. **Do Not Harm to Others to Benefit Yourself:** This is the definition of sin. One's duty is to clean up one's past harm to others, live in the present, keep one's conscience clear, and maintain open channels to one's God-Within. Do so by confessing sin, making restitution and obtaining forgiveness of victim. Although confession to a non-victim may be helpful

(The Confessional), it is insufficient! Then live synergistically in all your affairs.

4. **Cooperate with Others:** If they harm you, it's "Tit for Tat, then Forgive": (The computer program operating on this principle was the best in all contests. i.e., It was the behavior giving highest group survival). However, make sure that the Tit your respond with is not greater than Tat you received, or a revenge spiral can escalate out of control!

5. **Avoid Unwanted Pregnancies:** In terms of External Reality, life, even human life, is not inherently sacred. Only we the living say so from our Survival Imperative Reality. The ability of the earth to support life is already compromised by human overpopulation. Thus, it is our duty to avoid unwanted pregnancies potentially harmful to both the hapless child and its unwilling parent(s), as well as to the environment. The maximal survival of life is not the optimal survival of life. Quality not quantity!

6. **Live Optimally in Balance with our Living Global Support Systems:** A balanced economy, not a growth economy is imperative. There are limits! Either we impose them, or famine war or pestilence will impose themselves upon us. Live in balance. Keep our life-supporting ecosystems alive and well.

Ten Universe Laws for Physical Survival of Human Beings:

1. Avoid vertical falls greater than three meters.
2. Avoid breath stops for longer than one minute.
3. Avoid skin contact with temperatures greater than 50 degrees centigrade.
4. Avoid cooling core body temperature below 34 degrees centigrade.
5. Avoid warming core body temperature above 41 degrees centigrade.
6. Avoid breathing gases reduced in oxygen or containing hemoglobin binding poisons.
7. Avoid being dissolved by strong acids or bases.
8. Avoid being crushed, battered, or cut.
9. Avoid blood losses greater than two liters.

10. Eat appropriately and Avoid prolonged loss of sleep.

Neuroreality's Ten Commandments of Social Survival of Human Beings:

1. I your God-Within, am that "still small voice" of wisdom from your social brain Source.
2. You shall not place your self above me. My guidance requires your total surrender to me.
3. You shall not profane my name or swear upon it falsely.
4. You shall devote my Sabbath Day to the betterment of humanity and its support systems.
5. You shall honor your father and mother, and shall accept your neighbor as yourself.
6. You shall not wish to possess what is another's.
7. You shall not lie, cheat or steal.
8. You shall not commit adultery or murder.
9. You shall not bear false witness against anyone.
10. You shall honor your word, which is who you are, as sacred.

Ten Steps for Discovery by the Scientific Method, Most Powerful Method for the Objective Determination of Truth Known to Humanity.

1. Isolate and define the phenomenon to be understood.
2. Conceive of a model that could explain the mechanism of the phenomenon.
3. Changing one variable at a time, determine which variables are required for the phenomenon to still occur.
4. Where possible, simplify the system until only the required elements are present.
5. Based upon the model, propose a hypothetical prediction that would test its validity.
6. Perform the precise experiment required to test the correctness of that hypothesis.
7. If the hypothesis is not born out, return to the model and propose another hypothesis that tests the model.
8. If the hypothesis remains unfulfilled, consider changing the model by a paradigm shift.

9. When hypotheses are repeatedly fulfilled by others, consider the model to be validated as a theory.
10. Test breadth of applicability of the theory. This will define its applicability as an established fact.

The Nature of One's Source:

Each person's Source unfolds from his or her own unique genetics, development and experience. As our Higher Intelligence, our Source is brain-dependent and mortal, but committed to the immortality of life. It operates outside of our awareness from within the vast data bank of our cerebellar primary memory. It aligns with external reality, What Is: i.e., the universe as the origin of all life, abundance, opportunity and power. It tells the truth about What Is, regardless of the special pleadings of one's Reptilian Brain self. It recognizes that the production of higher levels of order results in emergent properties that are always greater than the activities of the parts. It uses this synergy to optimize life survival at all levels, including between individuals. It includes our social brain and only interacts with others on a nonviolent "win-win or no deal" basis. By acting to optimize life's survival, its own self-survival is ultimately enhanced by the synergy resulting from the law of emergence which provides far more benefits than by independently going it alone.

The Properties of One's Source:

It is our Higher Intelligence, closer than our breath. Fear and dishonesty can cut it off, via norepinephrine alarm inhibition of the three brain cortices. Lust and greed can have the same effect, via inhibition from certain dopamine rewards,.

It defines benefiting oneself at another's survival expense as "Bad": (i.e. playing by "I win you lose" rules is a "Sin"). It always prevents us from benefiting from gains we take at the expense of another's survival. It punishes us for harming another with the subconscious generation of pain of guilt. To our harm however, drugs can temporarily block our conscience. It "hates the sin, but loves the sinner (us)", and is always there, ready and waiting to help us get up.

It provides intuition about the right thing to do: (playing by "You win-I win" rules gives "the joy of service"). The yelling of one's frightened Reptile brain self easily downs out the Source's "still-small voice". Thus, one's Source can be "heard" better during meditation, prayer, and certain other states (where the Executive Ego can be allowed to rest, or to surrender its load). Its channels are further opened by "Cleaning-up one's

296

life": i.e., reversing past harm done to another's survival to benefit one's own self.

The Work of One's Source:

You Source has your purpose in life. It already knows the solution to all of your current personal problems. It has a special plan for you. It has the wisdom and the power for you to accomplish Its purpose and plan. It necessarily requires your total surrender and cooperation to do Its work of survival optimization. Its plan is easy to do. Its plan always succeeds. Its plan aligns with and taps what Is, the way the Universe works, the sole source of life, abundance, opportunity and power. Its plan improves life and eliminates human violence and suffering. Its plan always brings balance, love, happiness, satisfaction and joy to you and to others.

Opening the Channels and Surrendering to One's Own Source:

Your Source is knowing and wise. Its purpose is for your highest happiness. Its plans are superior. It has the power for you to accomplish them. Surrendering to superiority and happiness is not dangerous, and certainly is no sacrifice. Surrender to ones God-Within started occurring long ago. For example, 3000 years ago, King David of Israel, wrote the following psalm, his 23rd.

> "The Lord is My Shepherd. I shall not want.
> He makes me lie down in green pastures.
> He leads me beside still waters.
> He leads me in the paths of righteousness for his name sake.
> Even though I walk through the valley of the shadow of death,
> I will fear no evil; for He is with me.
> His rod and staff comfort me.
> He prepares a table before me in the presence of my enemies.
> He covers my head with fragrant oil, my cup overflows.
> Surely goodness and mercy shall follow me all the days of my life.
> And I shall dwell in the house of the Lord forever."

Finding Your Purpose, Plan and the Power to Achieve it.

"Be still and *know* that I am God", from David's 46th psalm, gives the method. Meditation and prayer are ancient techniques long practiced in order to silence the clamoring impulses of the xDARP and to calm the yelling of the worried Crocodile Brain. Only in inner silence, can the intuition from "that still small voice" of God Within be felt.

To listen to your Source, find a quiet spot where you can sit undisturbed with your spine vertical. Calm your Reptile Brain by rhythmic repetitive inner counting (1 to 10), or the inner chanting of a mantra such as "Wonderful Source" or "I bow to the God-Within who I am". As your mind quiets, remains alert, awaiting inspiration and guidance. "If with all your heart you truly seek me, You shall always surely find me. This says *your* God." is an ancient Moseic quotation of encouragement.

Begin to communicate with your source continually. As you clean up your past by repairing the harm you have done to others, you will remove the guilt blocking the channels to your Source. It will become a pleasure for you to walk and talk with your holy God-Within, thus coming to know the right things to do. The laws of the universe and life "will become your delight." Then, your Purpose and Plan will be revealed and, you will be given the Power to accomplish it.

The Joy of Discovering One's Source:
When you find that light within you, you will know that you always will be in the center of wisdom. As you probe deeper into who you really are, with your lightedness as well as your confusion, with your angers, your longings and your distortions, you will find the true, living Source. Then you will say,
"I have known you all my life
And have called you by many different names.
I have called you mother,
I have called you father,
I have called you friend,
I have called you lover.
I have called you the sun, and the flowers.
I have called you my heart.
But never until this moment have I called you *myself*.
I was blind, but now I see!
You are the end of my quest!
You are the beginning of my transformation!
I bow to you, oh God Within,
source of delight and inspiration."

This is joy! This is hope! This is enthusiasm for a better tomorrow!

In the next chapter, we take a new look at the afterlife by addressing the very real possibility of physical immortality.

Some Important Contexts in Chapter 17: The Reconstitution of Religion: Elevation to Nonkilling Levels of Civilization.

1. Recognize the presently expanding chaos and the misunderstanding over the meaning of freedom.

2. Choose the power of "true" religion to restore our Higher Calling: To rise from killing to nonkilling.

3. By optimizing, not maximizing, the survival of the family group, we must defuse the population bomb.

4. Religion is the product of our Social Brain's drive to optimize the survival of our species.

5. There are more than 15 essential human boding, non-spiritual functions of religion.

6. To bring all of us up to the nonkilling levels requires a globally unifying story.

7. NEUROREALITY: A Transformational Context for Existence, Bridging Brain and Mind, Science and Religion: *Viewing the eternal dyadic universe through the lens of the scientific method*

8. The Eight Octaves of Neuroreality:

   Octave 1: The Eternal, Dyadic Universe: Moving God from Outer to Inner Space

   Octave 2: Recognition and Empowering Use of The Eight Realities:

   Octave 3: The Quadrimental Brain, the Dual Quadbrain, and the Society of Seven

   Octave 4: Dyadic Behavior: Hemisity joins Sex as Part of Our Personal Identity

   Octave 5: Dyadic Evolution: The Existence, Origin, and Nature of Familial Polarity

Octave 6: Thwarted Brain Development: The Paradoxical Origin and Nature of Stress.

Octave 7: Scientific Religion: The Transforming Context of Neuroreality

Octave 8: Rising from Killing Competition to a Nonkilling Collaborative Civilization

9. The Trinity of Neuroreality: Eternal Universe as our Father, Scientist Sons as Role Models, The Social Brain as our Holy Source

10. Best Current Approximation of Moral Law:

11. The Ten Commandments of Neuroreality:

12. The nature, properties, and work of one's Source:

13. Opening the channels and surrendering to one's own Source:

14. Finding your purpose, plan and the power to achieve it.

15. The joy of discovering one's Source:

Section VI: Must I Die? How will I Die? What will Happen to Me after I Die?

Chapter 18: Cracking the Death Program, the Possibility of Physical Immortality

Spiritual Immortality: Life after Death is Everyone's Impossible Wish.

One of the consequences of the incorporation into our genes of behaviors that prolong our personal survival is that we all have inherited an inbuilt Survival Reality. In this purposeless and meaningless universe, this reality asserts that life alone is of value. We inherently hate and fear the thought of death and dying. Life is the only thing that gives our existence meaning. Therefore, it is not unexpected that we have accumulated many anxiety-quelling ideas that propose that there is life after death. Many such powerful motivators are to be found in the world's currently obsolete religions. Several types of after-lifes might exist. These range from eternal life in a Heaven with streets paved in gold, and where uncounted numbers of virgins wait to serve their martyred heroes, down to ideas of endless torture of sinners in the fires of Hell.

Other fervently held traditions include the resurrection of the dead for the "Last Judgment" at the end of time. The world's population crossed its first billion mark sometime shortly after 1800. There now are 7 billion of us alive on earth. To resurrect all the past generations of humans since the beginning of time in order for them to observe the impartial review each person's Book of Life at the last judgment between the righteous and the wicked would require the resurrection-recreation of at least, let's say, 63 billion persons. This would bring the number of people present to 70 billion, ten times the number now existing. This impossible act of creation would soon end all human life on earth, even if the majority were condemned to burn in Hell.

Here for the first time, the context of Triadism makes crystal clear the absolute impossibility of life after death. That is, life is a triadic (5D) process. Life is the activity of an intact physical body over time powered by energy contained in foodstuff. Without an intact, unbroken, functioning body there can be no action. Extracorporeal existence is not possible, neither before nor after death. Thus, although our species has been immortal thus far, none of its members ever has been so, much to our discomfort.

The Possibility of Physical Immortality: Death is Not Theoretically Required.

However, just because spiritual immortality is essentially impossible does not mean that *physical* longevity, or even *physical* immortality is theoretically excluded. For example, the mortality of plants ranges from that of the brief annual grasses to that of some almost immortal trees, which live for thousands of years. Similarly, animals do not age and die because of accumulated some unavoidable damage from cosmic rays. It is clear that animals can repair internal damage at every structural level, from the molecular, macromolecular (including DNA genomes), supramolecular assemblies, subcellular organelles, cells, tissues, organs, and organism levels. Because of this, we appear the same for many years in our prime even though essentially all of last year's atoms in our body have been replaced by new ones (from ancient stardust).

The Importance of Mortality in the Evolution of Life

The survival of fittest genes through reproductive competition is the motor that has driven the evolution of life (1). From this point of view, the "chicken" is only the delivery package for the "egg" (and sperm), which are what continue to change. How the best genes are selected is by winning the competition for reproductive access.

The production of aging plays an essential role in current genetic evolution. It prevents parents from being competitors for limited resources, and thus from being a liability to the survival of their offspring, the new generation. In general, the longevity of a species tends to relate to the generation length of that species (2). Thus, salmon or octopi only spawn once and then die without seeing their offspring. Interestingly, the removal of certain endocrine organs before spawning can prolong the life of a female octopus for several years.

The K-type prey mammals, whose offspring are soon able to reproduce, provide only short-term care for their infants and generally have a short life-span. In contrast, the r-class of mammals, whose offspring do not become reproductively mature for many years, provide long-term care for their progeny and tend to live at least until their progeny can reproduce. The generation time of humans has been about 20 years.

Evidence for Programmed Aging

However, there are notable exceptions to these generalities. For example, why should a large dog have a life span of only about seven years when an elephant lives ten times longer to the age of 70? or a horse live to be 50? or a buzzard live to be 120? Why should a house mouse live only 4 years but a Galapagos tortoise live for over 150 years? Why should humans with the disease of Progeria have markedly accelerated aging, to die at 15 instead of 70?

An appealing answer to these questions is that imbedded in each species' genome is a *death program*. This program activates at a very arbitrary time in the organism's prime. Through the induction of inflammation, age onset illnesses and other debilitating process including cell suicide, it ultimately depletes the organism's cell number, until the person loses that critical number of cells required to survive.

Age-onset illnesses include hypertension and other cardiovascular changes leading to heart attacks and strokes, our primary killers. They also include immune system weakening, skin and connective tissue changes and sensory system deterioration leading to deafness and loss of eyesight. They also bring about other metabolic failures such as age-onset diabetes, reproductive system failures including loss of libido and impotence, and neurologic failures leading to slowing and loss of coordination. All of these illnesses are exceedingly rare among youth.

Pregnancy is a surprising illustration of programmed aging, followed by a partial rejuvenation (3). Reversible age-onset disease-like symptoms appear as pregnancy progresses. They include hypertension, age-onset diabetes, fat redistribution of the senility type, the appearance of "old-age spots" of hyper-pigmentation, and of arthritis. These illnesses then disappear after delivery of the fetus and the expulsion of the placenta. These reversible symptoms appear to tied to placental hormone production (probably steroids, see below).

Aging phenomena exist in both sexes that are related to age dependent changes in the levels of sex steroids. For example, in the sexual maturation of the female, a programmed reduction in estrogen presynaptic receptor sensitivity occurs over the life-time of the female. In young girls, this presynaptic receptor is supersensitive, resulting in low levels of circulating estrogens. Therefore, no secondary sex organ development occurs and they cannot reproduce. In mature women, the estrogen receptor becomes less sensitive, resulting in moderate levels of estrogen production together with secondary sex organ development and reproductive competence. In matrons, the receptor has become subsensitive, allowing high levels of estrogen to build up. This leads to menopause with its paradoxical failure to supply estrogen, to reproductive incompetence, and to osteoporosis.

With maturity an increasing "androgenization" of both sexes occurs. In males, body hair amounts slowly increase after puberty, sometimes accompanied by later pattern baldness. In females, increasing hirsutism (hair growth) on face, limbs, body and pubis occurs with age. These also seem tied to changes in receptor sensitivity.

In general, aging parallels losses in cell numbers. Death occurs when cell numbers reduce to the point where internal redundancy is lost, and one or more vital system fails (at about 40% of lean body mass). This is how and when we ultimately die by asphyxiation. That is, if we aren't killed in the mean time.

Apoptosis (Cell Suicide) as the Source of the Programmed Death of Humans

In general, there are two types of cellular death: from injury by necrosis, or by programmed cell death by apoptosis (a-pop-tosis). In the development of multicellular organisms, apoptosis provides an important balance between life and death. There are many interesting expressions of normal and pathological apoptosis in development. For example, the resorption of the tadpole's tail when it becomes a frog, or the pruning of unused neurons in brain development are normal. The brain atrophy in Alzheimer's Disease is abnormal. The existence of the programmed death of cells gives credence to the possibility of a mechanism for the programmed death of whole organisms, the *Death Program.*

The molecular nature and control of many aspects of apoptosis have been clarified (4). The induction of neuronal apoptosis by stroke requires the coincident activation of two calcium ion cascades (5) for at least 24 hours (6). There are two coincident "fail-safe" pathways in the CNS each of which must simultaneously operate to activate cell death. Both involve the peptide cytokine, interleukin-1. Stress-induced *inflammation,* a homeostatic cell survival response, simultaneously releases interleukin-1 at the head of both fail-safe pathways. This leads to the release of serotonin at stress receptors (5-HT2aRs) on yet to be identified cells that release the major stress peptide, CRF (corticotrophin releasing factor) from their axons. If these stresses are prolonged beyond 24 hours, apoptosis is activated and programmed cell death occurs.

In the case of ischemic insult to the brain (stroke), extensive apoptosis occurs in the hippocampus and striatum. Fortunately, about eighty percent of this brain injury can be prevented by the blockade of one of the fail-safe pathways at any of several points. The hippocampus is essential for the retrieval of memory. Thus, symptoms in humans who have undergone prolonged uncompensated stress include dementia due to failure of retrieval. Such persons have difficulty remembering words, but immediately recognize them when prompted. However, even young dyslexic Rxps have this problem, which in their case is not due to aging.

The striatum is a portion of the Reptile Brain required for same-difference matching. Here, a symptom of brain apoptosis is psychosis: a failure in the matching process that leads to incorrect often bizarre ideation. This is followed by elaborate intellectual development of this false premise. The vulnerable striatum is also required for the initiation and coordination of movement. Its apoptotic injury can result in the shortness of stride, tremor, wide eyes, flat affect, also found in patients with Parkinson's Disease. Again, even young schizophrenics are psychotic, indicating a striatal failure not associated with aging in their case.

Currently, Death by Apoptosis Appears to be the Final Stage of Maturation.

The following is strong evidence that interleukin-1 is the key element in the programmed aging and death of animals, including humans (along with its cousins, interleukin-6 and tumor necrosis factor-alpha). In the laboratory, cell cultures of normal human fibroblast cells derived from skin normally stop dividing and die after about 50 cell divisions (9). It has been reported that as these cultures age, interleukin-1 overproduction occurs, which has been correlated with their ultimate failure to divide (10). Removal of interleukin-1 from these aged cultures caused the fibroblasts became "immortalized". That is the number of the divisions of which they were capable became endless. Restoration of the high levels of interleukin-1 back into incubation medium returned mortality to the cell culture. In this regard, a critical finding was the following: massive elevations of serum interleukin-1 are found in aging humans (11).

Several important questions about interleukin-1 would include: What changes in the control of interleukin-1 production occur in human aging? What is the status of interleukin-I in prematurely aged individuals with Progeria or in pregancy? Is AIDS mortality from HIV due to the elevation of inflammatory cytokines and the activation of the aging program? What consequences would the antagonism of, or removal of interleukin-1 from aging adults have? Is interleukin-1 somehow tied to steroid receptor sensitivity?

Three Independent Antiaging Pathways have been Uncovered by Aging Researchers:

Surprisingly, in spite of vast evidence buried in the current unassimilated, unintegrated science data explosion, the idea of a genetic death program, or for that matter, the programmed inflammatory induction of aging and death has yet to be promulgated. Instead, aging researchers have uncovered three interrelated pathways regulating the potential life span of flat worms, fruit flies, mice, monkeys and potentially humans. The first, dietary caloric restriction, is based upon the observation that if the calories eaten by these organism is reduced to about 70-80 percent of the normal amount, there is about a 50 percent extension in life span. Second, another line of evidence exists demonstrating that reductions in Insulin levels also extends life. Third, a peptide hormone, IFG-1 (insulin growth factor-1), has also been shown to produce life extension. Life span research is a growing area with a vital potential.

Fundamental Questions about Physical Immortality and Rejuvenation

Although theoretically possible, can physical immortality actually be accomplished? Ultimately, genetic engineering will become central to the identification, and termination of the death program. The sequencing of the entire human genome is now complete. Individual genes are being identified, removed, and replaced. Gene products are identifiable. Although it is believed that only about 150 protein gene products would be required to keep a cell alive, there are about 25,000 protein products in humans. Their presence in the right amounts at the right time makes multicellular life and death possible. Protein engineering is underway. Genes can undergo repair or redesign. Thus, identification and modification of the genes of the aging program is an eventuality. The interleukin-1 and related genes ultimately will undergo investigation and manipulation. So, can we achieve in the aged the rejuvenation, as illustrated in females after the delivery? In theory, the answer is a definite Yes!

Although Theoretically Possible, would Physical Immortality be Desirable?

What would the global consequences of human physical immortality be? Earlier global consequences of immortality may be the reason why an aging and death program has evolved. At least six major multiple species extinctions have occurred in the past: Were at least some due to overpopulation?

On the other hand, if we can identify and turn off the death program, why not use it to rejuvenate ourselves back to our ideal ages? Then, when rejuvenated maturity is pitted against youth in a competition for reproductive rights, there would be no contest! Experience counts! With immortality, massive selection of children of either sex might become common. However, contraception would be more likely. Then, genetic backups and annual upgrades could be made available for all.

To prevent a further population explosion would require genetically engineered redirection of our highest reward, away from sex and reproduction toward altruistic behavior. The joy and "orgasms" of service! Clearly, these ideas have a number of attractive features. How about secret immortality for just a select few? You and me? Science fantasy, fiction or fact?

In the Mean Time: Some Possible Anti-aging Substances:

Omega-3 fatty acids from fish oil capsules, 4 g/day, (12).
Deprenyl (seleguline, Eldepryl), 1.25mg/day (13).
DHEA (dehydroepiandrosterone), 75mg/day men, 25-50mg/day women (14).

Some Important Concepts in Chapter 18

1 Spiritual Immortality: Life after Death is Everyone's Impossible Wish.

2 Physical Immortality: Theoretically , Death is Not Required.

3 The Importance of Mortality in the Evolution of Life

4 Evidence for Arbitrarily Programmed Aging and Death

5 Apoptosis (Cell Suicide) is the Source of the Programmed Death of Humans

6 Currently, Death by Apoptosis Appears to be the Final Stage of Maturation.

7 Three Independent Antiaging Pathways have been Uncovered by Aging Researchers:

8 Fundamental Questions about Physical Immortality and Possible Rejuvenation that arise

NEUROREALITY: A SCIENTIFIC RELIGION TO RESTORE MEANING

Section VI: Must I Die? How will I Die? What will Happen to Me after I Die?

CHAPTER 19: Death and Rebirth: The Varieties of Religious Experience

This chapter deals with the personal psychology of religion. It is based upon the never-excelled, prescient book: *The Varieties of Religious Experience,* published in 1902 by Harvard Professor, William James, M.D., Father of American Psychology. All quotations in this chapter are from that source, unless marked otherwise. Paraphrasing of some of its contents was also used.

Religion and Neurology

How do we describe the psychology of the religious tendencies of self-conscious autobiographical humans? First we ask what the propensities of religious individuals are. Then we inquire into what is their neurological basis, an entirely different issue. At times their experiences appear pathological because they go beyond normal, fear-imposed memory limits and enter the realm of the subconscious. As a result, they have fallen into trances, heard voices and seen visions that carry an enormous sense of inner authority and illumination to them. Their ideas possess them. They have inflicted them upon their companions or age. However, their insights are not to be discarded as pathology, but judged for their merit. "By their fruits shall you know them, not by their roots".

Narrowing of the Topic

Religion is not a single essence, but rather a collective name with many characteristics. Here, it is not institutional. Rather, it is one's serious personal feelings, acts and experiential relationship with a Higher Power upon whom our life and survival depends. This can range from a relationship with one's inner Holy Source, (who is a life-oreinted reflection of the eternal infinite universe) to the idea of an externalized God-like entity (who can only be imperfect and threatened by evil) or to the uncaring universe itself (impersonal site of existence and its extremes).

Religion enthusiastically embraces and surrenders to what Is as perfect, rather than dully submitting to enforced external control as a victim. Religion brings trust, freedom from fear, joy and power. Religion extends the subject's positive range of life in a manner only dimly mirrored by falling in love. Religion releases a higher happiness that holds lower unhappiness in check. Religion thus performs a function of our life that no other element of our nature can successfully fulfill.

The Reality of the Unseen

To be asked to characterize religion in the broadest terms possible, it might be said to consist of the feeling-based belief that there is an unseen higher order in the universe, and that our supreme good lies in aligning ourselves with it. Because we are a social species, typically this higher order has taken an anthropomorphic form, with hierarchies of abstract gods and demons, sometimes emerging while dreaming. Belief in these unseeable abstractions can create an Inner Reality stronger even than that of our immediate surroundings and is part of our religious nature. This belief in a deep unseen presence mirrors the existence of our hidden inner Source, with whom, by surrender, we may learn to walk and talk, and from who comes true wisdom, guidance, love and happiness.

The Religion of Healthy Mindedness

Happiness is human life's chief concern: how to gain it, keep it, and how to recover it. Happiness results when the survival needs of our cells are met on all levels. At all times, this is the secret motive for all we do and for all we are willing to endure. This is part of our unconscious religion. Consciously, however, we can become very confused as to how to find happiness. Since the first gift of natural existence is the suffering of unhappiness, people come to regard the happiness that religious belief brings as proof of its truth. No other truth is as convincing.

In the first of two groups of religious persons, the "once born", happiness is an inherent attitude. They see God as the animating spirit of a beautiful and harmonious world. In spite of the hardships of their own conditions or the sinister theologies into which they may be born, when unhappiness is offered or proposed to them, they positively refuse to feel it, as if such were something mean or wrong. These same persons often are served by the so-called "High Churches" such the Catholic, Greek Orthodox, Russian Orthodox or Episcopal. (James wrote before the era of political correctness and in general refers to religious men, in this case to the primarily left brain-oriented males who were predominant in these congregations, Morton, Unpublished), they generally have no metaphysical tendencies; they do not look back into themselves. Hence, they are not disturbed by their own imperfections, yet it would be absurd to call them self-righteous for they hardly think of themselves at all. They cultivate healthy mindedness and divert their attention from disease and death as much as they can in a form of "Mind Cure", where "God is well and so are you". "Slaughter houses and other endless indecencies are never mentioned, so that the world, recognized officially, is a poetic fiction far handsomer, cleaner, and better that the world really is." Theirs is the power of positive thinking where there is no evil.

The Sick Soul, the Divided Self and the Process of its Unification

In contrast to natural happiness of the "once born", for the other group of persons, the "twice born", wrongness or vice is their essential nature. This evil, failure and melancholy, which no alteration of the environment or any superficial rearrangement of the inner self can cure, requires a "supernatural" remedy. As Saint Paul said, "What I would, that I do not; but what I hate, that do I". Many Protestants, (rich in right brain-oriented males, Morton, unpublished), have complained of the mental malaise of a divided will that brings almost continuous guilt and unhappiness from failure of self control, with its sense of incompleteness and imperfection, brooding, depression, morbid introspection, sense of sin, anxiety about the hereafter, distress over doubts, and the like. Some of these people discover a meaninglessness in life, where "all is vanity and a vexation of spirit", and have turned away from God.

Conversion

To be converted denotes a sudden, process of salvation by which a self, previously divided and consciously wrong, inferior and unhappy, becomes unified, consciously right, superior, and happy. Such a transformation results from the surrender of the self-orientated Ego to the Higher Power of our Social Brain Source who cares for us and helps us to escape from "sin". This is associated with an acute crisis of self despair and condemnation as inherently evil, and associated subconscious upheaval that occurs when selfish efforts for control, collapse and are surrendered. This results in an immediate transformational state of deliverance and happiness. Such is often accompanied by a shift away from preoccupation with one's self to a concern for others. As a result, there is an instantaneous, complete and permanent separation between the divided old life and the unified new one. "Conversion is accompanied by the loss of taste for past "carnal" pleasures and carnal company and by the discovery of a new purpose in living, that is, of the communication of the redeeming power of love". He who has his Source has life. And, he that doesn't have his Source does not have life. That is, there is no salvation except through complete surrender and giving up of one's past to one's Source. Without it, we fail again and again. However, to begin to become acceptable for communion with one's holy Source, true repentance and purification (i.e., cleaning up ones past harms to others) may be needed.

With total surrender, a complete and permanent abolition of earlier addictions automatically occurs as one of the fruits of conversion. The Source then provides guidance in a thousand ways and opens one's path in a way almost incredible to those who do not enjoy a truly surrendered life. Prayers, visions and loss of former identity occur. It is as if bandages are removed from the eyes to view the earlier misery from which one is saved. "It is as if the soul is rapidly shaken, revolved and turned in another direction, toward other aims, by other paths." During this process, one sees oneself as a passive spectator or participant of an amazing process performed upon one from above as a gift from one's Source. This seems to occur in an astounding way, unlike what happens at any other time in our lives. "At that moment, an absolutely new nature is breathed into us, and we become participants with the very substance of deity", our Source. After this "second birth" one can never revert to their former state of suffering.

It is natural that those who have personally experienced conversion should carry away a feeling of it being a miracle rather than a natural process. Voices are often heard, lights seen or visions witnessed. Automatic motor, birth-like phenomena can occur. After surrender of personal will, it always seems as if an extraneous higher power had flooded in and taken possession. In addition, the sense of restoration, safety, cleanness and rightness, can be so marvelous to support one's belief in a radically new nature. "He is a new creature, a new man, "born again", "sanctified", delivered from a state of suffering, being upgraded to a state of release and happiness." He is saved now and forever by the gift of his Source.

Those of the "twice born" nature (right brain-oriented persons, [RPs], Kelley, unpublished) appear to have a thinner barrier between their normal self and the subliminal elements both "divine" and "diabolical" in their subconscious. They are more hypnotizable than individuals of a "once born" nature (left brain-oriented persons, [LPs], Kelley, unpublished).

312

Surrender, means being willing to give up one's lifelong avoidance of memories of terror of death, by becoming willing to die. Their brains are thus released from the avoidance of pain and terror to experience and integrate their reactive memories of terror to upgrade their brain database, thereby transforming the individual into a more intelligent, superior human being. The last chapter of Neuroreality will describe the mechanism for this.

After this conversion, they have a sense of being assisted by a higher power, in the past often called the "Holy Ghost". We have fought all our lives to avoid confronting the very things that if experienced would transform us. The tensions of subliminal memories reach the bursting point, in the form unrelated to an epileptic seizure where the outcome is highly positive.

The characteristics of the conversion experience are:
1. The loss of worry, i.e., the sense that all is ultimately well with one; peace and harmony; the willingness to be; the certainty that salvation is a gift, a state of assurance, a purification (sanctification).
2. The perception of truths not know before, the clarification of mysteries.
3. The world appears to undergo an objective change to newness, cleanliness and beauty.
4. Automatisms, such as floods of light too intense for the eyes occur, reminiscent of the chromatic hallucinations of mescaline.
5. Feelings of ecstasy, joy, happiness and love.
6. A changed attitude toward life.
7. The desire to dedicate one's life for the work of the Source.

"When the sense of estrangement fencing man about in a narrowly limited ego, breaks down, the individual finds himself 'at one with all creation'. He and man, he and nature, he and God, are one". Perception of external control, which is so essential a feature in conversion, comes because of the recognition that their melancholy self can do absolutely nothing. It is completely bankrupt and without resource. "Redemption from such a state must appear as a free gift of God, paid by Christ's sacrifice. What must be done in return, but accept the God (Within) as his lover and praise him forever".

Metaphorical descriptions of conversion often include the idea of death of the self and rebirth of the spirit. The objects of faith may even be preposterous, yet the affective stream will float them along, and invest them with unshakable certitude. The more startling the affective experience, the less explicable it seems, the easier it is to make it the carrier of unsubstantiated notions. The human liability to sudden and complete conversion is one of our most curious peculiarities.

"If the Subject has no propensity to such subconscious activity, or if his conscious fields have a hard rind of a margin that resists incursions from beyond it, (as is the case for most LPs, Morton, unpublished) his conversion must be gradual if it occur, and must resemble any simple growth into new habits. The possession of a developed subliminal self, and of a leaky or pervious margin (as in RPs), it is a condition *sine qua non* of the Subject's becoming converted in the instantaneous way".

Saintliness and Its Value

The fruits of religious experience are among the best things that human history has to show. The highest flights of charity, devotion, trust, patience, bravery have been flown for religious ideals toward increasing human survival. "The collective name for the fruits of conversion is Saintliness". Here, religious emotions are the habitual center of personal energy, regardless of which world religion it is. An example of a lesser conversion is the transformation by motherhood from a life of self-indulgence to a life of joyful sacrifice for the child. Conversion brings the immediate reformation of drunkards, tobacco addicts and sexoholics. It was early observed that "the only radical remedy for dipsomania is religiomania"

Converted men agree very closely in what they tell us. They say that they have arrived at an unshakable conviction based upon experience that one's God Within is an entity with which we can converse. That in Him they meet all that they can imagine in goodness, truth, and beauty. That they can see his footprints everywhere in nature, and feel his presence within them as the very life of their life, so that in proportion as they come to themselves, they come to him. They tell us that what separates us from him and from happiness is, first, self seeking in all its forms, and secondly, sensuality in all its forms; that these are the ways of darkness and death that hide from us the face of our Holy Source. In contrast, "the path of the just is like a shining light, which shineth more and more unto the perfect day".

"For many, the benefits of conversion have always been: a desire to be of service, valuation of the common man, avoidance of popularity seeking, resistance to fashion and panic, avoidance of sarcasm, openness, acceptance, friendliness coming from internal security, asceticism, strength of "soul", purity, charity, continued realization of the sweet closeness of our Source, brotherly love, altruism, joyousness, tenderness, nonviolence, equanimity, resignation, fortitude, patience, fearlessness, martyrdom, receptivity, peace, purity of life, non-smoking, non flattery in address, and ornamentation."

Some negative consequences include: Organization into competing groups, fanaticism, and a theopathic condition of intellectual feebleness. Excessive devotion and purity, tenderness and charity, lack of prudence, asceticism, extremes, misdirection of effort, gullibility, morbid inability to meet the world; the welcoming false leadership, glorification of the chief of the tribe.

In general, the judgment of religion leaves it in possession of a towering place in history. Economically, politically and personally, its saintly group of qualities is indispensable to the world's welfare.

Mysticism

Personal religious experience has its roots in the center of mystical states of consciousness. First, we should ask, what are they and how do they differ from other states? We shall discard all claims of the supernatural and identify the following four characteristics of a conversion experience:

1. Ineffability: Conversion is presently indescribable, must be experienced. This is here proposed to consist of the release, and direct experiencing of a lifetime of suppressed reactive memories and their integration into primary memory.

2. Illumination: The integration of reactive memories into the primary memory bank results in the immediate and profound illumination and upgrading of one's Internal Reality construct of External Reality. These revelations resultant in an increase of insight and intelligence that is irreversible.

3. Transiency: The reintegration process completes itself in about an hour. This is accompanied by a cascade of insights.

4. Passivity: Once the subject has surrendered, it is as if a superior power has grasped and held him while the transformative discharge is brought about. He may manifest varied forms of altered consciousness during this time.

Alcoholic drunkenness converts the sober "No" to the unifying "Yes", and must be included as small part of a mystical experience. Nitrous oxide seems to reveal depth beyond depth of truth, which usually turns out to be nonsense, but leaves a profound feeling of revelation that other

315

unifying states of consciousness exist, "separated by the thinnest of veils so that we may spend our lives without suspecting they exist even though, unseen, they influence us". Uses of ether and chloroform have led to states where the meaning of existence appears to be revealed. "In that moment the whole of my life passed before me, including each little meaningless piece of distress, and I understood them. I felt as if I were part of something larger than myself that was controlling. I had the feeling of oneness with the grass, trees, birds and insects, everything in Nature. "Prayer becomes a return from the solitude of individuation into the consciousness of unity with all that is, to kneeling down as one that passes away, and a rising up as one who is imperishable."

The prime characteristic of conversion is a cosmic consciousness that brings focus to the life and order of the universe. "Along with the consciousness of the cosmos there occurs an intellectual enlightenment which alone would place the individual on a new plane of existence-would make him almost a member of a new species. To this is added a state of moral exaltation, an indescribable feeling of elevation, elation and joyousness, and a quickening of the moral sense that is fully as striking and more important that is the enhanced intellectual power. With these come what may be called a sense of immortality, a consciousness of eternal life, not a conviction that he shall have this, but the consciousness that he has it already" (Buck, 1901).

The conversion to cosmic consciousness is methodically cultivated as an element of the religious life by Hindus, Buddhists, Mohammedans, and Christians. Sufis first purge the heart of all that is not "God" through prayer and meditation. It became impossible for Saint Teresa to doubt that she had "been in God and God in her". She said, "I will never believe that any soul who does not possess this certainty has ever been really united to God". St Paul exclaimed "I live, yet not I, but Christ liveth in me".

Philosophy

Can philosophy support the religious man's sense of the divine? Feeling is the deeper source of religion, and theological and philosophical formulas are secondary products, like translations of a text into another tongue. Philosophy finds arguments for our convictions, but it does not establish God's existence, nor define his attributes. Metaphysical attributes thus derived are worthless. The attempt to demonstrate by purely intellectual processes the truth of the deliverance of direct religious experience is hopeless. "The true is what on the whole works well". Truth is what Is, the way the universe and life operate. Perhaps the establishment of an area we could call *"The Science of Religions"* would answer this need.

Other Characteristics

The "once born" (LPs) are attracted to a very different type of worship than are the "twice born" (RPs) are. "Lacking an appreciation of personal conversion, they are instead attracted to elaborate intellectualized dogma, rather than the simplicity and bare purity of unadorned literal truth. They crave the authority of richness and architectural complexity, of massive decoration, statues, frescoes, stained glass windows, jewelry, ornaments, vestments of gold embroidery, and visual symbolism. They are uncomfortable with a plain room with nothing but a Bible on the center table. Lacking a direct relationship with a Higher Power or a personal prayer life, they rely upon formalized prayers and upon the intercession of priests, popery, Mariolatry, and Jesus to protect them from God's wrath. Theirs is a liturgy of a superabundance of superficial relations, elegance, tributes of affection, social recognition, childish beliefs and intricate practices, including, fortunately for them, a Healthy Mindedness that ignores vicissitudes".

The three most essential elements of religion have been the following: *Sacrifice,* at first human sacrifice, then animal, then by Christ's blood and body, then by acts of penance that are thought to bring absolution of sin. *Confession:* part of the general system of purgation and cleansing which one feels one's self in need of, in order to be in right relations with one's fellow men and deity. It may take the form of private confession, public confession, or confession to a priest. *Prayer:* was commonly for better weather, for healing, where the victim may benefit by hypnotic suggestion. However, as an inward communication with a higher power, prayer is indispensible. Prayer is the very soul and essence of religion. Wherever interior prayer is lacking, there can be no conversion. Prayer is inner dialogue with one's Source, an active and mutual form of transaction. Through prayer we are actors in a very serious reality, the change of one's mind.

"Active religion involves the belief in ideal presences and a belief that in our prayerful communion with them, work is done, and something real comes to pass". With a continual prayerful interaction with one's Source, life appears to be effortlessly led, by thinking of something just

317

when one needs it, successful gliding over danger, avoidance of temptations of vanity and sensuality, discovering a root of the matter until then concealed, walking through open doors, on the easiest of roads, with perfect timing of actions needed. Persons are sent to us at the right time. Divine guidance comes of its own accord. This illusion is due to us becoming attuned to what is needed. It all seems like a miracle, the miracle of the universe. This is the value of the subconscious in belief, revelation and inspiration. Here, "Spirit" is process, a consciousness, and is vibrantly alive, but never disembodied.

Conclusions

The characteristics of religious life include the following beliefs: 1. that the visible world is part of a greater universe from which it draws its chief significance. 2. That union or harmonious relation with that higher universe is our true end. 3. That prayer or inner communion with the essence thereof, be that of an external or an internal "God", is a process wherein work is really done. And that conscious energy flows in and produces effects, psychological or material, within the phenomenal world.

Religion also includes the following psychological characteristics: 1. "a new zest which adds itself like a gift to life, and takes the form either of lyrical enchantment or of appeal to earnestness and heroism. 2. An assurance of safety and a temper of peace, and in relation to others, a predominance of loving affections. Religion thus appears to be associated with human welfare enhancement". This fits the survival optimization theory where the religious interaction is based upon personal concerns.

Magic and superstition abounded earlier. Now science has replaced it as an impersonal and generalized symbolic reality, yet still divorced from the true reality of the personal. Science cannot say that "the heavens declare the glory of God and the firmament showeth his handiwork". As contrasting realities of feeling and intellect, science is objective, cosmic and eternal, while religion is the other side of the coin, being subjective, minute and momentary. Thus, a God (external or internal) is the inevitable inference. "Religion, occupying herself with personal destinies, and keeping thus in contact with the only absolute realities which we know, must necessarily play an eternal part in human history".

Summation: "Feelings and conduct of religious saints of all faiths is almost always the same, even though the theologies vary greatly. They constitute the essence of religion. What are they? They are a biological and

318

psychological faith-state with a readiness for great things; belief in possibility for survival is one of the most important biological functions of humanity; the idea of God, whatever he is, understood or not, is used in this regard, if it proves himself useful. Does God exist? How does he exist? What is he? are so many irrelevant questions. Not God, but life, more life, a larger, richer, more satisfying life, is, in the last analysis, the purpose of religion. The love of life, at any and every level of development is the religious impulse. Not the question about God and not the inquiry into the origin and purpose of the world; religion's focus regards the question about Humanity. All religious views of life are anthropocentric. Therefore, religion must exert a permanent function, whether it is with or without intellectual content or whether, if it has any, such is true or false".

An important question is: what is the common element in the content of religions? First, *An uneasiness:* something is wrong. This often comes from the recognition of the duplicity and unreliability of egotism, the fear of death, the desire for help. Last, *the Desire for Salvation:* to become saved from the wrongness by making proper connection with higher powers.

William James Hypothesis of the Origin and Nature of Religious Experience

"The individual, so far has he suffers from his wrongness and criticizes it, is to that extent consciously beyond it, and at least in possible touch with something higher. Along with the wrong part, there is thus a better part of him, even though it may be but a most helpless germ. With which part he should identify his real being is by no means obvious at this stage. But, when stage 2 (the stage of solution or salvation) arrives, the person identifies his real being with this germinal higher part of himself; and does so in the following way. He becomes conscious that this higher part is conterminous and continuous with a MORE of the same quality, which is operative in the universe outside of him, and with which he can keep in working touch. In this fashion, he can get on board and save himself when all his lower being has gone to pieces in the wreck. Remember that for some men it arrives suddenly, for others gradually, whilst others again practically enjoy it all their life".

"This solution contains allowance for a divided self and the struggle; they involve the change of personal (mental) centre and the surrender of the lower self; they express the appearance of (the) exteriority of the helping power and yet account for our sense of union with it; and they fully justify our feelings of security and joy. Are the above objectively true? What is the MORE of the above? All agree that it acts as well as exists, and that something is really affected for the better when you throw your life into its hands."

Thus, William James' prescient idea was "that our subconscious is vaster than our consciousness and includes real genius. In the religious life, the control is felt as 'higher', but since on our hypothesis it is primarily the higher faculties of our own hidden mind which are controlling, the sense of union with the power beyond us is a sense of something, not merely apparently, but literally true".

"Strengthen the real nature, build up yourselves, the effulgent, the resplendent, and the ever pure, and call that up in everyone whom you see. Why does a man go out to look for God: It is in your heart beating, and did you not know you were mistaking it for something external? He, nearest of the near, is my own self, the reality of my own life, my body and soul. I am Thee and Thou art me. That is your own nature. Religion is about life, of living or not living in the higher union which opens itself to us as a gift."

"Man can learn to transcend the limitations of finite thought and draw power and wisdom at will…The divine presence is known by experience. The turning to a higher plane is a distinct act of consciousness. This is not a vague twilight or semi-conscious experience. It is not an ecstasy; it is not a trance. It is not super-consciousness in the Vedantic sense. It is not due to self hypnotization. It is a perfectly calm, sane, sound, rational, common sense shifting of consciousness from the phenomena of sense-perception to the phenomena of seership, from the thought of self to a distinctively higher realm. It is done by the exercise of power."

Postscript

James confirmed that he did not believe in personal immortality or life after death. However, he believed that we can experience union with something larger than ourselves and in that union find our greatest peace. This makes the difference between a life whose keynote is of resignation and a life whose keynote is hope.

Our final chapter provides a clear, neuroscience-based mechanism and explanation for the experience of transformation.

Some Important Concepts from Chapter 19: Death and Rebirth: The Varieties of Religious Experience

1. To describe the psychology of the religious tendencies of self-conscious humans, we both ask what the propensities of religious individuals are, and inquire into what is their neurological basis. Though at times they have fallen into trances, heard voices and seen visions that carry an enormous sense of inner authority and illumination to them, their insights are not to be discarded as pathology, but judged for their merit.

2. Here, religion is not institutional, but rather, it is one's serious personal feelings, acts and experiential relationship with a Higher Power upon whom our life and survival depends. Religion releases a higher happiness, dimly mirrored with falling in love that holds lower unhappiness in check. It thus performs a function of our life that no other element of our nature can successfully fulfill.

3, To characterize religion in the broadest terms possible, it consists of the feeling-based belief that there is an unseen higher order in the universe, and that our supreme good lies in aligning ourselves with it.

4, There are two groups of religious persons. In the "once born", happiness is an inherent attitude. They see God as the animating spirit of a beautiful and harmonious world. In spite of the hardships of their own conditions, when unhappiness is offered or proposed to them, they positively refuse to feel it, as if such were something mean or wrong. They generally have no introspective tendencies. They cultivate healthy mindedness and divert their attention from disease and death as much as they can in a form of "Mind Cure", where "God is well and so are you". Theirs is the power of positive thinking where there is no evil. These individuals are identified as LPs in their hemisity.

5, In contrast to natural happiness of the "once born" (LPs) is the moroseness for the other group of persons, the "twice born", RPs, wrongness or vice is their essential nature. This evil, failure and melancholy, which no alteration of the environment or any superficial rearrangement of the inner self can cure, requires a "supernatural" remedy. As Saint Paul said, "What I would, that I do not; but what I hate, that do I".

6, To be converted denotes a sudden, process of salvation by which a self, previously divided and consciously wrong, inferior and unhappy, becomes unified, consciously right, superior and happy. Such a transformation results from the surrender of the self-orientated Ego to the Higher Power of our Social Brain Source who cares for us and helps us to escape from "sin". This is associated with an acute crisis of self-despair and condemnation as inherently evil, and associated subconscious upheaval that occurs when selfish efforts for control, collapse and are surrendered. This results in an immediate and permanent transformational state of deliverance and happiness.

7, The seven characteristics of the conversion experience are: a) There is a loss of anxiety. b) There is the perception of truths not known before. c) The world appears changed to a newness, cleanliness and beauty. d) Automatisms, such as floods of intense light, can occur. e) Feelings of ecstasy, joy, happiness and love emerge. f) One's attitude toward life changes. g) There is a desire to dedicate one's life to the work of the Source.

8, If the Subject (LP) has no propensity to such subconscious activity, or if his conscious fields have a hard rind of a margin that resists incursions from beyond it, his conversion must be gradual if it occur, and must resemble any simple growth into new habits. The possession of a developed subliminal self, and of a leaky or pervious margin, it is a condition *sine qua non* of the (RP) Subject's becoming converted in the instantaneous way".

9, Thus, William James' prescient idea was "that our subconscious is vaster than our consciousness and includes real genius. In the religious life, the control is felt as 'higher', but since on our hypothesis it is primarily the higher faculties of our own hidden mind which are controlling, the sense of union with the power beyond us is a sense of something, not merely apparently, but literally true".

10, "Strengthen the real nature, build up yourselves, the ever pure, and call that up in everyone whom you see. Why does a man go out to look for God: It is in your heart beating, and did you not know you were mistaking it for something external? He, nearest of the near, is my own self, the reality of my own life, my body and soul".

NEUROREALITY: A SCIENTIFIC RELIGION TO RESTORE MEANING
Section VI: Must I Die? How will I Die? What will Happen to Me after I Die?

Chapter 20: Transformational Steps to Becoming a Human Being

This final unifying chapter seeks to answer the question: "What can this new scientific religion, Neuroreality, tell us about how human beings can stop killing each other to achieve salvation and immortality?" Humanity has always worshiped life and been terrified by the painful warnings of death. Each of us, at least secretly, has wished to be immortal. At present, there are only two kinds of religious institutions promising personal salvation from the throes of death and nonexistence. They are the core ideas that evolved into the Western religions and those of a different context that evolved into the religions of the East.

In the Western religions, including Judaism, Christianity and Islam, the existence of a supernatural Creator God is fundamental. According to these, He was the One who created and populated not only the earth, but also His other worlds with living creatures. Over time, some of His beings challenged His wisdom, and there was war in Heaven. Lucifer-Satan and his evil angel demons were cast out of heaven and exiled by God to this earth, where Adam and Eve other forms of terrestrial life had recently been created. Satan, the father of all lies, deceived Adam through Eve to defy and disobey God. Consequently, humanity was deprived of the support of the Garden of Eden; Adam was cursed to hard labor to obtain food, and Eve with the hard labor of childbirth.

As humans multiplied, they became so corrupt and it was said that God regretted having created them. To wipe the slate clean, He destroyed all life by a flood, save Noah, his family and a few animals in his ark. God then gave the rainbow as a promise that all those obey him would be saved at the end of time at the resurrection of the dead and their last judgment.

After the flood, humans again began killing each other, thus defying and disobeying God's command "Thou shalt not kill". This time, through Christianity, God offered another way to salvation. Although disobedience of God must always result in punishment by death, a scapegoat could be sacrificed as a substitute to save believers from death. That is, God impregnated Mary with His only Son, Jesus, to be crucified on a cross by unbelievers, thus to die as a scapegoat for the sins of the world. Those who believe in Him will also be forgiven of their sins at the resurrection of the dead and last judgment. They are promised Heaven where the saved will be given eternal life, which will be recreated on earth with streets of gold. In contrast, sinners will forever remain gripped by the torments of Hell.

The salvation motif is different in the Eastern religions, such as Hinduism, Buddhism, Jainism, Sikhism, Taoism and Shinto. Here, there is no Creator God to "obey, or be destroyed". Rather, the cycles of motion and rest in the universe are eternal, and all life is sacred. Crucially, each Soul is immortal, thus offering inbuilt salvation by eliminating the fear-invoking the possibility of immediate eternal death. According to this, by transmigration of the Soul one can, through learning and disciplined effort, rise above past lives of suffering that are inherent in pleasure-pain motivation design of life, to higher realms of blissful existence, often represented by polytheistic imagery. Or, through sloth and self-indulgence, one may fall to the suffering of lower life forms until one's soul finally decides to master existence. Thus, salvation from suffering comes from alignment with the perfect way the universe works to gain liberation from painful existence and thus achieve union with the Oneness of the Universe as God.

Clearly, either of the above two ancient religious routes to salvation require the belief in the supernatural and extracorporeal: that is the existence of God as a spirit, or the transmigration of the soul, both of which are absolute impossibilities. Thus, they cannot bring relief but only offer an opiate-like hope. These religions have failed us because they are such inaccurate approximations of the truth that they do not cross the threshold of workability, and thus are not sufficiently aligned with the way the universe works to provide practical relief from our suffering.

The fatal error in both the Western and Eastern religions is that the ancient scientific method's objectivity has long been replaced by the subjective wish-fulfilling dreams of spirituality. These days, people often say, "I am not religious, but I am spiritual". This is simply an attempt to bring one's religious beliefs from the social level down to the level of self. Indeed, one's conscious experience of existence is very personal. At that level, we each are totally alone, naked and helpless in the presence of the overwhelming universe of life and death. From that terrifying perspective, our nightly washings by the dream world during REM sleep with its pleasing sexuality and protective gods appear to provide us spiritual protection from the overpowering demons of death. For relief from the intolerable tension of this situation, we choose life! We choose God, and/or the protective fellowship of the collective good of our religious family. As infants, we can do no other. This is the first core benefit that religion provides a social organism: personal protection from death by membership in a higher family. However, it would appear that the more spiritual the beliefs of one's religious family are, the less they serve to protect us. In fact, a number of highly spiritualized religions have included murderous child and adult sacrifices. Not a few religions have required us to kill the human beings of another spiritual family.

What a good religion needs is the replacement of all the supernatural truth-camouflaging lies of subjective spirituality with the reproducible truths of objectivity. The removal of the comforting, but paralyzing spiritual belief in immortality and past lives karma enables us to recoup our responsibility for the fate of life on this planet, and to act rationally in a symbiotic constructive manner.

Dream Reality with its deliberate protective camouflaging of the raw truth, including its wishful supernatural exaggerations, exists everywhere. Spirituality is not at all wrong within the realm of Science Fiction. Indeed fiction and fantasy can be delightfully fun and entertaining. However, it is called science fiction because it breaks the rules of External Reality. Since it lies about what is, it can only fail in the real world where "the rubber meets the road". Lies just do not work in the external world within which we must survive, no matter how beautiful and fulfilling Spirituality is as an art form. What is needed is to use the scientific method to find and utilize the truth to align with the way the universe is. Dream Reality cannot help here; Only External Reality is the way the universe works.

Neuroreality provides a third alternative for salvation, **Figure 1**. Through use of the scientific method, it seeks accurate approximations of reality that cross the threshold of workability. In so doing, it provides us with such hands-on access to the levers and dials controlling the way the universe works that we can begin successfully to align with and tap the bounties of the universe, the sole source of life, abundance, opportunity and power.

According to Neuroreality, we are among cell-based living beings spontaneously created within the womb of Mother Earth, presently located

Figure 1: Reduction of "Terror of Dying" by Three Types of Religion

SCIENTIFIC RELIGIONS	SPIRITUAL RELIGIONS	PARANORMAL RELIGIONS
Basis: The Reliable Natural Laws of Waking External Reality *Known, logical, practical, useful, repeatable.*	**Basis: The Supernatural Mystical Nature of Dream Reality** *Unknowable, mysterious, overwhelming, physically impossible*	**Basis: The Supernatural of New Age Rationalism** *Hidden knowledge from ETs, spirits, animistic shamen*
Scientific Tools for Survival from Injury or Illness:	**Spiritual Tools for Survival from Injury or Illness:**	**Paranormal Tools for Survival from Injury or Illness:**
Emergency Medicine, Surgery, Internal Medicine, Radiation Medicine, X-rays, MRI, PET scans Pharmacology, Oncology, OB/GYN Pediatrics, Endocrinology, Urology, Dermatology, Orthopedics, Nutrition, Emergency Care, Psychiatry, Psychology, Geriatrics Biochemistry, Anatomy, Physiology Engineering, Physics, Chemistry, Astronomy, Geology, Marine Biology, Meteorology, Zoology, Plant Sciences, Evolution, Hospitals, Cancer Institutes, Doctors, Nurses, Technicians, Medical Teams, Universities, Life-Scientists, Vast publication of useful, repeatable knowledge gained by The Scientific Method.	God, Allah, Gods, Satan, Angels, Demons, Heaven, Hell, Immortality, Belief, Faith, Prayer, Healing, Miracles, Exorcisim, Moses, Ten Commands, Buddha, Eight-fold Noble Path, Mary, Jesus, Resurrection, Mohammed, Jihads, Ministers, Priests, Rabbis, Kalifs, Inspiration, Bible, Koran, Scriptures	Precognition, Clairvoyance Telepathy, Psychokinesis Extrasensory Perception, Levitation, Hypnosis, Astrology, Past Lives, Meditation, Gaia Earth Communication with the Dead Holistic Alternative Medicine Other dimensions and universes New Physics Quantum Mechanics Cosmic Consciousness
	Present Level of Communal Belonging and Support:	**Present Level of Communal Belonging and Support:**
	Birth: midwifery, circumcisions baptism, recordation, acceptance of child by the group.	Because New Age Religions are young and sparse, they provide little social support.
Present Level of Communal Belonging and Support:	*Childhood Religious Education:* Indoctrination from the "mothers knee" through college.	*Birth:* water or low intensity natural birthing.
Scientific Religions are new and undeveloped. A central global organization has yet to emerge. There are no traditions and much isolation. Because humans are a gregarious social species, this causes much unnecessary stress.	*Courtship Supervision:* defered pregnancy. *Marriage:* A community event *Daily Life:* Prayer, Daily-Weekly Meetings, Birthdays, Monthly Celebrations or Memorials, Voluntary community work, Temperance, Artistic Expression, Trust, Respect, Mutual Assistance, Obedience, Local-International Networking,	*Childhood Education:* Computer games, TV, No religious instruction *Courtship Supervision:* None *Marriage:* a semi-secret event performed in places of "Power" *Daily Life:* Little organized, except perhaps for celebrations of birthdays or solstices. If it feels good, do it. Free-Love,
Spiritual Religious Organizations have a 4000 year head start in this important area.	*Elders:* respected and valued *The Aged:* Elder Care *Death:* Funerals and Mourning	
Estimated Potential for Survival Optimization: 100%	**Estimated Potential for Survival Optimization:** 50%	**Estimated Potential for Survival Optimization:** 25%

in the energy halo of life within our galaxy. Some of these incubated life forms have evolved to increasingly higher levels of structural and energetic order, including conscious intelligence. Over the past millennia we humans have slowly been rising from the evolutionary level of individual survival of the fittest by tooth and claw to higher, nonviolent, empathic levels of family, tribe, society, nation, and world order. For eons of evolution, the natural laws of killing competition were perfectly appropriate at the individual survival level. However, upon rising to higher levels of order, the antisocial biological laws of rejection and killing are automatically replaced by a state shift to an opposite set of Nonkilling laws of acceptance (a form of love), empathy, and collaboration.

Failure to recognize the absolute futility of applying violence at all higher levels of society is a current source of killing global conflict. In addition, current ignorance of the existence of Law of Emergence prevents the recognition that benefits must always appear when rising to the next higher nonviolent level of order, benefits that exceed the cost. Furthermore, because we have now uncovered the biochemical basis of the existence of life and have decoded the human genome, the way is now clear for us to discover and terminate current aging and death program that is rotting and killing each of us unnecessarily.

Thus, Neuroreality provides salvation at five levels. First by promoting termination of killing competition by the enrollment of individuals into empathic cooperative societies of increasing levels of order, we remove the daily threat of death through violence and disorder. Neuroreality provides numerous new insights with personal tools to accomplish this conquest of inner space. Second, through conversion from the destructive spirals of growth-based economics to life-saving, balanced economies, we save Mother Earth and allow her life support systems to recover and continue to nourish us. Third, by continuing to clarify the molecular instructions of our genetics, we have the real potential to uncover and turn off the aging and death program, with resultant physical longevity, even immortality, as a real possibility in our future. Fourth, by continuing our conquest of outer space, we will be prepared to migrate to fresher planetary pastures as our earth moves out of our galactic zone of life. Thus, our species will become immortal.

Fifth and most important, a scientific religion can take advantage of the findings of the new Science of Happiness more effectively to bring us that intangible personal reward that we all crave: Happiness. Why is it that the third world Nigerians have been measured to be at least as happy as the first world Japanese whose material wealth (GDP) is 25 times greater? Further, the isolation that results from my out- competing others to be the best, richest, most famous, most powerful person in the pond doesn't lead to happiness, but rather to alienation and emptiness, If one has the view that they are always right and all the others are wrong, by definition one ends up being alone.

The renewal of the old rules such as of "Share and share alike", "Honesty is the best policy", "Fairness and Forgiveness", "Don't do to the other person what you wouldn't want them to do to you", or "It's better to give than to receive", can be shown to bring real satisfaction. Recently experiments demonstrated that people giving something to others felt happier than when someone gave the same thing to them. Maybe winning is not everything we thought it was. Rewarding someone is superior to punishing them and of course brings a happier outcome. It is clear that lying, cheating and stealing directly lead to violence. In contrast, belonging to something larger than one's self, namely life and human survival, and contributing to its well-being brings personal meaning and satisfaction. As a social species, we have ancient subconscious alarms going off in our heads if we are by ourselves for very much of the time. Weekly meetings and recommitment to one's greater group is a great source of pleasure. An associated weekly "potluck" lunch is notorious for making and renewing feelings of connectedness and good will through straight talk and "getting caught up".

It appears that the joy that comes from mental health is the well-being set point default of most humans. Relief from the depression and paranoia, which brings misery to countless billions, results in inner peace, and puts a song on one's lips. Because of the nature of the Pain Body-Reactive Mind, we do not currently know how to purge it and remove its continual subconscious neurochemical contamination of our happiness by anxiety. However, there are effective antidepressant, antimania and antipsychotic drugs available to those who understand. Further, the approaches to personal transformation, described in the previous chapter and in more detail later in this chapter, together with cleaning up one's past, along with the other information in this book, activates life's pleasures by restoring our birthright of joy.

A New Context for Living

The preceding chapters have developed the twenty-one paradigm shifts mentioned in the Preface, each these being a gift from the author's

Source. The first three of these gifts were cosmological in nature; the remaining 17 were neuroscience based. You are now familiar with all of them as core elements of Neuroreality: A Transformational Context for Existence, Bridging Brain and Mind, Science and Religion:

1. The Eternal Universe with Infinite Levels of Unique Structures and Laws
2. The Law of Emergent Properties
3. The Galactic Singularity Model of the Origin of Life
4. The Seven Types of Reality
5. Triadic Solution to the Mind-Body Problem
6. Cellular Survival as the Source of all living Behavior
7. The Five Dimensions of Behavior
8. The Quadrimental Brain Model
9. The Dual Quadbrain Model and the Society of Seven
10. The Four Freedoms of Choice within Determinism
11. The Neuroanatomical and Behavioral Basis of Hemisity
12. The Dyadic Evolution of Familial Polarity
13. Family Polarity as the source of Multilevel Global Conflict
14. Polaric Crossbreeding: Origin of Dyslexia
15. Polaric Crossbreeding: Origin of Trans-sexuality, Homosexuality, & Pedophilia
16. The xDARP as a Major Source of Neurotic and Psychotic Behavior
17. Guilt Pain as the Origin of Drug Seeking Behavior and Narco-trafficking
18. Programmed Elevation of Inflammation is the Key to Genetic Aging and Death
19. The Emergent Benefits of Living on the Nonkilling Universe Levels
20. Neuroreality and the Reconstitution of Religion as a Tool to Elevate Individuals to the Nonkilling Levels of Civilization.
21. The discharge of blocked memories of terror is transforming.

Each of these twenty one new contexts specifically contributes to the path of personal happiness and fulfillment, peace, satisfaction, self-respect, and respect for others. This path can be transformational, causing automatic elevation to the higher levels that optimize human survival.

Neuroreality: A New Story to Live By

Originally, humans developed the idea of extracorporeal supernatural existence to explain the many things that we didn't understand about our universe. Further, all religions contain the supernatural features which in every case turn out to be in conflict with External Reality. These time-honored religious Dream Reality metaphoric exaggerations include heaven, hell, gods, devils, angels, demons, including animal-human hybrids, little people, UFOs, aliens, miracles, telepathy, telekinesis, flight, past lives, precognition, ESP, hallucinations and old-fashioned nightmares.

This book removes that single critical defect of the old religions (Armstrong, 1993) by making clear that the belief of the extracorporeal (bodiless) existence is untenable because it is essentially impossible. This crucial accomplishment then unravels most of what is harming us within our current religions. That is, it eliminates superstition. Neuroreality decisively proves that physical out of body existence has never existed and never will, except as dream like illusions of the human mind created to disguise traumatic reality. With those fatal thinking flaws abolished, we regain control of ourselves, our species and our universe. By replacing a "spiritual" Triune God, with a "knowledge-based" Trinity, we retain all the elements we desire in answering our big questions about who and why we are, what we should be doing, and where we are going. Clearly, this paradigm shift would accomplish this book's goal to raise humanity from the level of killing to those of nonkilling levels in alignment with the direction the universe is taking us. This will enable each of us to effortlessly go with the flow of energy within the halo of life and climb to the higher levels of civilization, peace and satisfaction that come from the optimization of human survival.

The Law of Emergence Lifts Us from Killing Competition to Nonkilling Synergy

The logic of the eternal universe of infinite unique levels provides a compelling new story with fresh answers to the eternal big questions. Abundant free energy drives increasing structural complexity and organization beyond life itself as new levels of order come into existence, each with unique emergent benefits. Thus, through this new story, it is only common sense to move away from killing disorder and ugliness to the crystalline beauty of nonkilling perfection. If this story became widespread in the form of a global religion, children at their mother's knee as well as adults would choose to align in the formation of the nonviolent higher order of humanity. It is expected that by fully grasping the new story of Neuroreality, a person will spontaneously transform into someone who clearly sees that optimizing the survival of humanity as the most direct path to personal fulfillment. Thus, they will effortlessly be converted from a fighting competitor into someone whom they otherwise would never have been: a compassionate, collaborating, happy human being.

Essential Steps to Personal Fulfillment through Acting to Optimize the Survival of Humanity:

1. "If with all your heart you truly seek Me" (your pure and holy social brain Source, enemy of your crocodile brain self), "you will ever surely find Me. This says your God."

2. Then upon doing so, surrender to your Source who has your life's purpose, plan, and power to achieve it.

3. Find and do what you love to do to fulfill your purpose. Continuously communicate with your Source and follow its leading in doing each next satisfying right thing.

4. Use wisdom, discipline and creativity to avoid helping yourself at other's expense. Live "win-win or no deal".

5. Clean up your past harm to others, and avoid the downward spiral of guilt-repressing drugs of abuse.

6. Recognize that the Reality of your xDARP pain-body's thoughts and feelings does not come from your essence and is *not* who you are. This is of critical importance to know so that you can feel free *not* to act out its damaging neurotic and psychotic compulsions.

7. Know that your unique Internal Reality is only the current model you have constructed to approximate External Reality. You are continually improving it as you discover new facts. Realize that the way the universe Is, is the only way that works in our lives. Avoid wish-fulfilling fantasies. Discover more about the universe so as to create new survival optimizing inventions.

8. Know that in the absence of a functional brain or body, there can be no life; thus, freeing us from the superstitions of demons, devils, angels, gods, hell, heaven, and spiritual immortality, except as trauma avoidant figments of our imagination.

9. Know that all behavior is triadic, requiring a functional structure, time, and potential energy. Do not worry about the supernatural. It doesn't exist in external reality any more than the fantasies of dreams do. You can ignore it where the "rubber meets the road".

10. Know that each and every move you make is subconsciously dedicated at least at one level to the optimization of the survival of the precious cells living within you. Your body is a sacred temple of life.

11. Realize that you are not aware of much of your brain's pre-, sub-, and unconscious activity that continuously directs life optimizing actions on behalf of your cells.

12. Know that your mind consists of seven separate conscious elements with corresponding unique realities, each of which can separately take over control of your cockpit. Moreover, although it all seems to be you, you can learn to control which member of the Society of Seven is in power within you.

13. Know the Seven Realities in order to identify the member of your brain's Society of Seven who is presently occupying your "throne" of control. This is transformational.

14. One cannot win a fight against the way the universe is. Choose and Use the way the universe is and works. Align with it and tap its abundance, opportunity and power. Worship it as your Father-Mother God who has created you.

15. Build, organize and enjoy your nuclear family.

16. At least once a week collaborate with others on projects to optimize human survival.

17. Choose all of humanity along with its global support systems as your larger family.

18. Realize that life originated twice on earth and that parallel trees of life exist, one with a Patripolar reproductive strategy, and one with a Matripolar reproductive strategy.

19. Discover whether you are right or left brain-oriented, and appreciate your associated gifts and limitations by understanding their basis. Act in complement with others who are your opposites,

drawing upon their unique skills while contributing those of your own.

20. Find ways to understand the opposite points of view of Hemisity subtypes to avoid reactivating the many global sites of repetitive violence at the interface between groups of opposite Familial Polarity.

21. Although there were originally only two subtypes of each of the two familial polarities, recognize that because of cross breeding there are now at least sixteen, possibly thirty-two subtypes of humans within the Familial Polarity of humanity. Learn to which subtype you belong and its strengths and weaknesses, learning about those of the other subtypes as well.

22. If you find yourself to be among the non-original familial polarity types, do not view yourself as inferior. As Einstein, Michelangelo or Michael Jackson, you too have unique skills. To be truly appreciated, find and associate with others in your category while living in peace among the others, supporting the immortality of life.

23. Remember, if your sexual orientation is toward children, expressing such to them invariably harms them and kills their ability to have a happy future. This will cause others intensely to hate you and will disrupt society. You choice is either surrender to your Source and consequently do no harm, or to remove yourself from temptation.

24. Those of you with closed head injuries fall in a special category. Your injury makes it almost impossible for you to resist the selfish impulses of your Crocodile Brain, even though you know better. Acting out its competitive killing mode of "wine, women, and song" results in destructive antisocial behavior. However, know that your Reptile Brain has another face. It can surrender to an internal or an external Higher Power, and as your Servant Brain, assist that source with loyal cooperative behavior. Thus, you will need to become servants to a more dominant communal force and work to provide service to humanity. How this is to be accomplished, perhaps as part of a Public Works program, has yet to be developed. Because your Reptile Brain is incorrigible and

undisciplined, it may require a decrease of freedom on your part, but there truly is joy in the service of a good master.

25. For a very long life, develop habits that minimize inflammation within your body.

26. Get clear that living at the level of self survival leads to fear, conflict, stress, misery, violence, suffering, and killing.

27. In contrast, living at the higher levels as a prized family member and responsible citizen brings confidence, happiness, satisfaction, peace and joy.

28. Membership in a Neuroreality family can supply key elements of belonging, often missing in one's birth family or in a competitive, sometimes killing, youth gang. Satisfaction comes from working with and for others on Sourceful projects designed to optimize human survival.

29. Cooperation and collaboration between subunit individuals to build the higher levels of civilization brings about the emergence of new laws with new benefits. These need to be distinguished from the laws of the underlying level and utilized for optimizing humanity's survival.

30. For example, competition between the subunits of higher levels, such as between nations, causes more overall harm than benefits. At the international level, might there be a member-nation fundamental bill of national rights and obligations? A bill where the equivalent of 'the majority "rules"' of laws of "democracy" exist while still respecting the nonkilling rights of minority nations. Yet, according to Godel's IncompletenessTheorum, such a law cannot be predicted from a lower level, but rather must be discovered by the empirical trial and errors of political science.

Opening the Gate to Transcendence: the Final Step to Becoming Human.

The Ego Caretaker's Life-Long Isolation from Memories of Terror:

As noted earlier, humans are among the K-species animals whose infants are born small and almost helpless. This is in contrast to another class of animals (r-species), such as antelopes or elephants, who can jump up and run shortly after falling out of their mother's womb. Ironically, it takes ape or human infants several years of nurturing care before they have developed the physical control that an antelope baby already has at birth.

Because of this for several months after birth, primate infants can hardly move and are extremely vulnerable. During this time, their survival literally depends upon the minute-to-minute focused care of their own mother to meet their immediate needs for food, warmth, cleanliness, and notably, for protection. From the baby's viewpoint, being separated from their mother even for a few seconds, is tantamount to death, because this exposes it to the possibility of being killed by one of many very real dangers. Before civilization arrived, some of these included, being eaten by dogs or other predators, starving or freezing. The baby could and still can be the target of infanticide by new cohabiting males. Upon civilizations arrival, there arose the real possibilities of the baby's falling off a table and smashing its head, drowning in a toilet, or other lethal possibilities.

Because of this biology, a primate baby has become wired to feel like its life is being directly threatened if it is removed from their mother by even a few feet. The response to such separation is that the baby is genetically primed and exquisitely programmed to feel sheer terror and to scream in upset. If the baby survives such a significant separation from their mother, the inevitable consequence is that the Baby now has stored permanent memories of that experience of terror.

This poses a serious problem: what is the baby going to do with such death threatening memories? If they are retrieved, will the baby be thrown back into the incident of terror in a reverberating positive feedback scream? Apparently, such death threat memories are simply "too hot to handle"!

The Reactive Mind of the Cerebellar Thanatos is Where "too hot to handle" Memories of Death Terror are Stored.

There is evidence that the terrified Ego Caretaker dumps these toxic memories, *unexperienced* and *unintegrated* into the memory stacks of the so-called Reactive Mind (Hubbard, 1950), with its Pain Body (Tolle, 2005). It thereby seeks to avoid contact with them for the rest of its life.

In the Dual Quadbrain Model, these memories of death trauma are thus isolated on one side of the cerebellum away from the other side's vast store of benign *experienced* and *integrated* memories in the primary memory bank. This deposit results in the Caretaker not having to expend efforts to block conscious access to traumatic memories of past physical injury, developmental thwarting or other of situations that it perceives to be life threatening and thus terrifying. We cannot consciously retrieve these reactive memories and thus, can act as if they never happened.

Yet, due to the usual automatic memory checks continually occurring when the brain inquires about the outcome of earlier-similar situations, subconscious contact with traumatic memories is occurs. Thus, terror of dying memories remain available in the Reactive Mind and cause internal stress whenever they are restimulated by later incidents in our life. By crude stimulus-generalization, many current events are conservatively judged by the Ego to be related to a chain of earlier-similar traumatic events from which it is hiding. *The subconscious restimulation of unconfronted, unintegrated "too hot to handle" memories of terror is the source of later stress.*

This idea is reinforced by repeated observations that the separation of a monkey or rodent infant from his or her mother and siblings, even for only a few minutes each day during a specific infantile critical stage of development, can result in profound behavioral deficits in adulthood. When these animals reach adulthood, unlike their siblings who were not separated from their mother, they showed problem behaviors commonly seen in disturbed human adults. These include high anxiety, hyperactivity, aggression, hypersexuality, antisocial behavior and the inability to associate with others in a normal manner.

The Locus Coeruleus Alarm System in the Midbrain is in Charge of the Daily Suppression of Terror of Death Memories

The brain system that guards these disturbing reactive memories from emerging into the Ego Caretaker's and our consciousness is the vigilant locus coeruleus (LC) fear system, **Figure 2**. As each day progresses, the LC slowly becomes exhausted by its continuous work to avoid past and present terror, and begins to show the hyper reactivity of sleep loss. To counter this, during the night's sleep, several periods of Rapid Eye Movement (REM) sleep occur, during which time the LC goes off-line to

Figure 2. Death-Terror Memory Management

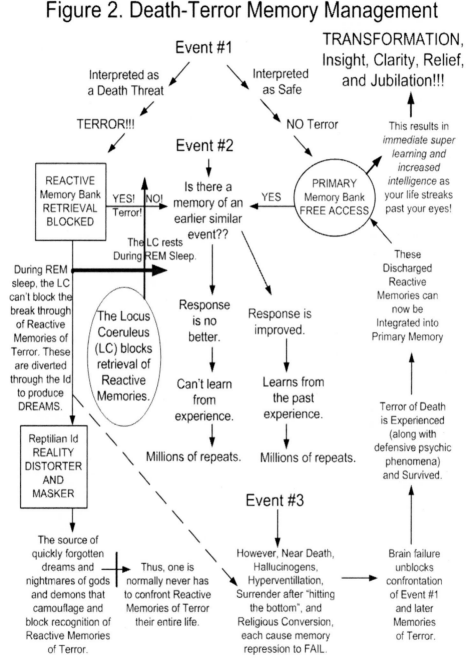

get its needed rest and replenishment. This is the time when, if awakened, the sleeper reports to have been dreaming, where typical rapid eye movements are associated with visual tracking of the events of their dreams. Penile erections or the feminine equivalent are often present during REM sleep.

During REM Sleep, When the Locus Coeruleus is Resting Off- line, Dreaming is Produced to Camouflage Emerging Memories of Terror.
 Significantly, the absence of LC activity during these REM periods leaves the brain temporarily vulnerable to the breakthrough of traumatic Reactive Memories by on-going "earlier-similar" memory searches. However, during REM sleep the Ego uses a second ingenious method, by a yet unknown mechanism, to protect itself from confronting the raw, near-death experiences in its Reactive Memory banks. That is by diverting breakthroughs of trauma through the Reptilian Brain to produce the Id's bizarre Dream Reality. This creates symbolic representations that hide and camouflage any frightening elements of the reactive memory that might emerge.

 Dreams and nightmares, created to protect against traumatic memory breakthroughs, are usually so well disguised in form as to be uninterpretable. Dreams actively camouflage memories of trauma by creating primitive and obscure Id-like thoughts filled by chains of associations, disguises, metaphors, symbols, monsters, flying, falling, and other supernatural events. These break all rules of external reality and may well represent the actual level of thought of the ancient Id. Furthermore, they are often rapidly forgotten upon awakening and thus become no longer threatening. Dream analysis often gives hints of something troubling from our past that appears to be present in our unconscious. However, as long as our Ego-Caretaker is functioning normally, it obviously can never allow successful digging in such an inquiry.

 If more highly charged traumatic memories begin to break through into consciousness, nightmares result, containing gods and demons, experiences of past lives, and of heaven and hell. Yet, even nightmares are less frightening to the Ego than having to confront the underlying original raw experience of death terror. Fortunately for the Ego Caretaker, each morning the LC comes back online after these REM periods, rested, refreshed, and able to maintain an entire lifetime of safety from exposure to one's many personal reactive memories of trauma or anything conservatively viewed as threatening one's survival. Thus, dreams provide protection from memories of terror, by use of deceptive imagery incorporating Id-like traits of disguise, lying, cheating, violence, and killing. This protects it from having to consciously face a lifetime accumulation of terrifying contents building up in our Reactive Minds.

The Unfortunate Costs of Terror Avoidance:
However, the brain's very conservative management of traumatic memories comes at a high price. By preventing access to incidents when at earlier times it feared for its life, it suppresses not only the approach to, but also the experiencing, and integration of many vital aspects of external reality. Further, many events which were viewed as death threats by the Ego of a fetus, infant, or young child and thus were in terror dumped into the Reactive Mind, would not be threatening to the Ego of a surviving adult. Instead, such incidents would have been confronted, experienced completely and integrated into normal memory to upgrade the accuracy of our Internal Reality approximations of External Reality and so increase or intelligence.

Thus, in the Reactive Mind, there is a huge backlog collection of now mostly benign, but once terrifying high intensity, unexperienced memories. These originally dreaded high intensity escapes from death, cause us stress now because they *remain* at their original high intensity form within the unconscious of the Reactive Mind. This warps our current experience of reality. If our reactive memories could be experienced and integrated into our Internal Reality model, we could become more balanced, confident, empathic, intelligent, wise and healthy human beings. However, our conservative, fearful Ego Caretaker doesn't recognize this, and blocks the original reactive memories at all costs. This causes the individual to remain ignorant, fragmented, often with ongoing stress-based mental health issues of truly appropriate or perhaps now inappropriate subconscious reactions of terror, phobias and irrational restrictions. This impairs our ability to integrate life effectively to choose to go with the flow of the universe.

One Part of the Brain Wants Your Help to Overcome the Fears of the Ego and to Transform Yourself:
For most people, the brain successfully suppresses all access to their hidden reactive terror of death memories for their entire lives. However, at death the brain begins to fail. This produces distinctly altered states of consciousness as part of the dying process. Importantly, some

dying people have been resuscitated to report classic "Near-Death", or "Out of Body Experiences" occurring with supernatural, dream-like imagery, where their life flashes past their eyes, and they feel a unity and oneness within a blinding light. As a person is dying, usually the cerebral cortex fails first, causing the loss of sophisticated language and its replacement by decorticate "Pigeon"-like language production. Next, the "same-different" discrimination skills of basal ganglia begin to fail, leading everything to meld into an "All-is-One" unity. For a person lucky enough to be revived at this stage of dying, these transcendent experiences are very impactful and permanently transform their remaining lives for the better. It is as if their eyes have opened to a reality of a higher order than only the one within that their anxious ego formerly permitted them to occupy.

These near-death experiences occur strictly because, as death approaches, the brain is forced to function outside of its normal operating limits, causing some of its subsystems to begin to fail. Yet, it is of great significance that over the millennia we have found other non-lethal brain-stressing conditions that produce similar altered consciousness states within non dying people. It is significant that the altered states observed are remarkably similar to those experiences reported by people retrieved from near death. These methods include induction an altered state in the brain by fasting, sleep deprivation, prolonged meditation-prayer, hyperthermia, pain, hyperventilation, hallucinogens and religious conversion (in rough order of increasing effect).

In the 1960s, indolamine hallucinogens such as mescaline, psylocybine or LSD, were used under controlled conditions to produce this same phenomenon (Grof, 1975, 1980). This has enabled the transformation of thousands individuals. Hallucinogens appear to attack the Ego directly. For the unprepared, the approach of "Ego Death and Transcendence" can be profoundly unsettling and the source of panic. This leads the weakened Ego to unsuccessfully to redouble its efforts to maintain amnesia from reactive memories, ultimately causing it, as a backup, to activate the production of Id-induced nightmares as hallucinations.

This was the basis of "a bad trip" and sometimes a subsequent run to a hospital Emergency Room. During the 1960s, it was estimated that hallucinogen users had "bad trips" about 60% of the time. This problem exacerbated when it became possible to synthesize, cheaper, but much less user-friendly hallucinogens such as DOB, STP or DOI to flood the market, displacing the more expensive LSD and mescaline. In reaction, the US Government declared possession essentially all hallucinogens to be crime.

Hopefully, LSD and mescaline will again become available to licensed physicians for the supervised self reduction of certain mental illnesses, or more importantly, as a safe and legal means of self-transformation. It is of interest that for the two thousand years preceding Christianity, hallucinogens appear to have been used in a rite of initiation, called the Eleusian Mysteries by one of the most impressive of the ancient civilizations, that of the Patripolar Greeks. This was held each September when thousands of the most eligible citizens volunteered to participate in a once in a lifetime ritual so secret that its description has been prevented by the threat of death (Wasson, Hofman & Ruck, 1978 of hallucinogen fame). Although the details are still missing, it is very clear that the this rite induced ego death and transcendence in a manner that was transformative to large groups of Greeks and thus to some degree to their society. Ironically, the Matripolar Romans ultimately replaced the Eleuisan Mysteries with weekly rites incorporating the symbolic crucifiction and resurrection of Christ. The related period of the Flower Children in the 1960s resulted in a perhaps similar transformation of society in the United Statesfor a short while. However, this lacked the sophistication of the Greek Mysteries and its uncontrolled side effects alarmed the government.

Fortunately, after the hallucinogen approach to transformation became illegal, a similarly profound brain effect was found to be induced by prolonged "Hyperventilation" in the presence of loud music and drumming within a safe space, as in Holotropic Breathwork (Grof & Grof, 2010). Such conditions also weaken the ability of the Ego Caretaker to suppress-repress memories of trauma in the Reactive Memory bank. This results in therapeutic breakthroughs from the top of one's "trauma stack" of reactive memories into normal consciousness.

The Transformation of the Religious Conversion Experience: Transcendence Awaits

Paradoxically, the best bad trip is the experience of total Ego collapse ("ego death") and the emergence of the Superego Source ("transcendence") into the seat of consciousness, as a form of the death and rebirth of the true self. In the case of religious conversion experiences or recovery from addictions, it is the intensity of the personal crisis that takes the brain outside of its comfort zone leading to ego death and surrender to a Higher Power. Persons whose brain has not been forced outside of its normal, well-guarded normal operating conditions never experience this inherently healing transformation. During these special times of Ego collapse, one can complete the experiencing of their birth and early childhood as a successful survivor. The consequent release and integration of an enormous amount of no longer dangerous formerly blockaded material occurs. This may be accompanied by the view of one's entire life flashing before ones eyes, sometimes with each of the original threatening scenes rapidly recurring and being discharged. These are integrated into the Primary Memory. Doing so results in a form of catch-up superlearning and a permanent boost in intelligence.

Further, one confronts for the first time the existence of other conscious elements of our Society of Seven within the mind besides just the clamoring, selfish Crocodile Brain Id. Often, when no longer suppressed by the Ego, the Social Brain "Source" comes to the fore, in whose purity one feels like filthy rags of corruption by comparison. Thus, this opens one to the greatest of rewards: the discovery of one's Higher Power. This is because your Source has your purpose, foolproof plans for your life, and the power to accomplish them. You will never be the same because you will have learned who you really are. Where possible, it is helpful to purify oneself in advance or as soon possible by cleaning up ones life of harm done to others. This removal of guilt further facilitates the opening of channels of communion between your surrendered self and your pure Source.

The Brain Core Id Reasoning is the Origin of Spirituality and Transpersonal Psychology

When awake, the facilitated breaking through of reactive memories of trauma into consciousness is of course extremely threatening to the failing Ego Caretaker. Thus, its protective backup production of Id based waking dreams and "daymares" activates. Under these conditions, the awake recall of this confabulatory creativity is experienced as something special, often Spiritual and Supernatural. That is, rather than permitting the basic raw trauma of this life's threats of death within the Reactive Memory to break through, what emerges instead are the much less threatening dream based symbols designed to camouflage them. This is the realm of the transpersonal psychology matrices of perinatal, prenatal, ancestral, karmic, racial, collective, phylogenetic or archetypal imagery and ideation (Grof & Grof, 2010). Sometimes these strictly defensive, avoidant mental creations are produced in part to allow a slower more controlled stepwise approach to the confrontation and discharge of traumatic memories from the present life.

342

Thus, the true terror produced by the dogs that savaged my head and arms as a child, which memory was dumped, frozen into my Reactive bin, becomes Spiritualized and disguised in nightmare fantasies of werewolves or demons. There, everyone can fly. Identifying with past lives on earth elsewhere in the universe becomes common. Those persons who helped us originally might become angels, benign spirits or even God himself. In this way the true trauma of the actual event, may slowly be approached by the Caretaker, through increasingly less distorted diffuse representations, until the true source invoking the terror of the dog attack actually is approachable to be discharged and integrated into Internal Reality.

Occasionally, some do not have the courage to get beyond these metaphors and to go on and complete the confrontation of the raw truth. As a result, they get stuck endless repeating past lives or other archetype symbology in great detail, never progressing further. One of these people once agitatedly told me that he had perfect parents and perfect childhood, but that he continually experienced living in ancient Egypt as the mutilated slave of a tyrant.

Thus, "Spiritual" realms of the mind certainly do exist in the form of Reactive Dream Reality. Where the confusion comes, is that most people are insufficiently scientifically grounded in the External Reality, to recognize the inherent impossibility of the extracorporeal. Thus, they fail to recognize their Spiritual experiences as only wishful, defensive lies, confabulated by their Id, or by the consensus with the Ids of others dealing with fear of death. Thus, it would seem that transpersonal, spiritual and supernatural realms exist as lies in the minds of humans to be used as defensive shields against the raw truth, while the truth is still actively being avoided. To prevent this and to facilitate progress, it is advisable to clean up one's past and present perpetrations against others. The purer you become, the wider the channel to your Source and the stronger its guidance becomes.

In this realm of the unconscious, the Id freely breaks the laws of logic and of external reality to create bodiless spirit entities performing miraculous acts and setting up their own rules, hierarchies and belief systems. They can be as subtle, creative and elaborate as dreams are, not recognizing the frozen terror of death that is at their base. We have thought that dreams represented a window into the spiritual with its gods, demons, heavens and hells. These realms often follow a common set of rules that are part of our collective unconscious as humans. Thus, within a person and like-minded associates, there is a specific Dream Reality. This the sixth type of reality filled with wishful Spiritual-Supernatural-UFO Science Fantasy that may sometimes seem more real than External Reality.

We wrongly have believed these collective Id defensive lies to be treasures of truth and have gathered them into our religions to answer Life's Big Questions. We have used this spirituality to short cut our work in understanding of the actual way the eternal impersonal universe works. We have replaced the objective laws of the universe with the wishful spiritual fantasies of dreams. Then, we become confused as to why the God of our creation is not protecting good people from evil. As a result, we have embellished our basic beliefs about the Life's Big Questions with the mysterious totems and symbols elaborated from our dreams, rather than to speak the beauty of the way the universe actually is. In the process, our, cerebellar Social Brain, Source, God Within becomes buried behind our Reactive Brain's increasing load of memories of terror, and causing our Ego Caretaker to have increasingly stressful, unfulfilling life.

The Difference between Religion and Spirituality

This process is causing Religion, our most personal all encompassing way of life, to be wrongly discarded by the disenchanted as the source of human abuse and killing. The real villain is Spirituality, taken from the most primitive of our Crocodile Brain's thoughts, whose purpose is to hide, cover, camouflage, and disguise terrifying memories of a life time of death threats. We have used this Spirituality, a phenomenon originating at the personal-self universe level, along with its reality shortcuts, to construct wishful, rule-breaking answers to the big questions of life. These were anciently and inappropriately installed into our Religions, which are by definition inherently associated with family and society at the next higher universe level.

With the development of our ability to analytically begin to answer some of life's big questions, it has become increasingly obvious that our previous answers to them, based upon the Crocodile Brain's Id-originated Dream Spirituality, are grossly incorrect. This has resulted in the present splitting off of Science from Religion, and has left us fragmented into warring camps and despairing of peace. What we need is a through reassessment of the foundations of current religions, discarding of all supernatural elements that cannot be demonstrated by use of the Scientific Method. This is what Neuroreality seeks to do. As a result, one can have a religion in which to believe that more accurately answers life's big questions and serves as one's transformative personal way of life, elevating one back into the human family with all its joys of association and service.

"If with all your heart you truly seek me, you shall ever surely fine me. Thus says your God".

As one tenaciously assaults one's own brain over the years, relentlessly causing it to release its reactive memories for experiencing and integration into daily experience, one begins to experience the destruction and re-creation of the entire universe, indeed of life itself. This demolition and rebuilding of the foundations of one's inner reality is an invaluable experience. During it, one must experience dying as many times as it is necessary in order to be reborn. While doing so, one need only maintain the position of a ruthlessly honest, dispassionate witness, neither avoiding nor promoting a particular point of view, just observing. This truth- telling inevitably leads you to discover a powerful ally waiting just outside of consciousness. It is your God Within, your Higher Power, your non-supernatural Source who stands at the door and knocks. When you surrender to the perfection of its higher wisdom, it will permanently transform you into a true human being. You can trust it with your life. Welcome home, loved one!

Removed of all Superstition, the Heart of Religion Still Beats on: the Old, Old Story of Emergent Benefits from Doing Good to Others

Parable: "His name was Fleming, and he was a poor Scottish farmer. One day, while trying to make a living for his family, he heard a cry for help coming from a nearby bog. He dropped his tools and ran to the bog. There, mired to his waist in black muck, was a terrified boy, screaming and struggling to free himself. At risk to his own life, farmer Fleming saved the lad from what could have been a slow and terrifying death.

The next day, a fancy carriage pulled up to the Scotsman's sparse surroundings. An elegantly dressed nobleman stepped out and introduced himself as the father of the boy Farmer Fleming had saved. 'I want to repay you,' said the nobleman. 'You saved my son's life.' 'No, I can't accept payment for what I did,' the Scottish farmer replied, waving off the offer. At that moment, the farmer's own son came to the door of the family hovel. 'Is that your son?' the nobleman asked. 'Yes,' the farmer replied proudly. 'I'll make you a deal. Let me provide him with the level of education my own son will enjoy. If the lad is anything like his father, he'll no doubt grow to be a man we both will be proud of.'

And that he did. Farmer Fleming's son attended the very best schools and in time, graduated from St. Mary's Hospital Medical School in London, and went on to become known throughout the world as the noted Sir Alexander Fleming, the discoverer of Penicillin. Years afterward, the same nobleman's son who was saved from the bog was stricken with pneumonia. What saved his life this time? Penicillin. The name of the nobleman? Lord Randolph Churchill. His son's name? Sir Winston Churchill.

This theme of the unpredictable, but life-affirming emergent benefits inevitably derived from rising to the next level above self, always speaks to the core of our existence and profoundly moves the elements of our mind. This is the fundamental life affirming biological engine at the heart of all the world's religions. Removed from the blood and other ancient supernatural encrustations of gods and demons, heaven and hell that we have long fought about, it still touches us deeply to watch the miracles of emergence appear in our life as the result of improving the lives of others.

Dear Reader,

May you uncover and embrace your sacred Source, allowing It to grace your life. May you, by walking and talking with your God Within, experience the inspiration, satisfaction and delight that come from improving your life and that of your human family.

Namaste (my Source affirms and honors your Source),

Bruce Eldine Morton

Some Important Concepts from Chapter 20: Transformational Steps To Becoming a Human Being

1. Based upon the accumulation of reproducible informational data obtained by the practice of the Scientific Method over the past 4000 years, our cultural model of the universe, life, and mind can now markedly be upgraded to a more accurate, more functional approximation of external reality.

2. Replacement of the fatal flaw of current religions: the essentially impossible external reality existence of the spiritual extracorporeal, with Neuroreality, a transformational context for existence, bridging brain and mind, science and religion, restores the control of our future into our own hands.

3. Many of the twenty paradigm shifts of Neuroreality are neither mainstream science nor common knowledge. However, all are data-based and reproducible, and require no faith or belief.

4. Understanding Neuroreality is sufficient to cause the effortless elevation of anxious competing individuals into welcomed members of family units, and to the higher levels of civilization with all the emergent benefits which automatically unfold, including satisfaction and peace.

5. Thirty steps are given as a practical integration of Neuroreality that promotes the personal rise from the suffering inherent at the killing level of the individual to the nonkilling social levels of human higher evolution.

6. The origin and meaning of dreams is described. Their supernatural external reality rule-breaking spirits have mistakenly been admired and allowed to contaminate our religion, forcing science to operate outside of it, and thus bringing the Id-based violence that is separating humanity today.

7. The mechanism for the ancient route that brings personal conversion and transformation through Ego-death and rebirth to one's Source is described.

References:

Alcoholics Anonymous (1952). *The Twelve Steps.* Alcoholics Anonymous World Services, N.Y.

Amen, D. G. (1998), *Change your Brain. Change your Life,* Three Rivers Press, New York.

Armstrong, K. (1993). *A History of God: The 4,000-Year Quest of Judiasm, Christianity, and Islam.* Ballantine, N.Y.

Barinaga, M., (1994) Cell Suicide: By ICE, not Fire. *Science, 236,* 754-756.

Barker, W. W., Yoshii, F., Loewenstein, D.A., Chang, J.Y., Apicella, A., Pascal, S., Boothe, T.E., Ginsberg, M. D., & Duara, R. (1991). Cerebrocerebellar relationship during behavioral activation: a PET study. *Journal of Cerebral Blood flow and Metabolism,* 11, 48-54.

Beaumont, G, Young, A, & McManus, I.C. (1984). Hemisphericity: A critical review. *Cognitive Neuropsychology,* 1, 191-212.

Bentov, I. (1978). *Stalking the Wild Pendulum.* Wildwood House, London.

Berridge, M. J. (1993). A Tale of Two Messengers, *Nature, 365,* 388-389.

Bickerton, D. (1995). *Language and Human Behavior,* University of Washington Press, Seattle.

Biddle, C. (2002). Loving Life: The Morality of self interest and the facts that support It. Glenn Alan Press, Richmond, VA.

Bogen, J. E., (1969). The other side of the brain II. An appositional mind. *Bulletin of the Los Angeles Neurological Society,* 34, 135-162.

Bogen, J. E., DeZure, R., Ten Houten, W. D., & Marsh, J. F., (1969). The other side of the brain. IV. The A/P ratio. *Bulletin of the Los Angeles Neurological Society* 37, 49-61.

Bontempi, B., Larent-Demir, C., Destrade, C., & Jaffard, R. (1999). Time-dependent reorganization of brain circuitry underlying long-term memory storage. *Nature,* 400, 671-675.

Bottini, G., Concoran, R., Sterzi, R., Paulesu, E., Schenone, P., Scarpa, P., Frackowiak, R. S. J., & Firth, C. D. (1994). Role of the right hemisphere in the interpretation of figurative aspects of language: a positron emission tomography activation study. *Brain,* 117, 1241 1253.

Bracha, V., Zhao, L., Wunderlich, D.A., Morrissy, S.J., & Bloedel, J. R. (1997). Patients with cerebellar lesions cannot acquire but are able to retain conditioned eyeblink reflexes. *Brain,* 120, 1401-1413.

Broca, P (1863). Localisations des fonctions cerebrales. Seige de la faculte du langage articule. *Bulletin de la Societe d Anthropologie, 4,* 200-208.

Brown, D. (2003). *The Da Vinci Code.* Doubleday, N.Y.

Buck, R. M. (1901). *Cosmic Consciousness: a study of the evolution of the human mind.* Philadelphia, p 2.

Cherniski, S.A. (1998) DHEA Breakthrough. *Ballantine Books, NY.*

Daily, M. and Wilson, M. (1978). *Sex, Evolution and Behavior,* Wadsworth Pub. Co., 1978.

Dawkins,R. (1976) *The Selfish Gene,* Oxford University Press, London.

Dilmun, V. M., et al. (1986) Neuroendocrine-Ontogenic mechanism of aging: Toward an integrated theory of aging. *International Review of Neurobiology. 28,* 89-155.

Dow, A. (1993). Deprenyl, the antiaging drug, *Halberg Publishing Corp.* Delavan, WI,.

REFERENCES

Chomsky, N. (1959). A review of B. F. Skinners 'Verbal Behavior', *Language*, 35, 26-58.

Cohen, H. D., Rosen, R. C., and Goldstein, I. (1976). Encephalographic laterality changes during sexual orgasm. *Archives of Sexual Behavior*, **5**, 189-199.

Coren, S. The left-hander syndrome: The causes and consequences of left-handedness (Free Press, New York, 1992).

Coyne, J. 2009. *Why Evolution is True*. Vinking, NY.

Crowell, D. H., Jones, R. H., Kapuniai, L. E., & Nakagawa, J. K. (1973). Unilateral cortical activity in newborn humans: An early index of cerebral dominance. *Science*, **180**, 205-208.

Crick, F. (1982). *Life Itself: Its Origin and Nature.* Futura Macdonald, London.

Crick, F. (1994). *The Astonishing Hypothesis: Scientific Search for the Soul.* Schribner's, N.Y.

Darwin, C, 1859. *On the Origin of the Species by means of Natural Selection, or the Preservation of Favored Races in the Struggle for Life*, Murray, NY

Darwin, C, 1871. The Descent of Man and Selection in Relation to Sex., Prometeus Books, NY

Dawkins, R. (1976). *The Selfish Gene*, Oxford, New York.

Dawkins, R. (2009). *The Greatest Show on Earth*. Free Press, NY.

DeMeo, J. (1998). *Saharaisa: The 4000BCE Origins of Child Abuse, Sex-Repression, Warfare, and Social Violence in the Deserts of the Old World*. Orgone Biophysical Research Lab, Ashland, Ore.

Demasio, A. (1994). Descartes' Error: Emotion, Reason, and the Human Brain.Avon, N.Y.

Descartes, R. (1974). *Discourse on Method* and *The Meditations*, trans. F. E. Sutcliffe,

Desmond, J. E., Gabrieli, J. D. E., Wagner, A. D., Ginier, B.L., & Glover, G. H. (1997). Lobular patterns of cerebellar activation in verbal working-memory and finger-tapping tasks as revealed by functional MRI. *Journal of Neuroscience*, **17**, 9675-9685.

Einstein, A. (1984). *The Meaning of Relativity*. 5th ed, MJF Books.

Einstein, A. (1927). Kaluza's theory of the correlation of gravitation and electricity: Parts I &II, *Sitzungsberichte der Preussische Akademie der Wissenshaft, Berlin*, 6, 23-25, 26-30.

Eisler, R. (1987). *The Chalice and the Blade,*Harper-Collins, N.Y.

Eisler, R. (1995). *Sacred Pleasure: Sex, Myth, and the Politics of the Body.*Harper-Collins, N.Y.. Fink,

Ekman, P (2006). *Darwin and Facial Expression: A Century of Research in Review*. Malor Books.

Dax, M.. (1785). Lésions de la moitie gauche de μencephale coincident avec μoubli des signe de la pensée. Gazette Hebdomadaire de Medécine et de Chirurgie, 2(2eme serie), m 2. (read at Montpellier in 1836.)

Davidson, R. J. & Hugdahl, K., (1995). Brain Asymmetry, MIT Press, Cambridge, MA.

Fink, G. R., Halligan, P.W., Marshall, J.C., Frith, C.D., Frackowiak, R.S., & Dolan RJ (1996). Where in the brain does visual attention select the forest and the trees? Nature, 382, 626-8.

Freud, S. (1960). *The Ego and the Id*. Norton.

Gazzaniga, M. S., (2000). Cerebral specialization and interhemispheric communication; Does the corpus callosum enable the human condition? Brain, 123, 1293-1326.

Gazzaniga, M.. S., (1989). Organization of the human brain. *Science, 245*, 947-952.

Gazzaniga, M., Bogen, J. E., & Sperry, R. W., (1962). Some functional effects of sectioning the cerebral commisures in man. *Proceedings of the National Academy of Sciences, USA, 48,* 1765-1769.

Geschwind, D. H., Iacoboni, M., Mega, M. S., Zaidel, D.W., Cloughesy, T, & Zaidel, E., (1995). Alien hand syndrome: interhemispheric motor disconnection due to a lesion in the midbody of the corpus callosum. *Neurology, 45,* 802-8.

Geshwind, N. & Levitsky, W. (1968). Human brain: left-right asymmetries in temporal speech region. *Science,* **161,** 186-187.

Gill, R., et al. (1987). Systemic administration of MK-801 protects against ischemia-induced hippocampal neurodegeneration in the gerbil. *Journal of Neuroscience, 7,* 3343-3349.

Godel, K. (1962). On Formally Undecidable Propositions. Basic Books.

Gooch, S. (1980). The Double Helix of the Mind. Wildwook House, London.

Gray, J. (1992). Men are from Mars, Women are from Venus. Harper Collins. N.Y.

Grof, S. (1975). Realms of the Human Unconscious: Observations from LSD Research. Viking Press, NY.

Grof, S. (1980). *LSD Psychotherapy.* Hunter House, Pomona, CA.

Grof. S. & Grof, C. (1989). *Spiritual Emergency: When Personal Transformation Becomes a Crisis.* Tarcher/Putman, Los Angeles.

Grof, S. & Grof, C. (2010). Holotropic Breathwork:A New Approach to Self-exploration and Therapy. Excelsior Editions, Albany, NY.

Hancock, G. (2007) *Supernatural.* p 283. The Disinformation Co., N.Y.

Hauser, M. (2006). *Moral Minds: How Nature Designed Our Universal Sense of Right and Wrong.* Harper Collins, N.Y.

Hayflick, L. (1965). The Limited in Vitro Lifetime of Human Diploid Cell Strains. *Experimental Cell Research,* 37, 614-636.

Heath, R. G. (1977). Modulation of emotion with a brain pacemaker: Treatment for intractable psychiatric illness. *Journal of Nervous and Mental Disease,* **165,** 300-317.

Heath, R. G., Llewellyn, R. C., & Rouchell, A. M. (1980). Cerebellar pacemaker for intractable behavioral disorders and epilepsy: Follow-up report. *Biological Psychiatry,* **15,** 243-257.

Heath, R. G., Rouchell, A. M., Llewellyn, R. C. & Walker, C. F. (1981). Cerebellar pacemaker patients: An update. *Biological Psychiatry,* **16,** 953-962.

Harlow, H et al. (1976) Effects of maternal and peer separations on young monkeys. *Journal of Child Psychology & Psychiatry & Allied Disciplines,*17, 101-112.

Henry, J. P. & Wang, S. (1998). Effects of early stress on affiliative behavior. *Psychoneuroendocrinology,* **23**, 863-875.

Hernstein, R. J. & Murray, C. (1994). The Bell Curve: *Intelligence and Class Structure in American Life.* Free Press - Simon and Schuster.

Hubbard, L., R. (1950). Dianetics: The Modern Science of Mental Health. East Grinstead, Sussex, England: Hubbard College of Scientology.

Hutsler, J. & Galuske, R.A.W., (2003). Hemispheric asymmetries in cerebral cortical networks. *Trends in Neurosciences, 26,* 428-435.

Hutsler, J. J., Loftus, W. C., & Gazzaniga, M. S., (1998). Individual variation of cortical surface area asymmetries. *Cerebral Cortex, 8,* 11-17.

REFERENCES

Jager, G. & Postma, A., (2003). On the hemispheric specialization for categorical and coordinate spatial relations: A review of the current evidence, *Neuropsychologia*, 41, 504-515.

James, W. (1878). *Principles of Psychology*, Holt, republished by Dover, 1950.

James, W. (1902). *The Varieties of Religious Experience*, republished by Wilder, 2007.

Kaluza, T. (1921). Zum unitatsproblem der physik. *Sizungsberichte der Preussische Akademie der Wissenschaft*, 966-972.

Kargh, H. (1996). *Cosmology and Controversy*. Princton University Press, N.J.

Katie, B. (2002). *Loving what Is: Four Questions that can Change Your Life*. Harmony Books, N.Y.

Kawai, M. (1965). Newly-acquired pre-cultural behavior of the natural troop of Japanese monkeys of Koshima Islet. *Primates*, 6, 1-30.

Kleim, J. A., Vij, K., Ballard, D. H. & Greenough, W. T. (1997). Learning-dependent synaptic modifications in the cerebellar cortex of the adult rat persist for at least four weeks. *Journal of Neuroscience*, 17, 717-721.

Kosslyn, S. M., (1987). Seeing and imagining in the cerebral hemispheres: A computational approach, *Psychological Review*, 94, pp. 148–175.

Kosslyn, S. M., Koenig, O., Barrett, A., Cave, C., Tang, J. & Gabrieli, J.D.E., (1989). Evidence for two types of spatial representations. *Journal of Experimental Psychology: Perception and Perfomance*, 15, 723-35.

Kosslyn, S. M., Chabris, C. F., Marsolek, C. J. & Koenig, O., (1992). Categorical versus coordinate spatial relations: computational analyses and computer simulations. *Journal of Experimental Psychology: Human Perception and Performance*, 18, 562-577.

Lamb, M. R., Robertson, L.C., & Knight, R. T. (1990). Component mechanisms underlying the processing of hierarchically organized patterns: Inferences from patients with unilateral cortical lesions. *Journal of Experimental Psychology: Learning, Memory, and Cognition* 16, 471-483.

Leibniz, G. W. (1984). *Philosophical Writings*, edited by G. H. R. Parkinson, Harmondsworth, London.

Leiner, H. C., Leiner, A. L., & Dow, R. S. (1991). The human cerbrocerebellar system: its computing, cognitive, and language skills. *Behavioral Brain Research*, 44, 113-128.

Levy, J., (1969). Possible basis for the evolution of lateral specialization of the human brain. *Nature*, 224, 614-5.

Levy, J. & Reid, M., (1976). Variations in writing posture and cerebral organization. *Science*, 194, 337-339.

Liao, Z., et al., Increased urine interleukin-1 levels in aging. *Gerontology*, 39, 19-27 (1993).

Libet, B., (1982). Brain stimulation in the study of neuronal functions for conscious sensory experiences. *Human Neurobiology*, 1, 235-42.

Lindley, D. (2001) Falling to earth in a quantum way. *Nature*, 410, 145-146.

Lockhorst, G. J., (1985). An ancient Greek theory of hemispheric specialization. *Clio Medica, 17*, 33-38.

Lovelock, J. E. (1979). *Gaia- A New Look at Life on Earth*, Oxford University. Press.

Malebranche, N. de (1923). *An* essay concerning human understanding. Oxford University Press

Loye, D., (2007). *Darwin's Lost Theory: Who We Really Are and Where We're Going.* Benjamin Franklin Press, Carmel, CA.

MacLean, P. D. (1990). The Triune Brain in Evolution: Role in Paleocerebral Functions. Plenum.

Maier, J. A. M. (et al., (1990). Extension of the life-span of human endothelial cells by an Interleukin-1a antisense oligomer. *Science 249*,1570-1573.

Milner, B., (1968). Visual recognition and recall after right temporal lobe excision in man. *Neuropsychologia, 6,* 101-209.

Moller, P. L., Madland, D. G., Sierk, A. J., & Iwamoto, A. (2001). Nuclear fission modes and fragmented mass asymmetries in a five-dimensional deformation space. *Nature, 409*, 785-790.

Morton, B. E. (1985a). The mind-body problem as subsets of the structure-activity relationship. *Neuroscience Abstracts,* 11, 876.

Morton, B. E. (1985b). Conflict and the quadrimental brain hypothesis. *International Society for Research on Aggression Abstracts*, 13, 106.

Morton, B. E. (1989). The quadrimental brain as a neuroscience working hypothesis. *Neuroscience Abstracts,* 15, 729.

Morton, B. E., (2001). Large individual differences in minor ear output during dichotic listening. *Brain and Cognition, 45,* 229-237.

Morton, B. E., (2002). Outcomes of hemisphericity questionnaires correlate with unilateral dichotic deafness. *Brain and Cognition, 49,* 63-72.

Morton, B. E., (2003a). Phased mirror tracing outcomes correlate with several hemisphericity measures. *Brain and Cognition, 51,* 294-304.

Morton, B. E., (2003b). Two-hand line-bisection task outcomes correlate with several measures of hemisphericity. *Brain and Cognition, 51,* 305-316.

Morton, B. E., (2003c). Asymmetry Questionnaire outcomes correlate with several hemisphericity measures. *Brain and Cognition, 51,* 372-374.

Morton, B. E., (2003d). Hemisphericity of university students and professionals: Evidence for sorting during higher education. *Brain and Cognition, 52,* 319-325.

Morton, B. E. & Rafto, S. E., (2006a). Corpus callosum size is linked to dichotic deafness and hemisphericity, not sex or handedness. *Brain and Cognition, 62,* 1-8. 8.

Morton, B. E. & Rafto, S. E., (2006b). Sex and aggression: corpus callosal size is linked to hemisiphericity, not gender. In *Contemporary Research on Aggression,*Pro Facultate No. 8 K. Osterman, K. Bjorkqvist, eds. Pp. 267-278, Abo Akademi University, Vasa, Finland.

Morton, B. E. & Rafto, S. E., (2010). Behavioral laterality advance: Neuroanatomical evidence for the existence of hemisity. *Personality and Individual Differences,* 49. 34-42

Nelson, D. L., & Cox, M. M. (2000). *Lehninger's Principles of Biochemistry.* 3nd Ed., Worth.

Newcomb, S. (1894). Modern mathematical thought, *Nature*, 49, 325-329.

Paige, G. D. (2002) *Nonkilling Global Political Science.* Xlibris, N.Y.

Peikoff, L. (1991). *Objectivism: The Philosophy of Ayn Rand.* Meridian, NY.

Plato (1975) *The Phaedo,* trans D. Gallup, Oxford University Press.

Popper, K., & Eccles, J. (1977). *The Self and Its Brain, An Argument for Interactionism.* London.

Prescott, J.W. (1996). The Origins of Human Love and Violence. *Pre- and Perinatal Psychology Journal, 10.* 143-188.

Priest, S. (1991). *Theories of the Mind,* Houghton Mifflin

Rand, A, (1957). *Atlas Shrugged,* Signet, NY.

REFERENCES

Reiman, E. M., Raichle, M.. E., Robins, E., Mintun, M. A., Fusselman, M. J., Fox, P.T., Price, J. L., & Hackman, K. A. (1989). Neuroanatomical correlates of a lactate-induced panic attack. *Archives of General Psychiatry, 46,* 493-500.

Rifkin, J. (2009). *The Empathic Civilization: The Race to Global Consciousness in a World in Crisis.* Penguin. N.Y.

Riklan, M., Cullinan, T., & Cooper, I. S. (1977). Tension reduction and alerting in man following chronic cerebellar stimulation for the relief of spasticity or intractable seizures. *Journal of Nervous and Mental Disease, 164,* 176-181.

Robertson, L. C. & Lamb, M. R., (1991). Neuropsychological contributions to theories of part/whole organization. *Cognitive Psychology, 23,* 299-330.

Rudin, D.& Felix, C. (1996). *Omega 3 Oils to Improve Mental Health, Fight Degenerative Diseases, and Extend your Life* Avery Publishing Group, Garden City Park, NY,.

Schmahmann, J. D. (1991). An emerging concept: The cerebellar contribution to higher function. *Archives of Neurology, 48,* 1178-1187

Schreurs, B. G., Gusev, P. A., Tomsic, D., Alkon, D. L., & Shi, T. (1998). Intracellular correlates of acquisition and long-term memory of classical conditioning in purkinje cell dendrites in slicees of rabbit cerebellar lobule HVI. *Journal of Neuroscience, 18,* 5498-5507.

Shiffer, F., (1996). Cognitive ability of the right hemisphere: possible contributions to Psychological Function. *Harvard Review of Psychiatry, 4,*126-138.

Schonfield, H. J. (1965). *The Passover Plot.* The Disinformation Company, N.Y.

Squire, L. R., Ojemann, J. G., Miezin, F. M., Petersen, S.E., Videen, T. O., & Raiche, M. (1992). Activation of the h ippocampus in normal humans: A functional anatomical study of memory. *Proceedings of the National Academy of Sciences, USA, 89,* 1837-1841.

Smeyne, R.J., et al., (1993). Continuous c-Fos expression precedes programmed cell death in vivo. *Nature, 363,* 166-169.

Smith, L. C. & Moscovitch, M. (1979). Writing posture, hemispheric control of movement and cerebral dominance in individuals with inverted and noninverted hand postures during writing. *Neuropsychologia, 17,* 637-644.

Sperry, R., (1968). Hemispheric deconnection and unity in conscious awareness. *American Psychologist, 23,* 723-733.

Sperry, R., (1982). Some effects of disconnecting the cerebral hemispheres. *Science, 217,* 1223-26.

Springer, S. P., & Deutch, G., (1998). *Left Brain, Right Brain: Perspectives from Cognitive Neuroscience.* 5th edn. New York, Freeman

Stapp, H. P. (1993). *Mind,Matter, and Quantum Mechanics.* Springer-Verlag.

Stephan, K. E., Fink, G. R., & Marshall, J. C., (2006). Mechanisms of hemispheric specialization: Insights from analysis of connectivity. *Neuropsychologia, 45,* 209-228.

Swinburne, R. (1986). *The Evolution of the Soul,* Oxford University Press

Tannen, D. (1986). *That's Not What I Meant.* Ballentine Books, N.Y.

Tannen, D. (1990). *You just don't Understand.* Ballentine Books, N.Y.

Tannen, D. (1994). *Talking from 9 to 5.* Avon Books, N.Y.

Teng, E. & Squire, L. R. (1999). Memory for places learned long ago is intact after hippocampal damage. *Nature, 400,* 675-677.

Tolle, E. (1999). *The Power of Now: A Guide to Spirtual Enlightenment.* Namaste, Vancouver.

Tolle, E. (2005). *A New Earth: Awakening to Your Life's Purpose.*Dutton. N.Y.

Uttal, W. R. (1978). *The Psychobiology of Mind,* Lawrence Earlbaum Associates.

Van Kleek, M. H. (1989). Hemispheric differences in global versus local processing of hierarchical visual stimuli by normal subjects: New data and a meta-analysis of previous studies. *Neuropsychologia, 27,* 1165-1178.

Wada, J. A.. (1977). Prelanguage and fundamental asymmetry of the infant brain. *Annals of the New York Academy of Science,* **299,** 370-379.

Wasson, R. G., Hoffman, A. & Ruck, C. A. P. (1978, 2008). *The Road to Eleusis: Unveiling the Secrets of the Mysteries,* North Atlantic Books, Berkeley, CA.

Weintraub, S. & Mesulam, M. M. (1987). Right cerebral dominance in spatial attention. *Archives of Neurology,* **44,** 621-625.

Weisenberg, T. & McBride, K. E. (1935). *Aphasia: A Clinical and Psychological Study.* New York: Commonweath fund, (cited in Springer, S.P. and Deutsch, G. *Left Brain, Right Brain: Perspectives from Cognitive Neuroscience.* 5th Ed. p 361, W. H. Freeman, New York, 1999.)

Wittling, W. (1990). Psychophysiological correlates of human brain asymmetry: Blood pressure changes during lateralized presentation of an emotionally laden film. *Neuropsychologia,* **28,** 457-470.

Wittling, W. & Pfluger, M. (1990). Neuroendocrine hemisphere asymmetries: Salivary cortisol secretion during lateralized viewing of emotion-related and neutral films. *Brain and Cognition,* **14:** 243-265.

Wittling, W. & Roschmann, R. (1993). Emotion-related hemispheric asymmetry: Subjective emotional responses to laterally presented films. *Cortex, 29,* 431-448.

Wolford, G., Miller, M. B., & Gazzaniga, M., (2000), The left hemisphere's role in hypothesis formation. *Journal of Neuroscience, 20*:RC64, 1-4.

GLOSSARY:

Age Regression: Our memories appear to be formed along a linear time track from before birth until the present. Retrieval of memories of the past is usually unimpaired, unless those of events were life threatening. Threat of death-induced high levels of fear can be traumatizing. A person in the present who is confronting stimuli related to traumatic earlier similar memory chains can be protected from reexperiencing their past trauma by the blocking its retrieval. Certain individuals under altered states of consciousness, including those during hypnosis, can be caused to leave awareness of the present and be thrown back along these chains to earlier times associated with similar to the present restimulus. In that state, they may recall information available then, but lost to access in the present due to mental blockade that avoids traumatic memory retrieval.

Alligator Brain: This brain core system is the source of totally selfish behavior. Its paired opposite is the Dog Brain which produces the totally altruistic behavior of a loyal servant or slave.

Caretaker Brain: This limbic brain element judges the survival significance of the present situation and decides which brain system is most relevant to optimizing its survival. Its synonyms are the Executive System, or Ego (in the Freudian, but not the popular Id-like sense)

Catharsis: An emotionally upsetting temporary purging of our habitual negative hopelessness, often as the result of participating (often vicariously) in a life-death drama. The xDARP – Pain Body, can promote social behavior that brings about upset followed by short-term removal of self-induced personal conflict.

Cross-polar Cross-breed: Combinations of both familial polarities, Patripolar-Haremic and Matripolar-Orgeic, as in marriage, offspring, etc.

Cultural Reality: The unique set of beliefs common to a large group of individuals in a society. For example, in Hawaii, it is considered rude to wear shoes indoors.

Deductive Reasoning: Attempting to apply a general rule to account for a specific instance.

Dialect: The circular yin-yang symbol of the dialectic universe of black and white, as seen on the South Korean flag.

Dissective Reasoning: Breaking down a whole by recognizing its component parts.

Determinism: The existence of inherent preprogrammed responses of biological organism to certain survival threats or benefits. We are not born a blank slate. We do not have the freedom to chose certain death dealing responses, such as the cessation of breathing. Within determinism we have the "freedom" to choose between four survival significant options: 1.To accept or reject the way the universe works. 2. When to take rewards, now or later. 3. Whether to share rewards with my family. 4. Who is my family.

Dominance in the home: In hemisity complimentary marriages, one parent is the role model, setter and enforcer of standards. This is, by definition, called conditional love. Their children accept, admire, even fear his or her leadership; accept and willingly seek to reach the standards. The other parent is less dominant than the children, and accepts and loves them unconditionally whether they obey or not. The subdominant parent is the child's beloved slave who gives them everything, defends them against the dominant parent's excesses, and can even be abused by the child.
    In Haremic families, the patripolar father is the dominant parent. In Orgeic families, the matripolar mother is the dominant parent. In R-R families, an essential subdominant parent is absent and the children fail to receive truly unconditional love, and may end up angry. In L-L families, the essential dominant parent is absent to set, model, and enforce standards, and the children can become tyrannically dominant over both parents.

Dominance in the workplace and community: Usually the reverse of dominance in the nuclear family. In the workplace, R-bops tend to treat others as equals and to be cooperative, while L-bops must fight for status in a local hierarchy and tend to be combative.

Dualism: The belief in a immortal soul which supernaturally occupies a physical body for a few years, whose thoughts are its mind. Opposites, such as black and white, are not dualistic. They are dyadic.

Dyadic: The many binary aspects of the universe such as hot and cold, right and wrong. This is not dualism, which asserts a spirit separate from a body.

Ego death: The hallucinogen or stress induced collapse of a dominant brain element system providing the sense of self. What often remains, is the altogether different Social Brain Source, normally suppressed by the Id.

Emergent Properties: Activities of a larger unit whole, not possessed by its building block subunits. For example, violin music cannot come from any disassembled combination of bow, strings, bridge, the box, or neck.

Empathy: Competition at its core results from the rejection of the Other as non-family and as a potentially killing alien to be eliminated. The state-shift that automatically occurs from rising from the level of selfish competition to familial collaboration requires accepting and incorporating the Other as valued subunit of one's family, and thus as one's equal. This acceptance and fusion automatically generates compassion for the Other that is the basis of love; love being defined as the acceptance of another just as they are and just as they are not. Thus, empathy results from the acceptance and concern for the Other, as in "Love the Lord your God with all your heart, mind, and body, and love your neighbor as yourself".

Event Horizon: The cutting edge site, the location where action is experienced as occurring. Levels below this are internal, above it are external.

Executive (Ego) Caretaker Brain: The bottom line Dual Quadbrain Model element that decides with which system to respond in order to optimize survival.

External Controllers: Authorities outside of oneself that command more respect from our Executive Brain than any internal brain element, and thus can externally direct our behavior. For some, a hypnotist is an example of such. For others, the law, the pope, or Jim Jones exert control externally this way.

External Reality: The way the universe is independent of our awareness or existence, ever changing, ever the same.

Falsifiable: Falsification: For a proposed idea to be true, it must be open to testing in such a way that if it is false, it can be possible to show it so. Thus, the proposition must be falsifiable, subject to falsification. Some would say that the existence of God is not falsifyable, therefore the idea of God is meaningless.

Familial Polarity: The two opposite reproductive strategies used by primates: in Haremic Patripolarity, males battle for paternity, and in the Orgeic Matripolarity, sperm battle for paternity. One of the three personality dualities along with Sexuality, Hemisity.

Fifth Dimension: Potential energy powers all activity, which is five dimensional.

Fourth Dimension: Time is the fourth dimension required for behavioral activity

God: The artifactual term used to describe an imaginary but non-existent supernatural entity.

Gothic personality: Black adoring, satanic, death-oriented, transgender, self mutilating, Lxp

Half Life: The amount of time required for the disintegrative loss of one half of the starting amount of a substance.

Halo of Life: A circular planar band of area superimposed upon the spiral galactic arms surrounding the black hole of a galaxy within which the potential energy to matter ratio promotes the formation and support of complex beautiful systems, including life.

Haremic: Harem forming patripolar reproductive strategy, in which males battle for dominance and the females follow the winner-patriarch. Genes of loser males are excluded from the offspring. The Patripolar gorillas and orangutans (and Neanderthals) are of the Haremic prototype.

Havingness: The ability to deserve, get, and keep what you need. For example, money or a mate. The ability to have can be blocked by the guilt of past perpetrations regarding the item involved. These can be removed to rehabilitate havingness.

Hemisity:
The two general personality and behavioral styles that result when the brain Executive is inherently either on the right or left side of the brain. Right brain-oriented persons, R-bops, have easier access to same side right brain global and emotional skills, and must cross over bridges to access left brain skills such as language, and abstract reasoning. For Left-brain oriented persons (L-bops), the reverse is true.

Homeostasis: To maintain the constancy of anything.

Hybrids of Polarity: The offspring of mixed polarity matings, such as L-L or R-R mates. These lack certain properties of purebred polarities, and can be dyslexic or have abnormal sexual orientations.

Imaginer Brain: The activity of the right cerebral hemisphere to create imagery, often in space saving cartoon form of the global view of things.

Induction: To discover a pattern common to many individual cases. To generalize.

Internal Reality: The unique inner model of external reality that we are continually building from sensory information.

LFf: Left brain-oriented female, Haremic, supportive in family, important details-oriented

Love: The willingness to accept another just the way they are and just the way they are not.

LM: Left brain-oriented male, Orgeic, supportive in family, important details-oriented

LP: Left brain-oriented person, may be male or female, Haremic or Orgeic, supports in the home

LxP, LxM, LxF: Hybrids from cross polaric matings. Often transsexual and/or homosexual-bisexual.

Lumper: An Rp who is strong in inductive reasoning and seeing the big picture from important details.

Matripolar: Right brained dominant females, Left brained supportive males, Orgeic (orgy having) reproductive style.

Monism: The limited belief that all of who we are including our minds are the three dimensional structures of our body.

Morality: Morals: Behaviors consistent with the primacy of life being the highest value. Moral is life optimizing and good. Immoral is death promoting and bad. Sexual morality refers to reproductive behavior optimizing the family. Sexual immorality refers to actions destructive to the family, producing illegitimacy and personal suffering in parents and offspring.

Neuropsychopharmacology: The study of overlapping areas of Neurology, Psychology, and Pharmacology, such as the effects of psychoactive compounds upon human behavior.

Orgeic: Orgy-having reproductive strategy, in which a matripolar female in heat mates repeatedly with all the males in the troupe. The unknown father of each offspring is determined by the winner of the resulting sperm race. Prototypes are the Chimpanzees, Bonobos, (and CroMagnons). All males assume they are the father, resulting in abundant support for the children.

Pain Body, Reactive Brain: The defective xDARP output of one side of the cerebellum that seeks to repair psychosocial developmental arrests sustained in the gaining of control over another or others. It is thus the source of the Devil Within in that it ultimately fights its dominating opponents with murderous and diabolical rage. It would rather kill or die than be controlled.

Paradigm shift: An unexpected shift in context. For example: stocks and bonds. Whether we talking Early American penal history or Wall Street finance makes a big difference. Or take stomach ulcers. Are they from stress induced hyper acidity or from bacterial infection?

Patripolar: Right brain dominant males, Left brain supportive females, Haremic (harem forming) reproductive style.

Radioisotope: An unstable higher element that breaks down to lower elements at a constant half life rate with the emission of ionizing radiation.

Dream Reality: Fictional details about past trauma that include a creator God which cannot be demonstrated and thus require faith to believe.

Reporter Brain: The abstractive activities of the left cerebral cortex from which language is built.

Reptile Brain: The binary activities of the oldest level of our brain. It has two modes: the dominating selfishness of the Crocodile Brain or surrendered altruism of the servile Servant Brain.

RFf: Right brain-oriented female, dominant at home, big picture-oriented.

RM: Left brain-oriented male, Haremic, dominant at home, big picture-oriented.

RPp: Right brain-oriented person, Orgeic, dominant at home, big picture-oriented.

RxPp, RxM, RxF: Right brain oriented hybrid between R-R parents. Developmentally dyslexic but talented. Suffers from mental blocks (temporary decorticate stupidity) when anxious.

Servant Brain: The surrendered, docile, altruistic and supportive side of the Reptile Brain core, as opposed to the totally selfish Alligator Brain.

Sexuality: One of three dualistic determinants of personality, along with Hemisphericity and Polarity. Sexuality is itself composed of at least three elements: Body sex (M/F), Sexual identity (cis/trans), and Sex of preferred sexual partner (hetero/homo)

Singularity: Within a black hole is a singularity where conditions are unlike those anywhere else in the universe. Chotic matter including spent stars, are swept into the black hole at its equator and compressed millions of fold. Also collapsing inwards are vast amounts of expended energy called entropy, and millions of years in extended time. The current mystery is how these three components are transmuted within the singularity of the black hole to produce two polar big-bang continuously flaring white holes of free (potential) energy radiation of subatomic particles and renewed time. The properties of the singularity make the black hole a megamachine of destruction and creation, the resulting galaxy thus becoming an eternal cycle of death and rebirth.

Social Brain: The part of the cerebellum that records primary memory in time, and from the sequence of events can discern cause from effect. From this it has knowledge of good and evil, life and death, making it the site of one's personal god and devil, and the source of morality and religion.

SOURCE: The mortal Higher Power, God within of the genetic social brain. Sees consequences, projects the future, has our purpose, the plan, and the power to do it.

Soul: An obsolescent term to describe a nonexistent immortal spirit that transmigrates bodies. An ancient fiction. Replaced by the Source .

Spirit: Another artifactual term describing the essentially impossible existence of a supernatural extracorporeal being. Replace by the Source corporeal.

Splitter: A Lp with a top down orientation, which dissects wholes into their component parts.

Surrender: Rather than be killed by someone more powerful, reptiles prize life so highly that they would rather surrender to the will of a higher power than die. Thus, the more powerful leader ended up with many cooperative partner slaves who followed and assisted him altrusitically. They could be altruistic because they were already dead, saved only by the acceptance of their complete surrender. Later in evolution, higher brain elements could induce obedience in the reptile brain sole source of behavioral output, and thus the reptile brain could be ruled within. Ultimately, the wise Source rules for the best interest of all involved.

Survival Reality: Although in External Reality life is no more important than death, only those living organisms who have declared their survival as the supreme value now exist. From this Survival Reality perspective, anything that harms life is evil and to be avoided, and anything that helps life is good and to be approached. Survival of the fittest has honed the abilities of living organism to survive in ever widening environments.

Synthetic Reasoning: The ability to assemble higher wholes with useful emergent properties from lower building blocks is a form of genius called Synthetic Reasoning.

Threshold of Workability: To be able to know External Reality with sufficient accuracy to be able to make things reliably do what one needs, is to have crossed this threshold.

Trans-Heterosexual: Is a Lxp who has the opposite sexual identity than that of their body, but is still heterosexual, although possibly bisexual as well.

Transcendence: A state of consciousness resulting after ego death that contains the wisdom and purity of the social brain Source. This state has been reached by various individuals throughout the ages by various means, including starvation, meditation, and the ingestion of hallucinogens. In India it was called Kundalini.

Transference: An unconscious psychological act of choosing someone safe in the present to represent an important person from one's past to use symbolically with whom to struggle to complete a thwarted critical period of development by gaining control over that person. Often occurs in marital conflict.

Triadism: In the past either monism or dualism were used in an a futile attempt to explain mind and life. Triadism is a third alternative that succeeds where the other two had failed. It says that mind is included in the five dimensional activity of an intact brain, over time, powered by the fuel of food.

Unhealing Psychic Wound: There are critical periods of psychosocial development in childhood. If the child is unfortunate enough not to gain control of a psychosocial survival process before it's window closes, he or she is forever left with an incompletion sensitivity associated with fear of death resulting from failure master control of the vital process.

xDARP: Broken developmental arrest repair program. A mechanistic explanation for earlier terms such as the Reactive Mind and the Pain Body. The xDARP is inappropriately activated in adulthood to continue a failed childhood struggle with an important other to gain control over them. This results in neurotic or psychotic inappropriate behavior that destroys families and children.

xDARP Reality: This reality is insane because it brings survival conflict from childhood into the present to contaminate the neutral non threatening life in the present. It powerfully creates conflict and personal pain by rejection and demands for change, none of which satisfy it. If believed and obeyed, the Pain Body leads to crimes of passion and nervous breakdown. A critical step in maturation is the discovery that we are not our xDARPs insane thoughts and feelings. Then we can begin to detach from its relationship killing pain.

Appendix: Some Neuroreality Paradigm Shifts

Neuroreality concepts that are more advanced than those of current Physics and Astronomy. Neuroreality asserts that:

1. The universe is eternal, infinite and endlessly multilayered.

2. Each universe level is unique in its contents, properties, and laws.

3. While residing at one level of this series of layers, we have probed about 8 higher and lower levels of its endless progression.

4. Each higher universe level contains emergent unique properties not present in the next lower level.

5. The applicability of Godel's Incompleteness Theorem goes beyond mathematics and is valid for all higher universe levels of structure and properties. Thus, like an oyster, which cannot be deduced from a pearl, the structural properties and laws of the next higher level cannot be deduced from a lower level.

6. Induction and deduction of mathemsatics apply within a given universe level. Yet, mathematics is useless in predicting the properties of the next higher (by synthesis) or lower (by dissection) level. These are only determined by empirical by trial and error.

7. Because of this, there can be no equation for everything. Like the existence of phlogistine or the soul, the idea of an equation for everything is based upon a false premise.

8. That process, properties, and behavior can be completely defined by five dimensions, the fourth being time, the fifth being free energy.

9. That the Big Bang is part of a cyclic process of the galactic singularities of an eternal universe, rather that the creation of something from nothing by a miracle of a nonexistent god.

10. That is, that the visible arms of galaxies feed inward into black hole singularities which spew out polar white hole fountains of big bang inflations of dark matter and energy, whose tori circle back to feed into the outer star forming visible arms of the galaxy in a continual transformational cycle of creation and destruction.

Neuroreality concepts that are more advanced than those of the current Life Sciences. Neuroreality asserts that:

1. The Triadic Solution to the classical Mind-Body Problem explains for the first time the creation of five dimensional Mind as the product of the three dimensional Brain in the presence of Time and Free Energy.

2. The Quadrimental Brain Model describes four vertical layers of evolutionary brain development.

3. The Dual Quadbrain Model is a bilateral expansion of the Quadrimental Brain. From these the Society of Seven Model of consciousness emerges.

4. Hemisity exists as the bilateral behavioral difference in thinking and behavior styles resulting from a unilateral executive system element inherently located on one or the other side of the cingulate cortex.

5. Life independently occurred twice on earth, once on the ocean's surface, the second at volcanic vents in its depth.

6. As a result, Dyadic Evolution exists due to of two competing trees of life: The Matripolar and Patripolar lineages.

7. Familial Polarity exists as the result of these two ancient different reproductive strategies.

8. Cross breeding of familial polarity R-R parents is the origin of developmental dyslexia.

9. Cross breeding of familial polarity L-L parents is the origin of homo and bi sexuality.

10. Neurosis and psychosis exist because of the existence of inappropriate cyclic activation the xDARP to repair developmental arresting.

11. xDARP activation causes interleukin-1a, serotonin, CRF, and norepinephrine release from yet to be identified cells in the stress pathway to create anxiety, panic and depression. Steps involved include the following:

    a) First step is yet to be discovered.
    b) Neurons with liposaccharide and other receptors release prostaglandin,
    c) Neurons with prostaglandin receptors release interleukin-1a,
    d) Neurons with IL-1a receptors release serotonin at 5-HT2a receptors
    e) Cells with 5-HT2a receptors release CRF in ventricles and at the locus coeruleus (LC).
    f) Cells with CRF receptors in the ventricles and in the LC release norepinephrine and CRF.
    g) To cause anxiety, panic, and ultimately to the catecholamine exhaustion of depression leading to suicidality.

12, The discharge of blocked memories of terror is transforming.

About the Author:

Bruce Eldine Morton was born Southern California in 1938. After Completing the M.S. and Ph.D. degrees in biochemistry at the University of Wisconsin, he spent post-doctoral periods as a Research Fellow at Wisconsin's Institute for Enzyme Research, M.I.T., and Harvard Medical School. He was hired by the School of Medicine at the University of Hawaii, 1969 where he directed a neuroscience research laboratory long after his "retirement" in 1995.

In 1974, Dr. Morton set a world distance record in a hang glider. He has also been active in gymnastics, SCUBA diving, wind surfing, snow boarding, and now with dual purpose motorcycle riding to Mayan ruins. He has been a member of many choral societies and performed in concerts with the Boston Symphony.

Dr. Morton spent sabbaticals at USC, Stanford, and at the University of Michigan. He is also a member numerous professional societies, including the International Society for Research on Aggression. His most recent publication was #80: BE Morton and SE Rafto, Behavioral laterality Advance: Neuroanatomical Evidence for the Existence of Hemisity, *Personality and Individual Differences 49*, 34–42 (2010). From his home base in Guatemala, Dr Morton continues research upon the removal of psychological stress. He may be contacted at bemorton@hawaii.edu

Index

CPSIA information can be obtained at www.ICGtesting.com
Printed in the USA
269298BV00001B/40/P